Brilliant Sanity:
Buddhist Approaches to Psychotherapy

Edited by
Francis J. Kaklauskas,
Susan Nimanheminda,
Louis Hoffman,
& MacAndrew S. Jack

University of the Rockies Press
555 E. Pikes Peak Avenue, #108
Colorado Springs, Colorado 80922

Copyright © 2008. University of the Rockies Press.

Brilliant Sanity: Buddhist Approaches to Psychotherapy
By Francis J. Kaklauskas, Susan Nimanheminda, Louis Hoffman, and MacAndrew S. Jack (Editors)

All rights reserved. No portion of this book may be reproduced, by any process or technique, without the express written consent of the publisher.

First Published in 2008, University of the Rockies Press.

> ISBN-10:   0-9764638-4-9
> ISBN-13:   978-0-9764638-4-9

University of the Rockies Press
555 E. Pikes Peak Avenue, #108
Colorado Springs, CO 80903

Cover Design by Laura Ross, 2007
Cover Photography by Sean Duggan, 2006

The Preface of this book, "The Meeting of Buddhist and Western Psychology," by Chöygam Trungpa, was originally printed in *The Journal of Contemplative Psychotherapy*, Volume 4, 1987; also published as the "Prelude" of the book *The Sanity We Were Born* by Chöygam Trungpa (edited and compiled by Carolyn Rose Gimian), published by Shambhala Publications. Reprinted with permission from Naropa University and Shambhala Publications.

Chapter 1, "Working with Existential and Neurotic Suffering," was originally published in K. T. Kalu (Ed.). *Meditation as Health Promotion: A Lifestyle Modification Approach*. Reprinted with permission of Eburon Publishers.

Chapter 5, "Psychotherapy as an Expression of Spiritual Journey Based Upon the Experience of Shunyata," was abridged from Edward Podvoll, *Recovering Sanity,* Boston: Shambhala Publications, 2003; "Preface to the New Edition," pp. XI-XVI and "Appendix I," pp. 319-352, abridged by Jeff Fortuna. Reprinted with permission from Shambhala Publications.

Chapter 16, "Contemplative Psychotherapy: Integrating Western Psychology and Eastern Philosophy," by Kyle Thomas Darnall, was originally published in *The Behavior Therapist,* Volume 30, October, 2007. Reprinted with permission from The Association for Behavioral and Cognitive Therapies.

This book is dedicated to Karen Kissel Wegela and Robert Unger, committed educators and clinicians who have, through vision and skillful means, enriched the lives of so many.

Table of Contents

Acknowledgements   i

Preface: The Meeting of Buddhist and Western Psychology   v
Chöygam Trungpa

Foreward: Awakening Mind's Potential   xiii
Dzogchen Ponlop

Introduction   xix
Francis J. Kaklauskas, Susan Nimanheminda, Louis Hoffman, & MacAndrew S. Jack

Part I: Ground

1. Working with Existential and Neurotic Suffering   3
   Han F. de Wit

2. An Existential Framework for Buddhism, World Religions, and Psychotherapy: Culture and Diversity Considerations   19
   Louis Hoffman

3. Therapist Subjectivity in Contemplative Psychotherapy   39
   Patricia Townsend & Francis J. Kaklauskas

4. Warriorship: A Tradition of Fearlessness and Its Impact Upon Contemplative Psychotherapy   65
   Matthew Tomatz

5. Psychotherapy as an Expression of the Spiritual Journey Based on the Experience of Shunyata   87
   Ed Podvoll with Jeff Fortuna

6. Buddhism, Psychology, and Neuroscience: The Promises and Pitfalls of a Neurobiologically Informed Contemplative Psychotherapy   99
   Michael Dow

Part II: Path

7. Large Group Process: Grounding Buddhist and 133
   Psychological Theory in Personal Experience
   Francis J. Kaklauskas & Elizabeth A. Olson

8. Group as a Mindfulness Practice 161
   Susan Nimanheminda

9. A Discipline of Inquisitiveness: The "Body-Speech-Mind" 175
   Approach to Contemplative Supervision
   Robert Walker

10. Maitri Space Awareness: Developing the Therapist Within 195
    James Evans, Alexandra Shenpen, & Patricia Townsend

11. The Body in Psychotherapy: Dancing with the Paradox 213
    Zoë Avstreih

Part III: Fruition

12. Listening Beyond the Words: Working with Exchange 225
    Karen Kissel Wegela

13. Resonance and Exchange in Contemplative Psychotherapy 239
    Farrell Silverberg

14. Exploring Countertransference, Emptiness, and Joy in the 259
    Path of the Therapist
    MacAndrew S. Jack & Abigail M. Lindemann

15. Windhorse Therapy: Creating Environments that Arouse 275
    the Energy of Health and Sanity
    Chuck Knapp

16. Contemplative Psychotherapy: Integrating Western 299
    Psychology and Eastern Philosophy
    Kyle Thomas Darnall

17. Mothering in the Moment: Explorations on Mindfulness 309
    in Mothering and Therapeutic Experiences
    *Elizabeth A. Olson, Helena Unger, Francis J. Kaklauskas,
    & Letitia A. Swan*

Part IV: Talks

18. From Eros to Enlightenment   337
    Mark Epstein

19. Psychoanalysis and Buddhism: Paths of Disappointment   347
    Robert Unger

20. Psychotherapy and the Paramitas: Walking the Bodhisattva's Path   355
    Lauren Casalino

21. A Personal Journal with Buddhist Psychotherapy   365
    Verónica Guzmán & Silvia Hast

    About the Contributors   381

    Index   389

Acknowledgements

The editors of *Brilliant Sanity* would like to begin by thanking Chöygam Trungpa and the countless other Buddhist teachers who brought the Dharma to the West. They have served as guides and inspiration to the ideas represented throughout this book.

Next, we would like to thank Naropa University, particularly the faculty, staff, and students of the Masters of Arts in Contemplative Psychotherapy Program (MACP) of the last 30 years. Without the support and dedication of these individuals, this book would never have been possible. In many ways, all these individuals deserve credit for the emergent content which resulted in this book.

The University of the Rockies Press and the editors would like to acknowledge many of the institutions and individuals that have supported this project. First we would like to thank Naropa University, and particularly Jane Rubenstein, for their collaboration and openness in this project. We would like to thank Lady Mukpo, Carolyn Gimian, and Shambhala Publications for their encouragement and the permission to use the work of Chöygam Trungpa. We also would like to thank Jeff Fortuna and Shambhala Publications for allowing us to use the work of Ed Podvoll in this text. We also would like to thank the Association for Behavioral and Cognitive Therapies for their permission to republish the chapter by Kyle Darnell.

It has been a pleasure working with the many talented contributors who offered chapters and talks to this book. Each of these authors sacrificed time and effort to share their wisdom and insight with the reader.

Last, we would like to thank a number of individuals who contributed to making this a higher quality book. Abigail Lindemann, Justin Heim, Lee Scher, Melissa K. Lawrence Hoffman, and Debby Patz Clarke provided important editorial assistance and consultation, including copy-editing, general feedback, and compiling an index.

Francis would like to thank: my family for their enduring love, support, and encouragement; my wife, Elizabeth, who has been endlessly supportive, patient, and wise in helping me achieve my dreams; my son, Levi, who has been an inspiration in all aspects of my life; my sister, Kathy, who from the time of my birth helped me to talk, write, think, and envision a meaningful life full of possibilities; and my brother, Edward, who showed me courage and encouraged me to live fully. Particularly, I would like to thank my parents: my father, Adolph Kalafski, who despite growing up in an orphanage and not attending high school, made it seem that everyone lived a life informed by Shakespeare and Goethe; and my mother, Eileen Perry Kalafski, who never gave up on me and believed that her children were special and unique. My hope is that my parents feel proud of the successes of their surviving children and know that their example of hard work helped us transcend the obstacles in our lives. I would like to thank my friends starting from childhood with James Camarano and the boys of New Jersey, my colleagues from college, particularly Chuck Kershenblatt, and my friends who have provided sustenance in my adult life: Charles Davis, Scott Seskind, Chris Randol, and the Dossett / Sell family. I would like to acknowledge my teachers, beginning with the blessings I have felt from Thrangu Rinpoche as well as my professors, supervisors, and analysts who skillfully showed me all that I did not know and inspired me to continue walking down the long road toward maturity. Finally, I would like to acknowledge my gratitude for the University of the Rockies Press and my other editors for their encouragement, trust, guidance and support throughout this process.

Louis would like to thank: Naropa University's Masters of Arts in Contemplative Psychotherapy Program (MACP) program, who initially welcomed me to present at *Buddhism and Psychotherapy Conference: Celebrating Thirty Years of Contemplative Psychotherapy* and introduced me to the wonderful things happening at Naropa. I would also like to thank the University of the Rockies for giving me the freedom, support, and time to dedicate to this project. In particular, I wish to thank Emory Cowan, Sue Cooper, Jim Ungvarsky, and Lorri White. My very talented co-authors/editors, Francis, Susan, and MacAndrew, who it was a privilege to share this project with, deserve much recognition for making this book happen. Many spiritual mentors and friends who helped me find freedom in spirituality also deserve recognition for their often indirect influence on this project: Robert J. Murney, Glen Moriarty, John Hoffman, Jay Gattis, Mike Mitchell, Roger Ray, H. Newton Malony, and many other unnamed individuals. Last and most importantly, I must share deep appreciation for Heatherlyn and Lakoda for their unyielding support and tolerance of the time it takes to pursue of projects such as this – you are my inspiration.

Susan Nimmanheminda would like to thank: Naropa's Contemplative Psychotherapy Department's Leadership Team: Karen Kissell Wegela, Robert Unger, Lauren Casalino, and MacAndrew Jack and Jennifer Hyatt, its Administrative Director, for the on-going energy, dedication and direction they give the Department. I feel an abiding appreciation of Helena Unger, the Group Process Leaders' Supervisor, for her vision, consistency, and example of a contemplative group leader. Finally, I would like to thank the students who have been members of my small group process classes over the last twelve years. Each of them has helped to make this program offering the valuable personal and professional endeavor it is for me.

MacAndrew would especially like to thank: my wife Anne for her selfless generosity and understanding, and my children Keegan and Tanner for their fresh love, humor, and boundless enthusiasm for life. Thanks to my mother and father for starting me on my way with love. I would also like to give thanks to some of the many people who have nurtured, prodded, or otherwise helped me along the way: David Ramirez, Nick Covino, Harbhajan Sing Khalsa, Rosely Traube, Rick Heimberg, Hardarshan Khalsa, Shigenori Nagatomo, Ted Grossbart, Steven Cooper, Jay Efran, Karen Kissel Wegela, Joy Von Steiger, George Fishman, Nelly Vanzetti, Jerry Resnick. Neil Rosen, and Tod Sloan.

Preface:
The Meeting of Buddhist and Western Psychology[1]

Chöygam Trungpa

Experience and Theory

Traditional Buddhist Psychology emphasizes the importance of direct experience in psychological work. If one relies upon theory alone, then something basic is lost. From the Buddhist viewpoint, the study of theory is only a first step and must be completed by training in the direct experience of mind itself, in oneself and in others.

In Buddhist tradition, this experiential aspect is developed through the practice of meditation, a firsthand observation of mind. Meditation in Buddhism is not a religious practice, but rather a way of clarifying the actual nature of mind and experience. Traditionally, meditation training is said to be threefold, including shila (discipline), samadhi (the actual practice of meditation), and prajna (insight).

Shila is the process of simplifying one's general life and eliminating unnecessary complications. In order to develop a genuine mental discipline, it is first necessary to see how we continually burden ourselves with extraneous activities and preoccupations. In Buddhist countries, shila might involve following a particular rule of life as a monk or a nun, or adopting the precepts appropriate to a Buddhist layperson. In the Western secular context, shila might just involve cultivating an attitude of simplicity toward one's life in general.

Second is samadhi, or meditation, which is the heart of Buddhist experiential training. This practice involves sitting with your attention resting lightly and mindfully on your breath. The further discipline of meditation practice is to note when your attention has wandered from the breath and to bring it back to breathing as your focus. An attitude of bare attention is taken toward the various phenomena, including thoughts, feelings, and sensations, that arise in your mind and body during practice. Meditation practice could be called a way of making friends with oneself,

---

[1] Originally published in Trungpa, C. (1987). The meeting of Buddhist and Western psychology. *Journal of Contemplative Psychotherapy, 4,* 3-14.
Note: This article was originally written before the move to gender inclusive language in academic writing. The editors have elected to retain the original version of the text with the gender specific language in order to insure preserving the integrity of the text.

which points to the fact that it is an experience of nonaggression. In fact, meditation is traditionally called the practice of dwelling in peace. The practice of meditation is thus a way of experiencing one's basic being, beyond habitual patterns.

Shila is the ground of meditation and samadhi is the actual path of the practice. The fruition is prajna, or the insight that begins to develop through one's meditation. In the experience of prajna, one begins to see directly and concretely how the mind actually functions, its mechanics and reflexes, moment to moment. Prajna is traditionally called discriminating awareness, which does not mean discriminating in the sense of developing bias. Rather prajna is unbiased knowledge of one's world and one's mind. It is discriminating in the sense of sorting out confusion and neurosis.

Prajna is immediate and nonconceptual insight, but at the same time it provides the basic inspiration for intellectual study. Because one has seen the actuality of one's own mental functioning, there is a natural desire to clarify and articulate what one has experienced. And there is a spontaneous curiosity about how others have expressed the nature and operation of mind. But at the same time, while one's immediate insight leads to study, it is necessary to maintain an ongoing discipline of meditative training. In that way, concepts never become merely concepts, and one's psychological work remains alive, fresh, and well grounded.

In the Buddhist culture of Tibet, where I was born and educated, a balance was always maintained between experiential training and theory. In my own upbringing, time was allotted in our regular monastic schedule to both study and meditation practice. During the year, there would also be special times set aside for intensive study and also for meditation retreats. It was part of our Buddhist tradition that such a balance was necessary for genuine learning to occur.

When I came to the West, to England in 1963, I was quite surprised to find that in Western psychology, theory is emphasized so much more than experience. Of course this made Western psychology immediately accessible to someone from another culture such as myself. Western psychologists do not ask you to practice, but just tell you what they are about from the very beginning. I found this approach very straightforward and something of a relief. But at the same time, one wonders about the profundity of a tradition that relies so heavily on concepts and opens its doors so easily.

On the other hand, Western psychologists do seem intuitively to recognize the need for greater emphasis on the direct experience of mind. Perhaps this is what has led so many psychologists to take an interest in Buddhism. Especially in relation to Zen, they are attracted to the enigma of it. And they are tantalized by the flavor of immediate experience, the possibility of enlightenment, and the impression of profundity. Such people seem to be looking to Buddhism for something they find lacking in their own traditions. This interest strikes me as appropriate, and in this respect Buddhism has something important to offer.

One important question always seems to come up when Western psychologists begin to study Buddhism. Does one have to become a Buddhist in order to learn about Buddhism? The answer is that of course one does not, but it must be asked in return, what does one want to learn? What Buddhism really has to teach the Western psychologist is how to relate more closely with his own experience, in its freshness, its fullness, and its immediacy. To do this, one does not have to become a Buddhist, but one does have to practice meditation. It is certainly possible to study only the theory of Buddhist psychology. But in doing so, one would miss the point. Without experience to rely on, one would end up simply interpreting Buddhist notions through Western concepts. A good taste of meditation is actually necessary in working with oneself and others. It is a tremendous help, whatever interest one may take in Buddhism as such.

Sometimes it is very hard to communicate to Westerners the importance of the experiential dimension. After we had started Samye Ling, our meditation center in Scotland, soon after I came from India to England, we found that a great many people with psychological problems came to us for help. They had been in all sorts of different therapies, and many of them were quite neurotic. They looked on us as physicians carrying out medical practice and wanted us to cure them. In working with these people I found that there was a frequent obstacle. Such people often wanted to take a purely theoretical approach, rather than actually experiencing and working with their neuroses. They wanted to understand their neuroses intellectually: where they themselves went wrong, how their neuroses developed, and so on. They often were not willing to let go of that approach.

The Training of a Therapist

In the training of a psychotherapist, theoretical and experiential training should be properly balanced. We combine these two elements in our Naropa Institute[2] psychology program: one begins with a taste of meditation, then applies oneself to study, then experiences meditation more fully, then does more intensive study, and so forth. This kind of approach actually has an interesting effect: it enhances one's appreciation of what one is doing. The experience of one's own mind whets the appetite for further study. And the study increases one's interest in observing one's own mental process through meditation.

In addition, when study is combined with meditation practice, it has a different flavor. Where direct experience is lacking, study tends to be mainly memorizing terms and definitions and trying to convince oneself of their validity. When balanced with meditative discipline, study takes on

---

[2] Now Naropa University.

much more life and reality. It develops clarity about how the mind works and how that knowledge can be expressed. In this way, study and practice help one another enormously, and each becomes more real and satisfying. It is like eating a sandwich—because of the bread, you appreciate the meat much more.

One question comes up when you try to balance the experiential and theoretical sides of training. How much time should be spent on each? Generally I would say it should be roughly equal. But at the same time the amount of hours put into practice, for example, is not as important as the attitude with which it is done. If the trainee is wholehearted enough, and if his practice is sufficiently intent, then his meditation will have its proper role and permeate his study and daily life.

All of this is not to say that there is no experiential training in Western psychology. But, from the Buddhist viewpoint, it is greatly underemphasized. And when it does occur, it seems to happen almost exclusively in the interpersonal situation of people talking to one another, such as the classical training in psychoanalysis. Some Western psychologists have asked me whether the direct experience of meditation practice is really necessary. They have wanted to know whether the *interpersonal training* is not enough. To this I would answer that the interpersonal training is not adequate in itself. First, it is necessary to study and experience one's own mind. Then one can study and experience accurately the mind in the interpersonal situation.

We can see this by looking at how the Buddhist tradition of abhidharma works. First, there is an exploration of how the mind evolves in itself and how it functions. The expression of this is the first half of the abhidharma. The second half is concerned with how that mind begins to respond to things from outside itself. This parallels how a child develops. In the beginning, he is mainly concerned with himself. Later, in adolescence, his world begins to grow bigger and bigger.

In order to understand the interpersonal situation correctly, you have to know yourself in the beginning. Once you know the style of the dynamics of your own mind, then you can begin to see how that style works in dealing with others. And, in fact, on the basis of knowing oneself, the interpersonal knowledge comes naturally. You discover that somebody has developed his own mind. Then you can experience how the two minds interact with each other. This leads to the discovery that there is no such thing as outside mind and inside mind at all. So *mind* is really two minds meeting together, which is the same mind in some sense.

Therefore, the more you learn about your own mind, the more you learn about other people's minds. You begin to appreciate other worlds, other people's life situations. You are learning to extend your vision beyond what is just there in your immediate situation, on the spot, so your mind is opened that much more. And that reflects in your work with others. It makes you more skillful in deeds and also gives you more of a sense of warmth and compassion, so you become more accommodating of others.

The Viewpoint of Health

Buddhist psychology is based on the notion that human beings are fundamentally good. Their most basic qualities are positive ones: openness, intelligence, and warmth. Of course, this viewpoint has its philosophical and psychological expressions in concepts such as bodhichitta (awakened mind) and tathagatagarbha (birthplace of enlightened ones). But this idea is ultimately rooted in experience—the experience of goodness and worthiness in oneself and others. This understanding is very fundamental and is the basic inspiration for Buddhist practice and Buddhist psychology.

Coming from a tradition that stresses human goodness, it was something of a shock for me to encounter the Western tradition of original sin. When I was at Oxford University, I studied Western religious and philosophical traditions with interest and found the notion of original sin quite pervasive. One of my early experiences in England was attending a seminar with Archbishop Anthony Blum. The seminar was on the notion of grace and we got into a discussion of original sin. The Buddhist tradition does not see such a notion as necessary at all, and I expressed this viewpoint. I was surprised at how angry the Western participants became. Even the orthodox, who might not emphasize original sin as much as the Western traditions, still held it as a cornerstone of their theology.

In terms of our present discussion, it seems that this notion of original sin does not just pervade Western religious ideas; it actually seems to run throughout Western thought as well, especially psychological thought. Among patients, theoreticians, and therapists alike, there seems to be great concern with the idea of some original mistake which causes later suffering—a kind of punishment for that mistake. One finds that a sense of guilt or being wounded is quite pervasive. Whether or not such people actually believe in the idea of original sin, or in God for that matter, they seem to feel that they have done something wrong in the past and are now being punished for it.

It seems that this feeling of basic guilt has been passed down from one generation to another and pervades many aspects of Western life. For example, teachers often think that if children do not feel guilty, then they won't study properly and consequently won't develop as they should. Therefore, many teachers feel that they have to do something to push the child, and guilt seems to be one of the chief techniques they use. This occurs even on the level of improving reading and writing. The teacher looks for errors: "Look, you made a mistake. What are you going to do about it?" From the child's point of view, learning is then based on trying not to make mistakes, on trying to prove you actually are not bad. It is entirely different when you approach the child more positively: "Look how much you have improved, therefore we can go further." In the latter case, learning becomes an expression of one's wholesomeness and innate intelligence.

The problem with this notion of original sin or mistake is that it acts very much as a hindrance to people. At some point, it is of course necessary to realize one's shortcomings. But if one goes too far with that, it kills any inspiration and can destroy one's vision as well. So in that way, it really is not helpful, and in fact it seems unnecessary. As I mentioned, in Buddhism we do not have any comparable ideas of sin and guilt. Obviously there is the idea that one should avoid mistakes. But there is not anything comparable to the heaviness and inescapability of original sin.

According to the Buddhist perspective, there are problems, but they are temporary and superficial defilements that cover over one's basic goodness (tathagatagarbha). This viewpoint is a positive and optimistic one. But, again, we should emphasize that this viewpoint is not purely conceptual. It is rooted in the experience of meditation and in the healthiness it encourages. There are temporary habitual neurotic patterns that develop based on past experience, but these can be seen through. It is just this that is studied in the abhidharma: how one thing succeeds another, how volitional action originates and perpetuates itself, how things snowball. And, most important, abhidharma studies how, through meditation practice, this process can be cut through.

The attitude that results from the Buddhist-orientation and practice is quite different from the *mistake mentality*. One actually experiences mind as fundamentally pure, that is, healthy and positive, and *problems* as temporary and superficial defilements. Such a viewpoint does not quite mean *getting rid* of problems, but rather shifting one's focus. Problems are seen in a much broader context of health: one begins to let go of clinging to one's neuroses and to step beyond obsession and identification with them. The emphasis is no longer on the problems themselves but rather on the ground of experience through realizing the nature of mind itself. When problems are seen in this way, then there is less panic and everything seems more workable. When problems arise, instead of being seen as purely threats, they become learning situations, opportunities to find out more about one's own mind, and to continue on one's journey.

Through practice, which is confirmed by study, the inherent healthiness of your mind and others' minds is experienced over and over. You see that your problems are not all that deeply rooted. You see that you can make literal progress. You find yourself becoming more mindful and more aware, developing a greater sense of healthiness and clarity as you go on, and this is tremendously encouraging.

Ultimately, this orientation of goodness and healthiness comes out of the experience of egolessness, a notion that has created a certain amount of difficulty for Western psychologists. *Egolessness* does not mean that nothing exists, as some have thought, a kind of nihilism. Instead, it means that you can let go of your habitual patterns and then when you let go, you genuinely let go. You do not re-create or rebuild another shell immediately afterward. Once you let go, you do not just start all over again. Egolessness is having the trust to not rebuild again at all and experiencing the psychological healthiness and freshness that goes with not rebuilding. The truth of egolessness can only be experienced fully through meditation practice.

The experience of egolessness encourages a real and genuine sympathy toward others. You cannot have genuine sympathy with ego because then that would mean that your sympathy would be accompanied by some kind of defense mechanisms. For example, you might try to refer everything back to your own territory when you work with someone, if your own ego is at stake. Ego interferes with direct communication, which is obviously essential in the therapeutic process. Egolessness, on the other hand, lets the whole process of working with others be genuine and generous and free-form. That is why, in the Buddhist tradition, it is said that without egolessness, it is impossible to develop real compassion.

The Practice of Therapy

The task of the therapist is to help his or her patients connect back with their own fundamental healthiness and goodness. Prospective patients come to us feeling starved and alienated. More important than giving them a set of techniques for battling their problems, we need to point them toward the experience of the fundamental ground of health which exists in them. It might be thought that this is asking a great deal, particularly when we are working with confronting someone who has a history of problems. But the sanity of basic mind is actually close at hand and can be readily experienced and encouraged.

Of course, it goes without saying that the therapist must experience his own mind in this way to begin with. Through meditation practice, his clarity and warmth toward himself is given room to develop and then can be expanded outward. Thus his meditation and study provide the ground for working with disturbed people, with other therapists, and with himself in the same framework all the time. Obviously, this is not so much a question of theoretical or conceptual perspective, but of how we personally experience our own lives. Our existence can be felt fully and thoroughly so that we appreciate that we are genuine, true human beings. This is what we can communicate to others and encourage in them.

One of the biggest obstacles to helping our patients in this way is, again, the notion of a *mistake*, and the preoccupation with the past that results from this. Many of our patients will want to unravel their past. But this can be a dangerous approach if it goes too far. If you follow this thread, you have to look back to your conception, then to your family's experiences before that, to your great-grandfathers, and on and on. It could go a long way back and get very complicated.

The Buddhist viewpoint emphasizes the impermanence and the transitoriness of things. The past is gone, and the future has not yet happened, so we work with what is here: the present situation. This actually helps us not to categorize or to theorize. A fresh, living situation is actually taking place all the time, on the spot. This noncategorizing approach comes from being fully here rather than trying to follow up some past event. We do not have to look back to the past in order to see what we ourselves or other people are made out of. Things speak for themselves, right here and now.

In my days at Oxford and since then, I have been impressed by some of the genuine strengths of Western psychology. It is open to new viewpoints and discoveries. It maintains a critical attitude toward itself. And it is the most experiential of Western intellectual disciplines.

But at the same time, considered from the viewpoint of Buddhist psychological tradition, there is definitely something missing in the Western approach. This missing element, as we have suggested throughout this introduction, is the acknowledgment of the primacy of immediate experience. It is here that Buddhism presents a fundamental challenge to Western therapeutics and offers a viewpoint and method that could revolutionize Western psychology.

Foreword: Awakening Mind's Potential

Dzogchen Ponlop

We might ask ourselves why, when our mind strives only for happiness, we often end up so far from our target. What is it that interferes with our aspirations and intentions? From the perspective of the Buddhist teachings, four profound truths are taught on the topic of suffering. First, suffering in this life is inevitable. Second, that suffering has specific causes. Third, there can genuinely be an end to that suffering; we can go beyond it. Fourth, the transcendence of suffering also has specific causes. Generating those causes is what we call *the path*. It is known as the path that leads beyond suffering, the path to liberation or the way to enlightenment. In other words, just as suffering has causes, just so transcendence has causes; it is not random.

Of all the suffering that we experience in this world, mental or psychological suffering is the deepest and most difficult to overcome. Physical suffering, such as hunger and pain, can be remedied easily with food and drugs. However, deeper and longer efforts are required to remedy mental suffering through the practices of therapy, counseling, and ultimately through one's own path of meditation.

In the context of the Buddhist spiritual path, the transcendence of suffering does not just mean that our relative suffering ceases and we achieve a continual state of relative happiness. Rather, we transcend the causes and conditions that obscure mind's true nature and achieve the state of full awakening. Our goal on this path is the realization of our inherent potential for wisdom and compassion, which is unconditioned, ultimate happiness. Being on this path means that we are willing to work with our minds, and we are willing to be uncomfortable at times in the process. It also means that we have a great curiosity about how things work, and we have a certain degree of passion—for truth and authentic experience.

Since our suffering and pain have causes, if we discover those causes, then we can remedy them. When we are looking for the causes of our suffering, the teachings of the Buddha direct us to look first at the mind as the source of our experience and the means for understanding it. Therefore, what is most important for us on this journey of awakening is to work with our minds. There are numerous teachings on mind, mental factors, and their ultimate nature in Buddhism that serve as an important basis for understanding and working with one's mind. It is a tradition rich in knowledge and contemplative experience in the field of mind and its psychology. Working with our minds is what we call *practice* in Buddhism—nothing more or less. Practice does not depend on meditation cushions, shrines, or images of Buddhas. To have a nice mala or thangka is wonderful, but it is not essential for the path. What is essential is for us is to work with our minds, no matter what tradition of practice we follow. In both formal meditation sessions and in postmeditation, the point is to try to see the true nature of your mind. What is that nature?

According to the view of the Buddhist philosophical tradition and to the experience of countless generations of accomplished practitioners, the true nature of mind—its absolute reality—is wisdom. Mind's basic state is primordially pure and fully awakened. This absolute reality is fully endowed with all the profound and vast qualities of enlightenment and, at the same time, is free from all defilements, all ignorance, ego-clinging, and mental afflictions, which are the ordinary experience of sentient beings. Yet, this originally pure essence is not truly or substantially existent. It is primordially empty. Far from being a vacuous state, however, that emptiness is full of energy; it radiates in all directions like the light of the sun, which illuminates the whole sky. In the same way, this luminous wisdom pervades all of samsara and nirvana, abiding inseparably with all phenomena. It is the life force of everything. It is taught that all appearances of samsara and nirvana are the display or creative energy of the true nature of mind. Everything arises from this nature and everything dissolves back into it. Whatever appears does not waver from the expanse of the true nature of mind.

While this pure essence cannot be seen directly by conceptual mind or expressed fully in words, it is described in many ways and known by many names. It is called the inseparable union of appearance and emptiness, luminosity and emptiness, and space and awareness. It is also known as buddha nature and ordinary mind. The great meditation master and pioneer in bringing Buddhism to the West, the Vidyadhara, Chogyam Trungpa Rinpoche, called this spontaneously present wisdom *brilliant sanity*.

Yet while it cannot be observed in a dualistic manner, there is a manner of seeing that is free of duality. When we can look at the appearances of mind—our perceptions, thoughts, and emotions—simply and directly, without concept or contrivance, we can recognize the very *nature* of those appearances. If we can genuinely see our emotions, senses, and thoughts just as they are, without trying to change them or improve our way of seeing them, then we can see the basic state of wakefulness. No matter what we experience in relation to these objects, the instruction is simply to look at the very nature of these appearances with the mind of nowness.

Consequently, samsara, with all its attendant sufferings, is nothing other than our failure to recognize our buddha nature in any instant. It is that simple. That is why all Buddhist schools teach the importance of meditating on the present moment. We bring our mind to the present moment, rather than getting caught up in past memories or anticipating the future. If we have the pointing-out instructions of the lineage or the courage and sharpness of mind to look at the present moment, then Buddha is everywhere, within and without.

If this is so, if wakefulness is inherent in every moment, then how is it that we fail to recognize it? If buddha nature is free from defilements, then how is it that we seem to be forever caught up in restlessness, discontent, and the turmoil of emotions?

Although all beings are at heart buddhas, our buddha nature is obscured by incidental stains: the disturbing emotions, dualistic fixations, and ego-clinging that cover our direct perception of the nature of mind. When those stains are removed, then mind's true nature is clearly apparent and we reach the state of buddhahood, which has always been with us.

It is taught that original wisdom is present at all times, even when we think it is absent. However, the intensity of this luminosity can be so strong that it has a blinding effect, like looking directly into the sun. We can't see—not because of the absence of light, but because it is too bright. The play of our awareness is so vivid that it fails to recognize its own nature. Because of the intensity of the brightness of awareness, we become confused. Our confused mind splits the intense brightness in two. We take one aspect to be a self: an *I* or a *me*, which provides a sense of reference point. We then see the self-play of this awareness as other: *you*, *them*, and all the objects that seem to exist separately. At this point, duality begins to dominate our mind. Through this duality, we accumulate karma. We engage in positive and negative actions. From these actions, we generate the results of samsara. From this perspective, we could say that the *creator* of our condition of suffering is simply the failure of awareness to recognize itself.

Within this intensity, there is a point where we discover a gap, a state of groundlessness or hopelessness, which is beyond the reach of any reference point. At that very moment, we are looking at the empty aspect of buddha nature. Because that experience of open space can be terrifying to ego, our usual response is to cover it over as soon as possible with thoughts and concepts. However, if we can rest within the gap experience, it is possible to feel the tremendous power and energy of ordinary mind. When we experience this field of energy, we are experiencing not just emptiness, but the union of emptiness and luminosity: the unceasing play of mind and its qualities of wisdom.

When our enlightened potential is not ripened, we do not know how to manifest this wisdom energy skillfully, in an unmistaken way. Instead, we project this energy outwardly through the filters of ego-clinging and concepts as passion, aggression, ignorance, pride, or jealousy—otherwise known as the *five poisons*. When our potential is ripened, however, we are never distracted from the state of nondual wisdom, the union of space and awareness. When that wisdom and compassion manifest outwardly, its energy manifests in five aspects, or particular qualities of wisdom. These five aspects are termed the five *buddha wisdoms,* or five enlightened qualities of awakened mind. These five wisdom energies are the pure essence of the five poisons. In other words, when the energy of our emotions arises, if we are under the influence of confusion, then we perceive that energy as one the five poisons. If we are free from confusion, then we recognize the emotion's essential nature and perceive it as the display of wisdom.

For Buddhist practitioners or any individual working directly with the principles of Buddhist psychology, it is helpful to understand the view of mind's ultimate nature, as well as its relative characteristics and functioning. The ultimate nature of mind is totally awake and free right from the outset, but failing to recognize this nature causes relative confusion or incidental stains to manifest. Yet all of these teachings remain a useless philosophy unless they are put into practice as a means of alleviating suffering, increasing happiness, and cultivating greater wakefulness. When we become skillful in putting the view and meditation into action in our lives, the dharma becomes a living teaching and support for our path. From the Mahayana perspective, *view* refers to the intellectual knowledge, the understanding of emptiness, and the interdependent nature of phenomena we gain from study. *Meditation* is the process by which we become accustomed to that view and gain a personal, experiential knowledge of its meaning. When view and meditation are joined, whatever we do naturally becomes ethical conduct, or mindful and compassionate action.

The key to the awakening, development, and maturation of the enlightened potential that exists within each of us is taught to be the cultivation of loving-kindness and compassion towards oneself and all other beings. At every stage of the path, compassion is the element that fosters the steady growth and ultimate ripening of this seed. It is the primary means by which we can reach the profound level of cutting through the very root of our suffering, which is ego-clinging. When ego is completely cut through, there is a sense of letting go of all delusion, all hope, and fear, as well as all anxiety, restlessness, and discontent. Consequently, we experience complete peace and full awakening.

The path of cutting through that leads to the cessation of suffering involves the *accumulation of merit,* which is simply the process of letting go, in each moment, of every aspect of our clinging. In this way, we transform our mindstream. We gradually shift the momentum of our actions from negative to positive, from self-cherishing to love and concern for others. Each time we let go of our clinging, we are dissolving the causes of negative actions. Hence, there is no arising of the five poisons, nor any suffering as a result of those actions. Working with mind's negative habitual tendencies in this way is a gradual process requiring effort and patience. Yet, there is a turning point—a moment where the cloudbanks of our obscurations can no longer conceal mind's luminous wisdom.

Therefore, the main practice of the Mahayana is the generation of the enlightened attitude, or the practice of giving rise to *bodhichitta*, which means *awakened* heart or mind. On the ultimate level, bodhichitta is the union of the wisdom of emptiness and boundless, unbiased compassion. However, relatively, we can think of it as the mind intent on enlightenment, and particularly as the desire to establish all sentient beings in the state of enlightenment, or complete awakening. Its essence is the desire that all beings see the highest truth—the actual nature of reality—and possess genuine wisdom. It is for this that Mahayanists dedicate their life.

Once we have entered this path, then, ideally, all our actions and relationships become infused with this motivation. Whether we are relating to our families or strangers, clients or competitors, friends or enemies, every encounter becomes an opportunity to bring our understanding from our heads to our hearts and put it into action in the everyday world.

However, when we set out to benefit others in this way, we must remember that no matter how hard we try, no matter how powerful our motivation or skillful our methods, it is impossible for us to be a *savior*, to liberate another sentient being from his or her own suffering. And just as there is no way that we can directly free other sentient beings through our efforts alone, there is no one outside of us who can release us from our suffering. We each must save ourselves, free ourselves. What we can do for others is create a positive environment in which they can discover their own wisdom and heart of compassion and work toward their own enlightenment. We can provide support for others to find their path, and once they have found it, help them to walk along that path, in the same way that parents do when they support and guide their children: never giving up on them or their inherent potential to awaken to a genuine and lasting happiness.

Introduction

Similarities between Buddhism and Western psychology are increasingly abundant in the academic literature. For instance, both psychotherapy and meditation have similar goals of reducing human suffering and understanding the human mind. Although these are an excellent starting point for dialogue, both traditions cover a very broad range of ideas with significant depth and intricacy. Although concepts from each view can be crudely compared on a cognitive level, developing proper understanding of either tradition takes years of practice, training, and guidance. The current volume hopes to deepen this discussion by bringing an impressive group of Buddhist oriented clinicians to a dialogue on developing a psychology informed by the insights of Buddhism and illuminating aspects of Buddhism through psychology.

The motivation for this book emerged from the *Buddhism and Psychotherapy Conference: Celebrating Thirty Years of Contemplative Psychotherapy* at Naropa University in May, 2006. Naropa University founder Chöyam Trungpa had the vision to invite psychotherapists and Buddhists together to discuss ideas and encouraged psychotherapists to practice meditation as a way of deepening their understanding of human nature and the mind. Naropa University has been at the center of this dialogue and the integration of these two disciplines from the initial 1974 summer forum, which featured Lou Ormont conducting psychotherapy groups. This continued through the recent conference, which included presentations from leaders in Buddhism and psychotherapy such as Mark Epstein, Harvey Aaronson, Gay Watson, and Karen Kissel Wegela.

We felt the energy from this recent conference at Naropa was too important to end when the conference concluded, so we invited some of the conference presenters to contribute book chapters or talks. Authors were asked to discuss how their experiences with Buddhist practice and worldview influences their clinical work. The results produced a rich diversity of ideas in which each chapter brings forth a unique voice in this dialogue. Previously published works were also included that demonstrated the combination of scholarship and wisdom. While many of the works pull from multiple traditions within Buddhism (Theravada, Mahayana, Zen, and others), the majority of the chapters draw most significantly from the Tibetan Buddhist tradition. The editors, authors, and holders of copyrighted material all agreed to contribute proceeds from this publication back to the Naropa University Master of Arts in Contemplative Psychology program (MACP).

This book's title, *Brilliant Sanity*, comes from Chöygam Trungpa. Trungpa used several English wordings to try to capture the Sanskrit word *tathagatagarbha*. Other translations include Buddha nature, basic sanity, and true nature. Brilliant sanity, or the nature of mind, has three primary qualities: openness, clarity, and compassion. Karen Kissel Wegela (1994) explains:

> The first quality is spaciousness. Our experience has within it a quality of space, emptiness, that can accommodate any state of mind whatsoever. Our mind is like the sky, and all the things that occur within it are like the weather. Just as the sky is not disturbed by the weather, our mind is not affected by the clouds, hail storms, pleasant and unpleasant emotions that come and go. The mind itself is spacious, empty. This quality is not graspable: we cannot hang on to it or even touch it. Yet, we can recognize it in our experience.
>
> The second quality of brilliant sanity is clarity. From the Buddhist point of view, an understanding of emptiness as space with nothing in it is incomplete. Emptiness is more than just a vacuum, more than the absences of experience. It is also a quality of awareness or wakefulness. We can join any experience with awareness, which is clarity, the perception of things as they are without distorting that perception in any way. It sounds very simple, but is quite difficult.... We generally filter our experience through our expectations, thoughts, preconceptions, and so on.
>
> The third quality of brilliant sanity is compassion. When the obstacles to spaciousness and clarity are dissolved, the impulse towards compassionate action arises naturally.... When we hear the cry of a child, our first instinct is to help. It is only in the flicker of the next moment that we can very quickly come up with reasons why we should not interfere, why we should hold back. If we look closely at our experience, that first reaction is a compassionate impulse, before confusion arises, an inherent warmth and tender-heartedness. (pp. 28-29)

The book is organized into four sections. The first section draws upon the Buddhist ground as outlined in the introduction by Chöygam Trungpa. This *ground* section highlights core beliefs and values that set the base for clinical work. The *path* section includes chapters that focus specifically on the training of psychotherapists. The *fruition* section provides examples of how these values are utilized in clinical work. The final section, *talks,* includes edited versions of public talks given on Buddhism and psychotherapy, and aim to follow in the oral tradition of Buddhist teaching.

Many of the chapters in this book draw heavily on Naropa's Master of Arts in Contemplative Psychotherapy Program (MACP). This is not intended as an advertisement or overview of the MACP program; rather, the authors utilize the program as a base or foundation to explicate important aspects of training and therapy from a Buddhist perspective. Readers are encouraged to consider how these training and psychotherapy perspectives can be incorporated, possibly with adaptations, into their own development as a therapist.

The Story of Naropa

The story of Buddhist abbot Naropa captures the heart of Buddhist path and Buddhist psychology (Trungpa, 1994). Naropa was born into a Brahman family and was always very curious, intelligent, and independent. He followed in the cultural traditions of his time and in an arranged marriage partnered with a beautiful bride, Vimaladipe. Despite his comfortable position in his culture, he and his wife dissolved the marriage and Naropa became a student monk at Nalanda University in India. Nalanda was recognized as the foremost religious and philosophical training institute in all the East. Students would travel from Indonesia, China, and even Greece to complete the rigorous 10-year program. Naropa was intellectually gifted and quickly made a name for himself with his excellent memory and debating skills. He quickly moved on to become a respected scholar and lecturer.

One day when Naropa was reading sutras, an old ugly woman approached him and asked if he understood the words of the books. "Yes, of course," Naropa responded. The old woman crowed with joyous laughter. She then asked if he understood the meaning. "Yes, of course" Naropa responded. The old woman broke into tears. When Naropa asked why she was crying, she told him that he had mistaken his intellectual understanding for wisdom. Naropa admitted she was correct. When she recommended that he study with her brother, Tilopa, Naropa had found his teacher. He resigned his post and spent the next twelve years studying under Tilopa. While Naropa wanted to discuss the meaning of the sutra, Tilopa had Naropa complete an endless series of contemplative practices from meditations on death to fetching Tilopa dinner. Eventually Tilopa slapped Naropa across his face with a sandal, which snapped Naropa from his intellectual stupor and arrogance and brought him into enlightenment. Naropa returned to Nalanda, and became one of the greatest Buddhist teachers in the history of India.

It is in the tradition of Naropa's union of academic knowledge with experiential wisdom that we have collected these offerings to the dialogue and integration of Buddhism and psychotherapy.

In closing, we would like to thank all those who have contributed to this project and we hope their merit will be beneficial to all those who read the book and beyond.

Francis J. Kaklauskas
Susan Nimmanheminda
Louis Hoffman
MacAndrew S. Jack
December 1, 2007
Boulder, Colorado

References

Trungpa, C. (1994). *Illusion's game: The life and teachings of Naropa.* Boston: Shambhala.

Wegela, K. K. (1994). Contemplative psychotherapy: A path of uncovering brilliant sanity. *Journal of Contemplative Psychotherapy, 9.* 27-51.

Part 1:
Ground

1

Working with Existential and Neurotic Suffering[1]

Han F. de Wit

Over the last decennia the literature exploring the relationship between the Buddhist and the Western view of human mind, experience, and behaviour has expanded at such a rate that it is hard to keep track of all the various approaches and analyses. In particular, the dialogue between the Buddhist understanding of mind and Western psychology and psychotherapy has gone through a major development; a brief look at the references of the papers in this book (which is just one among many) offers evidence of this fact. However, within this stream of publications there are a few recurrent themes that all circle around the practice of Buddhist meditation: what is its function and purpose? Is it therapeutic? Is it a method to objectively investigate mind and a way to knowledge of some kind? Is it both? Is its purpose to attain enlightenment as understood by Buddhists? If so, how is this notion of *enlightenment* to be understood in Western psychological terms?

Although the meditation practice of shamatha/vipashyana is common to all Buddhist schools, our attempts to answer those questions are complicated further by the fact that within the Buddhist tradition there is more than one way of speaking about the spiritual path and its goal of enlightenment. For instance, the language and conceptual framework that the Buddha used initially (and which later in the history of Buddhism has been coined the *First Turning of the Wheel of the Dharma*) defines enlightenment as *cessation of suffering*. In what came to be called the *Second Turning of the Wheel*, enlightenment is defined as the realization of *shunyata, emptiness*. In the Third Turning, it is defined as the realization of *Buddha nature, tathagatagarbha*. Finally, in the language of Vajrayana, Buddhist terms like *realizing ordinary mind, primordial purity* and the like are used to define enlightenment. It is said that the Buddha initially used the language of the First Turning because it is the most accessible to non-Buddhists. Because most readers will not be Buddhists, I will use primarily the language and concepts of the First Turning. This is also

---

[1] In Meditation as Health Promotion. A lifestyle Modification Approach, Proceedings, the 6th Conference. K. T. Kaku (Ed.), Delft, Netherlands: Eburon Publishers, 2000.

appropriate because the concept of suffering is central to both psychotherapy and the First Turning. Buddhism and psychotherapy aim at the cessation of suffering. In order to explore their relationship we will explore what is meant by *suffering* and its cessation in both traditions.

Two Famous Statements

In many Buddhist texts the Buddha is portrayed as the *ultimate doctor* able to cure the ailments of all sentient beings. A famous and often quoted statement from the sutra texts ascribed to the Buddha himself reflects this portrayal: "My teaching focuses on one and only one thing: suffering and the cessation of suffering" (Majjhima Nikaya, 1995, p.140). We might ask ourselves: What kind of suffering and cessation did the Buddha have in mind? Is it different from what psychotherapists see as their goal and if so, how?

Another equally often quoted statement in our Western culture comes from Sigmund Freud (1952) in his seminal study on hysteria where answers the question what his therapy can do by pointing out that it will transform neurotic suffering into ordinary suffering. Even though the term *neurotic* nowadays has fallen into disuse in professional circles (the DSM-IV avoids the term) the meaning of this statement is one that even our more optimistic therapists would still endorse. Again we might ask: What is meant here by *neurotic* and *ordinary* suffering? Let us first investigate the Buddhist meaning of suffering. After that, we will try to draw some conclusions about how this meaning relates to the notion of suffering that psychotherapists have in mind.

The Three Marks of Existence

In order to understand what Buddhists mean by suffering we have to go back to the view of life that the Buddha presented to his first students. Traditionally, this view (which is common to all Buddhist schools) is presented in what came to be called the Three Marks of Existence. This view certainly does not cover all the *marks* or aspects of our human existence, but it does cover the aspects that we tend to ignore or repress in our awareness. These three marks are emphasized in the teachings of the First Turning because they help the practitioner of the Buddhist path to become aware of this kind of ignorance and gain a more realistic and fearless view of life. This is necessary because only a realistic view can serve as the basis for spiritual development and for reaching enlightenment, the complete and unconditional acceptance and experience of the realities of human life. That acceptance and way of experiencing in itself brings peace or liberation.

What are the three marks, the three realities of life that we tend to ignore? According to the Buddha, they are: *pain, impermanence,* and *egolessness*. Let me briefly describe what is meant by those *technical terms* in Buddhism.

1. Existential & Neurotic Suffering

Pain

In the context of the Three Marks, the classical Buddhist term *duhkha* (Sanskrit) might be best translated as *pain* in the broad sense of dis-ease, discomfort, and as the opposite of *pleasure* (Sanskrit: *sukha*). Living beings are sensitive beings; they unavoidably experience pleasure and pain, both physically and mentally. Various types of pain are mentioned in the sutras. Some of them refer primarily to the physical level - like the pain of birth, sickness, old age and death - and others more to the mental level - like getting what one does not want, not getting what one does want, trying to get what one wants, and trying to keep what one likes. These eight types of pain are part of human life. Whether one is a Buddha or not the experience of these various types of pain will be there. But a Buddha, having accepted this reality of life unconditionally, will *experience* pain but *not suffer from* the experience of pain.

Not being enlightened we tend to think that the way to happiness is to seek pleasure and to avoid pain. As we will discuss below, suffering from pain as opposed to experiencing it results from trying to avoid, fight against, and ban these various types of pain from our awareness. Resisting what is unavoidable is obviously not the way to happiness at all. Because of our tendency to play deaf and dumb to this Mark of Existence, the Buddhist teachings of the First Turning draw our attention to the reality of pain; not in order to depress us, but in order to open our eyes, to make us more realistic.

Impermanence

The Second Mark of Existence goes by the Sanskrit term *anityata*, which is usually translated as *impermanence*. This term refers simply to the fact that nothing in our lives remains the same. Every meeting ends in a parting and whatever is composite will sooner or later disintegrate and vice versa. This is a fact of life - a mark of existence. Again, the reality of impermanence is experienced both by the Enlightened Ones and by us who are not enlightened.

Selflessness, Egolessness

The Third Mark of Existence is called *anatman* in Sanskrit, which is usually translated as *selflessness* or *egolessness*. This aspect of our existence is maybe the most difficult to understand and to experience in our everyday life. Generally speaking, the Third Mark points out that our experience is fluid and that no independently existing entities (objects and subjects) can actually be found in the ongoing stream of our life experience. What we do find is an ongoing flux of interdependent qualities of experience, which are technically known as *dharmas* that arise inter-dependently (Sanskrit: *pratityasamutpada*).

More specifically, no permanent entity that we could call *me* or *I* can be identified in our subjective field of experience. To be sure, there is a whole variety of ongoing and ever shifting inner experiences of bodily and other sensory sensations, of perceptions, thought patterns, and qualities of awareness to which we usually refer with the personal pronoun *me* or *I*. Nevertheless, we can neither locate and identify a permanent unchanging *entity* in this fleeting stream of experiences nor notice something that holds or *has* this stream of experience and that we could call *me*. According to the Buddhist view, this is not because of some kind of cognitive inadequacy on our part but because it is impossible to find something that does not exist. In fact, the outcome of the search for such an entity is supposed to be the liberating realization of the Third Mark: we do exist but in an egoless way, not as a solid entity that we could call *me* or *I*.

Maybe all this sounds a little philosophical, but practically speaking this realization is experienced as the opening up of a psychological space that is not conditioned by our ways of conceptualizing our stream of experience in terms of entities and with the entity *I* in the center. This space is a carefree space in which our painful attempts to hold on to and maintain the world as we think it to be and to ourselves as we think ourselves to be has been dissolved. Because the realization of no-self puts an end to our habitual pattern of conceiving our experience in a self-centered way, it also puts an end to egocentric emotions like greed, jealousy, aggression, pride, and so on. The illusory distance between *me* and *the world* has been dissolved into a warm and clear space of total intimacy with our moment-to-moment experience.

Of course, our mind still keeps its (in itself valuable) capacity to conceive our stream of experience in terms of entities. The Third Mark addresses our inability to experience the selflessness of phenomena and our tendency to mistakenly slip into the belief that these entities and objects, which are created by our mind, *really exist*. We then begin to live in and hold on to a self-conceived world, a world imagined by our mind to lie outside of our mind; holding on to this imaginary world as real and fighting against occasional experiences of egolessness that threaten its seeming reality lead to suffering.

The Three Marks of Existence point to fundamental qualities of our human existence mentioned above; unavoidable qualities that we have great difficulties accepting and living with because we are not enlightened. The spiritual path of the Buddha points out a way that enables us to develop a view that accommodates those realities and therefore enables us to relate to our ongoing life experience in an increasingly realistic and psychologically healthy way. Ultimately this leads to a total pacification of our anxiety about the realities of life. In terms of the First Turning, this is called *the peace of nirvana* or enlightenment. The Three Marks together with the view of nirvana as peace are also known as the Four Seals (Geshe, Lundrup, & Hopkins, 1989). Virtually all Buddhist schools say that whoever asserts the view expressed by the Four Seals can be called a Buddhist.

1. Existential & Neurotic Suffering

Existential Suffering

Let us now turn to the Buddhist concept of suffering. As I mentioned above, in the language of the First Turning enlightenment is understood as the cessation of suffering. What kind of suffering is meant here? Basically it is the suffering that is experienced by fighting against, resisting, ignoring, and pushing out of one's awareness the existential realities of life as described by the Three Marks of Existence. I will call this suffering *existential suffering*.

The difference between the Buddhas and ordinary beings is that the former unconditionally and fearlessly accept and embrace the fundamental realities of life while the latter do not and therefore suffer. Ordinary beings are scared by reality, try to escape from it and fight against it, just like Siddhartha Gautama when he first encountered it outside of the protected environment of his father's palace. In fact, it was his encounter with existential suffering that made him leave his palace and begin his quest to find a way and view of life that would put an end to this existential suffering. As we know his quest led him to become the Buddha, which means "the awakened one." It is interesting to note that Siddhartha is portrayed in Buddhist texts as a perfectly healthy young man, both mentally and physically, free from any kind of *neurotic* attitudes or behaviour. Even so, he had to come to grips with the great realities of human life. This is what he did and what his enlightenment is about.

Remembering why and in what state of mind he himself entered on a spiritual path, the Buddha began to address and teach about the suffering that he had freed himself from. So he presented in many sutras what later came to be systematized as the *Three Kinds of Suffering*. Within the Buddhist traditions, several slightly different interpretations of these three have developed over the centuries. I will briefly present only one of them that seems to be most relevant to our explorations.

The first type of suffering is called in Sanskrit *duhkhaduhkhata*, which we could translate as the suffering (*duhkhata*) of pain (*duhkha*). Sometimes it is translated as *ordinary suffering*. It refers to suffering from the eight kinds of pain that we mentioned above: birth, old age, sickness (physical and mental illness), death or dying, not getting what one wants, getting what one does not want, the effort of trying to get what one wants, and the effort of trying to keep what one likes. When we do not accept those eight kinds of pain but resist them, repress them, fight against them, then we suffer from them; we experience *duhkhaduhkhata*. This is the result of going against the experience of the First Mark of Existence. For instance, our *resistance to nakedly experience* the pain and disease of old age makes us *suffer from* the pain and disease of old age. Ongoing resistance to the acceptance that we did not have things go our way makes us suffer in the form of lasting disappointment and resentment. In this interpretation, *duhkhaduhkhata* is said to be experienced most strongly by beings that are born in what is called *the Human Realm* (Gampopa, 1998). For now, we can understand this term as being born as an unenlightened human being. We will discuss the Six Realms, of which the Human Realm is one, later on.

The second type of suffering is called *viparanamaduhkhata*, which is usually translated as the suffering of impermanence. If we resist, repress and fight against the experience of change, then we suffer from that change and we experience the suffering of impermanence. This results from resisting the reality of the Second Mark of Existence.

The third type of suffering is called *samskaraduhkhata*, which is usually translated as suffering of conditioned existence. In technical Buddhist language, this kind of suffering is explained as resulting from holding the so-called *five skandhas* to be realities. Another way of explaining this is that this kind of suffering results from holding our ego-centered experience of reality as real. This way of experiencing in turn comes about because of ego-centered mental patterns (samskaras) that condition it. This is why this suffering is called the suffering of conditioned existence. It goes against the experience of the Third Mark of Existence. In a way, this kind of suffering is the most deep-rooted and pervasive one of the three and therefore the most difficult one to liberate oneself from.

To summarize, these three kinds of suffering all come from a movement of mind that is common to all unenlightened beings: the movement of mentally turning away and separating oneself from one's experience by imagining oneself as an entity separate from one's experience. This is what is called the *birth of ego* in Buddhist thought. By creating this imaginary distance between *me* on the one hand and *my experience, my world* on the other, the possibility of *keeping a safe distance* is suggested, where in reality there is none. The idea of a safe distance already points at what the affective dynamic of this movement is: It is fear of life and fear of death, or more precisely fear of suffering.

Ego in Buddhism

The intricate dynamics of the movement of mind that leads to the birth of ego have been discussed elsewhere in detail (de Wit, 1999). However, the close relationship between fear, suffering, and *ego* that Buddhism maintains makes it clear that the Buddhist concept of ego is very different from the way the term ego is used in many Western psychologies and psychotherapies, where it often has the positive connotation of inner strength and self-confidence. According to Buddhism, an ego-centered way of structuring one's life experience is connected with a *lack of confidence* in one's existence as a human being. Its psychodynamic root is fear for and distrust of one's mental and sensory mediated experience. According to Buddhism, ego-mind is fearful mind. Therefore, saying "One needs a strong ego before one can (transcend or) let go of it" shows a misunderstanding of the meaning of ego in Buddhism and is misleading.

Stated in Freudian terms, the Buddhist notion of ego does not refer to ego in the sense of Freud's *reality principle* but rather to the collective triad of the reality principle, the pleasure principle, and superego (the principle of conscience). From a Buddhist point of view, Freud describes the psychodynamics of unenlightened ego-mind, but not the dynamics of the egoless mind of the Buddha. In Buddhist terms, ego is not an entity but rather a more or less ongoing mental activity, the activity of our mind (consciousness/awareness) grasping and holding on to itself (to its thought contents).

    Lastly, although the movement of mind that leads to the birth of ego defines the unenlightened human being, we should not view this human being as psychologically unhealthy in the conventional sense. If we want to speak in terms of *health*, we could say that the Buddha enjoys ultimate or *absolute sanity*. This sanity is the result of liberating oneself from the movement of mind that we discussed: the mental movement of warding off the Three Marks. The path towards this liberation goes in the direction of ultimately embracing existential suffering unconditionally. By embracing it unconditionally, existential suffering is transformed and experienced as *unconditional compassion* towards samsaric (unenlightened) existence. Within that experience the reality of pain, impermanence and egolessness is seen *as it is*, without obstruction, with absolute clarity of mind. That clarity is referred to in Buddhism as *ultimate wisdom*. The suffering of pain then becomes the naked experience of pain. The suffering of impermanence becomes the experience of impermanence and the suffering of conditioned experience is transformed into the experience of egolessness. So, what is experienced as existential suffering by ordinary beings is experienced by the Enlightened Ones as compassion. This amounts to the cessation of existential suffering, the Buddha's goal. This cessation itself is experienced as ultimate freedom and happiness. As is said in a Buddhist sadhana: "Now pain and pleasure alike have become ornaments which it is pleasant to wear" (Trungpa, 1990). In this way, the universal pursuit of happiness that all living beings share with each other is fulfilled. In the realm of action this way of experiencing manifests as the ability to act in a compassionate and effective way toward other living beings who are still under the sway of existential suffering.

    Compared to the Buddha we could say that ordinary beings enjoy a *relative sanity* - relative to how well they can live an ego-centered life and manage their ego-centered emotionality. In terms of what we discussed so far: their sanity is dependent on how well they can cope with the existential suffering that results from warding off the realization of the Three Marks. From this ego-centered perspective the pursuit of happiness is narrowed down to and understood as seeking pleasure for oneself and avoiding pain. If, at times, we are unable to do this or if we lose track of how to do this there might be other people who help us to get back on track.

A Buddhist View of Neurotic Suffering

As long as we somehow can cope with the three kinds of suffering that our fearful mind has brought us, we might view them as an unavoidable aspect of life and endure them while trying to maintain our relative sanity. However, when we are attentive we might notice that there are also moments in our life that are free of existential suffering, free from fear of the realities of life. Such moments might make us think twice. They might occur in times of prosperity or even in the midst of adversity. Those moments might inspire us to take a second look at our mind and experience and make us look for ways to explore them. Instead of warding off our existential suffering, we might now begin to look for ways to see through it and to give up our resistance to it. That means in fact that we, like the Buddha, enter the path of meditation that ultimately might liberate us from existential suffering.

What happens when we cannot cope with the three kinds of existential suffering? We apply the same movement of mind to this suffering that we applied to the Three Marks, which transformed the Marks into the experience of the three kinds of suffering: We will try to ward off this existential suffering, to escape from it, to resist it, fight it, suppress it, ban it from our awareness. This repression and suppression leads in turn to another kind of suffering, one that obscures the direct experience of existential suffering. Although the term is slightly old fashioned, we will call this *neurotic suffering*. What this kind of suffering has in common with existential suffering is that it is also caused by one's mind. According to Buddhism the habitual mental and behavioral patterns that we develop to that purpose go against our humanness; they make us inhuman. In traditional Buddhist terms, we develop patterns that, when we die, will potentially lead us to being reborn not in the Human Realm but in one of the other five realms.

Varieties of Neurotic Suffering

Neurotic suffering grows on the basis of existential suffering. When existential suffering is (experienced as) unmanageable then neurotic reaction patterns tend to develop. However, because these patterns are maladaptive they bring their own kind suffering. Nevertheless they are attempts to *overcome* existential suffering. The various ways of repressing/ignoring existential suffering are described in Buddhism in terms of the Six Realms. We could understand the term *realm* here as a psychological space, in which we experience both ourselves and the phenomenal world in a particular way. Each realm has its own particular cognitive distortion, its neurotic view of life. Each one has its particular affective/emotional fixation, its particular concept of happiness and its own kind of neurotic suffering. I will briefly characterize each realm (Gampopa, 1998; Trungpa 1973).

The Hell realm is a psychological space that has as its cognitive distortion that the world is exclusively seen as a place filled with violence

1. Existential & Neurotic Suffering

(Trungpa 1973). Life is hell, so to speak. Its emotional fixation is the feeling of oneself being the victim of ongoing aggression. Its particular suffering consists of various kinds of torture. Its idea of happiness is the absence of torture. In terms of modern psychology, we might see these patterns at work in anxiety disorders and depression.

The Hungry Ghost realm is a psychological space that has as its cognitive distortion that the world is exclusively seen as a place filled with unattainable riches (Trungpa 1973). The emotional fixation is a feeling of insatiable longing or hunger. The kind of neurotic suffering of this realm is a feeling of being deprived, left out, a deep sense of poverty. Naturally, happiness is here conceived as the absence of dissatisfaction. In terms of modern psychology the patterns of the Hungry Ghost realm might be visible as lack of any self-esteem and grief about unfulfilled ambitions and recognition; the grief of not being seen or acknowledged by others.

The Animal Realm is a psychological space that has as its cognitive distortion that the world is fundamentally unknowable, too overwhelmingly big and unpredictable to even try to understand it (Trungpa 1973). The emotional response to that is playing deaf and dumb, ignoring the world and building a very small world to oneself. The neurotic suffering of this realm is the constant feeling of having no control or the fear of losing it. Happiness is conceived as the absence of the unexpected, the unknown. In terms of Western psychology, the patterns of this realm might manifest in obsessive-compulsive disorders, schizoid personality disorders, and certain forms of autism.

Taken together these three realms are called the *Lower Realms* in classical Buddhism. What they have in common is that the person experiencing them feels victimized by and powerless in the psychological space he or she is in. The next three realms are called the Higher Realms. Here one feels that one has some personal power.

The God Realm is a psychological space that has as its cognitive distortion that the world is not worth knowing, not even worth bothering about. Its emotional quality is one of self-indulgence, combined with megalomaniac feelings of being on top of the world or excessive pride (Trungpa 1973). Happiness is conceived as the presence of blissful oblivion and self-absorption. This realm is the most successful one in terms of warding off suffering. It is hardly perceptible. However, this realm eventually (according to the texts it might take a very long time) exhausts itself. Staying in it drains one's energy and resources so that it is bound to collapse at some point. In terms of Western psychology, we see its patterns in some drug induced disorders and in certain forms of substance dependence (and this *substance* may well be material wealth, power, pleasure and leisure!) but also in narcissistic personality disorders and mania/hypomania.

The Jealous God Realm is a psychological space that has as its cognitive distortion that the world is viewed as a battlefield in which one has to walk around as fully armed as one can, because survival of the fittest is its norm (Trungpa 1973). Its emotional quality is jealousy, competitiveness, and distrust. Consequently the neurotic suffering of this realm is the threat of being undermined or defeated by others and the need to constantly take countermeasures in all possible directions. Happiness is understood here as the experience of victory, of coming out on top as number one. Some of the psychological patterns of this realm we can see in paranoid and antisocial personality disorders and in the paranoid type of schizophrenia.

The last realm is called the Human Realm; it is somewhat special in that its neurotic suffering is not as strong as the experience of existential suffering (Trungpa 1973). Put another way, it is a realm in which neurotic attempts to ward off existential suffering are the least successful. This realm has as its cognitive distortion that the world is viewed exclusively as a space filled with pleasant and unpleasant/painful qualities and that life is about making intelligent choices between them. So, the view here is a kind of intelligent hedonism, which seems to echo Freud's reality principle and pleasure principle. Its main emotional quality is passion or desire. Happiness is understood here as the presence of satisfaction. Its neurotic suffering consists in constantly and obsessively searching for pleasure (or rather, for what one thinks that will give one pleasure) as an antidote to the existential suffering that is so strongly experienced in this realm. Traditionally it is said in the teachings of First Turning (but not in the Mahayana teachings of the Second Turning) that it is in this realm only that one can hear the dharma that is the teachings of the Buddha and practice them. Because of the intelligence operating in this realm one might be open to the idea that the cessation of existential suffering may well be the greatest pleasure one can possibly experience.

How to Understand the Six Realms

It is easy to misunderstand what is presented in Buddhism by the Six Realms. So, some further remarks on them might be in order. First of all, they have in common that each of them is the result of maladaptive coping strategies, which aim at denying, resisting or escaping the reality of pain, of impermanence, and of egolessness, both on a personal and social level. However, although the mental and behavioral patterns that characterize and govern these realms also seem to manifest in various mental disorders that we distinguish in our Western psychology, we should be careful not to jump to the conclusion that the Buddhist theory of the Six Realms somehow suggests that these disorders are all *caused by* the mental movement of warding off existential suffering. For there can be and actually are many other factors (both of a biological and circumstantial nature) that lead to mental problems and disorders. So, the Six Realms *do not offer a causal explanation* of mental disorders as classified in the DSM-IV by Western psychology, even though we see many of the patterns of the Six Realms clearly manifest in them. Its explanation is neither saying nor implying that mental illness is caused by the mind resisting to relate to existential suffering. Rather, the Buddhist interpretation of *neurotic suffering* in terms of the Six Realms offers a description of what one's mind tends to do when existential suffering is experienced as unbearable. And the causes that make this suffering unbearable can be many. The analysis in terms of the Six Realms is primarily a description of mental and behavioral patterns that are maladaptive in the sense that they weaken one's ability to come to grips and make peace with the great realities of human existence. The value of this analysis lies in that it offers a diagnostic tool to determine whether and when a psychotherapeutic or a spiritual approach might be helpful. The mind reacting to unbearable existential suffering leads to the kind of *psychological* problems that seem to be the main focus of Western psychotherapy. It is here that the great contribution of the Western psychotherapy seems to lie, even though Buddhism is certainly not without ways of treating them (de Silva, 1984, 1996). As to the treatment of mental illness and psychosis, Buddhism has its own ways of treatment as well; ways that are in many aspects close to Western biological psychiatry (Clifford, 1984).

Secondly, one might wonder what the psychological gain is of moving into one of these realms. In particular why would any human being want to move into what has been called the *Lower Realms*? They do not seem to be conducive to real happiness at all. Only in relation to each other does there seem to be a difference in what they conceive as happiness. The answer is that moving into a realm is not based on a deliberate decision, but it is the result of developing (mostly step by step and without realizing the consequences) certain mental and behavioral patterns to ward off existential suffering. For instance, through focusing strongly on a particular view and emotional quality (let us say the view of the world as a place of torture, permeated by aggression) we might overshadow the suffering that we experience when confronted with an unbearable great loss. This movement of mind that initially performs the function of distracting us from this existential suffering might become a habitual pattern. It then becomes more and more ingrained and begins to shape or dominate the psychological space in which we live. And at some point, the remedy turns out to be worse than the disease. By that time, this movement of mind imprisons our experience. It is like escaping from danger by fleeing in blind panic to a desert or a jungle to find out that in the long run living there is even more dangerous and that there is no way back. One feels one has no other option than to cope with this environment.

Lastly, human beings may develop mental and behavioral patterns that belong to various realms. They will apply those patterns depending on how they view their actual situation. They will find themselves going through experiences that resemble living in one of those realms. That is why Buddhist practitioners, although they are born in the Human Realm, might say by analogy that they are at times experiencing other realms. Traditionally, the Six Realms are understood in a more literal sense: as different physical existences in which one can be reborn. Being reborn as a hell being, a hungry ghost, an animal, a human, or a (Jealous) God is viewed as the result of ingrained mental patterns that survive after physical death. These patterns are reborn in the corresponding realm.

Although the idea of multiple lifetimes is foreign to Western culture (certainly to its scientific community), it points to the fact that the neurotic patterns that define the various realms can be very persistent and hard to break. Buddhists might say that the cause of their persistency is that these patterns have been developed for a long time over many lifetimes. One is reborn with them and when the conditions are there they become active and manifest. In that sense they seem to be very similar to what we call *personality disorders* in our Western psychological classification. These disorders are notably hard to cure as well.

The Relation Between Existential and Neurotic Suffering

Our definition of neurotic suffering as a result of warding off existential suffering has two important corollaries. The first one is that when there is no existential suffering then neurotic suffering cannot arise. Neurotic suffering is symptomatic of and arises from unmanageable existential suffering. *Unmanageable* in the sense that we are unable to face, endure, and ultimately dissolve that particular suffering and therefore we seek to protect ourselves by strategies that lead to neurotic suffering. The causes that make us unable to stay with existential suffering can be many, depending on the person and the circumstances. I will not discuss them here. Discovering them and dissolving them is one the aims of psychotherapy.

The second corollary is implied by the function of neurotic suffering: When there is neurotic suffering then existential suffering cannot (easily) be experienced. Although neurotic suffering in itself is symptomatic of unmanageable existential suffering, it also obscures existential suffering, which makes it difficult to work with existential suffering directly.

Last, both forms of suffering result from the same movement of mind: resistance. Existential suffering results from resisting the reality of the three marks, resisting seeing things as they are. Neurotic suffering results from resisting existential suffering.

The Implications for the Relation Between Psychotherapy and Buddhist Spirituality

Let us now bring back to mind the two statements that were presented at the beginning of this chapter, one by Freud and one by the Buddha. We can rephrase the one by the Buddha as follows: "I aim at one and only one thing: existential suffering and the cessation of existential suffering." Freud's statement can be rephrased like this: "The only thing that psychotherapy can do is to transform neurotic suffering into existential suffering." Put differently, the Buddha claims to be able to remove existential suffering and not neurotic suffering. Freud and most psychotherapists claim to be able to remove neurotic suffering but not existential suffering.

This way of reading these two statements provides us with a criterion to determine when and where psychotherapy is in order, and when and where the Buddhist spiritual path might be the way to go. Whether a spiritual practice or psychotherapy is indicated depends on whether the individual can work with existential suffering directly or not. This is not a black and white issue; it can be that the neurotic reaction to existential suffering is very light and does not prevent the practitioner from working with his or her existential suffering directly. In such cases existential suffering might be overcome by Buddhist spiritual practice and in its wake the neurotic reaction will disappear as well, as far as it is based on that existential suffering. This explains why spiritual practice (in some cases) might have a psychotherapeutic effect. However, when the neurotic suffering is so strong that the underlying existential suffering can not be worked with directly, then psychotherapy is in order. In Buddhist terms, we could say that psychotherapy is a means to lead people to the Human Realm and out of the other five realms.

Let me add a subtle point here. Both kinds of suffering derive their painful quality from the mental act of resisting and the fear that accompanies and fuels resistance. This means that the transformation from suffering from neurotic patterns and from the Marks of Existence into nakedly experiencing them amounts in both cases to letting go of one's fear-ridden resistance. The implication is that it is possible to attain *cessation of suffering* or enlightenment in the Buddhist sense while still *living with* neurotic patterns. But these patterns have now become like dead shells. We do not *live in* them any more, that is we do not feed them the energy necessary to maintain them. As time goes by they might simply fade away or even be put to use in a constructive way, somewhat like using an empty shell or conch as a musical instrument.

Spiritual Teachers are Not Psychotherapists and Vice Versa

The criterion presented here for distinguishing between the function of psychotherapy and the Buddhist path has also some implications for spiritual teachers and psychotherapists that we will briefly discuss now. If one confuses or equates the Buddhist path and psychotherapy then one might run into two forms of unprofessional approaches. Buddhist spiritual teachers might think they are as good as psychotherapists and therapists might think they are as good as Buddhist spiritual teachers; or their students and clients might think that way.

When the distinction is not clear to a Buddhist teacher then he or she might not diagnose neurotic suffering correctly and apply spiritual disciplines to it. This will, in most cases, result in failure, both for the teacher and for the student. Consequently, the student who approached the teacher with (tacit or explicit) therapeutic expectations will loose faith in the spiritual path and in the teacher. Such a person will not be inclined to enter such a path later on, after his neurotic suffering has been successfully treated by a psychotherapist. In the sporadic cases that a spiritual teacher happens to successfully treat neurotic suffering the student will be reinforced to think that traveling on a spiritual path is a form of psychotherapy and will only be motivated to practice its disciplines as a means to solve his or her neurotic suffering. That means that both in the case of failure and in the case of success this person will not be motivated to explore the possibility that the Buddhist path offers: to work with his or her existential suffering and attain cessation of it.

When the distinction is not clear to a psychotherapist, then he or she might not diagnose existential suffering correctly and apply psychotherapeutic disciplines to it. This results in most cases in failure, for how many psychotherapists are there who fully and unconditionally have themselves made peace with their own existential suffering and who are able to guide their clients in that direction? The client who approaches the therapist with existential problems and then receives psychotherapeutic treatment will not be helped and therefore loose faith in psychotherapy. When neurotic suffering turns up later in life he or she will not again consider psychotherapeutic help. In the sporadic cases of success by the psychotherapist the client will be reinforced to think that psychotherapy is not different from traveling on a spiritual path and not be motivated to practice spiritual disciplines that go *beyond therapy* (Claxton 1986).

The Buddhist path and psychotherapy are different disciplines with different aims and different means. The aforementioned risks that are taken by mixing them together might make us careful, if not skeptical, about *integrating* a spiritual practice into a psychotherapeutic approach and vice versa. That does not alter the fact that it would be very valuable to be fully trained and authorized in both disciplines by qualified people, that is by lineage holders of both disciplines. That will certainly enhance our diagnostic ability to determine what is best for the person who seeks spiritual or psychological help. But having determined what kind of help is requested, it seems best, based on our discussion, to choose to have either a spiritual or a psychotherapeutic relationship with the student or client.

References

Claxton, G. L. (Ed.). (1986). *Beyond therapy*. London: Wisdom Publications.
Clifford, T. (1984): *Tibetan Buddhist medicine and psychiatry: The diamond healing*. York Beach, ME: Samuel Weiser.
de Silva, P. (1984). Buddhism and behaviour modification. *Behaviour Research & Therapy, 22,* 661-678.
de Silva, P. (1986). Buddhist psychology: Theory and therapy. In M.G.T. Kwee & T.L. Holdstock (Eds.) *Western and Buddhist psychology: Clinical perspectives*. Delft, Holland: Eburon.

de Wit, H. F. (1999). *The spiritual path: An introduction to the psychology of the spiritual traditions.* Pittsburgh, PA: Duquesne University Press.

Freud, S. (1952). "*Gemeines Unglück*" in *Gesammelte Werke, I.* London: Imago Publishing.

Gampopa (1998). *The jewel ornament of liberation.* Ithaca, NY: Snow Lion Publications.

Sopa, G. L. & Hopkins, J. (1989): *Cutting through appearances.* Ithaca NY: Snow Lion Publications.

Trencker, V. (Ed.). (1995). *Majjhima Nikaya.* (B. Ñ_namoli & B. Bodhi, Trans.) London: Pali Text Society.

Trungpa, C. (1973) *Cutting through spiritual materialism.* Boston: Shambhala Publications.

Trungpa, C. (1990) *Sadhana of Mahamudra.* Halifax, Nova Scotia: Nalanda Translation Committee.

2

An Existential Framework for Buddhism, World Religions, and Psychotherapy: Culture and Diversity Considerations

Louis Hoffman

Confusion about Buddhism in the West both entices and creates anxiety for many practitioners and scholars. Various challenges arise such as labeling Buddhism as a religion or a philosophy, trying to understand Buddhism in the context of its Eastern origins, and whether Buddhism can fit into a Western mindset. Regardless, it is evident that Buddhism in the West, particularly when applied within Western psychology, is very different than Buddhism in the East.

This provides an important starting point when considering Buddhism and psychotherapy in a Western context. No world religion or philosophy can be fully understood separate from the culture in which it emerged; however, this does not mean that they should only be applied or integrated consistent with these origins. Religions and philosophies evolve whether they acknowledge this or not.

The goal of this chapter is to understand how Buddhism can be integrated into psychotherapy in a culturally and religiously sensitive manner. This issue is particularly challenging in an increasingly pluralistic and international society, and one that often offers overly simplistic integrations. Joey Pulleyking (2005), in addressing the attempts to integrate the sciences with religion or spirituality, purports that a major problem in cross discipline integration is the maintenance of depth in both domains. For instance, often simplistic understandings of Buddhism are integrated into more sophisticated forms of psychology, or pop psychology is integrated into a depth understanding of religion. It is a focus of this book, and more specifically this chapter, to develop an approach reflecting the depth and richness psychology and Buddhism have to offer.

Buddhism as a Philosophy and as a Religion

The question has often been asked: Is Buddhism a religion or a philosophy? It does not matter what you call it. Buddhism remains what it is whatever label you may put on it. The label is immaterial. (Rahula, 1974)

Defining Religion and Philosophy.
There is neither space nor need for a comprehensive overview of the various definitions of religion; however, some prefatory discussion is beneficial. The historical understanding of religion has changed enormously in the late modern and into the postmodern periods (Ervin-Cox, Hoffman, Grimes, & Fehl, 2007; Wulff, 1997). Through the evolution of the term religion, spirituality and mysticism have been removed from many contemporary understandings of religion. Religion has become highly associated with organized (or communal), ritualistic, and content-centered aspects of the previous broader, more inclusive understanding of religion.

Religion often, although not always, has something to say about what happens after death. Religion is also often thought to include statements of belief about metaphysical realities, such as whether a god, many gods, or some sort of ultimate reality exists. Increasingly, however, each of the major world religions include sectarian groups with varied metaphysical statements and beliefs. Given these variations, *religion could be defined as the structured and communal aspects of belief.* Although valid, this definition of religion is inclusive to the point of being nearly meaningless.

Theologian and philosopher Paul Tillich (1957) defined religion in connection with an individual's ultimate concern. This concept narrows the definition of religion by connecting it to that which is most important or most deeply grips an individual. More specifically, *religion could be defined as the structured and communal aspects of belief related to one's ultimate concern.*

The term philosophy, as it is understood in popular usage, has parallels to the evolution of the term *religion.* Historically, philosophy meant the pursuit of wisdom and was primarily connected to the academic study of philosophy. Today, philosophy is often reduced to meaning an individual's worldview. This commonplace usage is often what is meant by *Buddhist philosophy:* a worldview rooted in Buddhist thought and tradition. All world religions can be understood to have their own philosophy in this sense.

Buddhist philosophy in the more traditional sense also exists. In contrast with the more common usage of Buddhist philosophy, the traditional understanding applies Buddhist principles to understanding the nature of knowledge and the world. As should be apparent, when dialoguing about Buddhist philosophy, it is important to be aware of how the term is being used.

Historical approaches to the terms religion and philosophy demonstrate that Buddhism can be both a religion and a philosophy, depending upon how one uses the terms. As a religion, more emphasis is placed upon the ultimate nature of reality and desired outcome of life. For example, when Buddhism is connected to recognizing the illusion of the self and escaping the repetitive cycle of life and death, it is functioning as a religion. However, when focused more on a way of living or what is deemed a moral or good life apart from the broader ultimate claims, Buddhism can function as a philosophy or world view.

Buddhism and Religion in the West. Religion has developed a bad name in the West. Much of this resulted from the abuses and perceived abuses of organized religion (Hoffman, in press; 2007). These abuses led to a mass exodus from the Judeo-Christian religions in the West, particularly the United States. For many spurned by the Judeo-Christian versions of organized religion, Buddhism was very appealing. Buddhism in the United States lacked much of the rigid structure and organization associated with the abuses of power and corruption in other religions.

Many of these new Buddhists retained their distaste for organized religion, and even the word *religion*. This contributed to some of the distinctive nature of Western Buddhism. But Buddhism did not escape other influences of Western culture. Individualism, pragmatism, an often excessive valuing of the self, a simplistic hedonism, and a quick fix mentality became associated with at least some approaches to Buddhism. As should be evident, not all Buddhist approaches in the West integrated these problematic features, and few integrated them all. However, these influences significantly changed the face of Buddhism.

Psychology was particularly susceptive to these new Western Buddhisms. Examples abound of this, including mindfulness-based relapse prevention (Witkiewitz, Marlatt, & Walker, 2005), tendencies to emphasize non-attachment to suffering while retaining attachment to the self, and using meditation solely as a relaxation technique.

The contemplative psychotherapy approaches, such as those taught at Naropa University, reflect a refreshing return to the roots and depth of Buddhism in psychotherapy. Unfortunately, most mainstream approaches seem to pick and choose aspects of Buddhism while readily changing traditional Buddhism to fit immediate needs. This is not to argue that aspects of Buddhism, or any other religion, should not change, evolve, or seek adaptation through dialogue with popular culture. Rather, it is a strong criticism of the way contemporary psychology and United States culture has often done this without serious reflection to recognize how they have changed what they are integrating.

It is important for Buddhist therapists to be aware of this history for several reasons. First, although the Buddhist therapist may view Buddhism as a philosophy, many of his or her clients may view it as a religion. Second, it is not an uncommon experience for therapists to experience resistance to meditation or mindfulness with non-Buddhist clients because of its being associated with Buddhism as a religion. While the therapist may view the incorporation of Buddhism as enhancing therapy, some clients will experience it as coercion into a different religious belief. Third, this brief history of religion has impacted many Buddhist clients and, furthermore, may help explain why and how they are Buddhist.

Existential Insights

Existential philosophy and psychology have long voiced strong critiques of religion, particularly organized religion (Hoffman, 2008, Mendelowitz, 2006, Nietzsche, 1886/1966). The intention of this critique, however, is often misunderstood. The intent is not to say that religion, even organized religion, is bad, but rather to strongly challenge religion without critical thought.

Two important applications from existential thought can inform the current discussion. First, existentialism would applaud the concerns about organized religion, particularly the abuses. Second, existential thought would raise strong concerns about the shallowness with which many individuals in the West and Western psychology have integrated Buddhism without much critical thought.

There is little doubt that Buddhism has much to offer psychology and psychotherapy, particularly when working with Buddhist clients. The integration of Buddhism and psychology in the West is also young enough to try to avoid some of the problems that other religions, such as Christianity, have made when attempting such integration. Christianity is replete with *Christian psychologies* that insult the richness of Christianity *and* psychology. By taking seriously the challenge of integration, Buddhism can avoid such mistakes.

Existentialism also points toward the potential for integration. Consistent with the idea of perennial philosophy, existentialism has attempted to identify certain existential givens, or struggles, that are universal for all people. Existentialism as a whole does not attempt to provide answers to these givens, but rather identifies them as universal struggles. Although individuals within existential thought have attempted such answers, most view the answers as something that individuals need to discover on their own.

Siblings in Wisdom and Essential Differences

Rudyard Kipling stated, "East is East and West is West and never the twain shall meet" (as cited in Roth, 2003). There is a great amount of truth to this statement, particularly when applied to Eastern and Western religions. There are also more similarities than are often recognized, but even the similarities are fraught with important subtle differences. Nonetheless, there is sufficient reason to believe that dialogue between the East and West, including religious dialogue, can be mutually beneficial. Masao Abe (1990), a leader in the Christian-Buddhist dialogues, states,

2. An Existential Framework

Over the past few decades the dialogue between Buddhism and Christianity has evolved considerably. It has gone beyond the state of promoting mutual understanding between the two religions, and is now entering a new stage in which the mutual transformation of Buddhism and Christianity is being seriously explored. (p. 3)

This respect for interfaith dialogue is shared by the Dalai Lama, who states, "Close contact with different religions helps me to learn new ideas, new practices, and new methods or techniques that I can incorporate into my own practice" (Gyatso, 2001, p. 52).

The purpose of this dialogue, however, is very different in the religious studies realm, from which Abe and the Dalai Lama are participating, and the realm of psychology and religion. In psychology, recognizing similarities between different religious backgrounds can be helpful in working with clients from a different religious background, but also is important in avoiding imposing beliefs when working with these clients.

Kenosis and No-Self

A key concept in Buddhism is non-attachment to the self or *no-self*, which is often cited as an essential difference from the Western religions (Gyatso, 2001, 2007). However, most religions value forms of self-denial or self-emptying and warn against the dangers of excessive self-focus. In Christianity, the concept of *Kenosis*, or self-emptying, resembles many aspects of the Buddhist idea of no-self (Abe, 1990, 1995).

Western culture, however, transformed the ideas of no-self and Kenosis. How this occurred in Buddhism has already been discussed. In Christianity the process was more gradual, emerging from the development of Western thought, particularly through the development of modernism. The development of this heightened view of self was not indigenous to Buddhism or the Judeo-Christian religious traditions; rather, it is an aspect of Western thought that transformed all religions in the West to some degree.

This is not to say that the original understanding of Kenosis is equivalent to the Buddhist idea of no-self. In Buddhism, the ultimate goal is to recognize that there is no independent self, whereas in Christianity the goal has traditionally been the unification of the self with the ultimate reality of God (i.e., the self still exists separately). Although this goes beyond the purpose of this chapter, some recent developments emphasizing *panentheism* (God is all things) and process theology (emphasizing that everything, including God and self, are more fluid) evidence some movement in a direction more strongly resembling Buddhist conceptions of the self.

The Dalai Lama, in his discussion of no-self, focuses on the lack of an independent self:

> the various schools of Buddhism... agree that the root cause of all our suffering and afflictions is the strong clinging to a sense of "I." To put it simply, they assert that there is no-self or individual that exists apart from, and independently of, the aggregates. (Gyatso, 2007, p. 120)

Existential psychology, evidenced in the writings of May (1981), similarly addresses the interconnectedness of various influences. May uses destiny to refer to the many determined aspects of human existence, those devoid of choice which inevitably influence, and sometimes determine, all individuals. However, despite the large agreement, existential psychology tends to retain a sense of *I* or agency that tends to reflect a different understanding of self.

From an existential perspective, it could be maintained that the difference in Buddhism, the Judeo-Christian religions, and existential thought on the self are cultural interpretations of the same existential given or reality. In this manner, concerns of the self take on a pseudo-universal or perennial quality. For existential theory, the universals are not necessarily in the content, but rather in the issues wrestled with. In other words, *the tension between attachment to the self and nonattachment signifies a universal struggle; however, existentialism does not necessitate a specific answer.*

Kirk Schneider (1990), the leading contemporary existential psychologist, conceptualizes the self in terms of paradox, which bears some similarity to the Buddhist view of absolute and relative truth. Attachment and non-attachment could be seen as one of the basic paradoxical tensions within the self; people both seek to attach and de-attach. The danger is in the extremes, at least in terms of unenlightened existence on earth (samsara). This is consistent with Epstein's (1995) integration of Buddhist thought in psychology. Accordingly, Epstein maintains that some conception and analysis of the self is necessary to achieve the end of no-self.[1] The extreme represented by trying to attain no-self too quickly without going through the process is just as dangerous as attaching too much to the self.

In discussing the danger of the ends, it is important to distinguish between the path and the destination. The destination often represents an extreme. As is evident, the Buddhist no-self is an extreme. Similarly, the idea of discovering one's essential self, which was integrated into many religious traditions and psychologies in the West, represents an extreme. When the extreme is obtained gradually without shortcutting the process, it can be a healthy end. It is when the extreme is too quickly sought or

---

[1] The self here needs to be distinguished from the ego; compare with the discussion of ego by de Wit in Chapter 1.

2. An Existential Framework

when it is forced that it becomes destructive. Unfortunately, Western culture tends to lack the patience to allow for such uncovering.

Although this deals with levels of abstraction, it has some very practical utility in the psychotherapy office. I have argued that the struggle with attachment and the self is a basic existential given that all people wrestle with and that this is reflected in the major world religions. Furthermore, the chapter has purported that the extremes of non-attachment and too much attachment are dangerous, at least at most points on the journey. The ethical therapist, however, must stay open on the desired ends or outcome of the client in relation to the self. Stated differently, therapists must be able to recognize this basic existential issue and at the same time bracket their beliefs when working with clients. In doing this, therapists can help clients of various world religions avoid the extremes (too much self or too much self denial) or short cuts (bypassing the necessary process to no-self).

Hoffman, Stewart, Warren, and Meek (2006), in their critique of the postmodern idea of no essential self, maintain that cultures and religions have various *myths of self* (i.e., conceptions of the self).[2] Different myths of the self may be associated with psychological health in different cultures and religions. For people rooted in Western culture, the move toward no-self, if this is their desired end, may be different because of their indoctrination with Western individualism and focus on the self.

Of particular importance is the recognition that different conceptions of the self, and different outcomes relevant to the self, may be beneficial for different individuals. Rarely, if ever, should this be dependent upon the therapist's belief or agenda. Mosig (2006) maintains that the view of self and conceptions of mental illness have important conceptual and lived differences. For example, the strong sense of self and high self-esteem promoted in Western thought may not be compatible or healthy for many Eastern individuals who tend to de-emphasize the self.

This conception is further supported in the writings and research of Krippner (see Krippner & Achterberg, 2000). Much of Krippner's research and writing has focused on indigenous healing techniques. He found that often indigenous approaches to healing are most apt to work in the culture in which they developed. In other words, cultural beliefs often dictate to some degree what is healthy and unhealthy and what is healing and/or benign; not just conceptually, but in a lived reality. This suggests that culture is more than merely a construct, but a powerful force in the lived experience of individuals.

---

[2] The postmodern and the Buddhist ideas of no-self, although sounding similar, do not share that much resemblance. See Hoffman et al. (2006).

Compassion, the Personal, and Beyond the Personal

Karen Armstrong (2001) asserts that a commonality of all the major world religions is compassion. This is also illustrated in Mark Ian Barasch's (2005) *Field Notes on the Compassionate Life*, which draws from all the major religions in developing a deeper understanding of compassion. Stated somewhat more broadly, the Dalai Lama makes a similar assertion, suggesting that love, compassion, and forgiveness are central to all world religions (Gyatso, 2001).

Similar to the attachment/non-attachment discussion, the religious teaching from various world religions points toward compassion as a perennial concern. Lest we confuse this with a universal, it is also important to acknowledge that compassion often is understood differently in different world religions (Gyatso, 2001). What is consistent is the concern for others and the connection of this to the good or moral life.

Suffering and Depth Work

Western culture, particularly in the United States, has become obsessed with quick fixes, the expanding of happiness, and overcoming suffering. Most world religions and depth psychologies have emphasized the impossibility of such a feat, yet some have been employed in the service of this cause. Buddhism is used to "just let go" and Christianity is used to "just let go and let God." Similarly, existential psychology has been associated with "just choose to be happy." Such simplistic notions demonstrate a lack of understanding of human nature.

Religion, when not distorted with some perversion of a prosperity ethic or outcome, provides an important corrective to the psychology of the quick fix. In Buddhism, this is quite explicit and self-evident, but it does not carry over into how Buddhism is often used. Western culture often presents Buddhists as people who are always calm, always in a good mood, and generally happy-go-lucky. Such characterizations reflect a basic misunderstanding of Buddhism.

Existential thought, in particular, provides a good integration with this aspect of Buddhism. As illustrated by May (1991), a critical Western myth illustrating the existential condition and process of existential therapy is Dante's *Divine Comedy*. This myth illustrates two aspects of a critical truth. First, you can not get to heaven or nirvana without going through hell, or immense suffering. Second, the journey that one must go on is a journey into the self, even if that self is a temporary structure which one ultimately abandons.

Existentialism and Buddhism both see suffering as inevitable, but also as offering potential for growth and understanding. To deny suffering is to be stagnant. Instead, suffering should be faced and even embraced. Suffering is one of the world's greatest teachers, but also one of the most neglected.

2. An Existential Framework

A Buddhist Corrective to Existential Individualism

Existentialism emerged in the late modernist period in the writings of Pascal, Kierkegaard, Nietzsche, and later Sartre. Early existential writings strongly reflected, and even accentuated, extreme individualism. In more recent times, existentialism has sought to become open to contemporary and postmodern insights (see Schneider, 2008). If existentialism is going to claim broad relevance consistent with its claimed nature, it must be willing to accept a critical corrective from Buddhist thought.

It seems ironic that today existentialism, once associated with extremist individualism, is now often viewed as similar to Buddhist thought, which strongly warns of the dangers of excessive self-focus and self-concern. This is not, however, an irreconcilable difference. Existentialism has de-emphasized individualism over time and, I would argue, opened itself to an approach that is less tied to individualism. Challenges still remain. Existential thought, although de-emphasizing the self, does not wish to fully let go of it. However, the idea of no-self is a challenge to much of Western psychology and Western thought.

Some postmodern thinkers (Gergen, 1991, 1995; Zweig, 1995), along with some Buddhist thinkers such as Epstein (1995), provide possibilities for overcoming this seemingly impossible difference. Postmodern thought has questioned the existence of a self, but done so in varying ways. Some, such as Gergen and Zweig, have argued for multiple conceptions of self; others have focused on the self as a social construction (Hoffman et al, 2006). The shift for these postmodern thinkers is on the recognition that the self, whether an illusion or not, is created in a cultural setting and is socially constructed.

Similarly, Epstein (1995), as referred to earlier, understands that identifying the self as a necessary process on the journey to recognizing the illusion of the self. This view, too, recognizes that although the self may be a necessary construct, it is simply that – a construct. It is not a necessary conception. Even at its most basic, the self can be said to be an arbitrary boundary among many boundaries. For example, one can distinguish between the heart, arteries and blood vessels, and the lungs, but these are all part of one's body. Similarly, in the Buddhist view, along with some views from process theology, quantum physics, and postmodern thought, the self is just one arbitrary boundary among many in the larger whole.

Implications and Applications for Psychotherapy

This section will build upon the previous section offering some specific therapeutic implications and examples. It will illustrate that many of these abstract concepts discussed have a very practical aspect, even though most of these concepts may not be directly discussed with clients.

Attachment and Non-Attachment in Psychotherapy

Mindy was a zealous new Buddhist convert determined to "become a good Buddhist." She grew up in a conservative Christian home and was very active in her church youth group. When she was 17, she decided to share with her youth group that she was a lesbian, expecting them to accept her. That same night, one of her closest friends shared this with their pastor, who approached her and her parents about a "plan of action" to "save" her. The pastor recommended an experienced Christian conversion therapist, who could "cure her of this disease."

Mindy's parents, who did not know about her sexual identity, required her to continue to see this therapist as long as she lived at home. At first, Mindy attempted to cooperate and change her sexual orientation, but eventually she recognized this was not possible. People at her church continued to publicly pray for her and the success of her therapy. When Mindy's parents would only pay for her to go to a Christian college where she could continue to receive "the support she needs," Mindy decided to pay her own way through college. She left Christianity with anger toward all organized religion.

In college, Mindy spent three months in therapy and came to accept herself as a lesbian. Much of her depression and anger faded through therapy and as she developed a healthier support system. After college, she started to experience loneliness and detachment which led to her exploring new spiritual avenues. She began reading Buddhist literature and referring to herself as a Buddhist because, "I could be spiritual without having to be involved with organized religion." This is when she resumed therapy.

Mindy remained strongly attached to labels, especially her label as being a lesbian. Her work identity as a teacher and spiritual identity as a Buddhist were also very important to her. One of her primary goals in therapy, however, was to "attain the recognition of no-self." She was eager for new relaxation and meditation techniques to help her achieve this and regularly asked for more "tools." When I encouraged her to slow down, she initially became very angry and did not return to therapy for several weeks.

Mindy's therapy progressed slowly while she was demanding quick fixes. Over time, she was able to recognize that her attachments to the labels of being a lesbian, a teacher, and a Buddhist were what she used to help her cope with her prior hurtful experiences with Christianity and that it would be dangerous to too quickly loosen her hold on these aspects of how she identified herself. As she accepted that the labels were part of her attachment to self, she was able to accept the need to move more slowly in her path to non-attachment.

After a year of therapy, Mindy joined a local Buddhist temple. This was a big step for her, as she began to accept that there were some healthy aspects of organized religion and being involved in a spiritual community. After joining, the pain from her experience of coming out as a

2. An Existential Framework   29

teenager resurfaced, but she persevered. Her religious community was also successful in helping her recognize that non-attachment was a goal that very few achieve. This led to her patience with herself increasing, which along with the connection from the community helped her feel she accomplished her goals for therapy.

Compassion as an Outcome Measure

Early in my work as a depth therapist, I found myself amazed with two therapy outcomes that I had not expected. First, many individuals who began therapy mad at organized religion began talking about a desire to return to religion in the latter stages of therapy. This occurred despite my honoring of their desire not to discuss religion in therapy. Over the years, I have continued to note that many individuals uncover a religious or spiritual longing toward the end of the therapy process.

These clients have transformed their understanding of religion. They began to distinguish between organized religion or representatives of religion, and the underlying religion. Often, this included a new compassion for religious individuals participating in the tradition that previously injured the client.

Second, clients developed a longing for something beyond themselves, something transcendent. This took many forms, sometimes similar to their prior religious beliefs and sometimes very different. For many, an important part of this longing for something beyond themselves was a desire for a religious or spiritual community. For others, they sought a connection with nature or the world in general.

Related to this longing for connection beyond the self was the development of compassion. As clients ended therapy, many of them wanted to give something back. There were many examples of this including a desire to become a therapist, volunteer in the community, or become more involved in their religious or spiritual community. This was not a mere giving of money, but rather a giving of themselves.

This development of wanting to give back also emerged as compassion in their relationships. One client noted in jest how much therapy had changed her friends. As she discussed this, she stated that she now saw them differently, through compassionate eyes instead of judgment. She noted that her friends also recognized this and interacted differently with her.

As an example, Mary, a Caucasian woman in her mid 50s, entered therapy for depression and relationship conflict. She had been involved in a number of unsuccessful romantic relationships and became estranged from her entire family, including her two children. She participated for a year in individual therapy before transferring to an interpersonal group I was running. She continued in group for nearly two years before graduating.

In Mary's individual therapy, she was able to develop a deeper understanding of herself and alleviate most of her depression; however, she was never able to apply what she learned to her individual relationships resulting in lingering loneliness and depression. When she first began group, she was not well received by the other group members. Although they described her as "fun," she seemed unable to relate to the experiences of others; her stories and contributions were always about herself.

Many participants in the group pushed her hard on developing more empathy and compassion for others. Gradually, she was able to recognize what others were feeling, but this was at a detached, cognitive level. Over time, as she continued to work through aspects of her previous relationship pain and her fears, she became more subjectively involved in the group, building her empathy and compassion. By the time she left group, she was recognized for being the first to have tears come to her eyes when another group member was experiencing genuine pain and suffering.[3]

Mary was profoundly impacted by this change and it allowed her to reconcile with her children and many of her friends. She continued to need the support of the group through this process, recognizing that developing compassion brought with it pain. This pain, however, was something for which she had developed an appreciation. She also recognized that the development of compassion was an important sign of the success of therapy.

Adler (1927/1965), who profoundly impacted the existential psychologist Rollo May, spoke of social interest as part of healthy functioning. As with many ideas of Adler's, this conception has become so pervasive in humanistic and existential psychology that the source of this idea has been lost (Yalom, 1980). From this perspective, a measure of compassion may be a more helpful outcome measure than a Beck Depression Inventory.

Embracing Suffering

Sam was first drawn to Buddhism early in his graduate studies to become a therapist. He took a class his first semester which talked about integrating mindfulness and meditation into therapy, which he felt was a good fit with his personality. According to Sam, he had always been a very optimistic and upbeat person, even though he had been through many difficult situations in his life. He stated he decided to become a therapist because his friends told him, "If you can stay upbeat through your life experiences you'd be great at helping others."

Midway through Sam's second year in graduate school, he began having difficulty sleeping, crying spells, and increasing irritability. At first, Sam tried to brush this off and deal with it by immersing himself in Buddhist literature. Sam finally reached "a breaking point" following a

---

[3] As noted by Barasch (2005) in his discussion on mirror neurons, this is often a reflexive action for people who have developed a capacity for empathy and compassion.

2. An Existential Framework

conflict with his supervisor at his practicum site. Sam began quoting Buddhist literature to all his clients, even those who were of a different religious background. When they became concerned about this, Sam interpreted this as a defense and resistance to therapy. When several of Sam's clients began dropping out of therapy, his supervisor suggested they begin reviewing recordings of the sessions leading up to them dropping out.

At this point, Sam had not told his supervisor that he had been quoting Buddhist literature and teaching mindfulness and meditation in therapy. When his supervisor discovered this, he immediately ordered Sam to desist until he had a better understanding of when this might be inappropriate with clients. Sam became very angry, yelling at his supervisor. The clinic Sam was working at decided that it was not appropriate for him to see clients until he underwent psychotherapy and received some training on diversity. They were, however, willing to be patient in working with Sam on these issues and retain him as a practicum student.

When Sam began therapy he voiced suicidal ideation and difficulty controlling his anger. He was obsessively reading popular writings which claimed to integrate Buddhism and psychology. I asked Sam to share some of these with me, which he gladly did. For two weeks he spoke with great intensity and excitement about this literature. He was very resistant to any feedback or redirection on topics during this time. After two weeks, I told Sam that I noticed that the literature he was reading all focused on the idea of using Buddhism to let go of problems. I also commented that this was a limited understanding of Buddhism.

Sam was stunned by my remarks and initially responded with anger. I suggested that he talk with a teacher from a local Buddhist community for some suggested readings in Buddhism and Sam agreed to sign a release for me to talk with this individual. The Buddhist teacher recommended readings on suffering from a Buddhist perspective. Over the next several weeks, Sam descended into a deeper depression, but the suicidal ideation fully disappeared.

Sam realized that he had been using his optimistic personality, and later Buddhism, to avoid dealing with personal pain. Sam gradually began talking about many of the painful experiences of his life in an authentic way for the first time. Over the next year, Sam worked hard in therapy and developed a greater balance between his optimism and openness to suffering. He also developed a more grounded approach to Buddhism. When he returned to his practicum after 6 months, his supervisors reported that he was much more empathic and connected with his clients. His new clients were staying in therapy with much greater consistency and Sam reported feeling like a much more competent therapist.

Working with Diversity

The Buddhist therapist must recognize the essential differences between being a Buddhist therapist in the East and being a Buddhist therapist in the West. Additionally, as previously noted, it is important to recognize that although the Buddhist therapist may not see Buddhism as a religion, many of their clients will. It is dangerous for the Buddhist practitioner to be insensitive to these issues. In this section, I focus on Buddhism with the implicit understanding of it as a religion. This is not done to advocate for this position, but rather to illustrate important applications when working with a diverse clientele.

Over the years, I have come to refer to myself as a therapist who specializes in religious and spiritual issues in therapy and have avoided referring to myself as a religious therapist. This is not to state that it is inappropriate to be a Buddhist therapist, a Muslim therapist, or a Christian therapist; rather, it acknowledges the difficult complexities around such issues. Furthermore, it may be more helpful to retain a religious or philosophical neutrality on such issues.

Research investigating therapeutic effectiveness in working with Christian clients suggests that non-Christian therapists who are open to religious issues are more effective in working with Christian clients than Christian therapists or non-Christian therapists not addressing the religious issues (Propst, Ostrum, Watkins, Dean, & Mashburn, 1992). Although I am not aware of any similar research with clients from different religious backgrounds, I would guess that the results would be similar.

The most effective therapists in dealing with religious and worldview issues are not necessarily the therapists who share the same beliefs and values as the client, but the therapists who are open to working with the client's value system. Often, the therapist sharing a value system with the client becomes problematic for a number of reasons. First, if the client is aware of it, they may be fearful of being judged as not being a good Buddhist (or Christian, Jew, etc.). They may limit disclosures and be inhibited in developing rapport due to this conflict. Second, they may look to the therapist for religious advice and guidance, often blurring the therapy boundaries and areas of the therapist's expertise. Third, the therapist may assume shared beliefs and values, not recognizing when they may be imposing their beliefs on clients. Last, people have different ideas about what it means to be a Buddhist, Muslim, Christian, or any other religious label. If you see Buddhism as a philosophy, and your client sees Buddhism as a religion, labeling yourself as a Buddhist could be unintentionally communicating a deception to the client.

As hopefully has been illustrated thus far in this chapter and the book, integrating Buddhism into psychotherapy is a complex, difficult process that should not be carried out without thoughtful consideration. This section helps the Buddhist therapist, or a therapist who is a Buddhist,

2. An Existential Framework

think through how to avoid the therapeutic and ethical pitfalls of integrating Buddhism and psychology.

Knowledge, Awareness, and Cultural Competency

Therapists who are not familiar with diversity often do not see it when it exists in their personal lives and therapeutic relationships. Yalom (1980) illustrated this with death issues. Many therapists with their own death issues, or lack of awareness of death issues, did not recognize or respond to these same issues with clients when they were brought up. Similarly, therapists unaware of diversity issues, or uncomfortable with them, including religious diversity, often will not see diversity.

A downside often exists with diversity awareness, too. Early approaches to dealing with diversity focused on teaching about different cultural groups. This often leads to stereotyping clients into cultural groups and treating these groups as if they were all the same. Therapists must recognize that all forms of diversity have significant within-group differences that often exceed the between-group differences. Knowledge of groups applied without recognition of individual within-group differences facilitates stereotyping, not effective therapy.

Cultural competency requires that therapists are knowledgeable about different groups and between-group differences. However, cultural competency should not stop here. Therapists should be rooted in their own self-knowledge and self-awareness, including awareness of their biases and prejudices. When considering Buddhism and psychotherapy, several examples are evident. First and foremost, the Buddhist therapist must be aware of their own feelings toward other religions and the variations within Buddhism.

If the Buddhist therapist has strong negative feelings about other world religions, they should not work with people from these backgrounds. Similarly, if the Buddhist therapist has strong negative feelings about a group representing a variation within Buddhism, such as Zen Buddhism, Pure Land Buddhism, or Buddhists conceiving of Buddhism as a religion, they should be cautious when working with individuals holding these beliefs. It is not that therapists should always avoid working with clients who represent views that the therapist finds distasteful; instead, it means the therapist needs to be aware of these reactions and be cautious because of them. Additionally, these are often times when it is good to seek out consultation or supervision.

Integrating Without Imposing

I have discussed the theme of not imposing one's world view onto clients many times in this chapter to stress its importance. In my experience as a supervisor and faculty member, I frequently have encountered students, as well as other professionals, speaking of *sneaking in their religious belief.* They often have voiced this with pride in their creativity in accomplishing this. This has occurred with therapists who were Buddhist as well as Christian, Jewish, and Muslim.

For most of these therapists, when I gently push them saying, "Now how would you feel if your therapist was sneaking in Christian (or Buddhist, or Muslim) ideas into your therapy?" they often respond with indignation, and most understand the point of this question. Others have responded with ideas such as, "Well, if it is on their death bed, then I'd do it." One obvious underlying message is that if the client will be unable to report the ethics violation, then it is okay. However, this, in many ways, represents the more reprehensible aspect of taking advantage of clients who are vulnerable.

Some Buddhist therapists have responded stating that since they conceive of Buddhism as a philosophy, not a religion, this is acceptable. However, when asked if their clients agree with this perspective, they often stumble. Imposing values is imposing values regardless of what label is placed upon it.

Avoiding imposing the therapist's values on the client is not as easy as it sounds. Even Carl Rogers (1980), early champion of values-free therapy, recognized that therapists cannot help but impose their values on clients at times. What therapists choose to respond to, their subtle increased interest, and what bores them all impact the client and, in subtle ways, imposes values.

The most important thing a therapist can do to decrease values imposition is to create the appropriate therapy climate and relationship. When therapists create a relationship of trust and one in which expressing different viewpoints is encouraged, it is more likely that clients will resist values imposition. From an existential viewpoint, this is creating a therapeutic relationship in which clients are encouraged to make their own choices. Therapists can model appropriate disagreeing, encouraging clients to do the same.

The more the relationship exudes mutuality, instead of the powerful therapist role, the easier it is to create a climate in which clients feel comfortable disagreeing with the therapist. When therapists hide behind their authority role or encourage a perspective of the therapist as expert, then clients become less free to make their own decisions and values imposition is more likely. Once an appropriate therapy relationship is constructed, it is easier for the therapist to risk integrating religion or spirituality without imposing values. Integration still should be done thoughtfully through examining the potential problems that may interfere with the therapy process; however, the general risk is decreased.

Integration should also address the potential of dual roles. For example, consideration should be given to whether it is appropriate for the therapist to also teach or instruct clients in meditation. It may be that some forms and levels of meditation may be acceptable to be taught by the therapist, but more complex or enduring teaching, or certain types of meditation, crosses into dual roles and compromises therapy. Similarly, it should be considered if it is acceptable for the therapist to take the role of guiding clients in Buddhist principles.

Generally, more directive Buddhist applications should only be considered with advanced training and, even then, is often best left to religious or spiritual leaders. Often, it is beneficial to obtain a release to talk with these leaders so that a collaborative relationship can be set up. Such collaboration often can help the therapist avoid crossing into inappropriate dual roles with clients.

Supervision and Consultation

Ongoing supervision and consultation should be a staple in psychotherapy. I would like to see an added requirement of a minimum number of consultation hours a year added to continuing education requirements. However, most therapists would likely resist this, seeing it as an additional unnecessary time consumption that interferes with their practice. Nonetheless, therapists may take their own initiative in committing to ongoing consultation and supervision.

Supervision and consultation are particularly important when working with a new client population, developing a new specialty, working with challenging clients, and working with clients representing a form of diversity the therapist is not familiar with. Several fairly evident implications of this emerged in the current discussion.

First, integrating Buddhism into psychotherapy should be understood as a new specialization. No therapist should attempt integrating Buddhism into psychotherapy without first seeking specific training in this realm and seeking appropriate supervision or consultation. Reading this book does not create a new specialty and should not be deemed sufficient to be applying Buddhist thought to psychotherapy. Similarly, merely being Buddhist and a therapist does not qualify you to work with religious and spiritual issues in therapy; training and supervision is still needed.

Second, it is important for Buddhist therapists not familiar with other religions to seek supervision when working with clients from other religions who are introducing religious issues into psychotherapy. It often can be helpful to set up a network of therapists from different religions who can consult with each other. Consultation with religious leaders from various faiths can also be very helpful when working with these clients.

Third, it is often important to seek consultation when working with clients with a very similar religious background to assure that you are not missing subtle differences. This is particularly important for therapists who are first working with these clients and therapists who have entered into a routine in many aspects of their therapy.

Conclusion

Ignoring religious and spiritual issues in therapy does a tremendous disservice to clients. It is important that therapists acquire the knowledge, training, and experience to be able to help clients explore these issues and, when appropriate (contextually and in consideration of the therapist's training), address the relevancy of these issues. Once therapists have begun to understand the foundational issues that are challenging to integrating Buddhism and psychotherapy, they can provide a fruitful alliance that enhances the therapy process for therapist and client (see Hoffman, Cox, Ervin-Cox, & Mitchell, 2005).

References

Abe, M. (1990). Kenotic god and dynamic sunyata. In J. B. Cobb, Jr. & C. Ives (Eds.), *The emptying god: A Buddhist-Jewish-Christian conversation* (pp. 3-65). Eugene OR: Wipf & Stock.

Abe, M. (1995). Beyond Buddhism and Christianity – 'Dazzling darkness.' In S. Heine (Ed.), *Buddhism and interfaith dialogue* (pp. 127-150). Honolulu, HI: University of Hawaii Press.

Adler, A. (1965). *Understanding human nature.* New York: Premier. (Original work published in 1927)

Armstrong, K. (2001) *The battle for God.* New York: Ballantine Books.

Barasch, M. I. (2005). *Field notes on the compassionate life: A search for the soul of kindness.* New York: Rodale.

Epstein, M. (1995). *Thoughts without a thinker: Psychotherapy from a Buddhist perspective.* New York: Basic Books.

Ervin-Cox, B., Hoffman, L., Grimes, C. S. M., & Fehl, S. (2007). Spirituality, Health, and Mental Health: A Holistic Model. In I. Serlin (Ed.), *Whole person health care* (Vol. 2: Psychology, Spirituality, & Health; pp. 101-134). Westport, CT: Praeger Books.

Gergen, K. J. (1991). *The saturated self: Dilemmas of identity in contemporary life.* New York: Basic Books.

Gergen, K. J. (1995). The happy, healthy human being wears many masks. In W. T. Anderson (Ed.), *The truth about the truth: De-confusing and reconstructing the postmodern world* (pp. 136-144). New York: Tarcher/Putnam.

Gyatso, T. (2001). *The compassionate life.* Sommerville, MA: Wisdom Publications.

Gyatso, T. (2005). *Essence of the Heart Sutra: The Dalai Lama's heart of wisdom teachings* (Trans. G. T. Jinpa). Boston: Wisdom Publications.

Gyatso, T. (2007). *Mind in comfort and ease: The vision of enlightenment in the great perfection* (Trans. M. Ricard, R. Barron, & A. Pearchey). Boston: Wisdom Publications.

Hoffman, L. (in press). Existential-integrative psychotherapy and the God image. In G. Moriarty & L. Hoffman (Eds.), *The God image handbook for spiritual counseling and psychotherapy: Theory, research, and practice*. New York: Haworth Press.

Hoffman, L. (2005). A developmental perspective on the God image. In R. H. Cox, B. Ervin-Cox, & L. Hoffman (Eds.), *Spirituality and psychological health* (pp. 129-149). Colorado Springs, CO: Colorado School of Professional Psychology Press.

Hoffman, L. (2008). Spiritual and religious issues from an existential-integrative perspective. In K. Schneider (Ed.), *Existential-integrative psychotherapy: Guideposts to the core of practice* (pp. 187-201). New York: Routledge.

Hoffman, L., Cox, R., Ervin-Cox, B., & Mitchell, M. (2005). Training issues in spirituality and psychotherapy: A foundational approach. In R. Cox, B. Ervin-Cox, & L. Hoffman (Eds.), *Spirituality and psychological health* (pp. 3-14). Colorado Springs, CO: Colorado School of Professional Psychology Press.

Krippner, S. & Achterberg, J. (2000). Anomalous healing experiences. In E. Cardena, S. J. Lynn, & S. Krippner (Eds.), *Varieties of anomalous experience: Examining the scientific evidence* (pp. 353-395). Washington, DC: American Psychological Association.

May, R. (1981). *Freedom and destiny*. New York: Norton & Company.

May, R. (1991). *The cry for myth*. New York: Delta.

Mendelowitz, E. (2006). Meditations on Oedipus: Becker's Kafka, Nietzsche's metamorphoses. *Journal of Humanistic Psychology, 46,* 385-431.

Mosig, Y. D. (2006). Conceptions of the self in Eastern and Western psychology. *Journal of Theoretical and Philosophical Psychology, 26,* 39-50.

Nietzsche, F. (1966). *Beyond good and evil: Prelude to a philosophy of future* (W. Kaufmann, Trans.). New York: Vintage Books: (Original work published 1886)

Propst, L. R., Ostrum, R, Watkins, P., Dean, T., & Mashburn, D. (1992). Comparative efficacy of religious and non-religious cognitive-behavioral therapy for the treatment of clinical depression in religious individuals. *Journal of Consulting and Clinical Psychology, 60,* 94-103

Pulleyking, J. (2005). The dynamics of faith: How can the psychologist understand religion and spirituality? In R. H. Cox, B. Ervin-Cox, & L. Hoffman (Eds.), *Spirituality and psychological health* (pp. 15-29). Colorado Springs, CO: Colorado School of Professional Psychology Press.

Rahula, W. (1974). *What the Buddha taught* (Rev. ed). New York: Grove Press.

Rogers, C. R. (1980) *A way of being*. Boston, MA: Houghton Miffin.

Roth, C. (2003). *The influence of Eastern or Western worldview on the perception of stress.* Unpublished doctoral dissertation, Forest Institute of Professional Psychology, Springfield, MO.

Schneider, K. J. (1990). *The paradoxical self: Toward an understanding of our contradictory nature.* New York: Plenum.

Tillich, P. (1957). *The dynamics of faith.* New York: Harper & Row.

Witkiewitz, K., Marlatt, G. A., & Walker, D. (2005). Mindfulness-based relapse prevention for alcohol and substance use disorders. *Journal of Cognitive Psychotherapy, 19,* 211-228.

Wulff, D. (1997). *The psychology of religion: Classic and contemporary views* (2nd ed). New York: John Wiley & Sons.

Yalom, I. D. (1980). *Existential psychotherapy.* New York: Basic Books.

Zweig, C. (1995). The death of the self in the postmodern world. In W. T. Anderson (Ed.), *The truth about the truth: De-confusing and reconstructing the postmodern world* (pp. 145-150). New York: Tarcher/Putnam.

3

Therapist Subjectivity in Contemplative Psychotherapy

Patricia Townsend
Francis J. Kaklauskas[1]

> We know that the first step towards the intellectual mastery of the world in which we live is the discovery of general principles, rules and laws which bring order into chaos. By such mental operations we simplify the world of phenomena, but we cannot avoid falsifying it in doing so, especially when we are dealing with processes of development and change.
> - *Sigmund Freud, [1937] Analysis Terminable and Interminable*

> Emotion is uncertainty regarding projections, and the projections have also been put out by us. What we label things makes the projections. The buildings or the houses or the trees or the people as such are not the projections. What we make out of them is the projections—our version of the buildings, our version of the landscape, the people, the trees. It is a new coat of paint that we put on them, the reproductions we make of them. And there is the possibility of not being able to relate with those, since we are uncertain of ourselves and thus uncertain of our projections.
> - *Chogyam Trungpa, [1992] The Lion's Roar: An Introduction to Tanta.*

Therapist Subjectivity in Contemplative Psychotherapy

Contemplative psychotherapy has grown out of a combination of Western and Buddhist psychological perspectives. As such, it represents a unique vision of therapy, one primarily informed by its integration of Buddhist perspectives of self-experience within a therapeutic model. From

---

[1] This chapter is primarily developed from *Therapist Subjectivity in Contemplative Psychotherapy* presented by Patricia Townsend at Naropa University, April 2007. Additions to this chapter are derived from *Integrating Contemplative Spiritual Perspectives in Clinical Work: Live Supervision of Cases* presented by Francis Kaklauskas and Louis Hoffman at Naropa University, May, 2006

the Buddhist perspective, the self is seen as impermanent, interdependent, and lacking any inherent existence. The self is impermanent in the sense that it is always changing; interdependent in the sense that its appearance is dependent upon causes and conditions; and lacking inherent existence precisely because it has no substantial essence or is empty in nature.

The Buddhist psychological use of the words *empty* and *emptiness* differs from Western usage. In the Buddhist perspective, the term *emptiness* is used primarily in reference to the ground of all experience. Rather than connoting a lifeless void, emptiness refers to an absolute potentiality from which all experience arises. The experience of emptiness is one that precedes and transcends the dualities of subjectivity and objectivity and all conceptual experience (Gyatso, 2005; Trungpa, 1973; Suzuki, 1973). In order to accommodate the idea of an experience, which is beyond conceptualization, the Buddhist view of emptiness is embedded within a two-truths view of reality. There is not only a relative truth to which we conceptually relate but also an absolute truth that transcends the duality inherent in conceptual experience. In relative truth, the self and all phenomena appear to be continuous, independent, and real in nature. In absolute truth, the self and all phenomena are impermanent, interdependent, and empty of any essential nature.

Several other contemporary Western psychological schools approach an interdependent and impermanent view of the self, but stop short of embracing a non-essentialist view of the self. In Contemplative Psychotherapy, acceptance of the ultimate non-existence of the self has far-reaching implications with regard to the practice of psychotherapy and to the management of the therapeutic alliance. It also shifts the understanding of therapist subjectivity in ways that are different from other Western contemporary models.

Brief Review of Western Philosophical Ideas about Self and Subjectivity

The question "What is the self?" is a very old one. Recent historical accounts suggest that ancient discourse on the topic demonstrated an interplay of ideas from various cultures, particularly ancient Greece and India (McEvilley, 2002). Monks, philosophers, and traders wandered thousands of miles, learning from other cultures and returning with new perspectives. Because ideas from ancient Greek philosophy and pre-Buddhist Indian philosophy converged, the similarities between Western models and Buddhist thought have been repeatedly discussed (de Wit, 1993; Epstein, 2007).

The ancient Greek philosophical tradition emerges out of a pre-existing sense of the self as essential. Descriptions in Homer's *Iliad*, for instance, already indicate a view of reality which is composed of discrete concrete physical objects (Toohey, 1992). Although some recent

3. Therapist Subjectivity

translations have used concepts of spirit or soul, these Western philosophical concepts were born from a language and mental construct of objects as discrete. In Homer's writing, *psyche* may most accurately be translated as blood or breathe and the view of psyche as soul developed later in this philosophical tradition. Under the Sophists, thinking about phenomena tended to be reductive (Kerfeld, 1981).

Protagoras's (ca. 490-420 B.C.E.) famous statement that "man is the measure of all things, of things that are, that they are, and of things that are not, that they are not" (cited in Stumpf, 1989, p. 32.), brought into the Western view a powerful statement of subjectivism, relativism, and uncertainty about knowledge. In many ways, this debate continues.

Plato, while not unwavering in the idea of a substantial self, generally spoke of the *soul* or *psyche* as that which has the ability for knowledge and wisdom. Socrates' most famous psychological perspective of self is found in *The Republic*, which depicts a tripartite soul comprised of reason, spirit, and appetite. His example of the charioteer (ego) managing two reins, one attached to a well-trained thoroughbred (superego) and the other to a wild horse (id), has been compared to Freud's structural theory of mind (Gallucci, 2001).

Aristotle (384 B.C.-322 B.C.E.) focused more on the use of *psyche* that allows for remembrance, imagination, and rational thinking. He focused on how the five senses bring information to the psyche and added a sixth aspect—common sense—to his epistemological model. Simultaneously in India, the Eastern philosophical tradition, including Buddhism, took up similar questions, but incorporated the idea of consciousness as the sixth means of knowing (Duerlinger, 2003).

With the advent and rise of Christianity, the self or soul became understood as more enduring than the physical world; in fact, the self came to be seen as eternal (Inagaki & Jennings, 2000). Western philosophers through the age of enlightenment generally held the view of a continuous enduring self. Continental philosophies, from Descartes' arguments on self-existence to Leibniz's monad theory, highlight how highly deductive methods can lead nevertheless to irrational and fantastical conclusions (Russell, 2002).

The rise of British empiricism brought conceptions of the self back into the forefront of western thought (Sellars, Rorty, & Brandom, 1997). The foundational epistemological question of how the self interprets reality comes to the forefront in the work of Berkeley and Hume. Kant's (1881/2003) *Critique of Pure Reason* attempted to define the nature of mind and self in an absolute categorical theory and is not without similarities to Buddhist thought.

Western philosophy began to revolt against both the emerging positivism of British philosophers and the purely deductive continental methods, as new heuristic and phenomenological forms of philosophy, as seen in Schopenhauer, Kierkegaard, and Nietzsche began to emerge (Kearney, 1994). During the last half of the 19th century, psychology and philosophy also began to become distinct areas of study. At that time, psychology primarily sought to understand the topics of anatomy, response effects, and psychophysics, while philosophy continued to seek answers to the questions of "What is the self and the mind?" and "What is ethical behavior?" Also during this period translations of Hindu, Buddhist, Taoist, and other Eastern philosophical texts began to enter the consciousness of Western academics and intellectuals, and this may have had some influence on the future development of Western views of self and subjectivity (Clarke, 1997).

Subjectivity and Self in Western Psychology

At the end of the 19th century, Wundt and Fechner were seeking the general and unifying principles that define the human animal through the creation of psychological laboratories (Wozniak, 1992). Francis Galton, profoundly influenced by Darwinian evolutionary theory, sought to understand how humans are different from one another. He went against the common belief that infants are born with similar attributes, arguing for individual differences, most notably in intelligence (Thorne & Henley, 2001).

William James (1890) attempted to unify the principles of these divergent sources in *Principles of Psychology*, and he brought conception of the mind and consciousness to the forefront of psychological inquiry. Following Wundt's experiments in which participants would close their eyes and track their mental processes (similar to meditation), James often used his personal experiences to illustrate and inform his evolving understanding of issues of consciousness. Although Wundt concluded that the study of consciousness was too complex and variable between individuals to be accurately measured, James presented his ideas on the stream of consciousness, habit, and emotions (Hilgard, 1987). James's views of consciousness suggested that subjective experience may be best studied through in-depth personal inquiry and case examples. He stressed that each individual is concerned with parts of objects and that consciousness and attention are selective. He also stressed the idea of impermanence, asserting that once a consciousness pattern is completed, it will never be duplicated due to the inevitable and unrelenting changes within one's mind and the environment.

Although James and others of his period were focused on understanding the underlying principles of human experience, Freud's work set forth the in-depth exploration of the clinical practice of psychology. Freud's view of self and subjectivity evolved throughout his life and his ideas of transference, countertransference, and projection became the foundation for the future study of subjectivity in the therapeutic process (Gay, 1998).

The next important wave in understanding the subjectivity of self in psychology was fostered by Post-Freudian theorists. Anna Freud (1936),

3. Therapist Subjectivity

Melanie Klein (1932), Frieda Fromm-Reichmann (1950), and Karen Horney (1937, 1939), although often disagreeing with one another, established many of the core concepts related to subjectivity (Sayers, 1991). Anna Freud's (1936) description of the various defense mechanisms that influence one's perception of the world and the self have such a resonance that her ideas of displacement, sublimation, repression and rationalization have become ingrained in the very vocabulary of contemporary culture (Mitchell & Black, 1995). Klein's (1932) emphasis on pre-oedipal interactions and relational desire paved the way for intersubjective approaches from attachment theory to somatic therapy (Weaver, 1999). Fromm-Reichmann's (1950) warmth and openness was a precursor to humanist approaches of seeing the self with more holism and less pathology. While Karen Horney (1991) originally developed her ideas independently of Buddhist thought, later in her life she found striking similarities to her views in Buddhist thought (Quninn, 1989). These include her view of basic anxieties, which resemble the idea of *Duhkha* or suffering, and her three forces of *moving towards, moving against, and moving away from,* which echo the Buddhist principles of three primary emotional responses of passion, aggression and ignorance.

Heinz Hartman, (1939, 1964) furthered the discussion of self through the inclusion of non-pathological self skills (memory, motor coordination, and reality-testing) that were later conceptualized anew in the work of Heinz Kohut (1971, 1977). Although all of these theorists continued to use a reductionist model to understand the self, Murray's (1938, 1967) view of personology attempted to rescue psychology from its increasingly diagnostic perspective by acknowledging both the nomothetical and idiographic elements, ideas that have gained renewed interest through the diagnostic and idiographic personality theories of Theodore Millon (1990, 2004).

The inter-subjective and relational movement pioneered by Harry Stack Sullivan (1953) questions the assumption of a distinct self. Sullivan felt that the self is constructed only through relationships with others (Mitchell, 1988). His strong relational views have been taken up by environmental personality theorists from Albert Bandura (1977) through Phillip Zimbardo (2004, 2007).

Recently three contemporary psychological movements shed new light on client and therapist subjectivity: the late, but vital, arrival of cultural diversity, rapid advances in neuropsychology, and postmodern psychology. Diversity training has become common in both clinical and academic settings. Building upon the feminist, racial political, and intellectual movements, multicultural psychology has finally brought a simple commonsense truth to clinical consciousness. Both the client and the therapist have cultural views that greatly influence their world views, their views of the self, and their views of relationships (Smith, 2003). Diversity highlights the subjective and inter-subjective dilemmas in the clinical encounter by bringing greater awareness to the unspoken implicit rules about relational dynamics, roles, values, and rituals that evolve from race, ethnicity, religion, class, gender, and sexual orientation (Sue & Sue, 2007).

Although the pursuit and rigor of contemporary neuropsychology provides convergent validation to previous psychological theories, neuropsychological research highlights our limited comprehension of brain mechanisms and our enigmatic understanding of mind (Fienberg & Farrah, 2003). For example, while neuropsychological research posits strong evidence that points to the prefrontal cortex as the organizing apparatus for experience and specifically to the autonoetic center as the specific area of the brain that holds the conception of selfhood, this mechanistic view has had limited implications for understanding the phenomenological experience of the self (Kolb & Whishaw, 2003). Perhaps the most important areas of neuropsychological discoveries as related to the idea of self are those that simply demonstrate that perceptions of the self and the world are capable of changing over time and that brain development is more complex and interrelated to environmental factors than some previous personality theories conceptualized. Neuroscience has also brought emotions back into clinical practice, as cognition and behavior appear directly linked to emotional processes (Siegel, 2007; Schore, 2002).

The history of Western ideas presented here can be seen as following the development of the paradigmatic thinking of pre-modern, modern, and postmodern thought (Hoffman & Kurzenberger, 2008). The pre-modern perspective relied heavily on intuition and revelation. The modernist movement, beginning perhaps with Aristotle, reached its philosophical zenith in logical positivism and found its psychological apex in the rise of empirically validated treatment approaches. In Thomas Kuhn's (1962, 2000) paradigmatic theory, postmodernist views got a foothold in current intellectual theory. Postmodernism has not rejected the pre-modern and modernist ways of knowing and understanding the self, but it does seek to expand the epistemological methodologies so as to be inclusive of a pluralistic perspective. The Dalai Lama's interest in finding connections between physics, psychology and Buddhist understanding could be seen as a postmodern pluralistic process of seeking truth (Gyatso, 2005).

Towards an Integrated View of Self

Recent Western psychological theoretical conceptualizations are expanding the portrayal of self-experience in a direction akin to Buddhist thought. Many of these ideas have emerged from the relational schools of psychodynamic approaches, as well as from the inclusion of relational theory in almost all present-day therapies. Yalom (1995) noted that all therapy is relational therapy and that Sullivan's ideas have become the norm across therapeutic theories and approaches. In contemporary

3. Therapist Subjectivity

theories, *the self* has grown increasingly tenuous, as seen in the relational view of self-experience, which entails "multiple and shifting self-organizations and self-states that are generated in interpersonal and social fields" (Mitchell, 1997, p. 21). Such views seem to accommodate the impermanent (multiple and shifting) and interdependent (generated in interpersonal and social fields) aspects of Buddhist perspectives of self; however, here again, these stop short of declaring the self empty of inherent existence.

One of the core foundations of relational psychology is its elucidation of the self as existing only in relation to others and the environment, and in this respect, relational psychology embraces an interdependent view of self-experience (McWilliams, 2004). Relational theory also portrays the self as "decentered and understands the mind as a configuration of shifting nonlinear states of consciousness in an ongoing dialectic with the necessary illusion of unitary selfhood" (Bromberg 1998, p. 7). In these ways, relational theory has partially embraced the Buddhist description of self-experience, which has led to interesting contemporary psychological debates about the very existence of the self (Safran, 2003).

When Western theorists debate the existence of the self, they most often seem hindered by the assumption that a no-self view dictates that experiences arise and dissolve in a lifeless void. For instance, when defending Bromberg's (1998) view of the self against perception as a no-self view, Pizer (2003) argued that it did not place self-experience in a void, "but in a potential space between disparate realities that remain somehow linked despite the dissociative nature of psychic organization" (Pizer, 2003, p. 153).

However, it is important to note that the no-self view of Buddhist psychology locates all conscious experience as arising not from a void, but rather from an emptiness which is filled with potential, clarity, and luminosity (Gyatso, 2005). Buddhist teachings on emptiness stress its potentiality and the paradoxical nature of self-experiences which arise within it. The Heart Sutra proclaims the famous caveat that *form is emptiness; emptiness is form; form is no other than emptiness; emptiness is no other than form*. This sutra points to an experience that transcends conceptual limitations of tolerating paradox; the realization of this experience is seen as the hallmark of enlightenment.

In a similar fashion, Pizer (2003) lauded the ability of the self to handle paradoxical experience within itself and within relationships as foundational to mental health. His view of the self as a bridging process that connects separate islands of subjective experience seems to stress the dynamism of the self over its solidity. However, he contended that the successful maneuvering of paradox, again, does not entail dissolution of self. Instead, he saw maturity and creativity in straddling paradox within the self.

In *The Self is Alive and Well and Living in Relational Psychoanalysis*, Bruce Reis (2005) took to task the critique that relational theory entails a postmodern dissolution of the self. Postmodernism emphasizes that knowledge and reality are socially constructed and that there is no core self or reality that exists outside the social matrix. When critics claim that relational theory entails a postmodern dissolution of the self, they are asserting that it deconstructs the concept of self down to a non-reality. Reis disagreed with this assertion, contending that relational theory fundamentally retains and redefines rationalist terms and concepts of ego psychology. Reis concluded that rather than dissolving the self, relational theory has expanded its boundaries to include "areas of subjective experiencing that were previously excluded from consideration" (p. 86). He contended that the concept of self has "surfaced within the spaces between... dissociated self states" (p. 93).

It seems possible that the missing link for embracing a non-essentialist view of the self in relational and other Western psychological schools is the absence of a two-truths theory of reality, which differentiates between a relative and absolute view of experience. Holding the view that there is an absolute ground of experience from which all relativity arises allows one to entertain the concept of an empty self. Since holding only an absolute view would preclude nomothetical conceptualization of relative experience, both views are held in Buddhism—pointing to the middle way by tolerating paradox and creativity in our experience.

Clinical Applications of Subjective Views

Despite the hesitation of Western psychology to fully embrace a non-essentialist view of the self, clinical theory and practice has become increasingly inclusive of the view of the extreme relativity of self-experience on the part of the therapist. The classical role of the therapist as a blank screen has moved towards a more responsive role as an active participant in a relational intersubjective field (Cohen & Schermer, 2001). The one-person psychology approach that expected a therapist to adopt an impenetrable mirror-like affect to allow for uncontaminated interpretation of client transferences has come to be seen as unrealistic even within post-classical schools of psychoanalysis (Livingston, 1999).

The subjective experiences of psychotherapists, once exiled from the therapeutic setting, are now recognized as useful monitors and tools for therapeutic interventions in most Western schools. Several aspects of the therapist's self-experience, including the therapist's empathy (Shapiro 2001), emotional availability (Wright 2000), and vulnerability (Livingston, 1999), are used to draw out, support, and explore the subjective experiences of clients in self psychology and intersubjective models.

The Concept of Self in Contemplative Psychotherapy

Contemplative psychotherapy embraces the Buddhist perspective of the self as being impermanent, interdependently arising, and empty of inherent existence. When we are able to abide in these truths, our experience displays its most basic nature: brilliant sanity. Brilliant sanity is seen as the ground of all experience and refers to the unconditional sanity or basic healthiness inherent in everyone (Wegela, 1992). It consists of three main qualities: spaciousness, clarity, and compassion.

The reason we often do not experience the brilliant sanity of our lives is because we are frightened by the groundlessness of it (Trungpa, 1973). We cling instead to a false view of self as being permanent, independent, and real in order to escape the intensity of a non-referential experience. This false view of the self is referred to as ego. The Buddhist idea of ego differs in meaning from the Western psychological usage of the term. In the Buddhist view, when we cling to this false sense of self, or ego, for security, we have a confused experience of life. The arising of ego brings fixation on duality and concepts, which distances us from a direct non-referential experience. In therapy, this would include fixating on the subject-object duality of the therapist-client relationship and on how to interpret or conceptualize the experiences that arise within it. By fixating on duality and concepts such as these, we miss or avoid the groundlessness of our experience. Instead, we identify ourselves with our thoughts and emotions.

Therapist Subjectivity in Contemplative Psychotherapy

One of the basic premises of a contemplative psychotherapeutic approach is that loosening attachment to our false sense of self, or ego, provides glimpses of the brilliant sanity underlying all experience. This focus applies not only to the self-experience of the client, but also to that of the therapist. However, it is no small feat to hold the contemplative view of self while immersed in therapeutic work with clients. Central challenges contemplative psychotherapists face are how to manage self-identifications they have as therapists within the alliance and how to let go of those identifications in order to open to a more direct experience of the therapeutic work.

To accomplish this, therapists hone in on the details of their self-experience and subjectivity with mindfulness. They train awareness on their felt sensations and cognitions. They track their experience throughout therapeutic sessions, with the primary objective of opening to what they are feeling and thinking, to touch the experience of self and relationship, and to let it go. In this way, they approach a direct experience of the therapeutic work and offer their clients a receptive and responsive presence (Wegela, 1998).

Chogyam Trungpa (1973) wrote that the greatest obstacle we generally face in opening to the brilliant sanity of our experience is "the fact that we are always trying to secure ourselves, reassure ourselves that we are all right. We are constantly looking for something solid to hang on to" (p. 91). What we hang on to tooth and nail is the perception of ego as being permanent, independent, and solid. When we are caught off guard and experience a sense of uncertainty in our daily lives, we often try to figure out how to return to a more comfortable state. In contemplative psychotherapy, when we are in sessions with clients and are feeling unsure of what to do, we open to this uncertainty, rather than avoiding it. We remain skeptical of any conscious intentions to be a healer or helper, since these intentions are often motivated by a desire to reduce our own anxiety or confusion.

Contemplative psychotherapy uses the term *therapeutic aggression* to describe any therapeutic activity that has either a conscious or unconscious intention of forcing change on a client (Wegela, 1988). This type of activity is tracked and avoided because it is seen as a rejection of the direct experience of the therapeutic work. Therapeutic aggression happens when we do not accommodate whatever arises in sessions with openness; it happens when we overlook the natural expression of the ground of brilliant sanity by attempting to control and fix a situation that is viewed as discrete and mechanistic.

Exchange and Touch and Go

A distinguishing characteristic of psychotherapeutic technique within the contemplative view is its focus on letting go of the fixation to therapist self-experience primarily through a process called *touch and go* (Wegela, 1988). The purpose of this technique is to nurture an environment within which the brilliant sanity of the therapeutic moment can surface in the awareness of both parties in the alliance. Rather than voiding the self-experience of the therapist, this technique encourages a more receptive and responsive presence and helps promote empathic attunement with the client, as well as helping therapists avoid therapeutic aggression and tolerate countertransference reactions.

Touch and go is intimately related to the contemplative concept of *exchange*, "a process by which we consciously or unconsciously experience another person's state of mind... [It] is not a therapeutic technique, but a constantly recurring moment in which the distinction between self and other flickers" (Leyton, 1992, p.45). In contemplative psychotherapy, opening to exchange provides the therapist a cognitive and felt sense of a client's self-experience. Since the ground of all experience is intrinsically healthy, the therapist accommodates the exchange rather than shifting or changing it. This entails loosening any fixation on self-experiences occurring in the exchange.

3. Therapist Subjectivity

The way therapists open to exchange is through the process of touch and go. The therapist touches into her experience of exchange and lets it go. She opens to whatever arises without grasping onto and without dissociating from the experiences of the therapeutic moment. When therapists can lightly touch and let go of their experiences moment to moment within sessions, it is hoped that clients receive a sense of this accommodation through the process of exchange as well. When clients learn to tolerate their self-experiences, they might relax enough to experience the spaciousness of their brilliant sanity. Likewise, moments of accommodated self-experience can break habitual patterns and repetitions and allow for the emergence of new experience.

Accommodation of Transference and Countertransference Experiences

In some Western schools, an emphasis on analysis of transference and countertransference issues allows therapists to explore tendencies of self-experience and convictions that arise for them with their clients. This information is often seen as invaluable in ascertaining client experiences and in planning treatment. In contemplative psychotherapy, therapists hone in on the details of these tendencies with mindfulness. Within sessions, we notice what types of feelings, impulses, thoughts, and convictions are arising for us in relation to our clients. Rather than finding the meaning of all these experiences in the session, we open to the experiences (including interpretations and other cognitive therapeutic action), touch them, and let them go. Through this simple effort, we avoid getting caught in countertransference reactions, and we open to a broader range of experience. Training in this way helps therapists not only to tolerate countertransferences, but also to recognize them as signposts toward opening to a less ego-clinging state and a more direct experience of the therapeutic work. Opening in this way allows for more spontaneity and the chance to offer clients access to new experiences of themselves.

Shamatha Meditation Practice

Within the contemplative psychotherapeutic model, meditation practice is the primary method used to train ourselves to monitor exchange, apply touch and go, and avoid therapeutic aggression. *Shamatha meditation* is valued within Buddhism as a means of becoming familiar with the workings of the mind, of loosening the grip of ego, and of approaching a more direct experience of our lives. In one form of shamatha, the breath is taken as the object of meditation. We turn our attention to our breath and watch what happens. We develop mindfulness of its movement and texture within our bodies. This type of meditation draws attention to the natural rhythm and flow of the breath. There is no fixation or clinging quality in the unconscious process of the breath. In this respect, the breath is a great teacher and model of non-attachment.

Another focus of meditation is to develop mindfulness of self-experience. When thoughts arise within shamatha meditation, we label them *thinking* and let them go. For therapists, practicing in this way illuminates the power that we have to free ourselves from attachment to self-experience as being solid and to diagnostic categories or developmental systems as being solid. The ability to let go of thoughts, interpretations, and emotions as they arise deepens our confidence that we can open to a more direct experience of life and of therapeutic work.

In fact, a major point of practice is to apply the meditative experience to post-meditation activity so that all experiences of life offer the potential for further mindfulness practice and exploration. We learn about the ways we self-organize in the face of groundlessness most often in post-meditation experiences. In moments when we are caught off guard by some aspect of life, we can find the greatest insight by watching what we cling to conceptually for security. By paying close attention to our thoughts, emotions, and felt senses, we learn about the self-experiences that we use to ground ourselves and to diminish anxiety.

When we are caught off guard by someone's response to us, there is often a moment of feeling off-balance and not quite sure of who we are. Should we be complimented or insulted? Should we know what this person is referring to? Before we land on some conviction of truth about what is going on, we can try to open to the groundlessness of feeling off-balance. When we can accommodate this experience with curiosity, we may find, if nothing else, that there are several self-convictions or certainties available for examination. When we cannot open to feeling off-balance, we can at least be mindful of the thought patterns and convictions upon which we are landing. In this way, we develop an intimate understanding of the storylines and felt-sense of our ego-clinging. This is an invaluable practice for alerting us to the ascension of similar clinging patterns when we are in sessions with clients. It also trains us to help bring the same type of awareness to our clients' patterns of ego-clinging.

Discriminating Wisdom

Buddhist teachings on *prajna*, or discriminating wisdom, offer helpful skills in managing the cognitive aspects of subjectivity within therapeutic work. Opening to discriminating wisdom involves actually relaxing the mind's attempts to figure something out. In Western society, the most valuable aspect of an analytic aptitude is often seen to be its ability to quickly reach logical conclusions, to solve problems. Within contemplative psychotherapy, we find a richer use for this faculty: We can use it to stay open to not knowing, to stay present in the groundlessness

3. Therapist Subjectivity

of a therapeutic moment, when neither we nor the client *know* what to say or do.

Shifting our perspective slightly, we can see that the aspect of mind that asks all the questions is also basically saying, "I don't know." Through *vipashyana*, or analytical meditation practices we learn that when we relax into a do-not-know experience, that is when discriminating awareness is most able to surface in our experience. In moments when we hold a question in mind, rather than scrambling for its answer, insights beyond the situation-specific focus of the intellect often arise. Discriminating wisdom arises when we relax our need to know an answer. This can be a valuable discovery, which helps diminish clinging to the cognitive processes of subjective experience as a therapist. Valuing discriminating wisdom over knowledge helps therapists stay present, curious, receptive, attuned, and responsive with their clients.

Tonglen Meditation Practice

The contemplative practice of *tonglen* meditation helps train one's ability to stay present when faced with the suffering of oneself and others. Tonglen meditation addresses the habitual tendencies of ego to cling to pleasant experiences and turn away from unpleasant experiences (Chödrön, 2001). Through the practice of tonglen, these tendencies are loosened and reversed to develop a more openhearted accommodation of the suffering of oneself and others. There are four parts to tonglen meditation as taught in the contemplative psychotherapy training program: flashing awareness on an awakened-heart experience called *bodhichitta*, exchanging qualities, taking, and sending.

In the first part, flashing on awakened-heart, one imagines a situation of feeling fully openhearted and present. In the second part, exchanging qualities, one breathes in negative qualities like claustrophobia, darkness, and suffering; and one breathes out positive qualities like spaciousness, light, and compassion. The third and fourth parts are called taking and sending. One takes in the suffering of oneself or others on the in breath, and sends out relief from that suffering on the out breath. The regular practice of tonglen meditation is a powerful adjunct for monitoring exchange and applying touch and go within therapeutic sessions as it supports a less referential view of suffering. By releasing the need to defend a self-experience, one can more fully accommodate the suffering of others without turning away.

Case Study[2]

I met Sarah in the first month of my year-long internship at a mental health facility. Sarah was a woman with ruffled white hair; she was

---
[2] This case study is a compilation of clients and experiences of both authors.

in her mid-fifties and of average height with a thin frame. Her voice was soft and gentle. She often squinted while speaking as if pained by what she said. She was a retired lab technician living with her husband. She regularly visited her daughter and grandchildren, but had no other social outlet. From her intake sheet, I learned that her sleep had been very poor for more than a year and that she reported always feeling overwhelmed by anxious feelings.

Approaching Sarah in the waiting room at our first meeting, I sensed the fatigue in her slumped posture. When she looked up, I read her facial expression as despondent and I felt a pang of sadness in my chest. Before she spoke, I already felt strongly compelled to help her. Her eyes seemed to plead for me to do so. As we walked down the hall to my office, she lagged behind me. I slowed down so we could walk side by side, but then she slowed down to remain behind me. When we sat down in my office, I asked her "What brings you in?"

She said, "I don't know." That was a real conversation stopper; other clients generally take that opening in the first session and talk quite freely. In the silence, I noticed myself scrambling for a reply, wondering if I should bring up what I already knew from her intake sheet. Remembering this information, however, I guessed she might be feeling overwhelmed with anxiety in the moment. I fell back on a more object-oriented question, "The aspens are full of color this time of year. How long have you lived in Colorado?"

"Six months," she said and went silent again.

After about thirty seconds, I remembered supervision I had received about the importance of making contact with clients and how just saying anything, even if it is ridiculous, is better than allowing a complete withdrawal. I resorted to even more object-oriented questions, "Did you see the aspens on your way into the building?

"I don't know... I mean yes. I guess they're pretty." she said.

Was she just giving me back what she thought I wanted to hear? Did she not want to burden me? As our first meeting went along, it developed into an awkward interview. In response to my eventual questions about her history of sleep disturbance and anxiety, she offered only minimal replies followed by silences. Although I shared several possible skills she could use for managing anxiety, I gathered they had not registered with her. When the session ended, she asked me, "What do you think I should do?"

"Schedule for next week and we can talk more about it." I said confidently, wanting to instill hope in her about our work and changes she could make.

Sarah elicited my wanting-to-know mind and my desire to be of help. Over the week, I thought of numerous questions I wanted to ask about her childhood, her marriage, her children, her work, and hobbies. When I remembered that we had not discussed the possibility of medicating her sleep disorder in the first session, I called her to set up an

3. Therapist Subjectivity

appointment with our psychiatrist. I read and photocopied several chapters of an anxiety workbook and wrote up note cards to prompt my memory in session of helpful techniques for alleviating anxiety. I noticed this heightened level of preparation, but regarded it as nothing more than good therapeutic practice. Looking back, it was the beginning of a slippery slope of wanting to self-organize as an expert for this client.

In the next session, when we sat down, I felt Sarah's silence envelop me like fog. Hoping she would release me from the fog, I asked tentatively, "What should we talk about today?"

"I don't know," she said.

"What are the possibilities?" I asked.

"You could tell me what you think I should do?"

"About what?" I questioned her back.

"I don't know," she replied.

So our work went. Sarah replied "I don't know" and "What do you think I should do?" multiple times in each session. This often led to a groundless sensation in me. I felt exposed and vulnerable, quickly followed by a strong urge to know and say what she should do. Possibly to distract myself from that discomfort, my thoughts in session often wandered to academic conceptualizations of her presentation. Perhaps she was putting me in a complementary countertransference role of the narcissistic parent who undermined the development of her own authority (Ziezel, 2006). Or perhaps her anxiety was producing an overstimulation of her parasympathetic nervous system response, leaving her dull and deadened.

Tracking my own experience of these interpretations, I noticed I felt relaxed while contemplating them, but also more distant from Sarah. I realized that I was placing these academic constructs on top of my direct experience of her. Given our brief time together and her extreme tentativeness, I knew better than to believe what I thought. I tried returning my attention to the technique of touch and go. I asked Sarah questions about her life and her experiences of anxiety, determined to accommodate whatever arose without intellectualization and without therapeutic aggression. Yet time and again, I felt compelled to be helpful by addressing Sarah's conviction that the direction of her life should be provided by a therapist and not by her.

My primary site supervisor assured me that she had dependent personality disorder and that I needed to optimally frustrate her into the development of a self. But that did not help me with my feelings. When I opened to Sarah's experience, I gathered that through the exchange with her emotional state I was uncertain, intolerant, and dull. Perhaps to escape these feelings, I hypothesized in the moment that she might be unconsciously using projective identification because she was unable to tolerate her feelings; and I was catching these terribly uncomfortable mental stances. I enjoyed the comfort and triumph of these *in-the-moment* interpretations so much so that I repeatedly decided I had figured her out and just relaxed in that knowledge. I viewed the two of us in this detached way until I realized I was escaping her experience again. It was very difficult to just stay in the uncertainty and discomfort of Sarah's experience.

I talked with my three site supervisors about these experiences and her "I don't know" and "What should I do?" imperatives. My humanistic supervisor recommended that she was not ready to know and that I should let her know that I accept her knowing or not knowing. My psychodynamic supervisor told me that these statements may be forms of resistance and that asking the client to make a guess may help her access her unconscious experience. My behaviorist supervisor insisted knowing is not important and if insight comes it usually happens after behavioral change. From this perspective, I should guide her through completing more self-efficacious and rewarding tasks each week until she was functioning at her peak.

I considered each of these elucidations throughout our first months together. However, my initial feelings of wanting to help Sarah eventually decreased as I began to notice my annoyance with her passivity. I started to dread the sessions and the inevitable moments when she would ask me what she should do. I came up with endless lists of ideas to explore. I asked her to tell me all about her anxious feelings: when she had them, what thoughts came with the anxiety, and what behaviors she employed to address them. She sometimes spoke about feeling anxious around other people, like her husband, because she often thought others were mad at her. However, these explorations quickly moved into masochistic self-condemnations, with her voice fading off until she mumbled into silence. She would then look up and ask, "What should I do?" In hindsight, I realized that in our emotional exchange the tone of my own thoughts also had become condemning toward her for not knowing what to do.

More out of frustration than sympathy, I often fell for her pleas for direction and she rewarded me with gratitude and praise for offering such useful support. This often relaxed my discomfort and seemed to relax Sarah's anxiety, if only briefly. She would listen earnestly as I went over progressive muscle relaxation and breathing techniques she could use to manage her anxiety. In later sessions, however, she did not mention using any of the techniques during the week. When I asked if she found them useful, Sarah said that she either forgot about them or tried them to no avail—giving up after one or two attempts. I felt quite bewildered when these statements were often followed by, "Oh, but do *you* think that is what I need to do?" Whatever my reply to this question, she requested a review of the techniques. She assured me that she saw their benefit and really would apply them all week. I took these events as strong signals to abandon the use of directives with Sarah and stay the course of tracking our exchange and applying touch and go to my experience. My attempts at using the best practice protocols for anxiety and dependent personality disorder did not appear to be helping her. Perhaps I had the wrong

3. Therapist Subjectivity

diagnosis. Perhaps it did not matter. After all, assessment is a continual process, mentally constructed, interdependent, and empty.

So, I went to the Buddhist lineage for guidance in her treatment. In the *Abhidharmakosha* of Vasubandu, the mind is viewed as having fifty-one mental factors that create our experiences. These factors included the omnipresent factors such as skandha activity. There are five determinative factors, including concentration and mindfulness; virtuous factors, such as considerateness and enthusiasms; and non-virtuous factors, such as envy, greed, dullness, and excitement. Also included are variable factors, such as regret, general examination, and precise evaluation. These variable factors can be beneficial in guiding one's action and understanding, but they can be limiting if taken to an extreme. While certain factors are seen as beneficial, all, even the non-virtuous factors are accepted. The non-virtuous factors such as greed, pride, and anger, are not to be gotten rid of, but rather accepted as transient mental states that one can bring awareness to in order to avoid unhelpful behavior.

In relation to Sarah, the virtuous factor that was not being recognized was self-respect or a sense of propriety. Similar to cognitive techniques, I highlighted the things she was able to do and accomplish, such as attending our sessions and making lunch for her grandchildren. Once she would acknowledge her competencies, she would immediately become fearful of feeling too good about herself or being prideful. From a Buddhist perspective, self-confidence and pride are viewed as separate mental states. Sarah and I discussed how feeling positive about oneself in a realistic manner is actually very different from non-reality based feelings of pride.

This discussion naturally led her to recall a story from her childhood. She said that her father was always so sure about himself and was often wrong. She retold a story of falling off her bike and breaking her thumb. When she ran home in tears, her father insisted that she was not hurt and was only pretending in order to get attention and sympathy. When her mother came home and saw her swollen hand, they went to the hospital and her broken thumb was put in a cast. We talked about her mother being confident enough to seek help, and the confidence of the doctor to treat her injury. Confidence was not negative. She could be confident without being prideful like her father.

The non-virtuous factor that stood out in Sarah was cruelty, particularly focused on herself. She appeared attached to the idea of herself as being bad and incompetent. From the Buddhist perspective, the mind's ability to solidify our ideas creates a misattunement to our environment, limits our ability to remain curious about the self and the world in new progressive manners, and is the root of suffering. Buddhism suggests the use of cognitive antidotes to work constructively with negative or difficult emotions. This practice is sort of a prescriptive technique to train one's mind.

Two mental afflictions that have many antidotes are the root experiences of lack of compassion and of attachment to one's view. Sarah could benefit in training in both these areas. Compassion is the inherent ground below drive theories and even below the self. It is an inherent quality of our brilliant sanity. Many antidotes are given for developing compassion, but the examination of the interconnected nature of phenomena, contemplating the experiences of others, and loosening attachment to self-perception are common approaches. I felt like Sarah was examining these issues in therapy, and that she was, in fact, developing more compassion for herself.

One antidote for attachment to one's view is to observe how the mind can exaggerate dualistic, positive or negative, perceptions. From a Western perspective, this could be described as the mind's primitive defense of splitting. Sarah had exaggerated the badness within herself while idealizing the positive qualities of those around her, like her husband, her daughter, and me. To address this propensity in Sarah, I brought attention to ways I had not played an idealized role thus far within our work, by not being able to find sustainable solutions for her problems of anxiety and overall uncertainty of what to do. We then explored her impulse to blame herself rather than me for the shortcomings of our work.

Discussions of this aspect of Sarah's experience brought forth developmental memories. She said that when she felt like she knew something, her father would get mad at her. But she knew that when she struggled her mother would try to comfort her, which Sarah enjoyed and appreciated. Without using Western psychological language, she came to realize the secondary gain she was expecting by being needy. If she were needy, she would be comforted. Although that worked with her mother, her husband, and her children, everyone else had different responses, often ranging from frustration to dismissiveness. At the end of that session, she smiled at me for the first time.

I thought I was on a roll and began to take more risks in treatment. I told her she should do what she wanted to do. When she would ask what to do if her husband or daughter did not like her actions, I told her that they should come talk to me about their feelings of dislike. This began to loosen Sarah's perception that she was omnipotent and the creator of other people's feelings. When we talked about her opinion of her family members, she talked more easily, as she was not the focus. She began to see, in part, that the feelings, thoughts, and behaviors that emerged in her family were co-created. She was not the sole karmic generator of their struggles.

I was beginning to feel good about our work, even prideful. She was actually developing a self. I felt inspired to call my self psychology instructor and tell him that through empathy and compassionate challenging I had helped someone become a better functioning self. I wanted to tell my Buddhist teacher that "Yes, I see the self exists and is

3. Therapist Subjectivity

needed, and also that it actuality doesn't exist." I thought I had figured it all out; I understood Sarah. Our work was simply about helping her create a unifying, reflective, open, creative, confident, yet not prideful, sense of self.

Soon thereafter, Sarah told me for the first time that she had worked with another mental health center in Texas before moving to Colorado. She asked if I would review her records to see if they could benefit our work even more. I had her sign a release and believed at face value that she thought the records would help build upon our recent work. When I received her records, the truth of the subjective nature of therapeutic work poured off the pages. She had seen three different psychiatrists who had diagnosed her with major depression, anxiety disorder NOS, and post traumatic stress disorder, respectively. She had tried over a dozen medications with modest results, at best.

For a period of several years, she saw two therapists: the first diagnosed her with bipolar disorder; the second with borderline personality disorder. She then went through several interns who saw her no more than twelve times a year. The intern notes initially reported major changes, but the notes became shorter and shorter, and each discharge summary stated that she was non-compliant with treatment. From her records, I also learned that she had been in a traumatic car accident in which she had been hit by a drunk driver and was in a coma for three days. She did not receive compensation from the uninsured driver, and had not sought neuropsychological evaluation or intervention. She returned to work for six months and then retired. That is when she and her husband moved to Colorado to be closer to the grandchildren.

After receiving the records my mind was spinning; I was now considering endless new conceptualizations of her case. Had our therapy actually helped? I recalled the disturbing evidence of Mike Lambert (2005), which showed how therapists are apt to overestimate clinical change. When she returned for the next session, I immediately wanted to get to work. I wanted to understand the string of symptoms described in her previous treatment records. I started our next session by informing her that I had received the records, was concerned about her head trauma, and wanted her to do something about it.

Unexpectedly she asked me, "What do you think is wrong with me?" I felt a slight jolt, realizing for the first time that I had unquestioningly bought into the idea of something being "wrong" with Sarah again. I slowed down and said I was not sure I wanted to pathologize her experience. She said that she did not care if her situation was pathological. She wanted to know how to get better, how to have more energy, be more confident, and have less fear; she felt ready for more progress. She thought the car accident had changed her and she wanted me to help her understand that better.

I felt invigorated by Sarah's sudden lack of passivity and remembered the pre-doctorate intern who was continually hounding me for neuropsychological assessment cases. I offered Sarah the referral.

She said that having been a scientist herself, she was curious about what these tests might say. We went ahead and set up an appointment for testing—both of us expressing our mixture of fear and optimism regarding how the testing and the results might affect her.

As it turned out, the assessment results could not have been worse, not in their conclusion of any significant pathology, but rather in their inconclusiveness. The student psychologist informed me that in fact *he did not know*. Her performance IQ was lower than her verbal IQ, but not to the point of significance. She may have lost some functioning due to the car accident or she might have always been more verbal. He informed me that it was hard to say if she was more depressed or anxious, and that she also had some indications of somatic disorders. The results showed she fell just short of meeting high suicidal risk on the Rorschach. Her MMPI indicated the possibility of substance abuse disorders, but not definitively. I relentlessly quizzed him to give me the answer, but he said he could not. He said he liked her, though, and he wished he could have been more helpful.

Before our next session I caught myself. What happened to the relational work we were doing before I reviewed her records? I thought back to the process factors that had helped the therapeutic process, therapeutic alliance, talking, occasional insight, and support (Walborn, 1996). I realized that I was ruining our therapeutic alliance with my renewed desire to understand the diagnostic convolution of her situation. I also reviewed the shock of receiving Sarah's records—how prideful I had been of our work before hand and how reluctant I now was to lose our momentum. I wondered what unconscious processes might have prompted Sarah to steer us toward the rocky road we had just encountered. Hadn't we just built up her self-experience beyond needing to be pathologized?

I paused to take a deeper look at my own subjective experience. I realized I had been sensing myself as being in relation to someone who desperately needed help, actually *my help*. I realized how much Sarah and I conspired to maintain a solidified view of her self-experience as being dependent on others' help and how often I bought into the role of the knowing therapist. In a way, through my excitement over "the success" of our work, I took some ownership of her experience, which she then took back by getting worse.

Somehow we accommodated the inconclusiveness of her assessment results and both became more comfortable with not knowing. In the next few sessions, I sat back. I endured uncomfortable silences and did not force my theories on her. She actually became more relaxed in the sessions. She reported that she was sleeping better and had more energy and thanked me for the referral to the psychiatrist. She thought the medications were helping. She also explored new avenues about understanding her life. She said life was bizarre; that even as she

3. Therapist Subjectivity

approaches sixty, she does not know what it means and that she continues to be unsatisfied, confused, and uneasy much of the time.

Despite bringing her up for more supervision, no clear diagnosis or prognostic treatment approach was ever agreed upon between my supervisors nor did I settle into these myself. Even my feelings about her changed over time from care, to frustration, to pity, to hope, and around again.

She came regularly to her appointments the last few months I worked with her. We talked more about her grandchildren, about how she started and stopped drinking again and even that she made love with her husband for the first time in more than a year, appraising it as very tender and sweet. She continued to have recurrent negative cognitions about herself, get frozen with ambivalence, and had intermittent bouts of sleeplessness. She said she felt different—still like herself, but somehow she was also not who she used to be.

As my internship was ending, I considered taking her to my private practice despite the fact she could not pay. My supervisors decided to have her work with a new intern at the center where more services would be available to her. Although I was having a hard time letting her go, she was agreeable to working with a new therapist. In my second to last session with her, I introduced the new therapist and she seemed quite open and pleasant toward him. He seemed quite warm and very competent to me.

In our last session, I tried to review some of our work together, but she was not interested. Instead she talked about her grandchildren and how unrealistic her daughter's expectations of her were and how she was going to tell her so. She said how excited she was to continue therapy with the new intern and that he seemed smart and nice. At the end, she got up and thanked me and told me to take care. I tried to walk next to her on the way back to the waiting room, but as I hurried to catch up with her, she sped up more. She opened the door and said "Ta-ta" and was gone. I went back to my office and wrote a discharge summary making sure that I noted progress so that she could continue in treatment and that the center continued to receive funding. I ended the note saying that Sarah seemed to have taken more responsibility for managing her own experience, to have increased her ability to deal with ambivalence, and to have shown resilience. Was I talking about Sarah, myself, or my understanding of the Buddhist path?

This might be considered an anti-case example as no clear or new antidotal intervention or conceptual psychological theory emerged from our work. Therapy offered no definitive answers for Sarah. In the contemplative sense, however, we did share experiences of accommodating her anxiety and uncertainty about not knowing what to do. Since that discomfort presented as the ground of Sarah's experience, it seems we caught glimpses within our work of something at least as relevant, if not more relevant than *answers* for application to her self-experience—accommodation.

From our work, I discovered nothing more tangible than this to inform my future clinical work. From my efforts to treat her, I learned a lot about various disorders, neuropsychological research, assessment procedures, and supervisor subjectivity. From my efforts to track exchange and apply touch and go, I also learned about the patterns of my own subjective experience, of wanting to know, of wanting to help, and of having difficulty letting go. I learned that these tendencies are not pathologies in me, in her, or in our dynamic. I developed the humility to accept that I would not cure her. In retrospect, I have sometimes wondered if our sessions were helpful to her at all, or if she might also just have adapted to her situation over time without treatment.

Psychotherapy is difficult work—to not know, to persevere, and to let go. Sarah comes to mind sometimes in my work with other clients, while I drive in the car, and even within my meditation sessions. I continue to notice my impulse to grasp onto her by wanting to call the center for an update or push against her by being angry at the center for making me transfer her. I get sick of thinking of her sometimes and desire to push her out of my mind. When I realize I haven't been thinking of her for months and she comes up, I notice both my guilt and my relief.

Conclusion

In contemplative psychotherapy, the two-truths view of absolute and relative reality is applied to clinical work through the therapist's ability to hold an absolute view of the impermanent, interdependent, and empty nature of her subjectivity within the relative framework of relationship building, diagnosing, and implementing interventions. She operates within the systems of Western and Buddhist psychological theory while simultaneously entertaining the knowledge that those systems are relative, changing, and potentially limiting. The goal of the approach is not to eliminate the self-experiences of the client or therapist, but to illuminate the fluidity and workability of those self-experiences.

One fascinating result of bringing awareness training to our subjective experience within therapeutic work is that the more we know about how our experiences of self arise, the easier it is to not cling to them for security. Viewing self-experience as impermanent, interdependent, and ultimately non-existent helps loosen identification with therapist subjectivity in order to open to more direct contact with clients and to offer them a more receptive, responsive, and inventive therapeutic environment. It is interesting to view our subjective experience as a creative tool for therapeutic work. The more tightly we hold a paintbrush, for instance, the more constricted we are in expressing our art. The more we expand our view of the paintbrush as one aspect of an unfolding expression of art, the more freedom we have to manifest a direct expression of the art of any moment.

For both client and therapist, psychotherapy heightens the experience of *duhkha*, the inevitable uneasiness that comes from being. Accepting this situation is also a form of liberation. Therapy, like meditation, is a place where client and therapist can accept what is: the limits of our knowledge, our misguided interventions, the frequent futility of our efforts, the resultant karma that goes beyond us and our best intentions, and the incandescence of each unfolding moment. Therapy remains an impossible profession. Knowing *not knowing* is the best path.

Cohen and Schermer (2001) note the remarkable evolution of our understanding of the subjective experience of therapists in Western psychology—it has passed from being viewed as "technical error to valuable source of information about patient transference to directly shareable source of the content of therapeutic interventions" (p. 55). As contemplative psychotherapists, we would add that the subjective experience of the therapist can be used to communicate accommodation, to notice when solidifying views of self and other arise, and to use that recognition as a signal to open to a more direct awareness and experience of the brilliant sanity within therapeutic work.

Chogyam Trungpa defined enlightenment, or the direct experience of life, as "Compassion for self; skillful means with others" (cited in Patton, 1994, p 130). When we open to self-experience and recognize it as impermanent, interdependent, and empty of inherent existent, it is much easier to show compassion toward that self-experience. There is no reason to defend it or cling to it. In this way, we can more easily touch it and let it go, which affords us more access to, and freedom within, the art of the therapeutic moment.

References

Bandura, A. (1977). *Social learning theory.* Englewood Cliffs, NJ: Prentice Hall.

Bromberg, P. (1998). *Standing in the spaces: essays on clinical process, trauma, and dissociation.* Hillsdale, NJ: Analytic Press.

Chödrön, P. (2001). *Tonglen: The path of transformation.* Halifax, Nova Scotia: Vajradhatu Publications.

Christensen, L. (1999). Suffering and the dialectical self in Buddhism and relational psychoanalysis. *The American Journal of Psychoanalysis, 59*(1), 37-57.

Clarke, J. J. (1997). *Oriental enlightenment: The encounter between Asian and Western thought.* London: Routledge.

Cohen, B. D. & Schermer, V. L. (2001). Therapist self disclosure in group psychotherapy from an intersubjective and self psychological standpoint. *Group, 25*(1/2), 41-57.

de Wit, H. F. (1993). *Contemplative psychology.* Pittsburg, PA: Duquesne University Press.

Duerlinger, J. (2003). *Indian Buddhist theories of person: Vasubandhu's refutation of the theory of a self.* London: Routledge.

Epstein, M. (2007). *Psychotherapy without the self: A Buddhist perspective.* New Haven, CT: Yale.

Feinberg, T. E. & Farah, M. J. (2003) *Behavioral neurology and neuropsychology.* New York: McGraw-Hill.

Freud, A. (1936) *The ego and the mechanisms of defense.* London: Hogarth.

Fromm-Reichmann, F. (1950). *Principles of intensive psychotherapy*, Chicago: University of Chicago.

Gallucci, G. M. (2001). *Plato and Freud: Statesmen of the soul.* Philadelphia: Xlibris.

Gay, P. (1988). *Freud: A life for our time.* New York: Norton.

Gyatso, T. (2005). *The universe in a single atom.* New York: Morgan Road Books.

Hartmann, H. (1939). *Ego psychology and the problem of adaptation.* New York: International Universities.

Hartmann, H. (1964). *Essays on ego psychology.* New York: International Universities.

Hilgard, E. R. (1987). *Psychology in America: A historical survey.* New York: Harcourt.

Hoffman, L. & Kurzenberger, M. (in press). Premodern, modern, and postmodern interpretations of the miraculous and mental illness from religious and psychological perspectives. In H. Ellens (Ed.), *Miracles: God, science, and the paranormal* (Vol. 3). Westport, CT: Praeger

Horney, K. (1937). *The neurotic personality of our time.* New York: Norton.

Horney, K. (1939). *New ways in psychoanalysis.* New York: Norton.

Horney, K. (1991). *Final lectures.* (D. Ingram, Ed.). New York: Norton

Inagaki, H. & Jennings, J. N. (2000). *Philosophical theology and East-West dialogue.* Kenilworth, NJ: Rodopi.

James, W. (1890). *The principles of psychology* (Vols. 1-2). New York: Henry Holt.

Kant, I. (2003). *Critique of pure reason.* (J. Meiklejohn, Trans.) New York: Dover. (Originally published in 1881).

Kearney, R. (1994). *Twentieth-century continental philosophy.* London: Routledge.

Kerfeld, G. B. (1981). *The sophistic movement.* Cambridge: Cambridge University.

Klein, M. (1932). *The psycho-analysis of children.* London: Hogarth.

Kohut, H. (1971). *Analysis of the self.* New York: International Universities.
Kohut, H. (1977). *The restoration of the self.* New York: International Universities.
Kolb, B. & Whishaw, I. Q. (2003). *Fundamentals of human neuropsychology.* New York: Worth.
Kuhn, T. S. (1962). *The structure of scientific revolutions.* Chicago: University of Chicago Press.
Kuhn, T. S. (2000). *The road since structure: Philosophical essays, 1970-1993.* Chicago: University of Chicago.
Livingston, M. (1999). Vulnerability, tenderness, and the experience of selfobject relationship: A self psychological view of deepening curative process in group psychotherapy. *International Journal of Group Psychotherapy, 49* (1), 19-40.
Leyton, M. (1992). Egolessness and the borderline experience. *Journal of Contemplative Psychotherapy 3,* 43-70.
McEvilley, T. (2002). *The shape of ancient thought.* New York: Allworth.
McWilliams, N. (2004). *Psychoanalytic psychotherapy: A practitioner's guide.* New York: Guilford.
Millon, T. (1990). *Towards a new personology.* New York: Wiley.
Millon, T. (2004). *Personality disorders in everyday life.* New York: Wiley.
Mitchell, S. A. (1988). *Relational concepts in psychoanalysis.* Cambridge, MA: Harvard University.
Mitchell, S. A. (1997). *Influence and autonomy in psychoanalysis.* Hillsdale, NJ: Analytic Press.
Murray, H. A. (1938). *Explorations in personality.* New York: Oxford University.
Murray, H. A. (1967). Henry A. Murray. In E. G. Boring & G. Lindzey (Eds.). *A history of psychology in autobiography. (Vol. 5, pp. 282-310).* New York: Appleton-Century-Crofts.
Patton, P. (1994). A contemplative view of addiction as experienced by a recovering alcoholic. *Journal of Contemplative Psychotherapy 9,* 113-134.
Pizer, S. A. (2003). Commentary: Imagining Langan: A transcendence of self. In J. Safran (Ed.), *Psychoanalysis and Buddhism: An unfolding dialogue* (pp. 146-158). Boston: Wisdom Publications.
Quinn, S. (1997). *A mind of her own: The life of Karen Horney.* Orangeville, Ontario: Summit.
Reis, B. (2005). The self is alive and well and living in relational psychoanalysis. *Psychoanalytic. Psychology, 22,* 86-95.
Russell, B. (2002). *A critical exposition of the philosophy of Leibniz.* London: Routledge.
Safran, J. D. (2003). *Psychoanalysis and Buddhism: An unfolding dialogue.* Boston: Wisdom Publications.
Sayers, J. (1991). *Mothers of psychoanalysis.* New York: Norton
Schore, A. N. (2002). *Affect dysregulation and disorders of the self.* New York: Norton.

Siegel, D. J. (2007). *The mindful brain*. New York: Norton.
Sellars, W., Rorty, R., & Brandom, R. B. (1997). *Empiricism and the philosophy of mind*. Cambridge, MA: Harvard University
Shantideva. (1997). *The way of the bodhisattva* (Padmakara Translation Group, Trans.) Boston: Shambhala. (Original work from the 8th century)
Shapiro, E. (2001). Dealing with masochistic behavior in group therapy from the perspective of the self. *Group 25* (1/2), 107-120.
Smith, T. (2003). *Practicing multiculturalism: Affirming diversity in counseling and psychology*. Boston: Allyn & Bacon.
Sue, D. & Sue, D. M. (2007) *Foundations of counseling and psychotherapy: evidence-based practices for a diverse society*. New York: Wiley.
Sullivan, H. S. (1953). *The interpersonal theory of psychiatry*. New York: Norton.
Suzuki, S. (1973). *Zen mind, beginners mind*. New York: Weatherhill.
Thorne, B. M. & Henley, T. B. (2001). *Connections in the history and systems of psychology*. Boston: Houghton Mifflin.
Toohey, P. (1992). *Reading epic: An introduction to the ancient narrative*. London: Routledge.
Trungpa, C. (1973). *Cutting through spiritual materialism*. Boston: Shambhala.
Walborn, F. S. (1996). *Process variables.: Four common elements of counseling and psychotherapy*. Pacific Grove CA: Brooks-Cole.
Wozniak, R. H. (1992). *Mind and body: Rene Déscartes to William James*. Washington DC: American Psychological Association.
Weaver, C. (1999). An examination of the relationship between the concepts of projective identification and intersubjectivity. *British Journal of Psychotherapy 2* (16) p 136-154.
Wegela, K (1988). "Touch and go" in clinical practice: Some implications of the view of intrinsic health for psychotherapy. *Journal of Contemplative Psychotherapy 5*, 3-23.
Wegela, K. (1992). Shock, uncertainty, conviction: Gateways between psychopathology and intrinsic health. *Journal of Contemplative Psychotherapy, 3*, 33-52.
Wright, F. (2000). The use of the self in group leadership: A relational perspective. *International Journal of Group Psychotherapy, 50* (2), 181-197.
Yalom, I. D. (1995). *The theory and practice of group psychotherapy* (4th ed.). New York: Basic Books.
Zimbardo, P. G. (2004). Does psychology make a significant difference in our lives? *American Psychologist, 59*, 339-351.
Zimbardo, P. G. (2007). *The Lucifer effect: Understanding how good people turn evil*. New York: Random House.

4

Warriorship: A Tradition of Fearlessness and its Impact on Contemplative Psychotherapy

Matthew Tomatz

> I honor those who try
> to rid themselves of any lying,
> who empty the self
> and have only clear being there.
> - Rumi

Kali

Kali is fearsome! The ferocious Hindu goddess is envisioned as a hideous and disheveled black crone adorned by a garland of 51 skulls with pendulous breasts, lolling tongue, and wild-eyes. Her four arms and hands strike fear and exude power, as she brandishes a bloodstained knife and a severed, blood-dripping, human head. Kali is frequently envisioned standing atop a corpse-like Lord Shiva, who has arrived at the battlegrounds to tame her fury. It is only when she realizes that she has slain her husband that Kali ends her killing rampage and ceases drinking the blood from her slaughtered foes. Through and through, Kali is a warrior. It is the spirit of the warrior that threads together the practice of contemplative psychotherapy.

Defining warriorship from two distinct vantage points reveals remarkable differences in understanding the essence of a warrior. The common or *earthly* view is grounded in fear. Reacting to the overwhelming nature of fear, the earthly warrior assumes a rigid stance that is aggressive and brittle. The earthly warrior, looking to seek shelter from fear that is embedded in inevitable change, is motivated to substantiate himself through material wealth, muscle mass, limited emotions, reactionary behaviors, weapons, and violence. This rigid response lends itself to further defensive tactics that perpetuate a pattern of disconnection and ultimately generate suffering. The *warrior of compassion* (referred to as warrior or warriorship throughout this paper) assumes a different stance. The warrior is fluid and free to react to all that arises in the world with the delicacy of a water droplet or the ferocity of a tidal blast. To move in this manner, the warrior is accepting and accommodating. The warrior is brave, courageous, and spacious enough to be affected by his life experience. The warrior is fearless in the face of suffering, and he or she uses a tender heart to reveal the wisdom of emotion to inspire compassionate action. By connecting deeply with others and the raw experience of life, the warrior finds great freedom and is able to effect the world. In this way, it is Kali's spacious and compassionate heart that causes her to react to Shiva and act in accordance with her emotional tenderness.

Kali is emblematic of the warrior's path and a metaphorical reference point for contemplative psychotherapy, which is a practice of warriorship and informed as such by the Buddhist teachings in the Shambhala lineage. As I began to consider writing about warriorship and contemplative psychotherapy, it became clear that the masculine archetype of warriorship was not complete. I sought advice, and my wise and powerful female friends pointed me in the direction of Kali. An inclusive image of Kali moves past the limitations of masculine and feminine into a composite essence of warrior.

The presence of a forceful and terrifying warrior spirit within the compassion-based practice of therapy introduces a paradoxical thread that weaves itself through the tapestry of contemplative psychotherapy and life itself. "Kali conveys death, destruction, fear, terror, the all-consuming aspect of reality…. She is death itself" (Kinsley, 2003, p. 30). Kali, the Mother of Time, devours all. As such, Kali is representative of the Buddhist teaching of impermanence. At some point we must relate with the fact that all things end. Existence is in a constant state of motion, and we are faced with the basic point of the Shambhala teachings: "to realize that there is no outside help to save you from the terror and the horror of life" (Trungpa, 1999, p. 3). So, where's the good news – the other side?

Kali's presence equates to the Buddhist first noble truth: *suffering exists* and infuses life including awareness of the unwavering reality of our own mortality. Thankfully, this is not an endpoint, or we would be lost to hopelessness and endless despair. There is a path to embrace suffering and encounter all aspects of life directly and inquisitively. As suggested by Wegela and Joseph (1992), "one can work with fear constructively, without needing to get rid of it" (p. 44). We can embrace all aspects of existence and move into a space of freshness and possibility. It is from the stance of embracing uncertainty that Kali's power and magic are revealed.

Kali is multifaceted. Upon closer examination, we can see that fearsome Kali is holding her bloody talons in the gesture of dispelling fear, and her feet, often understood to represent conquest, also convey security and mercy. It becomes clear that Kali also symbolizes the divine mother, whose aggressiveness, as represented by the garland of heads, is directed at removing elements of false personality in order to reveal clarity, space, and freshness. False personality is parallel to the Buddhist concept of ego, a mistaken belief in self as solid, separate, and permanent – a defensive mechanism to deny unbearable impermanence. Kali, as divine mother, holds weapons directed at protecting us from delusion and ignorance. Her warrior spirit is focused on liberating the devotee from ego-bound delusion:

> To meditate on the dark goddess, or to devote oneself to her, is to step out of the everyday world of predictable dharmic order and enter a world of reversals, opposites, and contrasts and in doing so to wake up to new possibilities and new frames of reference. (Kinsley, 2003, p. 35)

In many ways, psychotherapy and devotion to Kali are the same. They are both processes of paradox: We must move into suffering in order to achieve liberating change. We must embrace uncertainty, accept the realities of impermanence, and assume a stance of fearlessness. In so doing, acceptance of everyday and ubiquitous suffering transcends stagnation and frees one from the shackles of delusional security into a space of possibility, freedom, and change. This is an unknown and terrifying path. This is the path of a warrior.

Death

Facing death is fundamental to the warrior. Kali is called upon not to center on the grim and become mired, but rather as a reminder of the forgotten truth of impermanence and to illuminate the path and practice of contemplative psychotherapy. A devotee, an aspiring warrior, and, for that matter, the warrior therapist or client, seeks to find strength in the face of uncertainty by accepting and being empowered by a full recognition of Kali in her most direct manifestation as death. To grow, to change, the warrior must stand and face death. The warrior practices a stance of acceptance by allowing for, if not embracing, impermanence. It is from this place of finding ground within groundlessness that the warrior uncovers strength to transcend habitual patterns. Similarly, by facing death with a open heart and exploring its meaning, the philosophical underpinnings of contemplative psychotherapy are revealed, primarily, that one's allegiance to ego, and its concomitant suffering, will eventually wither when there is an acceptance of impermanence and a release into growth and transformation.

Full acknowledgement of death is a frightful proposition. Death, of course, is present. We all know that. However, we rarely recognize our habitual, unconscious response, which is to flee and then establish a sense of security by erecting a rigid and fabricated boundary called ego. These "defensive strategies... take on a myriad of forms in everyday experience, serving in great measure to sustain ego's supposed comfort, permanence, and stability" (Wegela & Joseph, 1992, p. 37). Supposed comfort is an illusion, a desire for life to be sustainable and static, and a denial of what is real and present. We tend not to face Kali because she is terrifying: "The terror of death is ubiquitous and of such magnitude that a considerable portion of one's life energy is consumed in the denial of death" (Yalom, 1980, p. 41). It takes tremendous effort to sustain ego, since ever-present Kali regularly uses her sword to penetrate ego boundaries. This ego effort leads to a powerful and forceful presence acting as "a smoke screen that allows us to distract ourselves from the scary groundlessness that underlies our life" (Welwood, 2000, p. 149).

Simply stated, we work hard to deny impermanence.

> Although we can buy this truth intellectually, emotionally we have a deep-rooted aversion to it. We want permanence; we expect permanence. Our natural tendency is to seek security.... We use our daily activity as a shield against the fundamental ambiguity of our situation, expending tremendous energy trying to ward off impermanence and death. (Chödrön, 2001, p. 24)

This description of our patterned response to death anxiety begins to illuminate the paradox of compassionate warriorship. Warriorship tends to connote aggressive and forceful acts. Where these may be qualities of war, they are inaccurate views of the warrior. In actuality, a warrior looks to wage war on those things that harden and stagnate movement, where ego looks to establish a fixed position and fight against movement. Ego is an aggressive act that looks to defeat the enemy of impermanence. The compassionate warrior balances aggression with a tender and warm heart and an attitude of acceptance.

When out of balance, the abstract concept of ego manifests in a very concrete manner, which we call psychopathology. "In other words, psychopathology is the result of ineffective modes of death transcendence" (Yalom, 1980, p. 27). Our fear of Kali, and our aggressive acts of refusal, are at the root of our suffering and manifest as a 'force-field of anxiety'" (Yalom, p. 161). As stated by Zilbourg (quoted in Becker, 1973):

> Behind the sense of insecurity in the face of danger, behind the sense of discouragement and depression, there always lurks the basic fear of death, a fear which undergoes most complex elaborations and manifests itself in many indirect ways... No one is free of the fear of death... The anxiety neuroses, the various phobic states, even a considerable number of depressive suicidal states and many schizophrenias amply demonstrate the ever-present fear of death which becomes woven into the major conflicts of the given psychopathological conditions. (p.16)

Psychopathology, the refusal to acknowledge impermanence and its associated suffering, gives direction to the practice of contemplative psychotherapy. Contemplative psychotherapy looks to unwind the tangled

4. Warriorship

threads of ego to gradually reveal a more direct connection with Kali, which fosters the opportunity for intimacy and rewarding life experiences.

Facing death directly is a delicate proposition. Abrupt appearances of Kali likely initiate retreat and fortification of ego defenses. The practice of psychotherapy necessitates an artistic sensibility in revealing impermanent reality in a manner that can be accepted. In treatment, it is often not necessary or even advisable to address impermanence as primary, at least while ego has its full power. "The fear of death is a primal source of anxiety" (Yalom, 1980, p. 42), but "primary anxiety is always transformed into something less toxic for the individual" (Yalom, p. 45). Everyday anxiety is an entrance point as the contemplative psychotherapist looks to reveal and assist clients in facing impermanence. The faces of ego are launching pads to meaningful work. We would die in short order if dropped on the summit of Everest without oxygen. The mountaineer chooses a less toxic path of acclimation by ascending through a series of base camps. The warrior's path to the summit is also gradual, grounded in the ordinary reality and limitations of being a human being.

A client of mine, James, traversed this landscape as he looked to overcome addiction and accept impermanence. James was deeply in love. The strength of James's devotion to his wife, and their combined strength as a couple, had helped him transcend a previous gangster lifestyle in favor of family, professional success, material prosperity, and personal growth. After 20-years of marriage, James began therapy with me. His wife had recently died after an agonizing multi-year bout with cancer. James witnessed Kali on a daily basis as he witnessed the cancer ravage his wife. Compassionately, James was grateful for her death; her suffering had ended. However, after being party to this torturous death and losing his wife, James had begun using heroin again.

After committing himself to treatment, James had another demon to face, his own impermanence. From an outside perspective, James sought treatment to end his heroin dependency, and this is where we began. After several months and much work, James discontinued illicit drug use. He felt a sense of reward and change. He maintained employment, deepened relationships with his children, initiated new romances, and pursued artistic hobbies. On one level, it appeared James had made significant progress, and if not for *the hook,* treatment might have ended. Even though James had discontinued use, he kept a small stash of drugs hidden in a secret place, and ego was its guard. We called this bag of heroin *the hook*, and after considerable time, we agreed it was time to face the subject directly. Over a few sessions, we talked about the hook, its meaning and importance. It became evident that the hook was keeping James from progressing, but it was not clear why. Intellectually he understood its limiting function. James would dance between the ideas of disposing the heroin versus keeping it for posterity, "just in case." After several sessions, James was particularly close to the edge. I assumed a warrior's stance and abruptly pushed him: "You could flush it?" The room stood still. James was stunned. He was no longer looking at the hook. He was, instead, staring at his life without any hook. For a moment, James was naked, facing his life without an ego defense. The room was pregnant with opportunity.

James was having a visceral reaction to the reality of his life and situation. James's attachment to the hook had aggressively denied the raw intensity he now faced. He was approaching the potential loss of his stash, his last vestige of security. More importantly, he was looking into Kali's eyes, remembering the loss of his wife and understanding that he, too, will someday end. A moment like this holds the magic of therapy. It's huge. Contemplative therapists are trained to witness and highlight these moments of poignancy. James was faced with accepting the path of warriorship and moving into a dance with Kali. Instead of remaining hooked by the vacillations of ego, he could enter a path of freshness and explore something new.

The emptiness of this situation represents the warrior's home environment and his stance within it. A warrior is "someone who is not afraid of space" (Trungpa, 1984, p. 155). A compassionate warrior sheds aggressiveness when faced with uncertainty and is able stand within space, in acceptance, not knowing what will happen next. Warriorship redefines our colloquial definition of strength. Muscles and shields give way to embracing the inherent vulnerability embedded in moments that reveal our impermanent nature. These moments can become the basis of what Welwood (1985) defines as a "moment of world collapse" (p. 148): where the meanings on which we've been building our lives crumble. We might even consider these as moments of narcissistic injury that often lead to relapses of habitual responses, as happened for James when he began using heroin again. However, they also, and more importantly, hold the opportunity for transformative change. If the natural uncertainty imbedded in these moments is embraced, a new and involved way of relating with the world reveals itself.

After a few seconds of what felt like eternity, James slid down in the chair and his chest collapsed. Space evaporated. "I can't give up the hook! ...I'm not ready. I can't face it." "The neurotic obliterates the present by trying to find the past in the future" (Yalom, 1980, p. 161). James closed down the vitality of the present possibilities by permitting a future of stagnant sameness. For that moment, facing Kali had reified ego, but, nonetheless, a door had been opened. After several weeks, James announced he had destroyed his stash. He was standing within the unknown, eyes open to a future of possibility.

Acceptance of impermanence frees one from ego manifestations or nihilistic despair and propels movement and growth.

> The Warrior traditions all affirm that, in addition to training, what enables a Warrior to reach clarity of thought is living with the

awareness of his own imminent death... Rather than depressing him, this awareness leads him to an outpouring of life-force and to an intense experience of his life that is unknown to others. (Moore & Gillette, 1990, p. 82)

Warriorship is a liberating pathway from ego's limitations. "Anxiety, meaninglessness, and despair do not have to be denied but can become stepping-stones to something deeper" (Welwood, 2000, p. 151). A warrior passionately moves past ego defenses, which liberates possibility. A warrior's energy moves past the typical definition of aggression and assumes a new meaning: "Aggressiveness is a stance toward life that rouses, energizes, and motivates. It pushes us to take the offensive and to move out of a defensive or 'holding' position about life's tasks and problems" (Moore & Gillette, 1990, p. 79). A warrior transforms aggression into passion, acknowledging impermanence, and penetrates life. "A confrontation with one's personal death ('my death') is the nonpareil boundary situation and has the power to provide a massive shift in the way one lives in the world" (Yalom, 1980, p. 159). Where confronting Kali is at first glance terrifying, it is the path to liberation. This liberating current is one of perpetual movement and impermanence. It is the lifeblood of the warrior.

Garuda

A warrior engages in a direct confrontation with impermanence, fully open, fueled by fearlessness, and willing to move. Movement is crucial if we are to grow and live within an impermanent reality defined by flow and change. Without movement, we become confined to an ego-bound landscape of stagnancy and suffering. On the warrior's path, the courage to embrace this flow is rooted in fearlessness. The Shambhala teachings on "The Warrior of Outrageousness" (Trungpa, 1984, p. 167) expose the power and direction of the warrior spirit, and are realized by "the achievement of fearlessness." Legendary Garuda, king of birds, represents outrageousness. Garuda, with the head, wings, and talons of an eagle and the body of a man, hatches from the egg full-grown and launches himself into outer space with wings stretched beyond limits. He represents space, vastness, and is often depicted devouring a snake, which characterizes jealousy and hatred. Garuda is impressively powerful. Garuda's strength, freedom, and flight offer inspiration to the warrior who aspires to achieve fearlessness.

Garuda exemplifies the wisdom of facing Kali, as well as the reason for acknowledging impermanence as fundamental to contemplative psychotherapy. Garuda, representing space, defines therapeutic movement as occurring in a spacious atmosphere. Habitually, we become so organized around our ego identities that we fear becoming anything more. As illustrated in Hamlet, "rather bear those ills we have than fly to others that we know not of" (Act III, Scene 1; as quoted in May, 1988, p. 193). In therapy, clients are drawn to take flight and transform. To reach this goal, one must first enter the space of not knowing. "In the ordinary sense, we think of space as something vacant or dead. But in this case, space is a vast world that has capabilities of absorbing, acknowledging, and accommodating" (Trungpa, 1984, p. 155). This is a space of vitality and texture. This space can vibrate so radically that it shatters the veil of ego and exposes an impressive and terrifying landscape of opportunity. "Although this emptiness is really freedom, it is so unconditioned that it feels strange, sometimes, even horrible. If we were willing for a deeper transformation of desire, we would have to try to make friends with the spaciousness" (May, 1988, p. 147). The opportunity of liberation is often an experience of undeniable impermanence, as something must end for space to enlarge. To grow, we must take flight and transcend the veil of ego's atmospheric layer. Garuda reminds us that to experience fearlessness, "it is necessary to experience fear" (Trungpa, 1984, p. 47). Therefore, fearlessness is not the denial of fear; fearlessness is a spacious attitude that accommodates and recognizes fear. Garuda is our guide away from limiting despair. "Buddhism does not try to fill this emptiness at all, but rather provides a way to enter into it more deeply" (Welwood, 2000, p. 151). We no longer have to view our spaciousness as a deficit; spaciousness "acts as a catalyst to plunge us into more authentic life modes, and it enhances our pleasure in the living of life" (Yalom, 1980, p. 33). Garuda invites us to enter life fully, bravely, and fearlessly.

The fearless warrior who takes flight within space is open to all experiences – including pain. Contemplative psychotherapists recognize that "we suffer when we resist the noble and irrefutable truth of impermanence" (Chödrön, 2001, p. 28). Problems arise from the refusal to be present for the entirety of our life, and the contemplative therapist recognizes it is not possible to be present for others without being willing to feel pain. The training of warriors through the noble practice of Tai Chi Chuan recognizes that if a person is "afraid to take pain, then there is no hope for progress" (Lowenthal, 1991, p. 26). We must work directly with pain to alleviate suffering and move forward. "The more a person can bear pain and adversities with equanimity, the less he or she will experience *suffering* and the greater is his or her mental capacity to achieve inner freedom, serenity, and happiness" (Chen, 2006, p. 77). Garuda's flight into space is movement toward sanity. From this perspective, "sanity is not a kind of experiential higher ground," (Wegela & Joseph, 1992, p. 51), but a space of openheartedness and vulnerability. It requires the willingness to be affected and it "definitely requires the training of a warrior" (Chödrön, 2001, p. 65). Accommodating pain allows us to wake up, accept Kali's power, and live fully within the reality of our lives.

Buddhism offers teachings on traversing space, which become the foundation of a warrior's stance. Contemplative therapists study these teachings in the *Tibetan Book of the Dead* to cultivate fearlessness and to assist another in navigating the foreboding landscape of change, or *bardo*. The bardo is an after-death realm of transition through which a disembodied spirit passes between reincarnations. The text's intention is to guide the dead person toward enlightenment's path.

> This transitional experience, most importantly, presents itself as a period of decision making: the dead person can choose either to become enlightened by giving up his or her 'unconscious tendencies' that inevitably led to suffering, or the person can choose to remain bonded to those dispositions and become fated to circle once more through the patterns of his or her former existence. (Wicks, 1997, p. 1)

Moments of change and the practice of therapy mirror this transformative realm, albeit less grand. Contemplative therapists work with clients to accommodate not knowing and find ways of progressing through an unfamiliar landscape without the familiar reference points of ego. It is important to acknowledge these teachings because they recognize direction and purpose. Contemplative psychotherapy is not just about therapeutic space, an accommodating atmosphere, or esoteric concepts of fearlessness. Amorphousness is penetrated by the warrior's courage, discipline, responsibility, and ability to choose. There is a path to follow.

Inspired by Garuda, the compassionate warrior enters space fearlessly, and is oriented toward the noble goal of addressing suffering directly in order to alleviate stagnancy and facilitate progress. The warrior "lives not to gratify his personal needs and wishes or his physical appetites but to hone himself into an efficient spiritual machine, trained to bear the unbearable in the service of the transpersonal goal" (Moore & Gillette, 1990, p. 83). The warrior therapist is available to others because it is her duty, her calling. The contemplative therapist is inspired to connect with others and use this relationship to offer benefit to the world. There is great authenticity in this endeavor, and a warrior must train to be genuine in every moment of life: "That is the warrior's discipline" (Trungpa, 1984, p. 71). When genuineness is embodied, the space of impermanence is acknowledged and embraced. This spacious atmosphere is punctuated by sadness because the warrior, not afraid to accept pain, connects directly to the suffering present in the world. The warrior feels the weight of impermanence and Kali's presence in all that she does. Feeling sadness is inspiring to the warrior. It is the siren's call to action, as she knows there is direction to alleviate suffering. Garuda is a liberating spirit who guides warriors to reconnect with the natural fluidity of our being and to help others do the same. This is the practice of contemplative psychotherapy.

Training

Training is hard! I remember my first semester at Naropa University when I felt alone, uncertain, and remarkably un-special. It felt awful. I discussed this feeling with my meditation instructor, at which he smiled wryly and said, "Yeah, you're one in a million." With the sharpness of Kali's sword, his direct and simple comment cut through my ego with ease. I began to realize what was in store for me as I trained to become a contemplative psychotherapist.

The contemplative therapist is asked to join the tradition of warriorship and to make a commitment to the well-being of the world. The warriors of nonaggression "are men and women who are willing to train in the middle of the fire" (Chödrön, 2001, p. 7). They aspire to walk into uncertainty, release reference points, embrace impermanence, and dive into space like Garuda. Edward Podvoll, founder of the contemplative psychotherapy program at Naropa University, defined Buddhism as a commitment to live in naked reality (personal communication, April, 2003). This guidance illuminates the path of the warrior trainee. Contemplative therapists train "to bring a quality of unbiased presence to experience just as it is" (Welwood, 2000, p. 144). This training is unique in the world of psychology. Welwood laments the absence of mindfulness training in traditional programs, which rarely teach "people to remain open and alert in the face of the unknown" (p. 142). Embracing the unknown is the hallmark of contemplative training and contemplative psychotherapy.

Contemplative psychotherapists meditate. Meditation is home base and the foundation for one's training to embrace impermanence. "Meditative awareness enables the warrior to take his seat properly" (Trungpa, 1984, p. 74). Meditation is a practice that avails the stance of warriorship, which allows one to contend with suffering by becoming "very sharp, naturally alert, and very inquisitive and powerful" (Trungpa, 1999, p. 62). These qualities serve a therapist in his endeavors and are supported by another function of the meditation practice. Meditation awareness unveils the quality and process of our individual minds, and in so doing "you find that you can't hold on to anything. This provides a direct experience of the lack of solidity of the self" (Welwood, 2000, p. 153). On a small level, and occasionally in grand fashion, Kali is present on the meditation cushion and we are faced with impermanence. Meditation teaches the practitioner to cultivate warmth for the uncomfortable nature of the present moment, no matter how irritating it might be.

Contemplative therapy training is diverse. It is important to recognize that training is more than spending time on a meditation cushion. After all, contemplative therapists have to work with managed care insurance bureaucracies, too. Warriors are warriors of the world and must be prepared to enter and function in society. Since training is intended to meet this goal, both Western and Buddhist psychologies are

4. Warriorship

studied. There are intense class loads, clinical tutorials, research projects, dense reading lists, papers, exams, and more papers. On one level, training looks a lot like school. At Naropa University, all training efforts are conducted under the model of contemplative education, which necessitates self-reflection and a combination of personal experience and academic rigor. The inclusion of personal experience is fondly referred to as *process*, which is a manner of personally incorporating learned material. Essentially it means sharing personal thoughts and feelings with vulnerability and is a method for cultivating relationship and understanding among the cadre of trainees who spend three years together – in every class, activity, and retreat. (It is of interest that contemplative trainees refer to the group as a cadre, a term often used in military, or warrior, circles.). There is great emphasis to this component of the training process, as it is fundamental to learning about relationships – the basis of therapy. After a long, relaxing summer vacation, I returned to Naropa for my second semester. A friend pierced me with his gaze and welcomed me dryly, "Are you ready to process?" My skin crawled. I dropped into the texture of training. I remembered there was no place to hide and he was wondering if I was ready to show up for whatever arose. I was. And if the material became intense, I could always sit with it. All things lead back to the meditation cushion.

Intense training, weighty process, dynamic relationships, and the accommodating zone of meditation shakes our foundation and begins to reveal a tender heart that becomes the basis of a warrior's stance. This is why training is so difficult; there is no hiding from the naked reality of impermanence. Trainees are asked to meditate, and "meditation is destruction to security... It's a danger to those who wish to lead a superficial life and a life of fancy and myth" (Krishnamurti, 1979, p. 62). Warrior trainees are asked to move past comfort and are guided into the unknown. "The central question of a warrior's training is not how we avoid uncertainty and fear but how we relate to discomfort" (Chödrön, 2001, p. 8). Trainees are given opportunity after opportunity to answer this question by witnessing through meditation that ego is finite. "We need to be told that fear and trembling accompany growing up and that letting go takes courage" (Chödrön, 2001, p. 13). Trainees are given support throughout training because it is such a revealing process that increases one's vulnerability. Trainees are encouraged to enter therapeutic relationships and self-care is a theme of great importance. With care and support, trainees move into the unknown, close to Kali, and learn to welcome the feelings that accompany expanding spaciousness. This process reveals our tender heart:

> Going beyond fear begins when we examine our fear: our anxiety, nervousness, concern, and restlessness. If we look into our fear, if we look beneath its veneer, the first thing we find is sadness, beneath the nervousness. Nervousness is cranking up, vibrating,

all the time. When we slow down, when we relax with our fear, we find sadness, which is calm and gentle... That is the first tip of fearlessness, and the first sign of real warriorship. (Trungpa, 1984, p. 48)

After sitting for several weeks during a meditation retreat, I experienced this release and understood the wisdom of contemplative training. I had been sitting with my training cadre for nearly two weeks. My back was sore, my shoulders hurt, and I was ready to sleep in my own bed. Thoughts continued to present themselves rather randomly, and my eyes rested on the same patch of carpet that I had surveyed time and time again. I had a flash of awareness, as things tend to present themselves. The flash exposed my incredible efforts to show up in a certain way and helped me understand how hard I work to maintain this construct. It was little more than a flash but it shone with the intensity of the sun. I was consumed with feelings, tears flowed, and I felt utterly vulnerable. As I felt a layer of my ego cracking, I was given a tremendous gift – I was able to relax. I believe moments like these are the hallmarks of contemplative training. In one moment I realized that I could have a tender heart and be affected fully. Although vulnerable, I felt strong and liberated enough to connect with my experience directly. And in this, I had advanced my training as a warrior.

As we train to have an open heart, we are training to become warriors of compassion, and by facing impermanence the shell of ego will crack. It has to. The natural response to this occurrence is retreat. Warrior training teaches one to practice in this painful spot, to assume an open stance in the presence of Kali, to discover the strength of Garuda's fearlessness, and to transform suffering into a path of awakening (Chödrön, 2001, p. 41). There is no need to leave or transform discomfort, for the discomfort is our deep connection to others and at the heart of therapy. Trainees look to have a sad and tender heart, it is the ideal of warriorship, and because of this, the warrior can be very brave as well (Trungpa, 1984, p. 50). We all share an awareness of Kali; she threads her way through the human experience. By facing her directly, ego defenses fall away, the heart is softened, and it is possible to connect directly with others.

Warrior

Contemplative therapists assume a stance of acceptance that is riddled with paradox and guided by an open heart. Contemplative psychotherapists are trained in classical techniques. Within contemplative psychotherapy, technique becomes part of the arsenal of tools to advance therapy and is woven into practice. Technique is also a necessary component of warriorship, as it is "another aspect of the warrior's interest in skill, his mastery of the technology that enables him to reach

4. Warriorship

his goal. He has developed skill with the *weapons* he uses to implement his decisions" (Moore & Gillette, 1990, p. 83). However, technique is not the driving force of contemplative psychotherapy. By unveiling our hearts and facing impermanence, we recognize our inherent spaciousness and see ourselves, not as islands of uniqueness wrapped in a sheath of skin, but as deeply connected to others. There is a natural outpouring of compassion when this recognition occurs, and confidence arises. This is not a confidence of arrogance, but a compassionate allegiance to *Brilliant Sanity* or inherent health in everyone. Contemplative therapists are confident that the qualities of brilliant sanity (clarity, spaciousness, and compassion) are fundamental to all. The contemplative psychotherapist's charge is one of revealing brilliant sanity and helping the client to follow its direction toward health.

A therapist's allegiance to brilliant sanity, a fundamentally ineffable entity, reveals the layers of paradox that infuse the practice of contemplative psychotherapy. How can it be that assuredness and confidence are honed from a state of existence that is fundamentally spacious and amorphous? The key to understanding the contemplative stance is the recognition of impermanence and the basic lack of solidity in existence. In actuality, we are not looking for anything solid. Assuredness is not something concrete, but, rather, a presence that allies with brilliant sanity. A collection of qualities that illustrate what it means to be a contemplative psychotherapist, qualities shared by warriors, best describes this stance.

> This means he has an unconquerable spirit, that he has great courage, that he is fearless, that he takes responsibility for his actions, and that he has self-discipline. Discipline means that he has the rigor to develop control and mastery over his mind and over his body, and that he has the capacity to withstand pain, both psychological and physical. He is willing to suffer to achieve what he wants to achieve. (Moore & Gillette, 1990, p. 83)

It is clear that accessing the warrior spirit offers great strength and drive, which is based in a tender heart and other paradoxical qualities of vulnerability. "We're talking about manifesting fearlessness and gentleness that can save the world" (Trungpa, 1999, p. 191). This warrior meets the remarkable charge of alleviating suffering with an open and tender heart.

Therapy has considerable power when it arises from the unknown. Accepting this teaching is a great challenge to the aspiring contemplative psychotherapist. The truth is, we don't know! Problems arise when we feel we should know or are asked directly for *the solution*. Some models of therapy support knowing, which certainly complicates matters for the trainee who is learning what it means to be a contemplative therapist. "Most Western therapies are based on theories of *personality*, they are geared toward knowing, rather than not-knowing. An unspoken assumption in the therapeutic world is that we should always know who we are, and if we don't, that's a real problem" (Welwood, 2000, p. 156). From a contemplative perspective, working from the known will cause premature shutdown by looking to compress a client's experience into a definable boundary. A therapist is presented with a considerable dilemma when expected to know and not know at the same time.

The discomfort inherent to the paradox of therapy arises from impermanence. I learned this lesson as I completed my clinical internship. I was struggling with wanting answers, confidence, and direction. I would make interventions with clients that would feel so right and so wrong at the same time. I wanted to know if I was doing therapy. My wonderful supervisor shared a story with me that helped a great deal. At a time when he was grappling with similar issues in his life, he posed a question to his meditation teacher. He stated with great frustration, "Is everything such a paradox?" The answer was, "Yes…and no." My supervisor shared this story with me to help me relax. It worked. It allowed me to connect indirectly to impermanence.

If recognition of impermanence is invited into the endeavor of contemplative psychotherapy, there needs to be space for both knowing and not knowing, simultaneously. When several experienced clinicians gather to discuss cases, there will be as many different ideas, opinions, and clinical options. On the other hand, when we are in supervision, maybe with those same clinicians, we ask, "Did I do it right?" There is a sense that we want to know what to do while fully realizing that there is no one right answer. This paradox is a representation of our nature. Erich Fromm framed this issue clearly when engaging in a philosophical discussion about the core of being human; he saw "that there was no essence, that the essence of man is really his *paradoxical* nature" (quoted in Becker, 1973, p. 26). Becker goes on to describe this existential paradox as the condition of *individuality within finitude*. Being human entails a symbolic self, outside of nature, complete with an identity, a history, and self-consciousness to see the entire production transpire. Yet, at the same time, people are worms and food for worms. This is the paradox; people are out of nature and hopelessly in it.

Simply stated, impermanence complicates matters. If we were only our egos, then we could rely on our scientific knowledge to conquer matters of substance. Since we are impermanent, there is another, more heartfelt side.

> Rothenberg (1988, p. xii) sees the essence of effective therapy as a paradox in that the best clinicians are scientific, objective, rigorous, consistent, and logical, yet they are also highly imaginative: 'They are scientific and rely on systematic data and theory, and they are aesthetic in their application of intensity,

4. Warriorship

narrative, interpretation, and leaps of understanding.' (quoted in Kottler, 1991, p. 116)

The contemplative psychotherapist looks to find balance and find a sense of knowing within a landscape of many possibilities. Through meditation,

> We learn to trust in the unknown as a guide to what is most fresh and alive in the moment. With this trust, therapists can begin to let go of their knowledge and let what is needed to help others emerge spontaneously from the fresh edge of the moment. (Welwood, 2000, p. 145)

Welcoming the unknown is fundamental to a warrior's stance. A warrior is willing to risk not knowing and expose himself to the phenomenal world, developing a powerful attitude of trust.

The practice of psychotherapy is riddled with risk. On a concrete level, therapists routinely risk being fired based on projection, not because of incompetence. We often stand as a target for overt frustration and aggression. We are at risk of purposeful manipulation, or facing time-consuming litigation with the potential of a career-ending blow. There is also the ever-present risk of burnout, overwhelming caseloads, lack of financial viability, failure, client suicide, being witness to utterly heart-breaking trauma and human suffering, and being reminded of impermanence on a daily basis. When I tell people that I'm a therapist, I rarely receive a reaction of "how cool." More often I hear comments like, "How do you deal with it," "Do you take it home with you," "It sounds hard," and, most telling, "Look out!" These comments all indicate knowledge that therapy is risky business.

Faced with risk, there is a danger of losing courage and retreating or becoming mired in dullness, routine, or aggressive use of technique. Avoidance of therapy's dangers could lead to "a pathological avoidance of risk that may reveal us to be impotent, ineffective, or inadequate" (Kottler, 2003, p. 156). To be potent therapists, we must own that the work is defined by doubt and uncertainty, while at the same time assessing the risks and moving forward. The warrior "through his clarity of thinking realistically assesses his capacities and his limitations in any given situation" (Moore & Gillette, 1990, p. 80). Warriors assess risk and take action, which, in therapy, is done to progress the client's process.

> Therapists who play it safe in their work may remain basically satisfied with their moderate gains... Under the guise of protecting their client's welfare, they will avoid confrontation and conflict, preferring instead to move at a pace consistent with the client's own tolerance for boredom. (Kottler, p. 156)

Effective therapy is about growth and movement. If we only play it safe, and keep things within known boundaries, we assist only in a reformation of ego. No change has occurred. As therapists we must relax our preformed concepts, be vulnerable enough to not know, and use warrior's courage to hold that spaciousness for the client to hear his or her own wisdom.

A warrior is informed by the recognition that the future can never be known and that we can never hide from uncertainty.

> To tap the healing power within us, we first have to let ourselves *not know*, so that we can make contact with the fresh, living texture of our experience, beyond all our familiar thoughts. Then when we express what we are feeling, our words will have real power. (Welwood, 2000, p. 142)

When one embraces uncertainty, then possibility, opportunity, and direction are revealed. In this way, the paradox gives direction to the warrior. "As attachments lighten and idols fall, we will enjoy increasing freedom. But at the same time our hearts will feel an even greater, purer, deeper ache. This particular pain is one that never leaves us" (May, 1988, p.180). This ache, our yearning to connect, fuels Garuda's first flight. It is the tender heart of a warrior.

The warrior's stance is open and awake to allow for connection and relationship. The warrior renounces anything in his experience that is a barrier between himself and others (Trungpa, 1984. p. 66). In this manner, relationship is the fruition of risk. By risking an open heart, alert to all possible connections, true relationship can progress. Warriors "wish to dissolve the myth that we are separate" (Chödrön, 2001, p. 70). Compassionate warriors seek connection and find reward in meeting another's energy.

Relationship

Contemplative psychotherapy is richly textured. Clients talk about relationships, jobs, children, aspirations, fantasies, history, future, and present moment happenings. It can be quite ordinary. The ordinary is enlivened, made rich, vital, and alive by embracing the unknown and risking unfettered connection. An inherently vulnerable and openhearted therapeutic relationship unveils an accepting space that offers an opportunity for clients to present the fabric of their lives, be it joyous or otherwise. This foundational relationship is the ground from which to enter the unknowns imbedded within the therapeutic process, and life. It is impossible to know where this relationship will lead. It is the nature of change to move into unknown territory. As such, the process of psychotherapy encourages clients to develop a relationship with

4. Warriorship

uncertainty, and contemplative psychotherapists inspire movement down a warrior's path.

I will never forget Darrell and Janet's first session. I had little knowledge of them when we first met. Darrell was terminally ill and contending with significant health challenges, and his lifestyle of addiction and street crime was rapidly exacerbating the situation. In short, he was out of control. Janet and Darrell shared a long-time, yet inconsistent partnership. They moved fluidly between being out-of-control and controlling, each taking his or her own role in the mix. The more Darrell moved toward reckless or erratic behavior, the more Janet would try to control him, provide structure, and carry his responsibilities for the children's needs. Continuing this cycle escalated mutual frustration and motivated the couple to seek therapy. At that point in time, my office was small. I noticed their postures; he defended and slumped, she upright and ready to attack. The atmosphere seemed familiar and tight, and surprisingly distant given that our knees were almost touching. Darrell and Janet had been here before, he loose, she tight, with vast space in the middle. They started in on each other. It was tense. I attempted some classic techniques to facilitate understanding or connection; there was none. They continued to entrench themselves and their statements began to repeat, at least in essence. As Darrell continued to shut down, I had a sense that the surface banter was hiding other truths, so I asked Darrell if there was something he needed Janet to know. This intervention felt like a risk. I was asking Darrell to take a chance, to move into the unknown and connect with Janet. I was afraid that he would close the gap and remain stagnant.

There was an opening accompanied by undeniable vitality and intensity. Darrell sat up and made eye contact with Janet for the first time. With great warmth, he said, "I need you to know that I'm dying." Darrell and Janet both began to cry as this obvious truth was spoken for the first time. In one statement, Darrell acknowledged Kali and thrust himself and Janet into the unknown. There was now opportunity for new connection grounded in the reality of their lives. By moving into impermanence, by releasing the concrete constructs of habitual repartee, Darrell and Janet were able to foster a relationship of support that ushered in Darrell's imminent death. Darrell's courageousness was an invitation to move the partnership into the expansive spaciousness of the unknown. This is a beautiful illustration of the essence of contemplative psychotherapy.

The process of moving into the unknown is difficult and requires great diligence and commitment. It would be wonderful if there were a quick fix, a pill that would alleviate suffering and free one to experience life long happiness, which would likely require a continued reification of ego. However, life is grittier than that. Contemplative psychotherapy, grounded in Buddhist teachings, does not attempt to resolve the grit. "Buddhism does not simply aim at relieving suffering to make people feel better, but more importantly, at freeing the mind from the bondage of delusion and the conditioning of blind impulses" (Chen, 2006, p. 88).

Being freed from delusion is multifaceted. To move into the layers of spaciousness requires great bravery and courage. Trungpa (1999) teaches that the development of bravery and fearlessness is followed by cowardice. As one approaches the unknown, he feels petrified and wants to run. The warrior's path is to recognize cowardice as a staircase and move through the challenge of not knowing rather than being frightened away (p. 65).

Julio entered treatment with some earthly warrior training. He had been raised a warrior, taught by his father to fight and respect physical prowess. His gang involvement encouraged his aggression and promoted violent acts. During his first sessions, he sat across from me with feet firmly planted and both hands held in open fists. I could tell that he could take care of himself. Our cultural and social distance was great and there existed a vast gulf between us. A successful course of therapy would require us to relate and bridge this distance. The distance was also represented in our divergent views on warriorship. To this point, Julio was allied to warriorship of aggression. He was invested in maintaining his ego and his devastating relationship history had necessitated this shield to protect him from abuse and trauma. Julio was beginning to realize that his self-imposed barriers were causing great difficulty. His aggressive stance had landed him in prison and into a situation of isolation and depression. Julio now wanted to walk a different path. He would have to travel a great distance to begin embodying warriorship from another vantage. To change his path, Julio would have to open his heart, be affected, and walk into the unknown.

After working with me for several weeks, Julio had a breakthrough. He began to trust me and we started addressing his emotions. Julio was beginning to recognize the consequences of his past and this knowledge was novel and frightening. Julio was struggling to accept the directness and intensity of his emotions. I guided him in a grounding exercise that essentially offered him the permission to emote. As we progressed, I could see his shoulder soften and his affect changed. He was receptive and still. When we concluded, he said he felt wonderful. He felt alive. He felt connected to a greater love for his girlfriend and children. He said he never wanted this feeling to go away. He fearlessly moved into his emotions and experienced a cathartic release. He felt invigorated and excited about his life. I said nothing but knew his therapy was just beginning. He had taken his first step into the unknown world of an openhearted warrior. The next week was different. Julio was shut down and defensive. After resting in emotional richness, Julio saw a side of himself that was completely foreign and frightening. He had retreated from the unknown.

"Humans abhor uncertainty" (Yalom, 1980. p. 188). Julio became fearful of his emotions and he did not like it. By moving into the unknown

4. Warriorship

and making room for a new way of living in the world, Julio's ego took a hit, and uncertainty was a reminder of his fluid nature. Perhaps there was an unconscious realization: If he could change, he could end, a terrifying recognition of impermanence. Schein (quoted in Kottler, 1992, p. 67) referred to this event in therapy as the *demolition stage*. Demolition occurs when clients begin to feel more and more confused and dissatisfied with present behaviors and they become more vulnerable. Moreover, they are deliberately encouraged to do so. Petone (quoted in Kottler, 1992) believes this demolition stage necessary to prepare for lasting change. For change to occur, one must move into a landscape of transition where familiar reference points of ego are demolished. As the defenses of ego are lowered, the fundamental impermanent nature of reality is exposed and it can be disorienting. "The natural uncertainty and ambiguity embedded in reality is quite often experienced as terrifying, overwhelming, complex, and chaotic" (Gemmill, 1989, p. 141). Dossey (1990) described this cluster of emotions as "spiritual agoraphobia," (p. 81) a state analogous to the fear of open spaces. The intensity of this open space can cause retreat into instinctive habitual patterns or it can free one to experience the arising moments of reality less defended and with an open heart.

I encouraged Julio to walk a compassionate warrior's path and return to his emotions. His emotions assumed a fearful, confusing, and pressured nature. Julio often said, "I don't like this and I don't know what to do." Welwood (2000) describes such moments of "I don't know who I am" (p. 155) as sacred. Julio was beginning to walk on sacred and uncharted ground. Julio's journey was reflected in a dream that he shared after several more weeks of therapy. He described a frightening dream where he shielded himself in a well-defended house from intruders intending to kill. Yalom (1980) believes "every anxiety dream is a dream of death; frightening fantasies involving such themes as unknown aggressors breaking into one's home always, when explored, lead to the fear of death" (p.173). Julio's ego structure was dying, and he was terrified. Julio was in "an in-between zone, which is the threshold of new birth" (Welwood, 2000, p. 155). Julio had entered a terrifying state of bardo, looking for a new path.

The process of therapy asks clients to walk a warrior's path, to be fearless, and to move into uncertainty, where new possibility is revealed. "The Warrior is often a destroyer. But the positive Warrior energy destroys only what needs to be destroyed in order for something new and fresh, more alive and more virtuous to appear" (Moore & Gillette, 1990, p. 86). Paradoxically, Kali's destruction is the path of awakening. The unknown is remarkably grounding when approached with an open warrior stance. Thurman describes the bardo experience: "Your outer breath stops and you experience reality stark and void like space, your immaculate naked awareness dawning clear and void without horizon or center" (quoted in Wicks, 1997, p. 5). As Kali is exposed to the client and the ground shifts, the therapist must remain present to all that arises while assisting a successful navigation of this transitional state into a fresh relationship with reality. *The Tibetan Book of the Dead* is pragmatically and existentially directed toward the *dead* who are still living and written especially for benighted and bewildered souls. It acknowledges

> that enlightenment is difficult, and that it takes many repetitions of the key message for there to be any significant spiritual effect. It repeats its message that we, and only we, are the source of our desires, our interpretations, our evaluations, our pleasures, and our fears, and that we can render such sources of suffering ineffectual, if we were only to interpret the apparent seriousness and significance of the world as the play of our own creation. (Wicks, p. 12)

The guidelines of this teaching were invaluable as I worked with Julio.

Julio was brave and he moved further into the unknown. I would often repeat, "You don't need to know." I said this to assure him that his feelings of uncertainty were necessary and expected. I shared his uncertainty in not knowing the end path of treatment. I worked to trust the space and all that was showing up. Over time, Julio learned to accept and relate with his vulnerability, seeing it as source of real inner power and strength. His previous stance of fake power of the macho kind – which is really a form of control, tightness, and tension, had no real strength in it (Welwood, 2000, p. 158). His burgeoning strength allowed him to enter unknown space and find a fresh quality of presence – more alive and connected. He was better able to connect with his girlfriend and embrace her children as his own. He smiled more and lessened his need to know what he was "supposed to feel." He gradually learned that he did not have to act on intense feelings of aggression and could actually walk away from situations of aggression without raising his powerful fists. Standing with an open heart in the face of inevitable impermanence, Julio was becoming a warrior of compassion.

Endless Movement

The powerful tradition of warriorship is the basis of contemplative psychotherapy. A warrior is fearless and cultivates strength from the inherent vulnerability that is woven into an impermanent reality. From this perspective, there is no ending. Ending is antithetical to impermanence, which is innately fluid and boundless. Contemplative psychotherapy acknowledges this fluid reality and relies on the ancient tradition of warriorship to navigate the paradoxical tapestry of impermanence. Facing terrifying Kali and riding the spaciousness of garuda free the warrior to experience possibility and follow the movement of previously unknown

4. Warriorship

opportunities. Honoring this tradition, I now end by inviting the movement of your mind as you consider what has been said. That is the point.

References

Becker, E. (1973). *The denial of death*. New York: Free Press Paperbacks.
Chen, Y. (2006). Coping with suffering: The Buddhist perspective. In P. T. P. Wong & L. C. J. Wong (Eds.), *Handbook of multicultural perspectives on stress and coping* (pp. 73-89). New York: Springer.
Chödrön, P. (2001). *The places that scare you: A guide to fearlessness in difficult times*. Boston: Shambhala.
Dossey, L. (1990). Personal health and the environment. In J. Rifkin (Ed.), *The green lifestyle handbook: 1001 ways you can heal the earth* (pp. 79-85). New York: Henry Holt.
Gemmill, G. (1989). The dynamics of scapegoating in small groups. *Small Group Behavior, 20*, 406-418.
Kottler, J. A. (1991). *The complete therapist*. San Francisco: Jossey-Bass.
Kottler, J. A. (2003). *On being a therapist* (3rd ed.). San Francisco: Jossey-Bass.
Kinsley, D. R. (2003). Kālī. In R. F. McDermott & J. J. Kripal (Eds.), *Encountering Kālī: In the margins, at the center, in the West* (pp. 23-38). Los Angeles: University of California Press.
Krishnamurti, J. (1979). *Meditations*. Boston: Shambhala.
Lowenthal, W. (1991). *There are no secrets: Professor Cheng Man-Ch'ing and his Tai Chi Chuan*. Berkeley, CA: North Atlantic Books.
May, G. G. (1988). *Addiction and grace: Love and spirituality in the healing of addictions*. New York: HarperCollins.
Moore, R., & Gillette, D. (1990). *King, warrior, magician lover: Rediscovering the archetypes of the mature masculine*. New York: HarperCollins.
Trungpa, C. (1984). *Shambhala: The sacred path of the warrior*. Boston: Shambhala.
Trungpa, C. (1999). *Great Eastern sun: The wisdom of Shambhala* (C. R. Gimian, Ed). Boston: Shambhala.
Wegela, K. K., & Joseph, A. (1992). Shock, uncertainty, conviction: Gateways between psychopathology and intrinsic health. *Journal of Contemplative Psychotherapy, 8*, 33-52.
Welwood, J. (1985). Vulnerability and power in the therapeutic process. In J. Welwood (Ed.), *Awakening the heart: East/west approaches to psychotherapy and the healing relationship* (pp. 148-162). Boston: Shambhala.
Welwood, J. (2000). *Toward a psychology of awakening: Buddhism, psychotherapy, and the path of personal and spiritual transformation*. Boston: Shambhala.

Wicks, R. (1997). The therapeutic psychology of 'The Tibetan Book of the Dead.'. *Philosophy East and West, 47* (4), 479-494. Retrieved February 7, 2007, from http://ccbs.ntu.edu.tw/FULLTEXT/JR-PHIL/robert.htm

Yalom, I. D. (1980). *Existential psychotherapy.* New York: Basic Books.

5

Psychotherapy as an Expression of the Spiritual Journey Based on the Experience of Shunyata[1]

Edward Podvoll
With Jeff Fortuna

Preface

The encounter of Buddhist meditation practice with Western psychological treatment has been gradual but continuous for the past thirty years, and the result has been both subtle and revolutionary. When trained psychotherapists began to experience the deeply personal insights of their meditation practice, it changed their lives. What they were learning turned Western psychology upside down because they were exposed to a whole new way of seeing mental suffering and mental healing. It is always tremendously exciting when a therapist discovers this fresh view, but at the same time it creates chaos in their life. In 1974, I became one of those therapists. Although I had completed extensive training in psychoanalysis and was already a teacher of that discipline, what I was discovering with the practice of meditation made it impossible for me simply to continue in the same way.

Almost as soon as I learned the technique of sitting meditation and started to practice it, it seemed as though I had been waiting my whole life to do just that. I resolved that meditation was to be at the center of my life. During the first three years of meditation, I experienced a more subtle level of mind and its movements than can ever be seen in psychoanalysis. It was below and before the level of speech and communication, far more fleeting and delicate than the most open levels of free association or stream of consciousness. Gradually, I understood a new dimension of mental suffering that I had only glimpsed during psychoanalysis. But I had no idea of its almost instant-to-instant activity:

---

[1] Abridged from Edward Podvoll, *Recovering Sanity*, Boston: Shambhala Publications, 2003; "Preface to the New Edition," pp. XI-XVI and "Appendix I," pp. 319-352, abridged by Jeff Fortuna

the continuous burden imposed on the mind for self-justification, self-righteousness, self-centered-ness. It was a microscopic view of subtle and deeply ingrained ego-habits in action, going on below the surface and becoming the basis of interpersonal dialogue. I recognized it clearly as a universal ordeal.

I began to understand my patients differently. No matter how disturbed they were, their basic psychological ordeal was the same as my own. I felt more openness and kindness toward them and spoke more easily and directly with them. But my communications with professional colleagues were not so easy. I was unskilled, or more often just unable to discuss with them the new directions that my work and life were taking.

A huge gulf separates conventional psychological treatment and the forms of therapy that emerge from the discipline of meditation. That gulf could be called the problem of ego. The singular effect of meditation is the gradual softening and dissolving of one's self-absorption and egoistic impulses, a gradual relaxation and opening. But conventional psychology insists that one strengthen the notion of ego-identity through various strategies of self-assertion, self-empowerment, distinctiveness from others, and personal security. From this point of view, sanity is related to the power of the ego's abilities to secure its territorial demands, and mental disturbance arises from a crisis, a breakdown of ego's stability, or its failure to develop along the genetic and cultural plans that shape it.

In my previous work, I have tried to bridge the differences between the Buddhist understanding of non-ego and the Western ideology of ego psychology by using the language of internal experience. The many clinical examples and case histories in this book point to the experience that the seed of madness is present in everyone, that there is a natural affinity for the mind to seek personal self-expansion, and it will create a continuous stream of illusions to do so. Any emotion can be used in this demand for a solid, expansive, self-defending illusion. Each emotion, when not kept in its own place, can become like a spreading poison that unbalances the mind. This is not technical or professional language, but living language.

There is also another seed within us, even more important than the seed of ego: it is the seed of sanity, a human instinct of clarity, present in everyone as a brilliant, clear awareness capable of spontaneously cutting through the self-deception of madness. It is an instant of opening and wakefulness that brings one back from wandering in the world of dream. It usually requires some attentiveness even to notice such an event, and certainly a background of meditative discipline makes these flashes of wakefulness more recognizable and frequent. But they are also made more accessible by a variety of disciplines that cultivate body and mind synchronization. Anything that can truly be called therapy or treatment should be able to make this clarity of mind available as much as possible. In fact, at Naropa University in 1981, we began to practice this kind of treatment and established therapeutic communities, collectively called the Windhorse Project, that continue to this day.

5. The Spiritual Journey

There is also another purpose behind much of my writing, and consistent with the purpose of this book, that goes beyond the needs of health professionals who care for deeply disturbed people. The principles and the work described here can serve as a companion to anyone on the spiritual path of compassion. There are now many more practitioners of meditation than there were when I began writing about this topic, and still more people than there were then who practice a variety of traditional mind-body disciplines who will find this work to be contemplative discipline in action.

For practitioners of meditation in particular, the integration of meditation and contemplative practice can serve as a guide to the extremes of mind that someone they know—perhaps they themselves, a family member, or a friend on a spiritual journey—has certainly endured. This integration provides immediately useful information about relating to the mind and environment of someone in crisis. It may be useful for personal spiritual understanding as well: a tour and reminder of the extremes of emotional realms, the ever-present invasiveness of ego distortions within one's practice, and the grotesque proportions that spiritual materialism and the greed for spiritual experiences can take. Through practice, one can become better able to recognize when someone is in trouble, and one can become more helpful in guiding psychologically fragile people who wish to practice spiritual discipline.

At the end of two years of work writing the first edition of *Recovering Sanity* in 1990, I felt relieved at completing what had to be done, but not nearly as much as one might expect. An uneasiness pervaded the conclusion of this work as I became keenly aware of my continuing ardor for meditation discipline and the huge task of internal work that faced me. I felt unable to continue my life in a meaningful way until I could follow this increasingly strong instinct that was growing in me, ripening over sixteen years of practice, moving me to do a long-term meditation retreat. All other future plans dissolved into insignificance.

Soon after the book was published, I traveled to India, first living in an ashram in southern India to continue my six years of practicing hatha yoga, with the intention of then making a traditional pilgrimage to Buddhist sites. But over the next three months my longing and devotion to my Buddhist teachers and lineage intensified, reaching a critical point of seizures of migraine headaches, day after day, until I felt my life to be in danger. Something was wrong, life was going quickly, and there was no time to waste.

Single-mindedly I left the ashram and traveled to New Delhi where I might have the best chance to find lineage teachers who could give me direction. Then suddenly came a remarkable series of meetings that quickly opened the way for me to enter a meditation retreat in France, where I remained for the next twelve years.

After such a fortunate opportunity to practice, many people ask, "What do you have to say?" It is in the form of a prayer, a wish, an entreaty for the people of the world who, during the time I have been away, definitively passed from the age of anxiety into the age of terror. This prayer comes from the practice of *Chod,* known as "cutting through ego clinging," or severance of emotions that become like demons who uncontrollably afflict the mind, as with the urge for revenge, for example:

> *May all Karmic debts come to an end,*
> *May the links of vengeance be cut,*
> *May there always be joy and happiness,*
> *And may there be liberation from suffering.*[2]

Psychotherapy

Although the practice of intensive individual psychotherapy had been at the center of my life for many years, when I wrote the first edition of *Recovering Sanity* I said almost nothing about it. Psychotherapy was also a large part of my work in the Windhorse Project, and my particular expression of it continued to mature. But at the time of writing, it was far more important and urgent for me to give the *recipe* and technology for Windhorse *environmental therapy,* which was by then my overriding concern and the direct result of my own and my colleagues' Buddhist practice and study.

There was also the political problem that the discipline of psychotherapy with severely disturbed people was disappearing due to the widespread belief that the so-called "antipsychotic medications" had made personal therapy unnecessary. But, when a few years later the Windhorse group asked me to write something to help train new psychotherapists, I decided to share the wisdom of the special lineage in which I was trained and to give some basic instructions that were becoming more clear to me when integrated with intensive Buddhist meditation.

There have always been bursts of compassionate concern to care for people overcome with disorders of the mind, but only as recently as a hundred years ago did that inspiration and energy come together to create an intimate, personal treatment now known as the psychoanalytic movement. Its most enduring heritage is the development of the skills of intensive psychotherapy, which flourished for a while, but now seem to have given way to a bewildering variety of short-term therapies, none of which have the depth and discipline for people who are, or are becoming, insane.

For this reason, I wish to discuss some principles of psychotherapy and how they relate to the practice of mindfulness-awareness meditation, and how an understanding of the two disciplines can allow the energy of compassion to reenergize our healing traditions.

---

[2] Quote taken from a protected Buddhist text.

5. The Spiritual Journey

Compared to Windhorse intensive psychotherapy, the usual psychotherapy seems secretive, technical, and overly precious. Of course, there are reasons given for such preciousness, such as preserving the *purity of the transference* upon which so much of psychoanalytically oriented psychotherapy is said to depend. But in the case of Windhorse therapy, when working with people in extreme states of mind, it is the earthiness, openness, and genuineness of communication that carries the transformative power.

Emotions

In psychotherapy with people who do not have much control over their minds and are at the mercy of their emotions, sometimes just the recognition and clear delineation of an emotion is the first step in the discovery that mind can be worked with and tamed at all. There are a great many different ideas and theories about how a therapist should relate to a patient's expression of emotions in the course of psychotherapy. But practically speaking, whatever idea one has of emotions, how a therapist relates to his or her *own* emotions is what leads the way in therapy. Especially when working with highly disturbed people one cannot simply be an impassive interlocutor or benevolent witness—one needs to be fully engaged.

It is amazing how most of us hold on to emotions, cherishing them even while they consume us. It is as if their very weight and seriousness assure us that we are alive and still exist. But, when we come to work with the intensity of emotions in psychotherapy, the quality of lightness eventually becomes more important. It is a more subtle level of emotional mind. At the gross or coarse level we see that emotions can simply carry the mind away into unlimited distraction, while at a more subtle level, emotions can be experienced as a sharpness and clarity. But seeing this requires some precision and quickness. That is, one needs to train in recognizing the energy of emotions at a point before they steal the mind away.

In general, this requires solitary situations and meditation disciplines to expose the more subtle aspects of mind, while at the same time developing in oneself an unwavering attention and courage to make such observations. But, in the present discussion, we are working in the context of an interpersonal discipline, so we need to look directly into the psychotherapy structure and try to discover what training, in observing subtle mind, might still be possible. That is, how can the precision and clarity of meditation discipline be brought into the interpersonal field of observation?

During the course of intensive psychotherapy the whole range and repertoire of our built-in emotions can be experienced by patient and therapist toward each other, and so there are many opportunities to observe these more subtle qualities. It is the same as in any communal situation of people living intimately together. An older monk once said about living with a small group in an extended retreat, "One day you love 'em, the next day you hate 'em. So what!" Although there are many varieties of basic aggression, the subtle or pure quality is sharp, penetrating, burning, inescapable. It returns again and again, like the sting and heat of a slap in the face can return: days—even weeks—later, the moment it is remembered. Anger doesn't let you rest: it demands attention, so it is continually wakeful. Obsessive thoughts of revenge are its lifeline; just when you are getting exhausted by the anger, they add brilliance to the fire.[3]

Loneliness

The profundity of the experience of loneliness needs to be recognized and appreciated for its great potential in any healing relationship or, more simply, in anyone. The exploration of the depth and variety of loneliness leads to the source of insanity and, at the same time, can become a well-spring of insight and courage.

Fromm-Reichmann (1950) observed in her patients a deep abyss of loneliness in which a natural and instinctual longing for intimacy, whether along with or independent of desire, had become so exhausted by failure that they became resigned to ultimate isolation. She believed that this state of almost non-being had become incommunicable through ordinary language, but that nevertheless it was the basic task of a psychotherapist to open up his or her own being to receive whatever despair and fear might emanate from such a person, thus nurturing and protecting a precious and fragile human contact. But this "opening" in the therapist is not so easy to achieve because of therapists' dread of recognizing a quintessential loneliness in themselves.

We are, of course, capable of all kinds of empathic *exchanges* with states of fear, hate, joy—even mania—that undercurrent of unbridled exhilaration, self-expansion, and universal connectedness. Yet, it is the pain of being out of contact, of no connection, being unreachable, eternally unloved and unable to love, unable to feel another person's suffering because of being so preoccupied with one's own—this is the particular sense of degradation felt by those who seem to be unreachable or, to a lesser degree, simply *loners*.

We do everything we can to avoid being invaded by others' seemingly alien sensations. This is a long-established habit in all of us. Some actual effort is required to overcome it; we might be taking on, or taking in, an undesirable burden. Thus, what is first needed is to rouse the intention to do so; we have to wish to do it. Then, we learn and practice the discipline of engaging, *exchanging oneself for others*.

---

[3] For a more detailed discussion of this topic, see Edward Podvoll, *Recovering Sanity*, Boston: Shambhala Publications, 2003.

5. The Spiritual Journey

What I have tried to describe in the preceding few pages is a particular expression of compassion as it has developed in the apparently esoteric discipline of intensive psychotherapy with people in extreme states of mind. Although psychotherapy itself may be on the verge of extinction, the experience of compassion and the impulse to cultivate its expression always remains as a basic element of our human nature.

So it has always been understood, practiced, and experienced within the Buddhist meditation tradition that *exchanging oneself for others* is the quickest and most direct means to develop and fulfill our basic nature of compassion. This is made possible by taking hold of what is already there: the spontaneous ebb and flow of exchange, our natural infrastructure of compassion. We need only to seize it in the service of caring for others. Then it becomes the faultless, egoless support for anything that can be called basic attendance or psychotherapy. As the eighth-century Indian teacher Shantideva (1979) said,

> *Thus whoever wishes to quickly afford protection*
> *To both himself and other beings*
> *Should practice this holy secret*
> *The exchanging of oneself for others.* (p. 118)

Retreat

There is a subtle dimension of loneliness that is a source of strength or power. Before loneliness disintegrates into its catastrophic form that Fromm-Reichmann predicted could imbalance the mind, or becomes the less extreme feelings of self-accusation and despair, there is a transitional state in which loneliness holds a quiet dignity. This quality can be called *aloneness*, or the ability to be alone, or a lack of fear at being alone. Usually, when one sees this in oneself, or in others—even in children—it is like a glimpse of some strength of character.

When Herman Hesse's (1957) novel *Siddhartha* first appeared in English in the 1950s, it seemed to open up a new vista of maturity for adolescents of the time and for successive generations. During the course of the young Siddhartha's journey through loneliness, he comes to embody the possibilities of human character strength. In his frequently repeated statement, "I can think, I can fast, I can wait," is the full expression of his dawning maturity. "I can think," means "I can see clearly and precisely everything that occurs in my mind; I am not shaken or controlled by anything that arises in it." "I can fast," means "I can endure lack of comfort or companionship; I can live simply on very little; I have forbearance for hardship and even ascetic self-discipline." "I can wait," means "I have a sense of stillness, naked beingness, complete in itself, a patience beyond the need for entertainment or baby-sitters."

All of this is about the willingness to be lonely and the intention to surrender to the experience of retreat. It has always been in just this way that the sanity of loneliness has been explored and cultivated. The alchemy of transforming the suffering of loneliness into the confidence of *aloneness* is one of the basic tasks of becoming a full human being. Whenever you find this activity, you find the mark of a spiritual life. The catalyst to make this transformation possible has always been the hidden province of traditional cultures, which preserve the skills and disciplines to guide one through the confrontation with loneliness. Universally, this is called the practice of *retreat*, pulling back from the complexity of worldly entanglements to the simplicity of coming face-to-face with oneself.

But, the true urge to do retreat does not come from cultural or religious prescription or expectation, or from personal ambition. The spiritual tradition only provides the opportunity and energy. The genuine need for retreat comes from a lonely place within oneself that, at certain moments of life, calls out to us to be heard, to be met. Naked moments of being alone appear unexpectedly—anywhere, at any time—as experiences of stillness, immovable. It might happen just at the end of a long and exhausting outpouring of emotion, like an emptying-out. Or it might happen when the deep conviction in what seemed an unbreakable friendship abruptly collapses, or when speed and a constant busyness of mind spontaneously reveal themselves as futile, or when it becomes piercingly clear that life's end is in sight. Usually, these are moments of sudden hopelessness, but they are luminous nevertheless.

Loneliness in search of itself is a reminder that an entire dimension of our being, something so intimate to us, remains to be acknowledged and known. But then, we may have a glimpse of this and feel it to be an awesome place, better left unnoticed. Or, we may become distracted by so many other interesting things to do. But we may simply lack the confidence, the examples, the instructions for how to proceed.

To begin, there needs to be the intention to be lonely, to do what needs to be done, to stand alone between the sky and earth, exposed, open, and valorous. This has nothing to do with surviving the elements, with visions, or with proving oneself. It is remaining steadily in one's vulnerability, able to be intimate with fear, looking into oneself, fragile but persevering, listening, waiting.

Early in retreat, one may experience the loneliness of all the elements: the whole world of trees, sky, rocks, all vastly lonely, resplendent in their loneliness. Soon, loneliness becomes more ordinary. Cooking and cleaning, smelling and tasting food, preparing firewood, all occur in the midst of great precision. Loneliness is appreciated as elegant simplicity.

A deep loneliness occurs when everything within one's mind is a rapid succession of causes and conditions, one after the other, and mind itself is empty except for its continual magical tricks of swift appearances and disappearances. Our close friend is without real substance, hardly worth talking to anymore. We are unable to say that this aloneness has dignity—it is stripped bare of such features. We did not expect this desolation. It is a time to invoke the instructions and courage of the retreat teachers, and to share in their aloneness.

5. The Spiritual Journey

Obviously, it is hopeless to try and make anything come out right, to create happy endings. Even the slightest move in that direction causes more confusion. There is not another being in the world to blame for it. Never has the *truth of suffering* been clearer, and yet it does not lead to despair or depression. It would be like getting depressed about the second law of thermodynamics. There are moments of fundamental relaxation, giving in to whatever appears in the mind but going along with none of it. Discipline takes less effort because the unique taste of aloneness itself spontaneously brings one back to meditation. Somehow, this sense of ease seems worthy of celebration.

Mutuality

It is a paradox, yet true, that the journey of uncovering basic aloneness could lead to feeling intimate with all beings. When you look around and see the extent to which others are struggling against loneliness, you have a view of the suffering in front of them.

When the despair of loneliness is transformed—or purified, we could say—into the heroism of aloneness, it becomes a reservoir of energy that makes exchanging oneself for others possible and, without knowing it, one's innate compassionate nature flourishes. From that, a suppleness of intelligence develops: one spontaneously sees what is needed to reduce the suffering of others, and creatively knows the practical steps to take.

The activity called basic attendance is one such natural outcome. Perhaps every attentive parent has experiences of this instinct. My father despairingly witnessed the unfathomable difficulties of my early years in school: until the age of nine I seemed unable to learn, had difficulty reading, and usually felt humiliated and isolated by failure. At one point, he either understood what was the problem or just decided to confront and explore it in a personal way. In any case, it was an act of simple basic attendance, intuition, and skill.

His medical office, on the first floor of our home, allowed him to come and go to the family residence between seeing patients, or whenever he had a break. It did not seem to be any real plan or strategy on his part; one day he just started doing it. While I was seated at my desk, supposedly doing my homework after dinner, he came in, sat down next to the desk facing me, and started reading to himself from a large medical book he had brought with him. I was quite surprised; he was just being there, studying alongside me. He did this a couple of times each evening for weeks, maybe months. After ten minutes, or sometimes thirty minutes, he would leave and go back to work. We did not talk much but just sat there doing our mutual studies. He said this was an opportunity for him to do some reading, which he had no time to do. Sometimes he would doze off from fatigue.

As soon as these visitations began I was thrown face-to-face with my problem. In fact, I had never before stayed still at my desk, nor had I ever attempted to control my almost constant restlessness, distraction, and frustration. Now I was stuck with it. But, when he sat with me, I tried not to move too much and just confronted my inability to concentrate. A sense of discipline appeared. I realized what I had to work with and, very gradually, I learned to hold my seat—just as he did—and I became a proper student. Sometimes, to this day, when my mind wanders erratically, an ineffable sense of presence and stability arises in the midst of my loneliness.

It seems inevitable that a child's first good experiences of basic attendance create a warm spot and an easy acceptance for all future experiences of basic attendance. One's openness or trust in this form of learning companionship makes it easier to enter when, in the successive phases of our life, it may become useful, skillful, or urgent. There is a freedom to enter into relationships with teachers, tutors, trainers, counselors, and spiritual elders. Thus, much of our ability to receive help from others rides on the success of our early basic attendance encounters. They are landmark events in our developmental history of sanity. Whatever else may happen in basic attendance, the main point is that the principles and disciplines to stabilize body and mind are communicated. This is not done intellectually; it cannot be learned in books. It comes only from human example, human transmission, and warmth. This occurs at different levels at the same time; when the natural flow of interpenetration— being guided by exchanging oneself for others, and a full appreciation of symbiotic relatedness—function together.   In the very specialized form of therapy of working intimately with disturbed people, the lineage of Frieda Fromm-Reichmann, Harold Searles, and others attempted to explore the capabilities for the human transmission of sanity to its full extent. Fundamental to all their discoveries is the living principle that such unique human relationships are, from beginning to end, a mutual discovery between therapist and patient: a mutual journey of becoming free from personal madness.

We have come full circle: at first the wonder and energy of psychoanalysis passed into the discipline of psychotherapy; and now it returns, while retaining its original inspiration, in the form of basic attendance. In this way, the original intention and brilliance of intimate human caring is capable of entering into the domains of child care, education, the elderly, and the dying, and gives all human services in general a more profound dimension.

References

Fromm-Riechmann, F. (1950). *Principles of intensive psychotherapy.* Chicago: University of Chicago Press.
Hesse, H (1957). *Siddhartha* (H. Rosner, Trans.). New York: New Directions Publishing.

Santideva (1979). *A guide to the Bodhisattva'a way of life* (S. Batchelor, Trans.). New Delhi: Dhamasala.

6

Buddhism, Psychology, and Neuroscience: The Promises and Pitfalls of a Neurobiologically Informed Contemplative Psychotherapy

Michael Dow

For a variety of reasons, contemplative psychotherapy, if defined broadly as any approach to psychotherapy which draws from both Western psychology and Buddhist meditative traditions, has become part of mainstream American academic discourse. While the dialogue between Buddhism, psychoanalysis, and humanistic therapies is long-standing (Suzuki, Fromm, & DeMartino, 1963; see also Molino, 1999; Epstein, 1994; Wegela, 1994, 1999), in recent years academic psychology and neuroscience have begun to enter the conversation in full force.

This paper proposes that the dialogue between Buddhism, psychology, and neuroscience holds the potential to fundamentally expand our understanding of all three domains. However, and perhaps less commonly considered, such a convergence also holds the potential to reduce each domain to the epistemological framework of the other, thus impoverishing our worldview. This chapter outlines both the promises and the pitfalls of the meeting of Buddhist philosophy and practice with science, in this case academic psychology and neuroscience, why a neurobiologically-informed contemplative psychotherapy might be useful, and the details of how such an approach might look in practice.

Buddhism and Psychology

In recent years Buddhist concepts and practices like mindfulness have been rapidly adopted by academic psychology. Mindfulness and the importance of *acceptance strategies* (as a complement to *strategies of change*) are employed by treatment approaches across the field. A short list includes: one of the most researched behavioral treatments to reduce stress and chronic pain called Mindfulness-Based Stress Reduction (MBSR; Kabat-Zinn, 1995), the leading empirically validated treatment for borderline personality disorder known as Dialectical Behavior Therapy

(DBT; Linehan, 1999), the treatment with the strongest empirical support in preventing relapse in depression called Mindfulness-Based Cognitive Therapy for Depression (MBCT; Segal, Williams & Teasdale, 2001), the so-called *third wave* of behavior therapy, Hayes and Strosahl's Acceptance and Commitment Therapy (ACT; Hayes, Follette, & Linehan, 2004; Hayes, Strosahl, & Wilson, 1999), and a new approach to relapse prevention by one of the top researchers in the addiction field (Witkiewitz, Marlatt, & Walker, 2005). UCLA now has a Mindfulness-Awareness Research Center (MARC) which hosts new research projects looking at the effect of mindfulness on Attention Deficit Hyperactivity Disorder (ADHD) in children and applying mindfulness in schools. The Santa Barbara Institute for Consciousness Studies is conducting a rigorous scientific study known as *The Shamatha Project*, which is looking at the effects of three months of intensive meditation practice on attention, cognition, emotional regulation, and their neural and biological correlates (Wallace, 2007c). That many of these researchers work at large, well-known, public universities and are funded by grants from the National Institutes of Health and other government agencies, makes it difficult to still consider a Buddhist-oriented psychology a fringe or an unknown approach.

At least one reason for the current popularity of mindfulness-based approaches might be that they are more helpful. Segal, Williams, and Teasdale's (2001) research suggests that depressed patients who regularly practice mindfulness meditation have more improvement of depressive symptoms than those who are taught standard cognitive-behavioral techniques oriented towards identifying and correcting *distorted* cognitions. They propose that what is helpful in cognitive therapy is not changing one's thoughts, but learning to take a *meta-level* relative to thoughts in general. Practicing simple nonjudgmental awareness of thoughts with no attempt to change them already accomplishes the cognitive therapy goal of loosening one's belief in them.

The discourse of psychology is shifting towards an understanding that awareness and acceptance practices are as important, if not more, than practices oriented towards change (Hayes, Follette, & Linehan, 2004). As Buddhist approaches to psychotherapy drawn from humanistic and psychodynamic orientations have emphasized for some time (Wegela, 1994; 1996), an approach to therapy that emphasizes the *basic goodness* or *brilliant sanity* of all states of mind offers something quite radically different from the conventional psychological approach oriented towards the treatment of pathology.

Psychology and Neuroscience

At the same time as this dialogue between Buddhism and psychology is taking place, psychology itself is being changed by the growing convergence between psychology and neuroscience, disciplines which have been split essentially since Freud. Although trained as a neurologist and involved in basic research, Freud abandoned neurological explanations of the mind, it can be argued, because the science of the turn of the century was inadequate to the task. When Freud was first formulating psychoanalysis in the 1890s, neuroscience as we know it did not exist. Ramon y Cajal's discovery of the neuron as the basic functional and structural unit of the brain, often cited as the beginning of modern neuroscience, was only published a few years later (as cited in Kandel, 2006). Psychology, or at least psychotherapy, and neuroscience needed to separate in order for both to develop. Psychology otherwise would have been hobbled by a primitive science.

Current neuroscience, however, is sophisticated enough that many are attempting to reweave the two (Solms & Turnbull, 2002). Freud himself anticipated this development in a manuscript he chose to leave unpublished until after his death, "Project for A Scientific Psychology." In words now sounding prescient, Freud said, "after we have completed our psychoanalytic work we shall have to find a point of contact with biology" (Freud & Breuer, 1895/1957, p.175) and,

> biology is truly a land of unlimited possibilities. We may expect it to give us the most surprising information and we cannot guess what answers it will return in a few dozen years...They may be of a kind which will blow away the whole of our artificial structure of hypothesis. (Freud, 1920/1961, p.60)

This *reweaving* of neuroscience and psychology has its roots in cognitive neuroscience which began in the early 1970s with the introduction of biological methods of exploration into cognitive psychology. Eric Kandel and his associates' research on the neurobiological basis of learning and memory would be one early example (as cited in Kandel, 2006). Kandel's research identified specific changes in synaptic structure and function as a result of learning in invertebrate animals. Although his research was not on humans, prior to Kandel's findings, it was thought that learning and memory could not be studied in a meaningful way on a biological level. The idea that a *mental* subject like memory had a clear biological pathway which could be studied was groundbreaking.

In the 1980s, cognitive neuroscience was given new energy with the advent of brain imaging technologies like positron emission technology (PET), which measures the brain's consumption of energy, and functional magnetic resonance imaging (fMRI), which measures its use of oxygen. With these technologies researchers could directly *see* the neural representations of previously unquantifiable things, such as thought, memory, and emotion. Thanks to these technologies, developments in molecular neurobiology, and the discovery of similar brain-mediated emotional pathways in nonhuman animals, the study of emotions has entered a new renaissance. The *cognitive revolution* has given way to the *affective revolution* in neuroscience as pioneered by LeDoux (1998,

2002), Damasio (1994, 1999, 2003), Panksepp (1998), Ekman (1999), and Davidson (1998, 2004), among others. Emotions and mental states are becoming acceptable realms of exploration because their biological correlates can now be reliably measured.

The joining of both first and third person perspectives as equally valid realms of exploration, as some writers have argued (Wallace, 2007a; Wilber, 2000; Solms & Turnbull, 2002), may be key to the fruitfulness of this conversation between neuroscience, psychology, and meditation. How consciousness feels from the inside may be as important as what it looks like in a brain scan for the development of neuroscience, especially in terms of understanding consciousness. As Wallace (2006, 2007a) argues, if we are to understand the relationship between mind and brain, in addition to looking at neural correlates of consciousness, we need to investigate the phenomena of consciousness directly. This is the branch of psychology proposed by William James (1890/1950) known as *introspectionism*, which was abandoned due to the lack of any unified system of investigation and to the inherent instability of mental states (Hayward & Varela, 2001). Direct empirical observation with reliable instruments is the way science has always advanced, argues Wallace (2006). Meditation training, which stabilizes the attention, may allow first-person subjective exploration of mind to become a more reliable method of collecting data. Additionally, the data available from the *second-person* (Wilber, 2000) or interpersonal experiences of therapists and clients is likely to be important as well.

Although hotly contested, it can be argued that the *mind-body* problem (or *brain-mind* problem) will only ever be resolved if the subjective explorations available through psychotherapy and meditation are valued equally as the objective ones available through neuroscientific research. A dialogue between subjective and objective perspectives may bring the field closer to understanding the intricacies of the relationship between mind and brain. Although a larger issue than this paper can cover, the Buddhist hypothesis, according to Wallace, is that subjectivity and objectivity are inherently interconnected even at subatomic levels of reality (Wallace, 2003).

Promises of Integration

Neuroscience, psychology, and meditation can be seen as three disciplines or realms of knowledge that can inform and enrich one another. As the neuroscientific study of both meditative states and the therapeutic process grows, new insights are reached into how meditation, psychotherapy, and the brain itself function. Consequently new frameworks and understandings are developed for all three.

To understand the potential for synergy here, a brief update of some of the latest developments in brain science with clinical and meditative applications is in order. Recent findings in neuroplasticity, structural and functional changes in the brain as a result of meditation and psychotherapy, and theoretical models of brain/mind functioning derived from affective neuroscience and mirror neuron research will be reviewed.

Neuroplasticity

Neuroplasticity refers to how the structure and function of the brain changes in response to experience and can be studied on various levels from cellular to behavioral (Kolb & Whishaw, 2003). As more research has pointed to unsuspected degrees of neuroplasticity even into late adulthood, this area of study becomes especially relevant to both psychotherapy and meditation (Begley, 2007). The possibilities for change are greater than was thought and can be seen concretely on a neurobiological level.

Early studies in neuroplasticity came out of molecular biology research, and looked at neurological changes on a cellular level as a result of learning. Kandel's (as cited in Kandel, 2006) research, mentioned previously, which found changes in synaptic strength in *Aplysia* (a marine mollusk) as a result of behavioral learning paradigms, is an early example of this level of neuroplasticity research. Learning something means that the nervous system has changed the way it fires. Unsurprisingly, this was found to also hold true in more complex animals such as humans.

Later developments looked at the plasticity of more complex brain systems, and especially the plasticity and vulnerability of the developing mammalian brain in response to experience during the first few years of life (Schore, 1994). The complexity of the early environment and the quality of the parent-infant attachment clearly contribute to what is known as experience-dependent (as opposed to genetically-dependent) maturation, or use-dependent organization of the brain. Challenging any simple sense of genetic determinism, a new field of *epigenetics* looks not only at how genes are switched on and off by environmental influences, but how such switches can themselves be inherited (Pembrey, 1996).

Perhaps especially plastic are the brain's representational zones in the various sensory cortices: auditory, visual, and somatosensory. Sounds discernible by infants, for instance, are of a much wider range than those discernible by adults, which is necessary for them to be available for adaptation by any of the diverse human languages (Werker & Tees, 1983).

Neuroplasticity, however, goes much further than initially thought, especially when considering the brains of children. Neurological systems once thought to be genetically determined can be recruited for wholly other purposes. For instance, brain imaging shows that the visual cortex, which is only known to receive visual inputs, is active when people who have been blind since birth read Braille (Sadato et al., 1996). Sighted people who close their eyes and touch Braille symbols have no visual cortex activity: their somatosensory cortex is what is activated. The surprising suggestion is that an area thought to be hard-wired for vision can be recruited for the processing of other stimuli. If blind at an early enough age, you can literally learn to *see* with your fingers, at least in terms of reading Braille. But even further, the visual cortex of people blind since birth has been found to be active when using spoken language (Amedi, Raz, Pianka, Malach, & Zohary, 2003). The visual cortex, which *normally* only receives visual stimuli, can not only be used as a processor of somatosensory stimuli, but also can be involved in processing spoken and written language. Interestingly, adults who are blindfolded for 5 days also begin to show significant activity in the visual cortex from tactile and auditory stimuli. It remains unclear if such findings reflect neuroplasticity, pre-existing connections that were previously unknown, or, as Amedi and colleagues suspect, some combination of the two (Amedi, Merabet, Bermpohl, & Pascual-Leone, 2005).

The adult brain is also much more plastic than previously thought. It was assumed that neuroplasticity in adults was something one only found, in any significant way, after traumatic brain injury. That our brain is constantly being re-mapped and reorganized in response to everyday experience was never suspected. Jenkins and colleagues (Jenkins, Merzenich, Ochs, Allard, & Guic-Roble, 1990), however, found large-scale changes in both sensory and motor cortices in adult owl monkeys in response to non-traumatic everyday experience. Their sensory and motor maps were quite different at baseline, apparently based on the differences in their everyday experience. To further explore this, they trained monkeys via food rewards to place their fingers on a spinning disk, a task requiring delicate manual coordination. After a number of weeks of mastering this task, the area of the somatosensory cortex mapping the fingers that were stimulated had expanded roughly 400%. This is a large change for cortical maps once thought to be fixed, especially in a relatively short amount of time.

A later study showed that, more than actual sensory experience, what matters in terms of neuroplasticity is where one's attention is placed (Recanzone, Schreiner, & Merzenich, 1993). Two groups of monkey were given the disk spinning task while simultaneously listening to a series of tones via headphones. One group was rewarded for indicating when the sounds from the headphones changed, while another group was rewarded for indicating when the movement pattern of the disk changed. Both groups were exposed to identical stimuli, but the group who attended to the sounds had significant changes in the auditory cortex and none in the somatosensory cortex, while the other group had entirely the opposite result. The only difference was attention. Assuming that such findings translate to humans, the implication is that what one attends to, especially over and over, becomes encoded into one's cortical maps. As will be discussed further below, some scientists argue that such cortical maps may play a large part in determining the contours of sensory experience which may form the background, ambient basis for our very sense of self (Damasio, 1999, 2003).

Additionally relevant to neuroplasticity, studies have suggested that not only can adult humans develop new neural pathways, but they can grow entirely new neurons, especially in areas of the brain involved in ongoing learning such as the hippocampus, although in other areas such as the olfactory bulb as well (Eriksson et al., 1998; van Praag et al., 2002).

Being engaged by sufficient external stimuli appears to be central to the growth of new neurons. Kempermann, Kuhn, and Gage (1997) found that adult mice placed in enriched environments (cages with lots of toys, mazes, etc.) had a 15 % increase in the formation and survival of new neurons in the dentate gyrus, a region of the hippocampus specifically involved with recognizing novelty. Additionally, such changes translated into significantly increased ability to learn, as measured by the mice's ability to navigate mazes when compared to controls. In terms of applying such findings to humans, it may be important to note that the control group, mice in cages without toys, may have had an especially impoverished environment in regards to stimulation.

Exercise may also play a central role. A later study also found that mice who were allowed to run on a treadmill doubled their production of new neurons when compared to sedentary mice (van Praag, Kempermann, & Gage, 1999). The researchers hypothesized that voluntary aerobic exercise (forced exercise did not have the same effect) increases the number of neuronal stem cells that divide and give rise to new neurons in the hippocampus, but that it's the enriched environment that supports the survival of the cells. That this effect was only found with voluntary exercise however, raises the question as to whether any activity pursued voluntarily and with vigor might also lead to new neuronal growth.

Applying Neuroplasticity Findings

But is such research important for psychotherapists to know about? On a practical level, what does neuroscience have to do with psychotherapy or meditation? Aren't they separate domains entirely? As one example of how neuroscientific findings, psychotherapy, and meditation might inform one another, there are a number of interesting findings that come together in relationship to depression. Multiple studies have suggested that anti-depressant medications may stimulate the growth of neurons in the dentate gyrus, the aforementioned region of the hippocampus that is associated with recognizing novelty (Malberg & Schechter, 2005). When neurogenesis in this region was blocked in mice, anti-depressant medications showed no behavioral effect (Santarelli et al., 2003). While the exact function of the dentate gyrus remains unclear, it appears to have the function of encoding information arriving from the senses before further processing by the hippocampus. It has been associated with the ability to recognize new places, new faces, and new stimuli, in general. Because it is so busy, it has been suggested that new neurons are often needed here for continued learning (Begley, 2007). Although not certain, evidence suggests that neurogenesis in this region may be the more primary antidepressant mechanism operating with anti-depressant medications, rather than some sort of chemical rebalancing. If depression, neurologically, represents primarily a chemical imbalance, why is there typically a delay of 3-5 weeks after starting anti-depressant medications before the onset of any significant antidepressant effect, despite the near immediate increase in available serotonin? Neurogenesis may be a more likely mechanism; it is found across different classes of anti-depressants that target different neurotransmitters. Given what is known about neurogenesis, 3-5 weeks would apparently be a reasonable time table for onset of action (Malberg & Schechter, 2005).

It is well-known that depressed and traumatized patients have shrunken hippocampi and, specifically, shrunken dentate gyri. In some studies, regular aerobic exercise, now known to stimulate the growth of neurons in the dentate gyrus, is as effective in alleviating depression as selective serotonin reuptake inhibitors (SSRIs), the latest anti-depressant medications (Blumenthal et al., 1999). High levels of stress and sleep deprivation are also known to inhibit hippocampal neurogenesis (Malberg & Schechter, 2005). Together these findings suggest that depression may be related to the lack of neurogenesis in the hippocampus, and specifically in the dentate gyrus. Given the dentate gyrus's function in recognizing novel stimuli, some have further speculated that depression, functionally, is an inability to recognize novelty (Begley, 2007). This fits with clinical experience with depressed patients who report that nothing changes and that life lacks all excitement and interest.

Of course, novel sensory stimuli are, in reality, always present. Even familiar faces and environments are never the same from day to day. The difference is whether we attend to the newness that is there or whether we operate on our stored memory, tagging the various incoming stimuli into various a priori categories. Resisting this tendency of mind and actively *recognizing novelty* in our moment to moment awareness might be another description of mindful awareness. Although this is surely a simplification, we might think of depression as an inability to be mindfully aware of the ongoing newness and immediacy of experience that expresses itself as the lack of neurogenesis in the dentate gyrus. This would explain the effectiveness that has been found for mindfulness-based approaches to depression (Segal, Williams, & Teasdale, 2001), while also accounting for the effectiveness of SSRIs. This hypothesis remains provisional and leaves unexplained, for one, why transcranial stimulation is effective for depression and yet shows no hippocampal neurogenesis (Malberg & Schechter, 2005). Nevertheless, such a hypothesis serves as an example of how weaving together these three domains of psychology, neuroscience and meditation can suggest new insights not available to any domain pursued in isolation.

Neuroplasticity and the Differing Epistemological Assumptions of Buddhism and Science

As just discussed, neuroplasticity findings suggest one arena in which meditation, neuroscience, and psychology can interact. But there are important differences. Mindfulness meditation grows out of Buddhist thought which has different epistemological assumptions than modern science. Although the differences are more than space allows to fully explore, one area of contention has to do with which is primary, mind or brain. The basis of modern neuroscience, after all, is that all conscious experience can be wholly reduced to neural events in the brain. Francis Crick (1994), the co-discoverer of the DNA's double helix, called this the *astonishing hypothesis,* that is that, "You, your joys and your sorrows, your memories and your ambitions, your sense of personal identity and free will, are in fact no more than the behavior of a vast assembly of nerve cells and their associated molecules" (p. 4).

Although all that has been *proven*, per se, is that most mental states have neural correlates, the assumption tends to be one of causation: Brain causes mind. Buddhist psychology might take issue with the *no more than* in Crick's statement above. Buddhism's underlying assumptions, while not anti-materialist, may be quite different from the materialism that generally undergirds the scientific worldview. For instance, in Tibetan Buddhism, mind may be understood as a continuum of mental states from gross to subtle to very subtle, not all of which are necessarily mediated by the brain. The Dalai Lama explains, "the grosser the levels of mind, the more they are dependent on the body. The subtler they are, the less dependent they are, and the very subtle consciousness is independent of the body" (as cited in Hayward & Varela, 2001, p. 157). Writers such as Wallace (2007a) suggest that just as Newtonian physics works pragmatically to explain the natural world in most cases, but breaks down as you approach the speed of light and ultimately is not entirely accurate, so does a materialistic explanation of consciousness work at most levels of consciousness, although is not entirely accurate, until attention is sufficiently refined through meditation, after which it too breaks down. Wallace proposes that the mind is conditioned by the brain but does not arise from it; both mind and matter may be part of some more fundamental non-dual reality (Wallace, 2007b). This position is similar in some ways to the *dual-aspect monism* proposed by Solms and Turnbull (2002) and other writers, which suggests that the dualities of mind/matter, mental/physical, or subjective/objective are two aspects or two ways of viewing what is essentially the same fundamental reality.

In addition to having no understanding of how the brain might give rise to consciousness, what David Chalmers (1995) terms the *hard problem*, we still have not been able to determine what the neural correlates of consciousness (NCC) are: the so called *easy problem*. We have no measurement for consciousness. We do not know what its necessary and sufficient conditions are, which is to say that we do not know how to define it in an objective way (Wallace, 2006, 2007b). Although the easy problem may be solvable, it is not clear if the hard problem is. What are the mechanics of how the activity of neurons in the brain becomes the richness of our immediate experience? Although typically assumed to be true, that mind or consciousness is wholly caused by and reducible to neuronal firing essentially remains an unproven and perhaps an unprovable hypothesis. Mind and brain may ultimately be two sides or two ways of looking at the same coin.

While it may be going too far to say that neuroplasticity findings overturn science's materialistic assumptions, they do point to how the mind/brain pathway can work in the other direction. The mind can change the brain. Conscious repeated effort over time can in fact change brain structure and function in certain ways. Mindfulness awareness practices may lead to improved emotional regulation. Exercise and *enriched environments* may lead to neurogenesis which counteracts depression. Such findings do not actually contradict a *brain-first* paradigm because those mind states that were able to effect changes surely themselves had neural correlates. But the notion that with regular behavioral practice, with mental intention and attention you can change your brain in significant ways, does powerfully counter a sort of neural determinism popular in the culture.

Neuroscience of Meditation and Psychotherapy

Meditation, as traditionally undertaken, is just such a behavioral, endlessly repeated practice and, in regular meditators of any tradition, one might expect to find evidence of neuroplasticity. In most forms of Buddhist mindfulness meditation, for example, at least initially, one brings one's attention back again and again to the breath, to the sensory experience of the body, or simply to whatever is arising in one's immediate experience (Kabat-Zinn, 1995; Mipham, 2003). This bringing back of the attention occurs many times over the course of one meditation session. Meditation sessions, in most traditions, are encouraged daily, as well as practicing mindfulness in everyday life. Such a relatively intensive mind training, by Western standards, is bound to have observable correlates in the brain.

There is an extensive literature on the study of electroencephalogram (EEG) and other physiological changes due to various types of meditation (Cahn & Polich, 2006), but there is little research that has used brain imaging to look at changes in the brain itself as a result of meditative practice. Along these lines, Sara Lazar and colleagues (Lazar et al., 2005), using magnetic resonance imaging (MRI), found significantly thickened areas of the middle prefrontal cortex (PFC), as well as a thickened right anterior insula in 20 long-term, daily practitioners of vipassana meditation (a type of Buddhist mindfulness meditation) with an average of 45 minutes a day when compared to matched controls. Although this was merely a correlative finding and further research with a pre and post design is needed (maybe thick insulaed people are more likely to meditate), the fact that there was an additional correlation between length of time meditating and degree of insular and medial PFC thickness would at least strongly suggest a causal connection. The working hypothesis these researchers propose is not that meditation causes insular thickening, but that it prevents what has been thought of as normal age-related cortical thinning. The insula is involved in coordinating brain, body, emotion, and thoughts, and is thought to be centrally involved in *interoception*, or the representation of somatic states. That the insula remains thickened in meditators versus controls makes sense given that mindfulness meditation involves tuning into one's own moment by moment sensory experience. Lazar speculates that the thickening in medial regions of the PFC is due to the attentional component of vipassana meditation where one brings one's mind and attention back over and over again.

Therapy, even if simply putting feelings into words, is a repeated behavioral practice. As such, it should lead to changes in the brain, and so it does. Goldapple and associates at the University of Toronto (Goldapple et al., 2004) found that subjects who underwent a 10-week cognitive-behavioral therapy (CBT) course for depression had decreased metabolic activity in the frontal cortices with increased activity in the hippocampus and anterior cingulate. Subjects successfully treated with paroxetine (an SSRI, commercially named Paxil) had increased PFC activity and decreased activity in the brainstem and subgenual cingulate. The contrasting results between the two groups, especially in terms of PFC activation, led Goldapple to speculate, "CBT works top down, whereas medications work bottom up" (the subgenual cingulate, incidentally, was the successful target for deep brain stimulation (DBS) as a treatment for depression). In other words, CBT slows activity in the prefrontal cortex by evaluating and redirecting *negative thinking*, whereas paroxetine decreases activity in deep brain regions which, apparently, are over active during depression.

Therapy clearly, at least functionally, changes the brain, and in ways different than medication. When these changes are tied to therapeutic *success*, they inform us as to what neurological *dysfunction* underlies or correlates with the impetus for therapy (in this case, depression). This, in turn, also suggests treatments, such as DBS, which more directly target that neurological system. One wonders if different therapeutic approaches would lead to different neural signatures of *success*. Or perhaps would more differences be found between the patients of different therapists than therapies?

An intriguing example of how neuroscience and psychotherapy can more directly interact is provided by deCharms and colleagues' (deCharms et al., 2005) study of *neuroimaging therapy*, a form of biofeedback utilizing sophisticated modern technology. Chronic pain patients were shown real-time functional magnetic resonance images (rtfMRI) of their brain via 3D goggles, specifically the rostral anterior cingulate cortex (rACC) which flares up during intense pain and is associated with the emotionally difficult aspect of pain. Simply by trying to change the image of the rACC in their goggles, patients were able to reduce their pain by an average of 40%, equivalent to the effectiveness of many pain medications, and more than twice as good as controls. This learning took less than a day and persisted after the experiment. The moment to moment direct feedback of the image (with some guidance from the researchers) taught subjects how to access the pathways to pain modulation that were there, but otherwise hard to pinpoint.

Such results raise the question: Can we learn to change other distressing pathways? Could we some day target the reward system and upregulate happiness by watching our brains on a monitor? Could neuroimaging enhance the process of psychotherapy in general, even help assess the quality of the relationship? Beginning research in this area is, in fact, already underway at deCharms and Mackey's lab on the cognitive therapy of depression, although with the obvious limitation that the patient has to lie inertly in a clunky and noisy fMRI machine.

Real-time fMRI can also be used to teach non-clinical populations to change brain function. In another recent study of the power of rtfMRI (Caria et al., 2007), subjects were able to learn, in a very brief amount of time, to modulate the right anterior insula in response to emotionally salient memories. This is the exact same region found to be thickened in vipassana meditators. Interestingly, the left insula, not affected in meditators, was not subject to modulation in this experiment (the right brain may be more involved in somatic interoceptive awareness). What are the clinical applications of such findings? An overactive insula has been implicated in social phobia while an underactive one is associated with psychopathology (Straubea, Mentzelb, & Miltner, 2005; Birbaumer et al., 2005). Would subjects who practiced this sort of direct neurofeedback repeatedly forestall cortical thinning of their insulas as the meditators from Lazar's study did? From a first person perspective, what are these subjects experiencing and does it feel anything like mindfulness meditation?

Affective Neuroscience

The neurobiological study of emotions has become central to an understanding of how the brain works, and thus to understanding the potential synergy between psychology, neuroscience, and meditation. Central to this emerging field of *affective neuroscience* is the work of Damasio (1994, 1999, 2003). His ideas about emotion and the brain grew out of his clinical work as a neurologist working with patients with damage to the ventromedial prefrontal cortex (VMPFC; Damasio, 1999). Damasio observed that many of these patients had intact cognitive abilities, appeared normal in conversation, and yet were entirely unable to

6. Buddhism, Psychology, & Neuroscience

function in their lives. For example, many would struggle with the simple decision of when to return for their next appointment. Although they still had emotions, as registered by objective measures like the galvanic skin response, studies suggested that they were unable to access them consciously. Damasio hypothesized that the damage to the VMPFC prevented the input from the insula regarding somatic states from becoming conscious.

Damasio (1994) argues, contrary to Descartes, that mind and body are not separate. Even the most elemental processes of rational decision-making involve accessing our somatic memories of how we have felt in the past as a result of making similar decisions, and anticipating, somatically, how we might feel in the future (the somatic marker hypothesis). Without being able to represent our own somatic states to ourselves via information from the insula, without knowing how we are feeling, we can think, but we cannot decide.

Drawing on Spinoza's idea that *the human mind is the idea of the body*, Damasio (2003) argues that emotions are essentially unconscious neural maps of the moment to moment state of the body. When we consider that some types of mindfulness meditation are a conscious mapping of the moment to moment state of the body, we can see many areas of resonance. Such types of meditation could be seen on a functional level as forms of emotional regulation. In fact, emotions are mediated via the cingulate cortex, the somatosensory cortices (the insula and a region known as SII), and the brain stem tegmentum, as Damasio's research has shown. But the insula, Damasio suspects, has a primary role in representing emotion. That this is the exact region affected by vipassana meditation may further argue for understanding meditation, in part, as a form of emotional regulation.

The centrality of emotions and feelings to not only decision making, but our very sense of self, is the subject of Damasio's subsequent writings. Damasio (1999, 2003) argues that feelings, our conscious or semi-conscious awareness of the moment to moment changes in our somatic states, lie at the origin of our very sense of self. Consciousness, he suggests, is a "second order map" that maps the changes in the first order map that is our bodily emotions. In other words, our sense of self is literally, at a basic level, "the feeling of what happens" (Damasio, 1999, p. 22-23) over time.

Before leaving Damasio, it is important to point out another intriguing study which corroborates his findings of the association between the activity of the insula, feelings, and representations of somatic states. On an inpatient unit, patients with damage to the insula were unexpectedly found to have spontaneous and craving-free remission from nicotine addiction (Naqvi, Rudrauf, Damasio, & Bechara, 2007). As one patient described it, he simply "forgot how to smoke" (Naqvi et al., 2007, p. 23). The researchers hypothesized that the insular damage prevented somatically experienced craving states from being represented in the brain (Naqvi, Rudrauf, Damasio, & Bechara, 2007). Further work in this area is needed, but given previously discussed findings (Lazar et al., 2005; Witkiewitz, Marlatt, & Walker, 2005), one wonders if the effectiveness of mindfulness meditation as a treatment for addiction has to do with its effects on the insula.

Mirror Neurons

Mirror neurons are another recent finding proving essential to this interface of psychology, neuroscience, and meditation. Research in this area suggests that there may be neurobiological bases for concepts such as empathy, Buddhist notions of *exchange* (Wegela, 1994, 1996) and psychoanalytic ideas about objective countertransference (Spotnitz, 1979).

Rizzolatti and colleagues at the University of Parma, Italy (Rizzolatti & Craighero, 2004; Rizzolatti, Fadiga, Gallese, & Fogassi, 1996) discovered a set of neurons in the premotor cortex of macaque monkeys which are activated both during movement and during the observation of intentional *object-directed* action. These neurons fire both when a monkey picks up a banana and when he watches another monkey do so. They *mirror* or reproduce in the monkey's brain what he is observing in the outside world. This is not a simple connection of the visual and motor systems (which we might expect), because these neurons are peculiarly sensitive to intentional goal-directed action (Siegel, 2007). Just random hand movements, for instance, would not trigger them. They only fire if a monkey is observing another monkey reach for something. However, they continue to fire if the object, say the banana, is hidden, suggesting that this system allows monkeys to represent intention and the beginnings of a theory of mind (Siegel, 2007).

The ethics of human subject research do not allow us to have direct evidence for a mirror neuron system in humans. Still, there is strong indirect evidence for it, which suggests that in humans the system may have expanded to respond to self-directed actions and pantomimed, or *as-if* actions (Rizzolati & Craighero, 2004). That we see activation in the premotor cortex, where planning for action takes place, would suggest that our brains prepare our bodies to perform the same actions as those we are observing. Such premotor cortex regions (specifically the precentral gyrus) are also activated in humans when merely listening to someone describe action (Rizzolatti & Craighero, 2004).

Mirror neurons may also be key to our sense of self. Ramachandran (2007) speculates that the mirror neuron system originally evolved adaptively to read the mind or intention of others, but later, applied to ourselves, had the side effect of engendering self-awareness. In this view, consciousness is a sort of evolutionary accident which turned out to be adaptive. From this perspective, our empathic and often nonverbal communication with others may be more immediate and primary, both historically and even perhaps neurologically, than self-awareness.

Essentially, what these initial results point to is that empathy may have a neural basis. We resonate with others because our mirror neuron system, our *Dalai Lama neurons,* as Ramachandran (2007) calls them, do not distinguish between self and other, but rather resonate with and in fact replicate in ourselves what we observe as the intentional activity of others. This is true, as mentioned above, even when listening to others describe their intentional activity. This finding has obvious implications for psychotherapists. The contemplative notion of exchange, that we have "a natural ability to directly experience the client" (Wegela, 1994, p. 15) may be concretely true on a neuronal level. It then becomes even more important for therapists to be in touch with their experience. The accuracy of our own self-awareness may be intimately connected with our ability to accurately intuit others.

Neurobiology of Happiness

The neurobiology of happiness is a key area which ties together some of the previous discussion on neuroplasticity, affective neuroscience, and the neuroscience of meditation. Davidson and colleagues at the University of Wisconsin at Madison have become famous for their brain imaging studies of Tibetan monks which actually grew out of two decades of research on the neurobiology of emotion (Davidson, 1998, 2004; Ury et al., 2004). Initially, they were curious about the clinical observation that brain injured patients had a different relationship to emotion depending on the side of the brain which was injured. Patients with injuries to the left prefrontal cortex (PFC) were often unable to feel joy, and suffered with increased amounts of sadness (Begley, 2007). Patients with damage to the right prefrontal cortex, in contrast, were well known for their indifference to the injury and proneness to inappropriate laughter.

Widely thought to be only a phenomenon of brain injury, these left-right differences interestingly showed up in normal people, too. Studies of healthy subjects found often pronounced differences in left versus right prefrontal cortex activation, even at baseline, which corresponded to enduring differences in a person's predominant emotional states. Davidson termed left-right activation differences a person's *affective style.* One style was a chronically higher left prefrontal cortex activation. These people had what Davidson termed an "approach" orientation to stimuli and positive affect. They were more responsive to positive emotional stimuli, had a greater ability to suppress negative affects, and an enhanced ability to recover from negative affects as evidenced principally by greater control over the amygdala, which among other things is associated with processing fear. They reported being happy, alert, energized, and joyous. In contrast, people who were less able to recover from negative emotions, with more dysregulation of the amygdala, showed chronically higher right prefrontal activation. These people reported feeling more negative emotions such as worry, anxiety and sadness. In essence, right PFC dominance, in the extreme, is associated with depression, whereas left PFC dominance is associated with happiness (Davidson, 1998, 2004).

Davidson later realized that it's actually more complicated than that. It would be more direct to say that what contributes to happiness are things such as purpose, a strong social network, self-efficacy, the ability to accept oneself, and the overall sense that life is satisfying (Begley, 2007; see also Davidson, 1998). Left PFC dominance is associated with a more active stance to life, and people who are more active in engaging happiness-inducing relationships and activities are, naturally, more likely to be happy.

Like Damasio's research, Davidson's work points to strong connections between emotion and thought. His research suggests that the activity of the prefrontal cortex, a region associated with higher thought, is strongly connected to activity in the limbic regions such as the amygdala, more typically associated with emotion. Such linkages naturally suggest that emotional control may be trainable by engaging cognitive faculties as will be discussed further below.

Is affective style fixed? Initial findings suggested that adult affective styles do not change. An influential twin study from the 1990s had suggested the existence of a happiness *set point*, or a baseline level of happiness, is at least fifty percent genetically determined, to which people return after life's temporary ups and down that we tend to think will change things more than they do (Lykken & Tellegen, 1996). Although one of the authors of this study has later modified his position (Lykken, 2000), they initially went so far as to say, "It may be that trying to be happier is as futile as trying to be taller" (Lykken & Tellegen, p. 189). Their initial findings were subsequently replicated by others (Seligman, 1994). The stability of Davidson's affective style began to suggest that it might be a good neurobiological marker for such a relatively immutable happiness set point.

However, Davidson found that affective style can change rather dramatically between late adolescence and early adulthood. This alerted Davidson to the likelihood that the happiness circuit is plastic, although it looked, initially, as if much of its plasticity is lost in adulthood. But what if there were a way to change affective style in adults that had not yet been investigated? What if there were a mental training that could do so? A longtime meditator himself, Davidson started bringing Tibetan lamas with years of meditation practice into his lab. To his surprise and delight, these lamas registered larger relative left-PFC dominance while practicing a compassion meditation than any subjects measured before (Ury et al., 2004). Was this just a fluke or did this suggest that perhaps the happiness set point is not fixed, that one can train oneself to be happy? Perhaps the happiness set point is only fixed relative to changes in one's external surroundings. The notion of ongoing intensive mental training

6. Buddhism, Psychology, & Neuroscience 115

that could fundamentally alter one's mental and neural organization had not been considered by western science.

Davidson's initial findings with the Tibetan monks were remarkable, but did not establish a cause-effect relationship. It was possible that people with *left-leaning* PFC signatures were simply more drawn to become monks. The next important question was whether subjects naïve to meditation could show similar results with training. In another study, Davidson and colleagues (Davidson et al., 2001) found that subjects with no prior history of meditation who completed an 8-week Mindfulness-Based Stress Reduction course had relatively more left prefrontal activation, even at baseline (when subjects were not meditating), along with self-reports of increased positive affect and decreased anxiety, and improved immune system response. More studies are needed to see if this effect is enduring; however, it would begin to seem that Davidson's affective style, and maybe happiness itself, might be trainable through meditation.

That the left PFC would become more dominant is somewhat counterintuitive, as we might think of meditation as being more of a right brain activity–the right brain being more associated with emotion, nonlinear thinking, and spatial awareness. On second thought, however, continuing to bring one's mind back to the breath or simply the present moment is a type of attentional training which we could see associated with left brain function, as the left brain is associated with sequential and linear processing which would be central to such attentional training.

Very experienced long-term meditators in Davidson's lab had large differences in another area as well. Experienced Tibetan Buddhist monks had more high-amplitude gamma band oscillation and *phase-synchrony* on an electroencephalogram (EEG) while engaged in compassion meditation that was without object (and at baseline; Lutz, Greischar, Rawlings, Ricard & Davidson, 2004). Other studies that have looked at EEG during more object-oriented practices, such as mindful breathing, mantra meditation, have demonstrated more slow alpha and theta wave activity. While it is still unknown what these findings really mean, Davidson hypothesizes that the more concentrative practices initiate a top down slowing process on brain function, whereas the results here of gamma wave activity and neural synchrony represent more of an integrated and pervasive state of being which might typify an objectless meditation: "objectless meditation does not directly attend to a specific object but rather cultivates a state of being...the practitioner lets his feeling of loving-kindness and compassion permeate his mind without directing his attention toward a particular object" (Lutz et al., 2004, p. 16372).

It is unclear whether these different EEG signatures reflect differences in type of meditation, differences in level of meditative development or something else entirely. Davidson's approach here which is sensitive to such issues is already more nuanced than many previous studies, and opens the way for further research that looks at exactly such differences.

Integration

An example of how some of the above findings might begin to change our understanding of how mind, brain, meditation, and psychotherapy actually work, is Daniel Siegel's book, *The Mindful Brain* (2007). Siegel proposes that mindfulness meditation may function as a form of self-attunement which activates the same social circuitry in the brain activated in secure attachment, but directed towards the self. If the mirror neuron system resonates with the intentions of others, Siegel speculates, given the rough similarity between brain regions stimulated in secure attachment and mindfulness meditation (middle prefrontal regions), maybe what individuals are doing in mindfulness meditation is resonating with their own intentions, in a sense:

> When we tune into intention, in others or in ourselves, we are attuning our state with that of the "being" with whom we are focusing our attention. Because the resonance circuitry not only detects intentional states but creates them in the self, attention to intention creates attunement. (p.178)

and

> We can propose that as we embed an image of what is happening now with an automatic readying for what is next, the brain is representing an intentional state. This is how we are aware of intention. Notice how this automatic anticipation is a form of priming, not a prefrontal planning process. Priming readies us for the emerging now that peaks over the "horizon of the future" (Stern, 2003). In the next *now*, what happens actually matches what our mirror neuron system anticipated and the coherence between that anticipation and the map of what actually came to be creates a profound state of coherence. If this is part of mindful awareness, we can refer to this as "reflective coherence"...This is intrapersonal attunement. (p. 174)

In previous writings Siegel (1999, 2001) hypothesized that successful psychotherapy can be understood as an integration of left and right hemispheric functioning. In fact, from a neurobiological perspective, the goal of therapy can be described as the creation of a coherent self-narrative which is both emotionally rich (right hemisphere) and logically coherent (left hemisphere). This, in turn, has also been a signpost of secure attachment as measured in the Adult Attachment Inventory (George, Kaplan, & Main, 1985). Siegel (1999), drawing on Schore's work in this area (1994), speculates that the orbitofrontal cortex, one of the middle prefrontal areas with connections to both the limbic regions and the prefrontal areas and also associated with self narrative, is key to this integration. Helping clients to tell their story may be also serving the function of neural integration between left and right hemispheres and between limbic and frontal regions, which are at least partly mediated by the middle prefrontal regions. So the finding that mindfulness meditation is also associated with improved functioning in middle prefrontal regions lends credence, argues Siegel (2007), to the idea that mindfulness meditation and psychotherapy have some important functions in common.

Although Siegel's approach to integration has more details than space here allows, what is important is that he uses both first and third person perspectives to work towards an integrated theory of mind and brain. His is just one example of a possible line of inquiry integrating these domains, but one can readily see that such an approach not only has implications for the practice of psychotherapy, but also suggests a new understanding both of what is happening in meditation and how the brain itself *works*.

Outlines of a Neurobiologically Informed Contemplative Psychotherapy

What might a therapy look like that is informed by both the contemplative and the neurobiological findings discussed above? First, it would need to base itself in the findings of *interpersonal neurobiology*. Based on the simple fact that our brains, especially our nonverbal right hemisphere, develop primarily in the first two years of life in the context of an attachment relationship with a primary caregiver, a new approach to neuroscience termed *interpersonal neurobiology* has been heralded (Cozolino, 2002; Siegel, 1994). In other words, the brain can be understood as inherently interpersonal because it develops in an interpersonal context. This leads to a renewed appreciation for the power and importance of the often nonverbal levels of interpersonal attunement in the therapeutic relationship. A neurobiologically informed therapy would help clients create an emotion-rich, coherent narrative in the context of a sensitive relationship. Looking at mirror neuron findings, therapists might place renewed importance on *feeling into the intention* of clients in therapy. Such efforts to give clients the *feeling of being felt* might be understood as being reparative of early attachment disruptions registered neurobiologically in the middle frontal regions.

There is also a renewed neurobiological validation for the importance of the practice of mindfulness on the part of the therapist: the more clinicians are in tune with their own somatic experiences during sessions, the more they will be able to tune into or resonate with what is happening for clients (another hypothesis ripe for experimental validation). Via the mirror neuron system, the contemplative notion of *exchange* (Wegela, 1996) is given a neurobiological basis.

Additionally, the results of neuroplasticity suggest the importance of behavioral activation. Promoting emotion regulation practices such as mindfulness meditation or other regular behavioral practices may be key to effecting any lasting change in psychotherapy. Studies tying the insula, interoception and emotional regulation give biological credence to the contemplative psychotherapy notion of discovering and promoting potential mindfulness practices hidden in patients' daily lives (Wegela, 1994). Helping clients to develop awareness, perhaps especially somatic, interoceptive awareness in the midst of their daily lives, need not involve formal meditation training, but can incorporate disciplines patients are already engaged in, including the transformation of *mindless* disciplines (Wegela, 1994).

The trainability of attention circuits suggests that helping clients attend to the inherent workability of difficult situations, a key notion in Buddhist psychology (Trungpa, 1969), makes sense neurologically. As discussed previously, cultivating a detailed awakeness to what is new and unexpected in our experience might function as a biological antidote to depression. What we attend to shapes our cortical maps which can profoundly affect our experience of ourselves and the world. Helping clients to develop an approach orientation, to move towards both problem areas and potential sources of happiness and to overcome avoidance strategies would also be key, as Davidson's (Davidson et al., 2003) research suggests.

Future Developments

The scientific and neuroscientific study of meditation and psychotherapy is in its infancy and it is important not to prematurely jump to conclusions. Many paths need more investigation. For instance, no study has yet been done that looks at the differential effects of meditation. In addition to questions about the effects of different types of meditation, there is the question of whether everybody is affected more or less the same by any one particular practice of meditation. Are there other factors mediating the effects of mindfulness, for instance, like gender, socioeconomic or educational level, or attachment status? Do some people get more benefit from certain forms of meditation than others and why (are they doing it *better* and if so, what is the key *it* here, neurologically speaking?)? Might different forms of mindfulness awareness practice be more suited to certain individuals and can neuroimaging help us to understand this? It might be possible to target those individuals for whom mindfulness is not *working* and figure out why. Many of these questions can also be applied to neuroimaging research of psychotherapy.

The neural pathways, as opposed to simple neural location, of mindfulness meditation, though speculated on by Siegel (2007), are far from being conclusively understood, but this may change. We might begin to be able to make a *neural map* of successful meditative practice. It might become possible to develop a real time neuroimaging tool which, as in the chronic pain study (deCharms et al., 2005), is able to facilitate meditative development, or become a sort of bench mark, much as say a heart rate monitor is used regularly by athletes. In terms of psychotherapy, as discussed previously, it might become possible to develop a sort of interpersonal biofeedback tool which traces the neural and physiological states of both therapist and client. Additionally, we might see some sort of neural empathy machine, which allows us to directly reproduce neural states from one person to another.

There is also the issue of different degrees of meditative experience and development. Most research on meditation has been conducted on subjects with comparatively minimal meditation background, given the hundreds of thousands of hours usually devoted to meditation and spiritual practice in traditional Buddhist training lineages. In this regard, meditation research is really in its infancy. In the Shambhala Buddhist tradition for instance, shamatha-vipassana, a form of mindfulness meditation, develops along a series of nine stages (Mipham, 2003) whose difference has yet to be explored on a neurobiological level. How to set up studies and training experiences that give people the depth of meditative experience necessary to progress to these stages (Wallace, 2007c) remains as an additional question.

On another level, results of neuroscience experiments, although measuring objective phenomena, may provide new insights into what is happening on the subjective level of different types of meditation. Such insights, when combined with sufficient meditative knowledge and experience, might lead to the development of new types of meditation. Many of these potential developments may raise concerns for Buddhist practitioners, which this chapter suggests are related to some of the often overlooked potential pitfalls in this larger meeting explored below.

Pitfalls

The most significant pitfall of this dialogue between Buddhism, psychology, and neuroscience is best described by Chogyam Trungpa Rinpoche's term *spiritual materialism* (Trungpa, 1973), which is also echoed in Shunryu Suzuki Roshi's term, *beginner's mind* (Suzuki, 1973). These two seminal Buddhist teachers point to the central paradox of Buddhist practice: The more one practices the more one realizes that there is nothing fundamentally *to get* from practice because there is no separate self to get it and no place and time other than *now* to get it from. From a Buddhist perspective, the ego does not exist in any separate, permanent way. As Buddhist meditation and practice brings one closer to this realization, practice becomes more about losing one's sense of specialness or expertise, and settling into the fullness of the present moment (*beginner's mind* or *basic goodness*) than gaining anything, including brain states of mind.

Brain imaging studies of long term meditators showing significant brain changes both functionally and structurally, could suggest to some that enlightenment is principally a brain state that an individual strives to achieve. There are a number of problems here. Even assuming that every conscious experience is brain-mediated and thus detectable with brain imaging, brain image still does not equal individual conscious experience. There is no inherent meaning in the objective reality of a brain scan, meaning being necessarily a subjective thing.

Additionally, meditation takes place in the context of a lived life. As discussed further below, traditionally in Buddhism, meditation is one of three trainings, which also include wisdom and ethics (Das, 2005). To put it simply, Buddhist practice is not just about achieving a meditative state, but about the entirety of how you live your life. Buddhist practice is traditionally not founded on a commitment to a brain state, but to a path of benefiting others. The development of meditative wisdom is seen as inseparable from the development of compassion for all beings. The life of the Buddha is no more reducible to a brain state than is Shakespeare's life. In other words, a brain state is merely and powerfully but one moment in time of a brain which exists in the context of an individual, a community and a moment in history. One would not get Shakespeare's works or the Buddha's accomplishments, even if one could mimic the exact pattern of their fMRI.

Wallace's (2007a) description of the vast majority of Tibetan yogis' reluctance to assist with their brain imaging research may be for similar reasons (Wallace, 2007). They do not have *gaining mind*. They do not view their practice in terms of individual achievement. The pitfall in doing neuroscience research on meditation is to fall prey to the idea that meditation is about achieving a better or even a more neurally integrated state of mind, which paradoxically leads us away from the openness of our inherent nature, as conceived in Buddhism. Both Shunryu Suzuki Roshi and Chogyam Trungpa Rinpoche warn against exactly this sort of individual achievement oriented approach to meditation practice:

> In the beginner's mind there is no thought, "I have attained something." All self-centered thoughts limit our vast mind. When we have no thought of achievement, no thought of self, we are true beginners. Then we can really learn something. The beginner's mind is the mind of compassion. When our mind is compassionate, it is boundless. Dogen-zenji the founder of our school, always emphasized how important it is to resume our boundless original mind. Then we are always true to ourselves, in sympathy with all beings, and can actually practice. (Suzuki, 1973, p. 22)

6. Buddhism, Psychology, & Neuroscience   121

and

> Whenever we have a dualistic notion such as, "I am doing this because I want to achieve a particular state of consciousness, a particular state of being," then automatically we separate ourselves from the reality of what we are. (Trungpa, 1973, p. 14)

It might also be said that there's a version of *therapeutic materialism,* which applies this same overly achievement-oriented mindset to the therapeutic encounter. This can be seen in aspects of the evidence-based practice movement which apply the scientific method to psychology to see what *works* empirically and what does not. Slife and colleagues warn that we are in danger of creating a monopoly of a narrowly conceived empiricism, which is to say a situation where the only evidence that is being deemed a valid indicator of success in therapy is that which is observable by the senses and measurable by external means (Slife, Wiggins, & Graham, 2005). While it is useful and even necessary to know if psychotherapy is able observably to reduce specific symptoms, when such a value becomes *the* determinant of what is valid in therapy, we invalidate and ignore that which is unobservable by the senses, like subjective experience itself:

> Observation is frequently thought to avoid values rather than be a value. Yet, a value is something that indicates what matters – which things we should pay attention to and care about (the things that matter) and which things we should ignore and not care about (the things that do not matter). Empiricism, as the adjective in "sensory experience" implies, functions in just this valuing manner. It tells us which of our many experiences matter most in science. Rather than subjective experiences – including opinions, emotions, and spiritual experiences – it tells us that sensory or objective experiences should matter most to scientists. (Slife, Wiggins, & Graham, 2005, p. 84)

As Slife and colleagues (Slife, Wiggins, & Graham, 2005) go on to point out, there are many important things in therapy that are not observable with the senses, such as meaning, the relationship, and narrative coherence. The usual scientific response to this is to operationalize the nonobservable: the relationship quality as measured by the self-reported positive feelings towards the therapist on scale X. But most researchers will then make the mistake, due to an *empirical* bias that favors the observable, of equating the subsequent operationalization with the nonobservable itself. The relationship, or even the relationship quality, *equals* your score on scale X. The main problem with this is that there is no way, empirical or otherwise, of knowing if this is true. At the very least, for instance, from a psychodynamic perspective, a relationship is also made up of unconscious feelings, which will by definition not be reported on any scale. To counter this monopoly, Slife and colleagues propose instead a methodological pluralism which would validate other methods of investigation such as qualitative research. Methodology should be adapted depending on the nature of the object of interest, with empirical, quantitative research being but one option. Going back to James's (1895/1950) original notion discussed earlier, another option would be to expand our notion of what is meant by empirical to include not only data observable by the five senses, but internal, subjective data observable by the mind as well.

This pitfall of therapeutic materialism may extend to the focus on mindfulness in psychology. While the practice of mindfulness is arguably at the core of Buddhism, in the context of Western science and removed from its daily practice, we can easily lose touch with the goal of mindfulness practice. What is the point of mindfulness? To be more relaxed? Why is that a good thing? Without a larger view, the integration of Buddhism and psychology becomes more and more about the application of a relaxation technique. While this may have its uses, it radically curtails the larger potential of such a meeting.

In traditional Buddhist practice, meditation and mindfulness are parts of a larger notion of enlightened living which is summarized as *The Noble Eightfold Path*. The eightfold path is subdivided into the three trainings of *sila* (ethical self-discipline), *samadhi* (mindfulness and meditation), and *prajna* (wisdom and love training). As Lama Surya Das (2005) colloquially explains it:

> Wisdom Training is broken out into the first and second practices of the Eightfold Path (1)Wise View: seeing things as they are, not as they ain't, and (2)Wise Intentions, including unselfishness and the like. Ethics Training consists of the next three: (3)Wise Speech, (4)Wise Action, and (5)Wise Livelihood or wise vocation—making a life, not just a living. Meditation Training is broken out into the practices of (6)Wise Effort, which means appropriate and balanced effort rather than compulsive drive, workaholism or spiritual materialism; (7)Wise Attention, or mindfulness and presence of mind; and (8)Wise Concentration, or focus. (*Root of the Bodhi Tree: The Four Noble Truths and the Noble Eightfold Path*, ¶ 5)

Many of the psychotherapy approaches that explicitly teach mindfulness to clients do so within a larger context: Linehan (1993) talks about creating a *life worth living*, Hayes and Strosahl (1999) talk about *value-based living*, Kabat-Zinn (2005) presents a rich and well-rounded approach to mindfulness in every day life. But without a systematic attempt to include a larger view and path, it might be easy to default to *just practice mindfulness* without clarifying the goal or vision behind it. This may be more of a pitfall for therapists who teach mindfulness, but do not practice it, given the important findings of Kabat-Zinn (1995) and Segal, Williams, and Teasdale (2001) that their programs are less successful if the leaders are not regularly practicing mindfulness themselves.

Practiced in an isolated fashion, mindfulness may have its uses, but it may also lose some of its power. There might be a tendency towards self-aggression. Without an emphasis on *maitri*, a Sanskrit word meaning loving-kindness or *unconditional friendliness* towards one's experience (Wegela, 1994), one might become judgmental for not being mindful enough. An overly gain-oriented practice can serve to strengthen the sense of a separate, permanent self, and thus ultimately increase suffering. There could also be a tendency towards social withdrawal. Lacanian philosopher Slavoj Zizek (2005) has criticized Buddhism for encouraging people to develop an "inner distance and indifference to the mad dance of accelerated process" which allows us to "fully participate in the capitalist economy while retaining the appearance of sanity" (¶ 11-12).

However, there may be a natural corrective here. Mindfulness as an isolated practice unintegrated from the context of one's larger psychic and social life is hard to maintain. One may not be able to maintain a selfishly oriented meditation practice in the same way that one might a selfishly oriented exercise program. Meditation does not have the immediate reinforcement of an endorphin release, and may be harder to habituate to. The view of Buddhist practice which is founded on *bodhichitta*, "the radiant heart that is constantly and naturally, without self-consciousness, generating love and compassion for the benefit of others" (Mipham, 2003, p. 165), suggests something quite different from Zizek's view of the distanced and indifferent Buddhist, and something altogether more invigorating and self-sustaining.

There is another area of pitfall in this meeting between Buddhism and science. The scientific method, to an extent often unappreciated, is a probabilistic enterprise, which is to say it deals with uncertainties. Research can only ever suggest with varying degrees of probability the likelihood of something not being due to chance. With neuroscience related research, we are additionally confronted with the fact that the object of study is the most complex material thing in the known universe. We now know, for instance, that neural function, especially the function of complex things like cognition, emotion, and awareness, is often best understood as existing in pathways and modules rather than being isolated to a simple location. The problem is, with an estimate of roughly 200 billion neurons and 5,000-200,000 connections per neuron, there are a lot of pathways, which may not all be visible in current neuroimaging technology, although rapid developments in molecular biology may change that to a degree. This then is yet another level of pitfall: the uncertainty inherent in the still nascent technologies of neuroimaging. In addition to various technical issues, it becomes problematic if neuroimaging is used to indicate only *where* activity is occurring rather than asking what functional role the activity imaged reflects (Donaldson, 2004).

Conclusion

The conversation is still just beginning between neuroscience, Buddhism, and psychology. We are not certain where it will lead, but already it has suggested new models for what is happening in all three fields. The interweaving of first, third, and second person or interpersonal accounts of consciousness is likely to be fruitful. It will be interesting to see how ongoing developments in brain imaging facilitate more targeted interventions in psychotherapy and add more texture and nuance to our understanding of meditation.

At the same time, there is the danger that as these disciplines interact, a materialistic approach will become predominant. While there is nothing wrong with measuring outcomes in psychotherapy or studying the brain scans of meditators (the argument here is that these things can be useful), it is important to realize the limits of such investigations. It is crucial to make an effort not to be seduced into equating third person perspectives with first person, brain scans with feelings, or research findings with facts.

There is much to learn in both directions. Buddhism may be able to teach science some things: the power of the mind to effect change, the limitations of a grasping, materialistic orientation to reality, and the interdependence of all phenomena which does not allow one to separate the mind into parts without distortion. According to Buddhism, the fundamental nature of mind itself is basically good and cannot be improved on. If you meditate in order to reduce emotions, or in order to become someone other than yourself, you are misunderstanding Buddhist meditation. One may be simply reinforcing the hold of ego. Similarly, if you practice psychotherapy with an eye to obtaining certain observable results, while a legitimate and even appropriate endeavor in some settings, you necessarily constrain the possibilities of what might occur.

On the other hand, scientific and specifically neuroscientific inquiry may be able to enrich Buddhist practice and psychotherapy. Being able to see more clearly what's happening in the body, including the brain, as a result of various practices, experiences, and relationships will help enhance these disciplines. Despite their development in different arenas, Buddhist practice and psychology are fundamentally interested in things that are at least scientifically approachable: the alleviation of suffering, the promotion of happiness, and the nature of reality and mind. An orientation that is actively interested in multiple ways of approaching this topic—from the personal practice of mindfulness awareness disciplines, to the interpersonal practice of psychotherapy, to the objective information available from scientific studies—holds the most promise.

References

Amedi, A., Merabet, L. B., Bermpohl, F., & Pascual-Leone, A. (2005). The occipital cortex in the blind: Lessons about plasticity and vision. *Current Directions in Psychological Science, 14*, 306-312.

Amedi, A., Raz, N., Pianka, P., Malach, R., & Zohary, E. (2003). Early 'visual' cortex activation correlates with superior verbal memory performance in the blind. *Nature Neuroscience, 6*, 758-766.

Begley, S. (2007). *Train your mind, change your brain: How a new science reveals our extraordinary potential to change ourselves.* New York: Ballantine Books.

Birbaumer, N., Veit, R., Lotze, M., Erb, M., Hermann, C., Grodd, W., et al. (2005). Deficient fear conditioning in psychopathy: A functional magnetic resonance imaging study. *Archives of General Psychiatry, 62*, 799-805.

Blumenthal, J. A., Babyak, M. A., Moore, K. A., Craighead, W. E., Herman, S., Khatri, P., et al. (1999). Effects of exercise training on older patients with major depression. *Archives of Internal Medicine, 159*, 2349-56.

Cahn, B. R., & Polich, J. (2006). Meditation states and traits: EEG, ERP, and neuroimaging studies. *Psychological Bulletin, 132*, 180-211.

Caria, A., Veit, R., Sitaram, R., Lotze, M., Weiskopf, N., Grodd, W., et al. (2007). Regulation of anterior insular cortex activity using real-time fMRI. *NeuroImage, 35*, 1238-1246.

Chalmers, D. J. (1995). Facing up to the problem of consciousness. *The Journal of Consciousness Studies, 2*, 200-219.

Cozolino, L. (2002). *The neuroscience of psychotherapy: Building and rebuilding the human brain.* New York: W.W. Norton.

Crick, F. (1995). *The astonishing hypothesis: The scientific search for the soul.* New York: Scribner.

Damasio, A. (1994). *Descartes' error.* New York: Harcourt.

Damasio, A. (1999). *The feeling of what happens: Body and emotion in the making of consciousness.* New York: Harcourt.

Damasio, A. (2003). *Looking for Spinoza: Joy, sorrow and the feeling brain.* New York: Harcourt.

Das, S. (2005). Landscape of dharma: An overview of Buddhism and an appreciation of our tradition. Retrieved January 8, 2007 from http://www.dzogchen.org/teachings/talks/ndtapp.htm

Davidson, R. J. (2004). The neurobiology of personality and personality disorders. In D. S. Charney & E. J. Nester (Eds.), *Neurobiology of mental illness* (2nd ed; pp. 841-854). Oxford: Oxford University Press.

Davidson, R. J., Kabat-Zinn, J., Schumacher, J., Rosenkranz, M., Muller, D., Santorelli, S., et al. (2003). Alterations in brain and immune function produced by mindfulness meditation. *Psychosomatic Medicine, 65*, 564-570.

Davidson, R. J. (1998). Affective style and affective disorders: Perspectives from affective neuroscience. *Cognition and Emotion, 12*, 307-330.

deCharms, R. C., Maeda, F., Glover, G. H., Ludlow, D., Pauly, J. M., Soneji, D., et al. (2005). Control over brain activation and pain learned by using real-time functional MRI. *Proceedings of the National Academy of Science, 102*, 18626–18631.

Donaldson, D. (2004). Parsing brain activity with fMRI and mixed designs: What kind of a state is neuroimaging in? *Trends in Neuroscience, 27*, 442-444.

Ekman, P. (1999). Basic emotions. In T. Dalgleish & T. Power (Eds.) *The handbook of cognition and emotion* (pp. 45-60). Sussex, UK: John Wiley & Sons.

Epstein, M. (1994). *Thoughts without a thinker: Psychotherapy from a Buddhist perspective.* New York: Basic Books.

Eriksson, P. S., Perfilieva, E., Bjork-Eriksson, T., Alborn, A. M., Nordborg, C., Peterson, D. A., et al. (1998). Neurogenesis in the adult human hippocampus. *Nature Medicine, 4,* 1313-1317.

Freud, S. & Breuer, J. (1957). *Studies on hysteria.* (J. Strachey & A. Freud, Trans.). New York: Basic Books. (Original work published 1895)

Freud, S. (1961). *Beyond the pleasure principle.* (J. Strachey, Trans.). London: Hogarth Press. (Original work published 1920)

George, C., Kaplan, N., & Main, M. (1985). *The attachment interview for adults.* Unpublished manuscript.

Goldapple, K., Segal, Z., Garson, C., Lau, M., Bieling, P., Kennedy, S., et al. (2004). Modulation of cortical-limbic pathways in major depression: Treatment-specific effects of cognitive behavior therapy. *Archives of General Psychiatry, 61*, 34-41.

Hayes, S. C., Follette, V. M., & Linehan, M. M. (2004). *Mindfulness and acceptance: Expanding the cognitive behavioral tradition.* New York: Guilford.

Hayes, S. C., Strosahl, K. D., & Wilson, K. G. (1999). *Acceptance and commitment therapy: An experiential approach to behavior change.* New York: Guilford.

Hayward, J. H. & Varela, F. J. (2001). *Gentle bridges: Conversations with the Dalai Lama on the sciences of mind.* Boston: Shambhala.

James, W. (1950). *The principles of psychology.* (Vol. 1). Mineola, NY: Dover. (Original work published 1890)

Jenkins, W. M., Merzenich, M. M., Ochs, M. T., Allard, T., & Guic-Roble, E. (1990). Functional organization of primary somatosensory cortex in adult owl monkeys after behaviorally controlled tactile stimulation. *Journal of Comparative Neurology, 258*, 281-96.

Kabat-Zinn, J. (2005). *Full catastrophe living: Using the wisdom of your body and mind to face stress, pain, and illness.* New York: Random House.

Kandel, E. (2006). *In search of memory: The emergence of a new science of mind.* New York: W.W. Norton.

Kempermann, G., Kuhn, H. G., & Gage, F. H. (1997, April 3). More hippocampal neurons in adult mice living in an enriched environment. *Nature, 386,* 493-495.

Kolb, B. & Whishaw, I.Q. (2003). *Fundamentals of human neuropsychology.* (5th ed.) New York: Worth Publishers.

Lazar, S. W., Kerr, C. E., Wasserman, R. H., Gray, J. R., Greve, D. N., Treadway, M. T., et al. (2005). Meditation experience is associated with increased cortical thickness. *Neuroreport, 16,* 1893-1897.

LeDoux, J. (1998). *The emotional brain: The mysterious underpinnings of emotional life.* New York: Simon & Schuster.

LeDoux, J. (2002). *Synaptic self: How our brains become who we are.* New York: Viking.

Linehan, M. (1993). *Cognitive-behavioral treatment of borderline personality disorder.* New York: Guilford.

Lutz, A., Greischar, L. L., Rawlings, N. B., Ricard, M., & Davidson, R. J. (2004). Long-term meditators self-induce high-amplitude gamma synchrony during mental practice. *Proceedings of the National Academy of Science, 101,* 16369-16373.

Lykken, D. & Tellegen, A. (1996). Happiness is a stochastic phenomenon. *Psychological Science, 7,* 186-190.

Lykken, D. (2000). *Happiness: The nature and nurture of joy and contentment.* New York: St. Martin's Press.

Malberg, J. E. & Schechter, L. E. (2005). Increasing hippocampal neurogenesis: A novel mechanism for antidepressant drugs. *Current Pharmaceutical Design, 11,* 145-155.

Mipham, S. (2003). *Turning the mind into an ally.* New York: Penguin Books.

Molino, A. (1999). *The couch and the tree: Dialogues in psychoanalysis and Buddhism.* New York: North Point Press.

Naqvi, N., Rudrauf, D., Damasio, H., & Bechara, A. (2007, January 26). Damage to the insula disrupts addiction to cigarette smoking. *Science, 26,* 531-534.

Panksepp, J. (1998). *Affective neuroscience: The foundations of human and animal emotions.* New York: Oxford University Press.

Pembrey, M. (1996). Imprinting and transgenerational modulation of gene expression: human growth as a model. *Acta Genetic Medical Gemellol, 45,* 111.

Ramachandran, V. S. (2007). The neurology of self-awareness. Retrieved July 29, 2007 from http://www.edge.org/3rd_culture/ramachandran07/ramachandran07_index.html

Rencanzone, G. H., Schreiner, C. E., & Merzenich, M. M. (1993). Plasticity in the frequency representation of primary auditory cortex following discrimination training in adult owl monkeys. *Journal of Neuroscience, 13*, 87-103.

Rizzolatti, G. & Craighero, L. (2004). The mirror-neuron system. *Annual Review of Neuroscience, 27*, 169-92.

Rizzolatti, G., Fadiga, L., Gallese, V. & Fogassi, L. (1996). Premotor cortex and the recognition of motor actions. *Cognitive Brain Research, 3*, 131-141.

Sadato, N., Pascual-Leone, A., Grafmani, J., Ibañez, V., Deiber, M-P., Dold, G., et al. (1996, April 3). Activation of the primary visual cortex by Braille reading in blind subjects, *Nature, 380*, 526-528.

Santarelli, L., Saxe, M., Gross, C., Surget, A., Battaglia, F., Dulawa, S., et al. (2003, August 8). Requirement of hippocampal neurogenesis for the behavioral effects of antidepressants, *Science, 301*, 757-805.

Schore, A. (1994). *Affect regulation and the origin of the self: The neurobiology of emotional development.* Hillsdale, NJ: Erlbaum.

Segal, Z. V., Williams, J. M., & Teasdale, J. T. (2001). *Mindfulness-based cognitive therapy for depression: A new approach to preventing relapse.* New York: Guilford.

Seligman, M. (2004). *Authentic happiness: Using the new positive psychology to realize your potential for lasting fulfillment.* New York: Simon & Schuster.

Siegel, D. J. (1999). *The developing mind: Toward a neurobiology of interpersonal experience.* New York: Guilford.

Siegel, D. J. (2001). Toward an interpersonal neurobiology of the developing mind: Attachment relationships, "mindsight," and neural integration. *Infant Mental Health Journal, 22*, 67-94.

Siegel, D. J. (2007). *The mindful brain: Reflection and attunement in the cultivation of well-being.* New York: W. W. Norton.

Slife, B., Wiggins, B. J. & Graham, J. T. (2005). Avoiding an EST monopoly: Toward a pluralism of methods and philosophies and methods. *Journal of Contemporary Psychotherapy, 35*, 83 – 97.

Solms, M. & Turnbull, O. (2002). *The brain and the inner world: An introduction to the neuroscience of subjective experience.* New York: Other Press.

Spotnitz, H. (1979). Narcissistic countertransference. *Contemporary Psychoanalysis, 15*, 545-559.

Stern, D. (2004). *The present moment in psychotherapy and everyday life.* New York: W.W. Norton.

Straubea, T., Mentzelb, H., & Miltner, W. (2005). Common and distinct brain activation to threat and safety signals in social phobia. *Neuropsychobiology, 52*, 163-168.

Suzuki, D. T., Fromm, E., & DeMartino, R. (1963). *Zen Buddhism and psychoanalysis.* New York: Grove Press.

Suzuki, S. (1973). *Zen mind, beginner's mind.* New York: Weatherhill.

Trungpa, C. (1969). *Meditation in action.* Boston: Shambhala.

Trungpa, C. (1973). *Cutting through spiritual materialism.* Boston: Shambhala.
Ury, H. L., Nitschke, J. B., Dolski, I., Jackson, D. C., Dalton, K. M., Mueller, C. J., et. al. (2004). Making a life worth living: Neural correlates of well-being. *Psychological Science, 15,* 367-372.
van Praag, H., Kempermann,, G. & Gage, F. H. (1999). Running increases cell proliferation and neurogenesis in the adult mouse dentate gyrus. *Nature Neuroscience, 2,* 266-270.
van Praag, H., Schinder, A. F., Chrisite, B. R., Toni, N., Palmer, T. D., & Gage, F. H. (2002, February 28). Functional neurogenesis in the adult hippocampus. *Nature, 415,* 1030-1034.
Wallace, B. A. (2003). *Buddhism with an attitude: The Tibetan seven-point mind training.* Ithaca, NY: Snow Lion Publications.
Wallace, B. A. (2006). *Toward the first revolution in mind sciences.* Retrieved November 25, 2007 from http://www.youtube.com/watch?v=AhntEOGslbs
Wallace, B. A. (2007a). *Contemplative science: Where Buddhism and neuroscience converge.* New York: Columbia University Press.
Wallace, B. A. (2007b). *Hidden dimensions: The unification of physics and consciousness.* New York: Columbia University Press.
Wallace, B. A. (2007c). *The shamatha project.* Retrieved November 24, 2007 from http://www.sbinstitute.com/research_Shamatha.html
Wegela, K. (1994). Contemplative psychotherapy: A path of uncovering brilliant sanity. *Journal of Contemplative Psychotherapy, 9,* 27-51.
Wegela, K. (1996). *How to be a help instead of a nuisance: Practical approaches to giving support, service & encouragement to others.* Boston: Shambhala.
Werker, J. F. & Tees, R. C. (1983). Developmental changes across childhood in the perception of non-native speech sounds. *Canadian Journal of Psychology, 37,* 278-286.
Wilber, K. (2000). *Integral psychology: Consciousness, spirit, psychology, therapy.* Boston: Shambhala.
Witkiewitz, K., Marlatt, G. A., & Walker, D. (2005). Mindfulness-based relapse prevention for alcohol and substance use disorders. *Journal of Cognitive Psychotherapy, 19,* 211-230.
Zizek, S. (2005). The revenge of global finance. *In These Times, 20,* 12-15.

Part 2: Path

7

Large Group Process: Grounding Buddhist and Psychological Theory in Personal Experience

Francis J. Kaklauskas
Elizabeth A. Olson

> The attic fan rattles in its perfect tin house.... The mind is more than a simple container, the junk drawer beside the stove.... The Eternal City, Brodsky writes, is like a gigantic old brain, one that's grown a little weary of the world. And what have we here? Tarnished keys. A chipped teardrop from some dining room's chandelier. The trick must be to love both the blade & the air it shatters.
> - *From Eternal City* by Kathleen Graber[1]

When Chögyam Trungpa moved to England in 1963, he and Western psychologists immediately became intrigued with one another. He was curious to learn about how Western culture understood the workings of the mind; he also hoped that his 2,500 year old tradition could contribute to Western psychology (Midal, 2004). Although both traditions study human suffering, cognitions, and behavior, the approaches towards training were markedly different. As a monk in Tibet, he trained extensively in both meditation practices and scholarly activities. During certain periods of each year, the monks intensively practiced meditation, while at other times of the year formal academic study became the primary focus. He was surprised to find that Western psychology, compared to his Tibetan Buddhist tradition, strongly valued theory over personal experience. Even the experiential psychoanalytic trainings of that time required only several hundred hours of personal treatment, while most monks engaged in thousands of hours of meditative practices as part of their training. While Trungpa offered many contributions to Western psychology, his initial impression continued to influence his primary advice

---

[1] Originally Published in *American Poetry Review, 36(5)* September/October, 2007

to therapists. Trungpa suggested that academic learning be balanced with contemplative practices and in depth personal examination (Midal, 2004).

Building upon Trungpa's recommendations, Naropa's Masters of Arts in Contemplative Psychotherapy (MACP) program was, in part, modeled after his monastic experience. MACP students are expected to meditate regularly in addition to becoming proficient in the concepts and practices of western psychology. The students engage in intensive contemplative practices such as the Maitri program each year, while at other times focusing on academic learning, such as completing and presenting one's master thesis. As in monastic students, MACP students embark together on this rigorous two method journey and, if possible, stay in the same cohort until graduation.

Program History

The clinical training program at the Naropa University has always had a strong cohort and community emphasis. The students from each incoming year take all of their academic classes together, in addition to spending ten weeks together in meditation retreats through out the three year program. When the program started in 1975, many of the program's designers were simultaneously psychotherapists and students of Chögyam Trungpa. The American psychological zeitgeist of this time included therapeutic community models, personal growth-oriented group work, and systems theory. The collectivist, societal view found in Asian and other cultures, in addition to the allure of Buddhist thought, was also more fully entering the American consciousness. This amalgamation fashioned the Naropa University's passion for the cohort model.

The large group process class developed later as faculty and students grew increasingly interested in the power of large groups. The Naropa large group model continues in the earlier Naropa University tradition by incorporating influences across the spectrum of psychological theory and research, with a strong emphasis on Buddhist thought. This chapter shares some of the program's historical developments and foundational ideas regarding the experiential large group process class. The aim is to introduce the reader to a selection of primary influences on this approach.

Buddhism is Distinct from Psychology

Many Western and Buddhist ideas appear similar; however, to comprehend Buddhist thought only through associations to Western ideas will not provide a proper understanding. The similarities presented in this paper demonstrate the manner in which Buddhist and Western psychological ideas have shaped the large group process class. Although the authors hope to provide a basic introduction to both traditions, more

7. Large Group Process

in depth analysis demonstrates the discreteness of these ideas. Buddhist traditions have embodied a multicausal and impermanent view of the self and the world for over 2,500 years, yet Western languages and culture developed a markedly different perception of the self. Similar to the view of physical objects, the self in the Western psychological world traditionally has been understood as discrete, stable, and enduring. Only through rigorous meditation practice can one gain the proper understanding of Buddhist thought (Rahula, 1994).

Buddhism has acknowledged the practicality of the Western view through the discussion of relative and absolute reality. The mind comprehends the self and the world in a relative and discrete manner. This allows for communication regarding people, objects, and the study of cause and effect. This relative view is necessary for human interactions. Buddhism utilizes this relative view for practicality, but understands that this view is a construction that rests upon the ground of the absolute view. In absolute view, multicausal phenomena arise and fall away, and no enduring discrete self or physical object exists (Rahula, 1994).

The Dalai Lama (2005) outlined three features of the world: *matter* or physical objects, as is the focus of the Western and relative view, *mind* or subjective phenomenological experience, and *abstract mental formations*. The Dalai Lama drew on the philosopher Karl Popper's work regarding the first world, the second world, and the third world as a type of concurrent validity for these Buddhist beliefs. The Dalai Lama encourages comparative discussion and believes the ideas of Buddhism should be corroborated through evaluations by multiple western methodologies including philosophy and science.

The Three Jewels: Buddha, Dharma, and Sangha.

When a student of Buddhism desires to deepen his understanding, the three jewels of Buddha, dharma, and sangha are viewed as primary teachers (Gyatso, 2006; Trungpa, 1973, 2004). The Buddha's teachings suggested that the possibility of compassion, clarity of thought, and ethical action exists within each person. Each person is a Buddha and possesses brilliant sanity. While the Western tradition's primary goal is to increase a student's knowledge base, in the contemplative tradition this is balanced with the rigorous training of one's mind through meditation practices, so that understanding, compassion, enthusiasm, insight, and wisdom are revealed (Nhat Hanh, 2003; Trungpa, 2004).

The narrow definition of Dharma refers to the understanding and teachings of past and present Buddhist teachers and the study of Buddhist writings; however, many contemporary Buddhist teachers believe this approach limits communication and understanding across cultures (Gyatso, 2005, 2006; Suzuki, 1960, 1973; Trungpa, 2005). With this in mind, these teachers believe that through the study of

Western psychology, literature, and culture, they will be better able to communicate Buddhism to a Western audience. As part of this cross cultural dialogue, the meaning of Dharma has expanded to incorporate the knowledge and wisdom of other traditions. The Dalai Lama (2005) has strongly endorsed the need for kinship between Buddhist thought and scientific inquiry. When a reporter asked the Dalai Lama what would happen if Western science could disprove an aspect of Buddhist thought, the Dalai Lama responded that Buddhism would need to change in order to incorporate this new scientific understanding. From this perspective the Dharma is inclusive of Western science and the study of psychology (Gyatso, 2005, 2006; Jung, 1994; Suzuki, 1960, 1994; Trungpa, 2005).

The Buddhist teachings on sangha are at the heart of the Naropa contemplative training program's intensive cohort model. During his lifetime, a large group of individuals followed the Buddha on his journey throughout northern India; they set up camps around the location where the Buddha taught. This community of students was referred to as the *sangha*. The word *sangha* is repeatedly found in early Buddhist texts from the closely related languages of Sanskrit and Pali, and is most commonly translated as *assembly*, *community*, or *association* (Rahula, 1994). While the most limited understanding of sangha refers only to a community of monks practicing Buddhism, most scholars and teachers view sangha as those who follow a Buddhist, spiritual, or human growth path. Contemporary Buddhist teachers understand sangha to include all beings of the past, present, and future (Gyatso, 1984, 2005; Nhat Hanh, 2003; Trungpa, 2005). The goal of this wide view is to expand the practice of cultivating compassion and awareness to encompass all sentient beings.

The Naropa MACP program conceptualizes sangha as consisting of the entire community of students, professors, administrators, and also extends to the wider society. This vision is similar to the therapeutic community models postulated by Maxwell Jones and Thomas Main (Clarke, 2004). From this perspective, if one is open to examining one's reactions, all people and events can be seen as teachers and each moment is a chance to work constructively in the world. Buddhism is not a system of dogmatic beliefs, but rather a journey of understanding one's own experience. One of the most commonly repeated teachings of the Buddha stressed that one should believe nothing unless it resonates with their reason and experience (Gyatso, 1984, 2005; Trungpa, 1973, 1976). Similar to the dharma discourses of the Tibetan monastic tradition, Naropa students are asked to bring forth their ideas and questions, and engage in public discussions in order to sharpen their understanding of philosophical and psychological principles.

Community Meetings

With the importance of sangha in mind, MACP initially used the community meeting model from the therapeutic community and hospital

7. Large Group Process

traditions (Clarke, 2004; Rice, 1993). These groups of about a hundred included all students, faculty, and support staff. Following a brief period for program updates to be voiced, the community meeting would open into an unstructured large group in which participants shared thoughts and feelings about the program, each other, world events, or other topics. Hierarchical themes were common in these meetings. Discussion often revolved around an inquiry into the degree to which a graduate training program in psychology should be a democratic process where the students' ideas are valued equally with those of the more experienced faculty. Some meetings materialized into esoteric discussions of the proper understanding of a Buddhist idea, while others brought forth personal confessional disclosures that were unnecessarily revealing of the speaker.

This large group meeting was unlike any other interpersonal event in that participants' feelings were stronger and rationality vacationed. These meetings were always lively and appeared to encourage some additional cohesion among participants. In addition, they led to some productive administrative program changes. During and after these meeting, the MACP community discharged the built up tension with an endless supply of unprocessed feelings and interpretations of group dynamics. While the community meeting was always a provocative experience, the program's growth put increasing time restrictions on the participants. Eventually the community meeting was replaced by multiple administrative work groups devoted to program development. Although the additional structure and clarity of goals led to productive administrative work, the absence of the community group left members of the community longing for the excitement, power, and mystery of large group process experiences.

Development of an Academic Large Group Process Model

While the popularity of the therapeutic community models have significantly decreased over the last several decades, the availability and popularity of large group process training experiences has increased. Organizational consultants are increasingly using large group meetings in their work (Cummings & Worley, 2001, 2004). National and international psychology conferences are also increasingly making opportunities available for attendees to meet in large gatherings. Following repeated requests from students, the MACP program established the large group process class as a format to work with and process the intensity of the cohort model. The initial experiments included having the cohorts meet with faculty or outside consultants for a series of groups. These processes were generally facilitated by the particular training of the group leader. When the large group process class was added to the curriculum, the need for a model reflective of the program's values became apparent.

Building on the values of the past, an inclusive, and multi-theoretical approach began to take form.

For the development of this class, three primary Western academic traditions were brought on board: psychodynamic large group theory, industrial organizational psychology, and social psychology. Each of these models are academically inclusive and tolerant, as well as open to continual development ensuring a healthy coexistence with the contemplative program's emphasis on Tibetan Buddhist teachings. Further, the veracity of these models has withstood systematic and comprehensive study and the combination of these streams of knowledge are complimentary.

Prior to enrolling in the large group process class, the students have studied meditation and participated in an intensive retreat. In addition, students have completed courses in Buddhist psychology, group psychotherapy, family therapy, and the history of psychology. The students also bring their individual life histories and the history of the cohort into the room. All of these form the matrix of influences emerging moment to moment in the large group process experience. In the class, each academic tradition is viewed as providing a useful lens to understanding the dynamic of large group behavior while no one tradition in particular is accepted as doctrine. The goal of the class is to expand the students' comprehensive knowledge of psychology, and when possible, to ground these ideas in personal experience.

Experiential Learning

The large group provides a unique environment with countless opportunities for learning (Shields, 2001). Dé Mare and Schollberger (2003) postulated that in large group, the human mind is revealed as a mix of dialogue and free association. Large group experiences allow participants to better understand themselves and group dynamics. Large group also provides the object of the group itself, against which various psychological ideas can be examined. Although a large group may contain therapeutic elements, the goal of most large groups, across theoretical conceptualizations, is to move towards learning and personal growth. Recent neuropsychological research on learning has demonstrated the enduring Buddhist belief that experience is more important than knowledge. By providing an emotional experience within the learning environment, students more fully encode didactic understanding (Begley, 2007; Siegel, 2007; Siegel & Hartzell, 2003; Weiss, 2000).

The importance of being a group member as preparation for clinical work has repeatedly been endorsed (Hopper, Kaklauskas, & Green, 2008; Welber, 1988). As Bion (1962) clarified in *Learning from Experience,* remaining open to the continuous transformation of emotions and ideas is not just the property of psychotherapy, but the business of life. The Buddhist path is also not psychotherapy. The goal of meditation practice and training is not designed for specific symptom reduction, but rather to deepen understanding of the interplay between the phenomenological world and the mind in order to be of greater service to others (Tsoknyi, 2004).

Psychodynamic Theories of Large Group Dynamics

Psychodynamic theory often uses deductive reasoning to form explanations of behavioral phenomena with a causal emphasis on a biological drive and personality theory perspectives. Psychodynamic ideas are often primarily hermeneutic theory-driven explanations of phenomena, and, although very informative, many of the psychodynamic concepts are difficult to measure due to current methodological restraints. Industrial organizational and social psychologies approach human experience from a different angle and use both descriptive and statistical methodologies with deductive reasoning to inform exploratory hypotheses. Proponents of these various research methodologies have been dismissive of other approaches; however, by drawing upon the common findings, the resultant dialogue strengthens and broadens knowledge and understanding (Kaklauskas, 2005).

Le Bon's (1895) *Psychologie des Foules* has become an oft used starting point for discussion of large group phenomena. Although not translated into English until 1920 under the title *The Crowd: The Study of the Popular Mind*, Le Bon's ideas circulated throughout academic circles at the turn of last century (Triest, 2003). Although complex, much of Le Bon's work remains theoretically sensible even in today's contemporary context. His most popular ideas suggest that an individual is moved by forces outside of his awareness or consciousness:

> Whoever be the individuals that compose [a large group], however like or unlike be their mode of life, their occupations, their character or their intelligence, the fact that they have been transformed into a group puts them in possession of a sort of collective mind which makes them feel, think, and act in a manner quite different from that in which each individual of them would feel, think, and act were he in a state of isolation. (Le Bon, 1895/1920, p. 73)

Continuing, Le Bon pointed to the experience of an individual as he or she becomes part of a group:

> the disappearance of the conscious personality, the predominance of the unconscious personality, the turning by means of suggestion and contagion of feelings and ideas in an identical direction, the tendency to immediately transform the suggested ideas into acts... He is no longer himself, but has

become an automaton who has ceased to be guided by his will. (Le Bon, 1895/1920 p. 77)

Other topics discussed by Le Bon regarding large group include the pull towards extreme and concretized thinking patterns, changes in behavior towards authority, and interpersonal and group tolerance (Le Bon, 1895/1920).

Having adopted Le Bon's (1895) interests, McDougall (1920) added new views that included the increased frequency of primitive behaviors in unstructured groups and the level of increased civility in more organized settings (Triest, 1988). Freud drew upon Le Bon's and McDougall's observations and added his ideas regarding primitive drives, defenses, and structural theory in *Group Psychology and the Analysis of the Ego* (1922/1959) and *Civilization and Its Discontents* (1930/1961). Freud suggested that group dynamics are related to primitive drives and transference and noted the draw towards an idealizing of the societal leaders. Both Freud and McDougall were influenced by the emergence of anthropological study during the early part of the last century. Each asserted that while some cultural groups may appear primitive and difficult to understand from a European perspective, these groups have functioning rules, conventions, norms, and traditions.

After World War II, as individuals struggled to understand the horrors of the Holocaust and the destructiveness of the war, interest in understanding large group dynamics dramatically increased. Pioneered by Maxwell Jones and Thomas Mane, England led the formation of therapeutic community work (Clarke, 2004). Bion, Rickman, and Foulkes worked with returning veterans in large groups at the Northfield Hospital and brought forth ideas that remain central to the psychodynamic understanding of large group dynamics (Harrison, 2000). Drawing from the work of the Gestalt movement, the large group setting was not focused on any particular individual; rather, the community and organization became the client to be understood. Therapeutic community large group meetings served multiple purposes from sharing information to the disrobing of secrecies behind decision making and power structures. Large group conductors and participants were viewed as equals in the creation of the emerging group process.

Perhaps the best known psychodynamic ideas relating to group functioning come from the work of Wilfred Bion and Sigismund Foulkes. Bion created a canon of work that powerfully influenced the future of psychodynamic large group literature. Bion's (1961) classic text, *Experiences in Group*, is an exciting and witty qualitative analysis of the unstructured groups he conducted at the Tavistock clinic in London after World War II. He proposed that groups continually move from the group task to three basic assumptions: dependency upon the leadership, primitive flight/fight responses, and the process of pairing (Schermer, 1985). Bion also conceived the group's primary task as a movement from not-knowing to knowing (Billow, 2002). Miller and Rice (1967) added the widely accepted notion that a substage of counter-dependence occurs in the later stages of dependency. According to this view, the group rebels against its dependency needs and rejects the object of the leader through ignoring or minimizing the leader's importance (Billow, 2003).

While Bion eventually lost faith that groups could overcome their inherent destructiveness and chose instead to focus on individual character theory, Foulkes remained optimistic and active in small and large group work (Brown, 1992). Contrary to Bion's movement toward the individual psyche, Foulkes championed the group matrix: the dance of interactions between individual psyche, group mind, and social context (Brown, 1992). He suggested that the group rather than the therapist provided the treatment and used the term *conductor* in place of leader (Foulkes, 1964). Foulkes (1975) indicated that the group should be viewed with patience like a child learning to speak. Over time, the group progresses from childish individual monologues into mature group dialogues.

Building upon the work of Bion and Foulkes, Earl Hopper (2003) elucidated a fourth basic assumption particularly applicable to large group phenomena: incohesion or aggregation/massification. In a large group, this aggregation process occurs as members align together around beliefs, feelings, and behaviors. This creates a battle between individuals and subgroups for power, moral superiority, and the future direction of the collective. Hopper proposed that such common destructive elements in this process were scapegoating, assassination of others' characters, and psychic banishment. Eventually the spokesperson of varied subgroups will attempt to destroy the formal leadership and take control of the collective. In this stage, more formal and often unconscious patterns of behavioral norms are established. Stumbling upon a fitting metaphor during a trip to Ireland, Hopper pointed to aggregation as a collection of separate, unique potatoes while massification would be a bowl of mashed potatoes. Ultimately, individuals in a group alternate between the desires for both (Hopper, 2007).

Collective Unconscious and Roles

Carl Jung's construct of the collective unconscious is frequently misunderstood. While similar to Freud's belief in a personal unconscious, Jung broadened his ideas to include the "reservoir of the experiences of our species" (Jung, 1921). This primordial and universal group of archetypes is enacted by various participants in the large group. Subgroups often align within such Jungian spectrums as masculine/feminine energy and introversion/extroversion. In other instances, the group may attempt to identify a specific student's behavior as emerging from this collective unconscious in such roles as the hero, the devil, the scapegoat, or the crone.

The discussion of roles is a common theme in the class. As elaborated upon in later group analytic literature, each group needs individuals to fulfill roles to function effectively (Foulkes & Anthony, 1957). This idea was later expanded by the small and large group work of Yvonne Agazarian (Agazarian, 1997; Agazarian & Gant, 2000; Agazarian & Peters, 1981) in her *living human systems* and *system centered* perspectives. According to these perspectives, the progressive shifting of functional roles in nature's adaptive living organisms manifests continually in group process. While functional role taking can be adaptive for both the individual and the group, role locks occur when a group member stops acting and being seen in his complexity and instead becomes identified solely as a role. Common roles may include the voice of discontent, the sad participant, or the caretaker (Agazarian, 1997). Agazarian's solution to this dilemma corresponds closely to the contemplative psychological practice of bringing awareness to resolve impasses. When the group and the individual can identify the roles and the interdependent causation, roles are loosened or dropped. Similar to other large group theorists, Agazarian stressed the role of projective identification in this process. While an individual may not usually act as the role leader, the unconscious needs of the other participants for a leader can lead to atypical behaviors in participants.

Although projective process is the common explanation for the emergence of new behaviors and feelings in the large group, the contemplative perspective hinges on the concept of *exchange*. Given the Buddhist view of separation as illusion, individuals are continually open to the feelings of other group members (Wegela, 1988). Through awareness of one's phenomenological experience and the ability to skillfully communicate, these role-suctions and illogical feelings can be explored and better understood. This training is essential for clinicians, for just as psychodynamic thinkers deeply believe in the continuous occurrence of transference, contemplative clinicians remain aware of this exchange process to inform their work.

Social Unconscious

The social unconscious asserts that individuals and groups are intensely affected by societal and cultural forces and constraints that remain outside of awareness (Hopper, 1981). These societal and cultural restraints can be beneficial or deleterious, as many unexamined norms of behavior can be helpful to communication processes and community functioning (Hopper, 2003). The goal is to bring increased awareness to these forces in order to better understand why the large group acts as it does. Often, beliefs and myths of past generations continue to emerge in the present. Archaic American concepts of individualism and self-reliance as well as the Puritan beliefs of faith and sin repeatedly affect the large group behavior through the unconscious perpetuation of blindly accepted

7. Large Group Process

shared values and norms. Further, it is the depth of this social conditioning that has, in part, led to the difficulty Westerners have understanding many Buddhist ideas.

As students gain increasing awareness of negative feelings in large group, the possible roots of aggression may be explored. While such primary drives as sex and aggression, elucidated by Freud (1920/1961), Kernberg (2003), and many other psychoanalytic thinkers, are distasteful to many students, most are willing to accept the object relations perspective of Fairbairn (1952) and Winnicott (1965). Providing an even more convincing resonance, Adler's views (1929) on belonging and self-actualization inspire the way many students prefer to understand member participation. For example, students find Foulkes' idea (1975) that each group member of the group is driven not by innate aggression, but by the desire to form meaningful relationship as more palatable and useful for framing group interactions. Holding Foulkes' view, the leader may be able to understand and resolve destructive behaviors such as maladaptive attempts for intimacy, cohesion, and cooperation.

Group members take up the work of examining their experience through various large group theoretical perspectives. Pines (2000) suggested that the destructive power of the collective experience occurs through a heightening of projective processes that result in extreme intrapersonal and interpersonal chaos. Nitsun (1996) proposed that regression is connected with ideological controls for safety. System-centered views and dialogue group perspectives hold that difficulties arise mainly from miscommunication; the leader's task is to continue to elicit detailed emotional experience from the members while highlighting similar themes and feelings between opposing subgroups (Agazarian & Carter, 1993).

Challenges of Membership

The challenge of membership in large group training is parallel to the challenge of the individual in society. While in Bion's stage of fight/flight the individual feels drawn to take control or abandon the process in search of security and order, but the individual must resolve this dilemma by eventually gaining an understanding of how he or she can effectively influence others and also how impotent he or she may be in a collective (Schneider & Weinberg, 2003). de Maré (1989) stressed that to think clearly and contribute to the process of either a large training group or society is the challenge of citizenship. As the individual becomes better able to work constructively in the large group training, he or she becomes more accurate and effective in working in the larger societal context (de Maré, 2003).

Large Group and Organizational Development

For decades, organizational psychologists have used large group formats as part of organizational development consultation (Cummings & Worley, 2004). This format offers many benefits: an open forum in which all voices can be heard, an opportunity to directly discuss varied perceptions about organizational dynamics, and the placement of responsibility for the direction of the organization onto its members. Depending upon the organizational goals, the consultant chooses the appropriate amount of structure. When the goals are well defined, such as teaching communication skills, the consultant may provide a combination of psychoeducation and experimental processes. The Naropa large group class is significantly influenced by the process consultation models of Saul Eisen (2005) and David Campbell (1999). According to these views, in a less structured encounter, the organization and its members enact their strengths and challenges. Common topics the consultant addresses are communication styles, cultural norms and taboos, and the stages and challenges of organizational development. Process consultation is the continuous unfolding of new levels of disclosure and understanding; it seeks to bring into communication and awareness the formerly unspoken and unknown. In this way, visibility is brought to the invisible (Agazarian & Peters, 1995; Gant & Agazarian, 2005).

Large group consultations capture an organizational snapshot and seek to provide perspective by placing the present moment into a larger temporal perspective. The influence of iconic figures, myths, and legends of the past can be re-examined for current relevance and enduring core values can be re-established (Smith & Simmons, 1983). *Futuring* or visioning discussions help to unlock the potential in the organization (Cummings & Worley, 2001). The tension between realistic and unrealistic fantasies about the future moves the process from being abstract and idyllic to concrete and realistic. The qualities of the relationships between the members in an organization may be the most important influence in achieving group satisfaction, and in the large group all participants play a role in the present relational texture.

Another common theme in large group consultation work is deciphering the effects of the environment on the organization. In the large group class, students examine the effects of close events, such as the last class that they attended, views regarding the professors' level of competence, administrative edicts, and past cohort events upon current group dynamics. The influences of external world events, such as the country being at war, are also discussed. From a Buddhist perspective, the mind's tendency to fixate on past events and to move into hopes and fears about the future undermines the ultimate goal of uncovering the reality of how things actually are (Trungpa, 2005). In the large group process class, the members enact this tension as they strive to avoid getting lost in the world of abstract ideas, and instead remain aware of the present moment and their current experience.

While remaining unstructured enough to allow for new discoveries, the large group process class has defined goals and consistent form in order to lower the anxiety of participants (Kaul & Bender, 1994; Rice, 1993). Because this class shares many goals with leadership trainings, the large group process class syllabus is drawn significantly from organizational psychology models. The empirically researched approaches and best practice principles of effective management and leadership training are adapted into this new setting (Cummings & Worely, 2001; Gibber, Carter, & Goldsmith, 2000; McCauley, Moxeley, & Velsor, 1998). The student goals listed in the large group include increasing self-awareness of how to interpret the behavior of others, how one's behavior effects others, and increasing knowledge of group and systemic dynamics.

Students are also asked to become citizens of the group (Chazen, 1991; de Maré 2003). Hopper (2003) summarized citizenship in a large group as being, "willing and able to try to create the social, cultural and political conditions that are necessary to move towards the development and maintenance of hopeful attitudes for others as well as oneself" (p. 200). The member's first step is to understand the group's current state to the best of his or her ability. According to Bion (1961), in spite of one's inevitably frustrated efforts to meet the individual's personal needs, the needs of others in the group, and the needs of the group as a whole, one remains a group member with the need to participate and belong. Bion's quote harkens back to Klein's (1975) depressive position that integrating the good and bad of objects is an accurate and also heartbreaking understanding of living in reality. Akin to this journey of citizenship, Trungpa (1988) offered ideas on secular warriorship:

> Although the Warrior's life is dedicated to helping others, he realizes that he will never be able to completely share his experience with others. The fullness of his experience is his own, and he must live with his own truth. Yet he is more and more in love with the world. That combination of love affair and loneliness is what enables the Warrior to constantly reach out to help others. By renouncing his private world, the Warrior discovers a greater universe and a fuller and fuller broken heart. (p. 69)

This paradox of aloneness and connectedness is found repeatedly in Buddhist thought and ideas on citizenship.

Large group membership and the practice of citizenship are an ideal situation to practice the Buddhist paramitas of the Mahayana path of the Bhodisattva (Trungpa, 1973). Members are asked to have *generosity* that transcends irritation and defensiveness and allow others into their world. *Discipline* is the practice through not resorting to habitual cognitive, emotional, and behavioral responses. The traditional metaphor for the third paramita of *patience* is walking like an elephant. Members practice avoiding destructive impulsiveness and rigid avoidance, but seek a way to steadily and continuously engage with the group. The forth paramita of *energy* reveals that life is a continually unfolding and creative process. Each moment is fresh and can be joyful; if one remains awake, there is never a dull moment. The fifth paramita *meditation* is staying open in the present and being willing to honestly acknowledge one's experience and one's surrounding. *Meditation* is not a blissful or trance experience, but the practice of accepting whatever arises. The sixth paramita is *prajna* (knowledge or wisdom). This is closely linked with *upaya* (skillful means), and is the primary focus of students' large group experience. Large group membership provides the perfect, relative, state of affairs for the exploration of *prajna* and *upaya*. Prajna reflects a type of knowing that creates the possibility of accepting the world as it is. It is not an educational or technical accomplishment, but one that emerges from being present in the moment (Trungpa, 2004, 2005). Prajna moves beyond well fitting schemas or insightful interpretations. While the journey towards prajna is filled with educational learning, the actual experience is separate from ego, academic knowledge, or cognitive strategy.

Part of the power of group is that it offers the possibility for learning and wisdom. Group members are always attempting to move from the unknown to the known (Billow, 2002). The large group provides a unique opportunity for developing the humility needed to develop prajna and to actually understand the group dynamics. Rarely is any one member's view accepted without revision or challenge. Participants are often stunned when their ideas about the group's process are disputed or challenged, and more insightful alternatives are offered. Through this occurrence, participants realize the limitations of their ideas. From the perspective of contemplative psychology, this process of diminishing certitude and heightening compassion and curiosity is a prerequisite for the development of prajna.

From the open space of prajna, upaya is born. Frequently translated as *skillful means*, upaya is predicated on the notion that understanding opens the door for wise action. In the group experience, students are encouraged to consider skillful means for participating as a citizen in the group's unfolding process. Upaya does not mean attempting to show how intelligent or insightful one is, but rather to move the group process compassionately forward toward greater understanding and insight. The practice of developing skillful means is inevitably awkward and filled with misguided steps. Students are encouraged to see their relational mistakes with compassion towards self and others and as opportunities to further refine their communication skills.

The practice of skillful means includes taking time to predict how one's behavior may affect others. Elaborating on this, Trungpa delineated

7. Large Group Process

the similarities and differences present in the relationship between upaya and prajna:

> These two qualities, in fact, are sometimes compared to the two wings of a bird. Upaya is also described in the scriptures as being like a hand, which is skillful, and prajna as being axlike, because it is sharp and penetrating. Without the ax it would be impossible to cut wood: one would simply hurt one's hand. So one may have the skillful means without being able to act properly and skillfully. Otherwise the skillful means might become foolish, for only knowledge makes one wise. (Trungpa, 2004, p 100.)

Practical guides for developing skillful means in the large group class have been adapted from several works. From the Buddhist perspective, being a citizen in the large group is meditation in action. Members are instructed to observe their thinking and feelings, to return to their sense perceptions, and to allow compassion for themselves and others to well up. Members touch in fully with the current emotional and cognitive field of the moment, and then let go into the next moment (Wegela, 1988).

Instructions from Western approaches are also utilized to help ground the goal of increased awareness into a practical plan. The empirically supported approaches from industrial/organizational psychology and leadership and management development research are strikingly similar to the Buddhist instruction of practicing the paramitas. Group members are asked to be persistent and courageous in remaining open and present in each unfolding moment and to not allow the inevitable anxiety to prevent them from contacting and dialoguing with others (Gibber, Carter, & Goldsmith, 2000; Van Velsor & Guthrie, 1998).

Theoretical approaches, such as the group analytic or group relations models, instruct group members to observe not only the content of the discussions, but also to notice that context influences the present and the symbols and metaphors expressed in group (Chazen, 1991). An adaptation of the immediacy approach to group work suggested by Elliot Zeisel (2006) is also commonly utilized. Before speaking, members should consider the following questions: "What am I feeling? Why am I feeling this way? What are the other members of the group feeling? What would I like to say to the other person or the group? How might that person or the group feel or react?" Considering the answers to all of these questions, the group member arrives at the final inquiry: "What might I want to say now?"

Social Psychology

The large group is often conceived of as an enactment of societal behavior (Kernberg, 2003; Schneider & Weinberg, 2003), yet rarely are the findings of social psychology integrated in large group theories and practices. Social psychology research findings are extremely relevant to understanding large group dynamics. Social psychology research regarding group functioning discusses four factors: cohesion, roles, status, and norms (Baron & Byrne, 2003). Although it would be unusual for organizational consultation goals to have the group conductors elucidate links between group processes and social psychology, the academic setting that offers students this knowledge provides another useful lens for understanding individual and organizational dynamics. This section highlights some of the findings of social psychology that are regularly explored in the large group process class at Naropa.

Most graduate students are familiar with such popularized social psychology ideas as the conformity studies of Asch (Asch, 1956, Bond & Smith, 1996) and studies of obedience to authority by Milgram (1974). Regrettably, the unique perspective of social psychological research regarding group dynamics has not yet been integrated into many clinical training programs. Naropa's large group process class, however, attempts to bridge this gap as it allows students to understand these ideas not only cognitively, but also experientially.

Cohesion

The group psychotherapy concept of cohesion (Rutan & Stone, 2000) and the social psychology construct of entiativity have marked similarities (Hamiltom & Sanders, 1995; Lickel, et al., 2000). Cota, Evans, Dion, Kilik, and Longmon (1995) demonstrated that high-status members feel more cohesion than do low-status members. The importance of this is illuminated in how much more the leaders and well-respected group members experience group entiativity than do newer or less popular members. When a student joins an existing cohort after a leave of absence, the cohort without exception struggles to understand how the new member continues to feel outside the group despite their efforts to include him or her. Attractive students are also more likely to feel a greater sense of belonging than those students who are less aesthetically endowed (Prestia, Silverston, Wood, & Zigarmi, 2002). From the Buddhist view, the various responses to the sangha are a reflection of the perspective with which one understands the world and the workings of the mind. Thus, understanding how and why various group members experience cohesion is the work of both the spiritual path and clinical training.

Group members want to believe that the groups they are in are unique and important (Billow, 2003), as well as fair and morally advanced (Cropanzano, 1993; Scher, 1997). External threats, real or imagined, are used to increase cohesiveness. The exploration of the external threats to group cohesiveness inevitably mixes reality and fantasy. Commonly voiced external threats in the large group process class range from the inadequacy of the conductors to paranoid ideation surrounding the unresolved sadistic impulses of the program administrators.

Conformity behavior is also highlighted in large group process. Repeated field and heuristic studies have shown that both conformity behaviors and the subjective pressure to conform increase as group size increases (Asch, 1956; Baron & Burn, 2003; Bond & Smith, 1996). Although the size of the large group applies conformity pressure, the complimentary presence of the desire for individuation is strengthened (Maslach, Santee, & Wade, 1987; Snyder & Fromin, 1979). The extent of this individuation desire appears to be related to the degree that the member's culture is individualistic or collectivist (Hamilton & Sanders, 1995). The greater the individualistic value of a culture, the greater the members of that culture desire uniqueness. An example that is often used to illustrate this is that Western culture is individualistic and interested in the welfare of each person while Eastern culture tends toward collectivism and is more interested in the positive progression of the whole (Zimbardo & Gerrig, 1999). Research highlights that although the desire for conformity (Duambum, 1993) and yielding to authority (Baron & Burn, 2003) reduce anxiety regarding behavioral choices, these drives also counter the universal human desire for self-efficacy and self-determination.

The issues of conformity and individuation from a Buddhist perspective are seen as emerging from the desire to avoid suffering by clinging to a solid, separate sense of self. Here again we return to the paradoxical notion of the relative and absolute worlds. Although in the relative world, the individual experiences her existence as separate from another's, the absolute perspective illuminates Einstein's observation that such a separation is merely the optical illusion of self. Navigating this paradox is essential to effective functioning in the context of the group and one's culture (Gyatso, 2006).

Role

In the large group, individuals take up common social or familiar roles through forces of personal choice, persuasion, or induction. Some group members repeatedly carry the messages of emotion while other members present the voice of reason and realism. Some members consistently express outrage while others repeatedly express appreciation. Some members agitate the process and others attempt to quell the chaos and emotional intensity. From a systems perspective, the membership of the large group seeks homeostasis (Agazarian and Gant, 2000; Agazarian & Peters, 1995).

From a Buddhist perspective, homeostasis is a false pursuit and an illusion. In group, this is illuminated in the ever shifting states of the members' experiences, roles, and interpersonal dynamics. Impermanence is a core belief of Buddhist psychology and also of modern science (Gyatso, 2005). Although human nature clings to a sense of permanence, understanding the reality of change fuels the possibility and motivation for continuous growth regardless of how rigid one's roles may seem. Even

Freud (1930/1961) noted the limitedness and pointlessness of this clinging to permanence: "Civilized man has exchanged some part of his chances of happiness for a measure of security" (p. 79).

Status

As explored earlier, issues of popularity affect the status of group members. Tiedens (2001) found that proper displays of anger are most directly related to the attainment of status in group. Although impulsive anger, yelling, or continual protest may lower status in social settings, thoughtful complaints or assertiveness increase status. For Naropa students, many of whom are initially attracted to the non-aggressive, pacifist position of Tibetan Buddhism, learning assertiveness and boundary-creating skills are an important part of their personal and professional development. Meanwhile, from the contemplative perspective, the pursuit of status is another attempt for the mind to escape the truth of impermanence. In large group process, the achievement of status is usually as short-lived and ever-changing as assessments of the class's benefit from the experience and the facilitators' level of competence.

Norms

From a social psychology perspective, norms are established in the group as they are in the social world; through a variety of influences that include the social learning factors of associated outcomes, instrumental conditioning, and observational learning (Baron & Burn, 2003; Brown, 1998; Reno, Cialdini & Kallgren, 1993). Even though the large group class syllabus stays consistent from one year to the next, the interaction of the unique collection of students, group conductors, and external real world events lead to each cohort developing certain norms. Each cohort debates between typical descriptive behavioral norms of society, such as not interrupting others, and injunctive behavioral norms of how one ought to behave in the group (Brown, 1998). The goal of exploring behavioral norms is not to achieve the implementation of agreed upon norms, but rather to bring awareness to the tension between habitual behavioral patterns and other behavioral possibilities. True to Tuckman's (Tuckman, 1965, Tuckman & Jensen, 1977) observation of organizational and group dynamics, the group must move through storming endlessly about accepted behavioral norms, and find tentative agreements that can always be revisited and changed.

The first few minutes of each group class, and especially the first few classes of the semester, set a tone for future sessions (Rosenthal, 1987). Early in this process the conductors educate the group on normative focus theory and ask the group members to observe what behaviors, such as complaining, interpersonal praise, and vulnerability, are accepted and rejected by the group through verbal and nonverbal communication patterns. Certain behaviors receive positive attention while other behaviors are interrupted or ignored (Kallgren, Reno, & Cialdini, 2000). These initial group moments can inform the classification schemas for acceptable and unacceptable behaviors.

Regression

The prevalent large group theory repeatedly stresses the regressive or irrational tendency of large groups (Kreeger, 1975; Pines, 2000; Schneider & Weinberg, 2003; Hopper, 2005). Explanations for this include the breaking down of ego defenses through the high input of projective process of the large membership, the extremely high stimulation of multiple level processes that extend beyond cognitive grasp and elicit primitive defenses and drives. From a social psychology perspective, this experience is discussed as social facilitation theory (Zajonc, 1965; Geen, 1989; Zajonc & Sales, 1996). When an audience is present, individuals are more likely to act with their dominant responses. The larger the audience grows, the greater the heightening of arousal. In a structured setting, like an artistic or athletic performance, the struggle to balance internal focus and attunement to the audience creates a higher level of behavioral mastery. In a less structured setting, such as a larger process group, anxiety increases and individuals may act in a variety of uncharacteristic manners to lower their anxiety. This heightened anxiety produced by the audience of other large group participants may in part explain the intense emotions experienced in large group and the progression of varied and often unrelated utterances as each member attempts to regulate anxiety, cognitive confusion, and fear of performing poorly.

Related to this dynamic is another disturbing finding of social psychology that emerges in large groups known as the *bystander effect*. The bystander effect became part of social consciousness as an attempt to explain how at least thirty-five witnesses did not intervene when a women was murdered in an attack that lasted forty five minutes in New York City in 1964 (Darley & Latane, 1968). As a group increases in size, the members may experience a diffusion of responsibility and citizenship (Darely, 2001). In the large group, members are less apt to intervene if others engage in interpersonal verbal attacks or if communications become mundane and unsatisfying because they will wait for other members to take responsibility to intercede. In the large group, as occurs occasionally in clinical practice, one falls under the spell of regressive, primitive, or dominant ways of being. By becoming mindful of this state, the clinician can bring awareness to the pitfalls of impulsiveness, countertransference reactions, and projective identifications in psychotherapy practice.

Karma

Many Buddhist ideas can be observed in large group interactions, but the study of *karma* is particularly important and luminous. The idea of karma, like several other Buddhist ideas, was adapted from Hinduism. The Buddhist idea of karma has continued to gain interest and popularity in the West with comparisons often drawn to quantum mechanics and contemporary physics. From the Buddhist perspective, karma is simply the law that actions have reactions. The famous Haiku by Zen Monk Basho can be conceived of as an example of karma. Allen Ginsberg provided this translation, "The old pond/A frog jumps in/Kerplunck!" (Sato, 1995). Jumping into the pond, the frog set off echoes of water sounds, and although not mentioned but implied in the poem, the frog also stirred rings of water moving towards the shore. In Buddhism, actions are seen as causing a set of ripples in the environment.

In the book *Path to Bliss*, the Dalai Lama (Gyatso, 1991) clarified the Buddhist view of karma. He suggested that,

> Some people misunderstand the concept of karma. They take the Buddha's doctrine of the law of causality to mean that all is predetermined, that there is nothing that the individual can do. This is a total misunderstanding. The very term karma or action is a term of active force, which indicates that future events are within your own hands. Since action is a phenomenon that is committed by a person, a living being, it is within your own hands whether or not you engage in action. (p. 111)

The Buddhist view is that an action's result may not be immediately understood but rather may manifest over time. For some schools of Buddhism, the results of one's actions may not manifest for many generations or lifetimes. This is not a large leap, as history has taught us that the results of conflicts and alliances can last for centuries.

Karma is often understood as having four laws or truths (Gyatso, 1984). The first is that the results of an action are similar to the cause. If one is impulsive, open, or reactionary in a group, the subsequent actions of other group members may likely be similar. Process group research on self-disclosure, support and other factors suggest that this reaction process occurs (Burlingame, Fuhriman, & Johnson, 2004). The second law is that there are no results without a cause. In a group, members can understand all individual and group behavior as resultant from causations that include cultural history, organizational history, personal history, and biological forces. The third law is that once an action is done, the result is never lost. This idea is popular across group models, as leaders highlight how earlier events in group may be shaping current behavior. According to the law of karma, these results may have a long maturational period. During the last session of a large group, a leader may refer back to the initial session to highlight such a connection or a leader may reach back to the historical data of generations ago to help highlight the subtlety of influences on the current group's behavior. The forth law is that karma expands. From a psychological perspective, karma supports the idea of nurturance so that earlier life events manifest later in life (Siegel, 2003).

This understanding of the subtlety and multi-causality of group events concurs with the emerging ideas in social attribution theory. The factors for incorrectly linking cause and effect are influenced by an individual's personal attribution patterns as in self-serving bias (Brown & Rogers, 1991), cultural heritage (Brown 1998; Oettengen, 1995; Oettingen & Seligman, 1990), and current mood (Blazer, Kessler, Mcgonagle, & Swartz, 1994). In the group, members are likely to seek an obvious concrete cause for the sense of increased anxiety or dissatisfaction. This may take the form of finding a scapegoat or the membership vehemently asserting that a process-oriented group in an academic setting can be of no use. From the Buddhist perspective, acceptance of these simple answers is an act of ignorance. While the true statistical analysis of attribution factors for any group event is most likely impossible to determine, the search for causes increases an understanding of the complexity of the world, group dynamics, and the mind's individual tendencies.

Conclusion

The large group experience is an excellent container for students not only to learn about the ideas of psychology and Buddhism, but also to observe and even enact them. Although not designed to be therapeutic in changing symptoms or personality structure, students do appear to mature through this process. The experience may initially provoke anxiety. Yet, the students' tolerance for the complexity of larger group processes increases over time. The limited quantitative data collected by Naropa on this class has shown that the students' ability to learn from the large group experience increases with the number of sessions attended. After seven sessions, students report dissatisfaction with the learning that is taking place, while after twenty sessions students find this forum very valuable. Qualitative data from students at the end of the experience has repeatedly shown paradoxical statements, such as "I love the class," "I hate the class" or "It was horrible," "it was great." Further research is greatly needed, not only for the Naropa large group class, but on the general topic of the effects and benefits of large group experiences (Greene, 1979).

Large group process asks the member to transition from not knowing into knowing and back again to not knowing. The students learn to apply their dyadic studies of Buddhism, philosophy, organizational, and social psychology to their phenomenological experience and to the group processes, while touching into their personal experiences of anxiety, hope, fear, alienation, and connection. Tolerating one's fluctuating states of mind and exploring the subtle complexity of one's phenomenological experience are at the heart of Buddhism and the Naropa contemplative training. The large group has become a unique and important container for helping students, faculty, and the department offer increased awareness to the self, group dynamics, and the multicausality of experience. From the moment of silence following the bow at the beginning of the first group to the final bow at the end of the last semester, the students and conductor repeatedly glimpse the luminous and complex nature of the world and mind.

References

Adler, A. (1929). *The practice and theory of individual psychology.* New York: Harcourt, Brace & World.
Agazarian, Y. M., & Peters, R. S. (1995). *The visible and the invisible group: Two perspectives on group psychotherapy and group process.* London: Karnac.
Agazarian, Y. M., & Carter, F. (1993). Discussions on large group. *Group, 17,* 210-234.
Agazarian, Y. M. (1997). *Systems-centered therapy for group.* London: Karnac.
Agazarian, Y. M., & Gantt, S. P. (2000). *Autobiography of a theory: Developing a theory of living human systems and its systems-centered practice.* London: Jessica Kingsley.
Asch, S. (1956). Studies of independence and conformity: A minority of one against unanimous majority. *Psychological Monographs, 70,* (Whole No. 416).
Baron, R & Byrne, D. (2003). *Social psychology.* Boston: Person Education.
Begley, S. (2007). *Train your mind. Change your brain: How a new science reveals our extraordinary potential to change ourselves.* New York: Ballantine Books.
Billow, R. (2002). Bonding in group: The therapist's contribution. *International Journal of Group Psychotherapy, 53,* 83-110.
Billow, R. (2003). *Relational group psychotherapy: From basic assumptions to passion.* London: Jessica Kingsley.
Bion, W. (1961). *Experiences in groups.* London: Tavistock Publication.
Blazer, D. G., Kessler, R. C., McGonagle, K. A., & Swartz, M. S. (1994). The prevalence and distribution of major depression in a national community sample: The national community survey. *American Journal of Psychiatry, 151,* 979-986.
Bond, R., & Smith, P. (1996). Culture and conformity: A meta-analysis of studies using Asch's line judgment task. *Psychological Bulletin, 119,* 111-137.
Brown, D. G. (1992). Bion and Foulkes: Basic assumptions and beyond. In M. Pines (Ed.), *Bion and Group Psychotherapy* (pp. 192-212). London: Tavistock/Routledge.

Brown, J. D., & Rogers, R. J. (1991). Self serving attributions: The role of physiological arousal. *Personality and Social Psychology Bulletin, 24,* 712-722.

Brown, L. M. (1998). Ethnic stigma as a contextual experience: Possible selves perspective. *Personality and Social Psychology Bulletin. 12,* 165-172

Burlingame, G. M., Fuhriman, A. J., & Johnson, J. (2004). Current status and future direction of group psychotherapy research. In J. L. Delucia-Waack, D. A. Gerrity, C. R. Kalodner, & M. T. Riva (Eds.), *Handbook of group counseling and psychotherapy* (pp. 651–660). Thousand Oaks, CA: Sage.

Campbell, D. (1999). *The complete inklings: Columns on leadership and creativity.* San Francisco: Jossey-Bass.

Chazen, R. (2001). *The group as therapist.* London: Jessica Kingsley Publishers Ltd.

Clarke, L. (2004). *The time of therapeutic communities: People, places, and events.* London: Jessica Kingleys Publishers.

Cota, A., Evans, C., Dion, K., Kilik, L., & Longmon, R. (1995). The structure of group cohesion. *Personality and Social Psychology Bulletin, 21.* 572-580.

Cropanzano, R (1993). *Justice in the workplace.* Hillside, NJ: Erlbuam.

Cummings, T. C., & Worley, C. G. (2004). *Organizational development from organizational change.* Cincinnati, OH: Thomson South-Western.

Cummings, T. C., & Worley, C. G. (2001). *Organizational development and organizational change.* Cincinnati, OH: Thomson South-Western.

Darley, J. M., & Latane, B. (1968). Bystander intervention in emergencies: Diffusion of responsibility. *Journal of Personality and Social Psychology, 8,* 377-383.

Darely, J. M. (2001). Citizens' sense of justice and the legal system. *Current Directions in Psychological Science, 10,* 10-12.

Daumbum, K. (1993). *The self threat of receiving help: A comparison of the threat-to-self esteem model and the threat-to-interpersonal-power model.* Unpublished Manuscript, Gettysburg College.

de Maré. P. (1989). *The large group phenomena.* New York: Brunner/Mazel.

de Maré, P., & Schollberger, R. (2003). The large group as a meeting of minds: A philosophical understanding. In S. Schneider, & H. Weinberg (Eds.), *The large group re-visted: The herd, the primal horde and masses* (pp. 214-223). London: Jessica Kingleys Publishers Ltd.

Eisen, S. (2005). Future OD practice and practitioner competencies. In W. J. Rothwell & R. L. Sullivan (Eds.), *Practicing organization development: A guide for consultants* (pp. 664-671). New York: Pfeifffer.

Fairbairn, W. R. D. (1952). *An object-relations theory of the personality.* New York: Basic Books.

Foulkes, S. H. (1964). *Therapeutic group analysis.* New York: International University Press.

Foulkes, S. H. (1975). *Group analytic psychotherapy: Methods and principles.* London: Karnac.

Foulkes, S. H., & Anthony E. J. (1957). *Group psychotherapy.* London: New Impressions.

Freud, S. (1959). *Group psychology and the analysis of the ego* (J. Strachey, Trans.). New York: Norton. (Original work published in 1922)

Freud, S. (1961). Beyond the pleasure principle (J. Strachey, Trans.). New York: Norton. (Original work published in 1920)

Freud, S. (1961). Civilization and its discontents (J. Strachey, Trans.). New York: Norton. (Original work published in 1930)

Freud, S. (1965). New introductory lectures on psychoanalysis (J. Strachey, Trans.). New York: Norton. (Original work published in 1933)

Gantt, S. P., & Agazarian, Y. M. (2005). SCT® in Action: Applying the systems-centered approach in organizations. Lincoln, Nebraska: iUniverse.

Gibber, D., Carter, L. L., & Goldsmith (2000). *Best practices in leadership development handbook.* San Francisco: Jossey-Bass.

Geen, R. (1989). Alternative conceptions of social facilitation. In P. Paulus (Ed.), *Psychology of group influence* (pp.100-137). New York: Academic Press.

Greene, L. R. (1979). *Participants' perceptions in small and large group contexts. Human Relations, 32*(5), *357-365.*

Gyatso, T. (1984). *Kindness, clarity, and insight.* Ithica, NY: Snow Lion.

Gyatso, T. (1991). *The path to bliss.* Ithica, NY: Snow Lion.

Gyatso, T. (2005). *The universe in a single atom.* New York: Morgan Road Books.

Gyatso, T. (2006). *The essential Dalai Lama: His important teachings.* New York: Penguin Press.

Hamilton, V., & Sanders, J. (1995). Crimes of obedience and conformity in the work place. *Journal of Social Issues, 51,* 67-88.

Harrison, T. (2000). *Bion, Rickman, Foulkes, and the Northfield experiments: Advancing on a different front.* London: Jessica Kingsley Publishers Ltd.

Hopper, E. (2003). On the nature of hope in psychoanalysis and group analysis. In *The social unconscious: Selected papers.* London: Jessica Kingleys Publishers Ltd.

Hopper, E. (2005, February). *The large group.* Paper presented at the 63rd American Group Psychotherapy Association Conference, New York.

Hopper, E. (2007, March). *Moral corruption and ethical dilemmas in professional life.* Paper presented at the 64th American Group Psychotherapy Association Conference, Austin, Texas.

Hopper, S. J., Kaklauskas, F. J., & Greene, L. S. (2008). Group psychotherapy. In M. Herson (Ed.), *Handbook of clinical psychology* (pp. 647-662). New York: Wiley.

Jarrar, L. (2003). A consultant's journey into the large group unconscious: Principles and techniques. In S. Schneider & H. Weinberg (Eds.), *The large group re-visited: The herd, the primal horde and masses.* London: Jessica Kingsley Publishers Ltd.

Jung, C. G. (1994). Forward. In D. T. Suzuki, *An Introduction to Zen Buddhism.* New York: Grove.

Jung, C. G. (1921). *Psychological types: The psychology of individuation.* Princeton: Princeton University Press.

Kaklauskas, F. J. (2005, February). *Defending our turf: Integrating group theory with process and outcome research.* Paper presented at the 62nd American Group Psychotherapy Association Conference, New York.

Kallgren, C., Reno, R., & Cialdini, R. (2000). A focus theory of normative conduct: When norms do and do not affect behavior. *Personality and Social Psychology Bulletin. 26,* 1002-1012.

Kaul, T. J., & Bendar, R. L. (1994). Pretraining and structure: Parallel lines yet to meet. In A. Fuhriman & G. Burlingame (Eds.), *Handbook of group psychotherapy: An empirical and clinical synthesis* (pp. 155-188). New York: Wiley Interscience.

Kernberg, O. (2003). Socially sanctioned violence: The large group as society. In S. Schneider, & H. Weinberg (Eds.), *The large group re-visited: The herd, the primal horde and masses* (pp. 125-149). London: Jessica Kingsley Publishers Ltd.

Klein, M. (1975). *The writings of Melanie Klein, volume III: Envy and gratitude and other works.* New York: The Free Press.

Kreeger, L. (1975). *The large group: Dynamics and therapy.* London: Constable.

Le Bon, G. (1952). *The crowd.* London: Ernest Benn. (First published as La psychologie des foules, Paris, 1896)

Lickel, B., Hamilton, D. L., Wieczorkowski, G., Lewis, A., Sherman, S. J., & Uhles, A. N. (2000). Varieties of groups and the perception of group inactivity. *Journal of Personality and Social Psychology, 78,* 223-246.

Maslach, C., Santee, R., & Wade, C. (1987). Individuation, gender role, and dissent: Personality mediators of situational forces. *Journal of Personality and Social Psychology Bulletin, 25,* 1196-1207.

McCauley, C. D., Moxeley, R. S., & Velsor, E. V. (1998). *Handbook of leadership development.* San Fransisco: Jossey-Bass.

Meadow, P. (2003). *The new psychoanalysis.* Lanham, MD: Rowman & Littlefield Publishers.

Midal, F. (2004). *Chögyam Trungpa: His life and vision.* London: Shambhala.
Milgram, S. (1974). *Obedience to authority.* New York: Harper.
Miller, E. J., & Rice, A.K. (1967). *Systems of organization.* London: Tavistock.
Mullan, H. (1992). Existential therapist and their group therapy practices. *International Journal of Group Psychotherapy, 42,* 452-468.
Nhat Hanh, T. (2003). *Creating true peace: Ending violence in yourself, your family, and the world.* New York: Free Press.
Nitsun, M. (1996). *The anti-group: Destructive forces in the group and their creative potential.* London: Routledge.
O'Leary, J. V. (2001). The postmodern turn in group therapy. *International Journal of Group Psychotherapy, 5* (4), 473-87.
Oettingen, G.(1995). Explanitory style in the context of culture. In G. M. Buchanan & M. E. Sligman (Eds.), *Explanatory style* (pp.209-224) Hillsdale NJ: Erlbaum.
Oettingen, G., & Siligamn, M. E. (1990). Pessimism and behavioral signs of depression in East versus West Berlin. *European Journal of Social Psychology, 65,* 494-511.
Pines, M. (2000). *The evolution of group analysis.* London: Jessica Kingsley.
Prestia, S., Silverston, J., Wood, K., & Zigarmi, L. (2002). The effects of attractiveness on popularity; an observational study of social interaction among college students, *Perspectives in Psychology,* Spring, 2002.
Rahula, W. (1994). *What the Buddha taught.* Boston: Grove Press.
Reno, R., Cialdini, R., & Kallgren, C. (1993). The transitional influence of social norms. *Journal of Personality and Social Psychology, 64,* 102-112.
Rice, C. A. (1993). The community meeting. In A. Alonso & H. Swiller (Eds.), *Group therapy in clinical practice.* Washington, DC: American Psychiatric Press.
Rosenthal, L. (1987). *Resolving resistance in group psychotherapy.* London: Jason Aronson Inc.
Rutan, S., & Stone, W. (2000). *Psychodynamic group psychotherapy.* New York: Guilford Press.
Sato, H. (1995). *One hundred frogs: From Matsuo Basho to Allen Ginsberg.* Weatherhill: Boston.
Schermer, V.L. (1992). Beyond Bion: the basic assumption states revisited. In M. Pines (Ed.), *Bion and group psychotherapy* (pp 139-150). London: Routledge.
Scher, S. (1997). Measuring consequences of injustice. *Personality and Social Psychology Bulletin, 23,* 482-497.
Schneider, S., & Weinberg, H. (2003). Introduction: Background, structure and dynamics of the large group. In S. Schneider, & H. Weinberg (Eds.), *The large group re-visited: The herd, the primal*

horde and masses (pp. 13-26). London: Jessica Kingsley Publishers Ltd.

Siegel, D. J. (2007). *The mindful brain: Reflection and attunement in the cultivation of well-being.* New York: W. W. Norton.

Siegel, D. J., & Hartzell, M. (2003). *Parenting from the inside out: How a deeper self-understanding can help you raise children who thrive.* New York: Tarcher.

Siegel, D. J. (2001). Toward an interpersonal neurobiology of the developing mind: Attachment relationships, "mindsight," and neural integration. *Infant Mental Health Journal, 22,* 67-94.

Shields, W. (2001). The subjective experience of the self in the large group: Two models for study. *International Journal of Group Psychotherapy, 24,* 205-223.

Smith, K. K., & Simmons, V. M. (1983). A rumplestiltskin organization: Metaphors on metaphors in field research. *Administrative Science Quarterly, 28,* 377-392.

Snyder, & Fromin, (1979). *Uniqueness: The human pursuit of difference.* New York: Plenum.

Suzuki, D. T. (1960). Lectures on Zen Buddhism. In E. Fromm (Ed.), *Zen Buddhism and Psychoanalysis* (pp. 1-76). New York: Harper Collins.

Suzuki, D. T. (1994). *An introduction to Zen Buddhism.* Grove: New York.

Suzuki, S. (1973). *Zen mind, beginner's mind.* New York: Weatherhill.

Tiedens, L. Z. (2001). Anger and advancement versus sadness and subjugation: The effects of negative emotion expressions on social status conferral. *Journal of Personality and Social Psychology, 80,* 86-94.

Triest, J. (2003). The large group and the organization. In S. Schneider, & H. Weinberg (Eds.), *The large group re-visited: The herd, the primal horde and masses* (pp. 162-174). London: Jessica Kingsley Publishers Ltd.

Trungpa, C. (1973). *Cutting through spiritual materialism.* Boston: Shambhala.

Trungpa, C. (1976). *The myth of freedom and the way of meditation.* Berkeley: Shambhala.

Trungpa, C. (1988). *Shambhala: The sacred path of the warrior.* Boston: Shambhala.

Trungpa, C. (2004). *Meditation in action.* Boston: Shambhala.

Trungpa, C. (2005). *The sanity we are born with: A Buddhist approach to psychology* (C. Gimian, Ed.). Boston: Shambhala.

Tsoknyi, R. (2004). *Carefree dignity: Discourses on training in the nature of mind.* Berkeley, CA: North Atlantic.

Tuckman, B. W. (1965). Developmental sequence in small groups. *Psychological Bulletin, 63,* 384-399.

Tuckman, B. W., & Jensen, M. (1977). Stages of small group development. *Group and Organizational Studies, 2,* 419-427.

Van Velsor, E., & Guthrie, V. A. (1998). Enhancing the ability to learn from experience. In C. D. McCauley, R. S. Moxeley, & E. V. Velsor (Eds.), *Handbook of leadership development* (pp. 242-261). San Francisco: Jossey-Bass.

Wegela, K. K. (1988). "Touch and go" in clinical practice: Some implications of the view of intrinsic health for psychotherapy, *Journal of Contemplative Psychotherapy, 5*, 3-23.

Weiss, R. P. (2000). Emotion and learning-implications of new neurological research for training techniques. *Training & Development, 11*, 45-48.

Welber, D. (1991). Growth and training of a modern group analyst. *Modern Psychoanalysis, 16*(2), 183-193.

Winnicott, D.W. (1965). *The maturational process and the facilitating environment.* New York: International Universities Press.

Zajonc, R. B., & Sales, S. M. (1996). Social facilitation of dominant and subordinate responses. *Journal of Experimental Social Psychology, 2,* 160-169

Zajonc, R. B. (1965). Social facilitation. *Science, 149,* 269-274.

Zeisel, E. (2006, Febuary). *A modern analytic approach to working with immediacy.* Paper presented at the 64th American Group Psychotherapy Association Conference, San Francisco, CA.

Zimbardo, P. G., & Gerrig, R. J. (1999). *Psychology and life.* New York: Addison Wesley Longman, Inc.

8

Group as a Mindfulness Practice

Susan Nimmanheminda

This chapter is an attempt to discuss the commonalities between Buddhism, Buddhist meditation and mindfulness practices, and Western psychotherapy, particularly psychoanalysis. After an introduction in which I attempt to lay out some of the main points of this East-West dialogue, I will focus on issues discipline, contract, resistance, and the ego's activities of mental and verbal reflection. Finally, I will apply these theories to group work – group therapy and especially the group process class offered as part of Naropa University's Masters in Contemplative Counseling Psychology program.

Introduction

In the early 20th century, William James, who was nearing the end of his life, halted one of his Harvard lectures when he recognized in the audience a Buddhist monk from Sri Lanka. James is reported to have said to the monk, "Take my chair. You are better equipped to lecture on psychology than I. This is the psychology everybody will be studying twenty-five years from now" (Epstein, 2005, pp. 1-2). James had an interest in Buddhist thought throughout his life and led the way for the flourishing dialogue we see today between Buddhism and Western psychology. In the 1950s and 1960s, the psychoanalyst Karen Horney developed additional parallels. The three psychological forces she defined of *moving towards, moving against,* and *moving away from* reflect the essence of the Buddhist three poisons: passion, aggression, and ignorance (Nimmanheminda, Kaklauskas & Sell, 2004). In the 1970s and 1980s, this East-West dialogue continued in the works of Alan Watts, Chögyam Trungpa, and D. T. Suzuki. In the last couple of decades dozens of books have been published in the West regarding the relationship between Buddhism, mindfulness, and mental health. Safran's (2003) observation that "Buddhism gives every sign of being here to stay within our culture, and its influence on psychoanalytic thinking [and the theory and practice of psychotherapy in general] is growing" (p. 1) seems well justified.

Psychoanalysis has perhaps a stronger kinship with Buddhism than many other orientations toward psychotherapy because of its commitment to truth. As well as a method of assuaging mental suffering, psychoanalysis is an endeavor to investigate and understand the nature of mind. Freud's *fundamental rule* that the patient free associate was also a rule of honesty (Thompson, 2004). As Hanna Segal, a Kleinian psychoanalyst expressed it, "What is new about analysis is that it is the only discipline that considers that the search for truth is in itself therapeutic.... The fact is that the search for truth, for psychic truth, is the therapeutic factor" (as cited in Hunter, 1994, p. 50). The prominent British psychoanalyst, Wilfred Bion, emphasized this aspect again. He "placed truth – the need for truth and the need for truth seeking – as the focal point of his metapsychology" (Billow, 2004, p. 322). According to Bion:

> There is a need for awareness of an emotional experience, similar to the need for an awareness of concrete objects that is achieved through the sense impressions, because lack of such awareness implies a deprivation of truth and *truth seems to be essential for psychic health*. The effect on the personality of such deprivation is analogous to the effect of physical starvation on the physique. (italics added, as cited in Billow, 2004, p. 322)

Similar to psychoanalysis, Buddhism places a high value on honesty; to refrain from lying is one of its primary precepts. As a non-theistic set of beliefs and practices, Buddhism can be seen as a secular attempt to influence the mind in its effort to reduce emotional pain and self-imposed suffering. Psychoanalysis (and many other depth psychotherapies) and Buddhism offer practices to increase awareness, lift repression, develop the mind's ability to suspend judgment and increase its capacity for observation. Both orientations share the assumption that observation and awareness can lead to insight, new perspectives about oneself and the world, and psychic growth.

Psychoanalysis holds that mental exploration, reflection, and interpersonal processes address maturational deficits and inner conflicts, which allows for greater satisfaction in love and work. From the Buddhist perspective, insight and awakening come from a process of purification. Through practices which tame and train the mind, one's true, that is, *awakened* nature is accessed (Karr, 2007; Mipham, 2003; Rahula, 1959).

> The goal of the Buddhist path is to transform ourselves into what we have always been. Rather than strive to become something better, which is ego's game, we learn to remove the mask of ego to reveal our true nature. (Karr, 2007, p. xi)

Many types of Buddhist meditation take place sitting on a cushion. These practices are broadly divided into two types: *shamatha* and *vipashyana*. Shamatha, usually translated as tranquility, is the practice of

8. Group as Mindfulness Practice

focusing or resting attention on various objects in order to calm and center the mind. Buddhism maintains that the quality of mind developed during shamatha is one of calmness and attention with an absence of either grasping or avoiding mental contents. Cultivating this mental state is a necessary condition for recognizing the true nature of reality. Shamatha can result in blissful states of deep absorption, but these states are not its goal. The peace attained through this practice is considered only a temporary relief from suffering or *duhkha*; restlessness and dissatisfaction can return when internal and external conditions change.

The truth that psychoanalysis seeks is perhaps not the ultimate truth sought through Buddhist practices (Segal, as cited in Hunter, 1994, p. 50). Buddha's goal was to offer a path from psychic suffering through seeing and accepting both relative *and* ultimate truth. From the relative perspective, we are individuals with discrete lives and experience, but from the ultimate view, we are void of any consistent, permanent essential nature or self. Regarding *emptiness* of transient mental factors, Mark Epstein (1995) says:

> They [the emotions and mental states we come to call "I"] do exist, but we can know them in a way that is different from either expressing or repressing them. The Buddhist meditations of emptiness are not meant as a withdrawal from the falsely conceived emotions but as a means of recognizing the misconceptions that surround them, thereby changing the way that we experience them altogether. (p. 101)

The ultimate truth of the emptiness of self and all phenomena is achieved through vipashyana, a mental condition that can arise through shamatha. Shamatha can be considered a prerequisite to vipashyana, and vipashyana a prerequisite to *prajna* or insight and intelligence regarding the nature of relative and ultimate realities.

Along with mental training achieved through meditation, the tranquility that is considered essential for prajna also requires discipline and proper ethical conduct. Buddhist ethics are laid out as precepts for lay and monastic life. In the Theravada tradition these teachings are the *Eightfold Path* (Rahula, 1959, and in the Mahayana tradition they are delivered in the *Way of the Bodhisattva* (Chödrön, 2005). These ethical codes include practices and training in speech, action, livelihood, and concentration through which some mental factors and positions are cultivated and others are avoided. A foundation for meditation and ethical conduct is the practice of neutral attention – mindfulness.

Mindfulness

Mindfulness refers to awareness of the present, moment-by-moment experience. It is this aspect of Buddhism that Western psychology has embraced more than any other (Langer, 1989, 1997; Hayes et. al., 2004; Germer et. al., 2005; Safran, 2003; Siegel, 2007; Segal et. al., 2002). Traditional Buddhist teachings on mindfulness are given in *The Four Foundations of Mindfulness*: mindfulness of body, feelings, mind, and mental objects. As Gunaratana (2001) observed, these teachings incorporate "our whole life into meditation practice" (p. 197). Mindfulness practices that train us to be attentive to raw, non-conceptual experience of the present moment are conducive to tranquility and to insight, and they "directly improve the functioning of body and brain, subjective mental life with its feelings and thoughts, and interpersonal relationships" (Siegel, 2007, p. 3). These practices cultivate an open, spacious state of mind that is focused and present. Sogyal Rinpoche explains that the Buddha taught that ignorance was the cause of suffering and "the root of ignorance itself is our mind's habitual tendency to distraction. So mindfulness is the gateway to liberation" (cited in Tart, 1994, p. *ix*).

> The condition of mindfulness leads to insight and truth, the truth of ordinary living and of ultimate truth – the truth of reality that exceeds changing conditions. Because we unknowingly perceive ourselves and the world around us through thought patterns that are limited, habitual, and conditioned by delusions, our perception and subsequent mental conceptualization of reality is scattered and confused. Mindfulness teaches us to suspend temporarily all concepts, images, value judgments, mental comments, opinions, and interpretations. A mindful mind is precise, penetrating, balanced, and uncluttered. It is like a mirror that reflects without distortion whatever stands before it. (Gunaratana, 2001, p. 191)

Some mindfulness practices aim directly at developing shamatha. For example, the basic instruction of mindfulness of breath is to sit in a comfortable but erect position, rest the mind on the breath (or perhaps a particular aspect of the breath), and as thoughts occur, note them and then gently turn the attention back to the breath. For most meditators, this practice eventually leads to states of calmness. Other mindfulness exercises focus more directly at bringing about insight or vipashyana. For example, the Buddha's instruction, *Mindfulness of the Parts of the Body*, is a very systematic process of analytic meditation. In it the Buddha recommended that the meditator dissect the body into thirty-two parts and contemplate them according to their elemental natures and functions. This exercise is to be practiced with an attitude of equanimity or radical openness and non-clinging. Because it leads to awareness of our deep identification with our bodies, it can be very difficult; it is not surprising that the Buddha referred to it by the Pali word that means "going against the grain" (Gunaratana, 2001, p. 206). The purpose of this meditation is to lead the meditator to the conclusion "that there is nothing stable about the body and its parts. Everything is changing. Everything is impermanent. This is reality" (Gunaratana, 2001, p. 207). The same realizations come through *Mindfulness of Mind*, instructions for watching the various mental states – such as greedy, generous, calm, anxious, concentrated, distracted – come and go, and through *Mindfulness of Mental Objects*, which is the practice of bringing neutral attention to thoughts. Some instructions recommend labeling thoughts according to various categories and others encourage simply observing them as they come and go. The goal of all of these practices is the same: the meditator's progress toward increasingly enlightened states where phenomena are seen for what they are – composites or aggregates of ever-changing causes and conditions – and a sense-of-self that is more fluid and less identified with that which is transitory.

Parallels in the Paths and Goals in Group Work

The desire that most often draws people to study and practice Buddhism and to seek psychotherapy is often similar. People want to feel better, be happier, and have less discomfort and stress. Both Buddhism and psychotherapy "are concerned with the nature and alleviation of human suffering, and they each have a diagnosis and 'treatment plan' for alleviating human misery" (Rubin, 1999, p. 9).

As the discussion above shows, both practice and discipline are central to the Buddhist path. Although not usually considered as such, Western psychotherapies also incorporate practice and discipline; the contract or frame of psychotherapy can be viewed from this perspective. Freud (1913) initiated the discussion about the frame of the therapeutic relationship as a core aspect of treatment. In his work with individuals, his first requirement and *rule* was that the patient free associate, that she say whatever comes to mind without selecting or omitting anything. The analyst was advised to practice listening with a neutral attitude which would allow her unconscious to engage with the patient's and then to interpret what she heard. This contract has changed considerably since Freud's day, but contemporary analysts actively continue to study, experiment with, and debate the subject, attributing no less import to it than did Freud.

Group leaders also use the contract as a primary tool of the therapeutic process. Contracts vary depending on the therapist's orientation and the purpose of the group, but they are generally recognized as essential for promoting the group's goals and for understanding what impedes the process. Typical contracts ask group members to come at a certain time, talk to each other, and pay the therapist's fee. Beyond this, there may be rules prohibiting certain behaviors in and outside group. Irvin Yalom (1985) speaks not so much of a contract as of "culture building" and of the effort to establish "a code of behavioral rules, or norms" (p. 115). Louis Ormont's (1968) psychoanalytic groups stress immediacy. The contract is for members to talk about meaningful experiences, to share the talking time, and to communicate verbally. Group members are asked to refrain from *acting out* behaviors, such as missing appointments, coming to group intoxicated, and making important decisions without discussing them with the group. Stressing the aspect of immediacy, the contract is that members "keep communications within the emotional current of the group" (Ormont, 1968, p. 148). With such a contract, resistances naturally surface easily (Ormont, 1993). Members will talk about the past or future, and about life and people outside the group. However, resistances support the therapeutic process by bringing out the genesis of members' flight from the present. Once in the open, resistances can be understood, and intrapsychic dynamics can become interpersonal and undergo process and change (Ormont, 1993).

An experiential and academic process group is part of Naropa University's Masters of Arts in Contemplative Psychology program. The central objectives of this weekly group practice are for students to become familiar with their own and other's minds and behavior within a small group and to practice mindfulness and skillfulness in this interpersonal setting. In these Buddhist-inspired contemplative groups, the contract is that students show up physically, mentally, and emotionally, and verbalize their experience to other members. The contract prioritizes mindfulness over psychological change, although practicing skillfulness of speech is gradually given greater emphasis. Some of the leader's interventions encourage members' awareness of what they are seeing, hearing, sensing in their bodies, and thinking. For example, "John, did you notice the expression on Tom's face when he said that?" "Where did your mind go when you heard Jane's tone of voice?" Sensual, cognitive, non-verbal, and verbal phenomena occurring in the present become the objects of intentional awareness. Other interventions facilitate mindfulness by reducing or enhancing tension, and naming and exploring typical group dynamics such as subgrouping, aggression, competition, and cohesion. Some interventions attempt to encourage a group culture of equanimity, non-judgmentalness, and compassionate responsiveness towards all that is witnessed intra- and interpersonally. The contract is that students think and talk about their experience and this entails its challenges and resistances. Resistances are considered to be behaviors such as coming late, withholding verbal communications, and touching each other rather than putting feelings into words. Probably most challenging of all is learning to practice equanimity and non-judgmentalness. They are worked with by developing a group culture of mindfulness and equanimity – radical openness to whatever is thought,

8. Group as Mindfulness Practice

felt, and said. Verbal and non-verbal language become objects of attention and students are encouraged to listen to words and intonations, to see expressions and gestures, and explore the meanings of all forms of communication and experience. This process helps make *folk psychology* (Bruner, 1990) explicit; group members recognize and investigate the assumptions, prejudices, desires, and beliefs that are implicit in group and life.

The rules or contract of therapeutic groups and Naropa's contemplative group process are similar to Buddhist instructions in at least three ways: when cooperated with they help people achieve the group's stated goals; they are often met with resistance; and they provide opportunities for learning about oneself and others or, as Buddhists might say, they help create conditions in which truth can be realized.

Instructions, rules, and precepts – whether in regard to individual or group psychotherapy or Buddhist sitting and conduct practices – often evoke an accelerated experience of the mind's habitual responses to structure. People find themselves automatically complying with or defying the structure and can see more clearly "the self-protective strategies that analysts have termed *resistance and defensive processes* in psychoanalysis and the *hindrances, fetters, and impediments* in Buddhism" (Rubin, 1999, p. 9).

Resistance is the term many psychoanalytically informed therapists use to refer to individual and group behavior that interferes with progress. Freud initiated the use of this term because his model was based on a thermodynamic paradigm of drives and tension discharge and inhibition. Initially, he saw transference – the patient's tendency to see the doctor/analyst as her father, mother, lover, or persecutor – as the major resistance and impediment to free association and healing. But eventually he came to "appreciate the awesome leverage of transference" (Ormont, 1995, p. 399). Perhaps Freud's coining the dynamics as resistance was an unfortunate labeling because of the word's negative connotations, when, as mentioned above, resistances can be a royal road to therapeutic progress. Contemporary analysts generally recognize that working cognitively and emotionally with transference and other resistances in the immediacy of the therapeutic relationship is central to analysis, self-knowledge, and psychic growth.

In Buddhism, resistances are referred to as *hindrances* and *fetters*. Buddhism recommends that we practice mindfulness when meeting with habitual tendencies, such as aggression, craving, torpor, ignorance, jealousy, envy, and pride. Epstein (1995) provides an excellent personal example that captures the Buddhist view of resistance.

> At my first meditation retreat, a two-week period of silent attention to mind and body, I was amazed to find myself sitting in the dining hall with an instant judgment about each of the hundred other meditators, based on nothing besides how they looked while

eating. Instinctively, I was searching out whom I liked and whom I did not: I had a comment for each one. The seemingly simple task of noting the physical sensations of the in and out breath had the unfortunate effect of revealing just how out of control my everyday mind really was. Meditation is ruthless in the way it reveals the stark reality of our day-to-day mind. (Epstein, 1995, p. 110)

In group therapy and in contemplative group process, members inevitably experience similar dynamics. They hear their mind's judging and evaluating, and feel the pulls of desire and avoidance. Both on the meditation cushion and sitting in the contemplative group, the contract first and foremost is to endure the often unpleasant, if not painful, process of witnessing one's unruly, aggressive, lustful, impatient mind. But this challenging practice of mindfulness has its pay-off: it naturally cultivates the *paramitas* – qualities of generosity, discipline, patience, enthusiasm or exertion, meditation (also thought of as concentration or focus), and wisdom. Paradoxically, the willingness and ability to sustain this type of discomfort is a condition for the reduction of suffering. As described by Pema Chödrön (1998), it is a process wherein ever-so-gradually mental factors such as attachment, conceit, restlessness, and ignorance are eradicated and both relative and ultimate truths are directly known. To sustain this process of familiarizing ourselves with our minds requires patience, compassion, a sense of humor, and often a trustworthy guide, spiritual teacher or psychotherapist.

Mindfulness vs. Mentalization

Practices of mindfulness bring us into the present moment, which is the only moment of change. However, most individual and group psychotherapies are concerned with thoughts and feelings of the past and future. Being in the present moment with the past and future involves mental activities such as reflection, introspection, metacognition, self-awareness, imagination, and fantasy. *Mentalization* (the noun) and *mentalizing* (the verb) are the latest additions to our attempt to name and discuss these psychological activities.

The term *mentalization* was first introduced by Peter Fonagy et.al. (2002) in their description of the infant's and young child's mental process of constructing a sense of self. This complex process was subsequently succinctly defined by Bateman and Fonagy (2004) as "the mental process by which an individual implicitly and explicitly interprets the actions of himself and others as meaningful on the basis of intentional mental states such as personal desires, needs, feelings, beliefs and reasons" (p. 21). Mentalizing includes "attending, perceiving, recognizing, describing, interpreting, inferring, imagining, simulating, remembering, reflecting, and anticipating" (Allen, 2006, p. 6). Reviewing various diverse treatment modalities, Bateman and Fonagy (2006) found that the capacity for mentalizing experience was the primary element determining the therapeutic progress of those patients with the diagnosis of borderline personality disorder. It is an integral part of various psychotherapeutic modalities with diverse clientele (Allen & Fonagy, 2006) and is considered a critical factor in the outcome of therapy. It is this same process that Bion (1967) described as the capacity for containing and transforming *beta elements*, which are unformulated experience, into *alpha elements*, which are elements of experience that can be thought and spoken about. Bion (1977) considered the process of establishing a "mental relationship with a personality, either the individual's own or that of another person" (p. 53) to be a central developmental milestone.

Contrary to the term's most obvious connotation as purely cognitive, "at its most meaningful, mentalizing is suffused with emotion" (Allen, 2006, p. 8); it is very much tied to feelings – one's own and the other's affective states. Fonagy and others found that this ability to think about one's own feelings and to empathize and think about the feelings of others, is very dependent upon the status of one's attachment style (i.e., disorganized, anxious, secure) and upon the attachment style of the person with whom one is communicating. Basically, the more secure the attachment, the greater the capacity for mentalizing, "for holding mind in mind" (Allen, 2008, p. 4). This conceptualization helps to clarify why the therapeutic alliance with an individual or group leader, as well as the factor of a group's cohesion, are critical for creating an atmosphere where feelings, thinking, and communication can occur.

Initially, the processes of mentalizing that occur in psychotherapy and contemplative groups may seem inimical to the emphasis on nonconceptuality that is often associated with the Buddhist path. However, in *Contemplating Reality*, Karr (2007) asserts that "we need to use thought to get beyond thought. Real nonconceptuality arises from recognizing the true nature of conceptuality, not through blocking thoughts or getting rid of them" (p. 10). Buddhist practices compliment mentalization by cultivating attention, equanimity, and *touch-and-go* (Wegela, 1998). Touch-and-go is how Karen Kissel Wegela named the practice of engaging the phenomena of our attention actively yet without clinging. One must *touch* in with sufficient awareness to vividly contact an experience, another person or oneself, and then *go*, releasing the mind's tendency to grip on to and construct identity around the story. In group, touch-and-go can enable members in mentalizing their experience without becoming duped by its relative truth and it helps them learn to discriminate their actual, immediate experience from their narratives and concepts.

Buddhist Ego and Self vs. Western Ego

In Buddhism, the ego is often considered the primary source of suffering. "If the ego is well fortified and strong, suffering is great" (Chödrön, 2006). The ego to which Chödrön refers is likened to a *cocoon*, depicting its holding, protecting, containing, and, ultimately, its limiting and imprisoning capacities. It is a protective mechanism that tries to build and sustain a situation imagined as comfortable or agreeable. To the extent that the ego is a closed system, allowing little exchange with the world and its ever-changing conditions, there is a rigid self-structure. But greater curiosity, openness, and creativity are present when the self-structure has boundaries that both: allow for exchange between the unconscious and conscious and between one's internal and external world, and give it the capacity for containing and mentalizing disorganizing and chaotic experience.

All Buddhist practices work with the ego and the sense-of-self that is experienced as a solid, consistent, stable, *true* entity. Practices both on and off the meditation cushion help one recognize that one's prized self is empty of any enduring, stable, cohesive constituents; like all phenomenon the sense of self is a result of causes and conditions which have come together and will eventually become unstable and shift.

In ordinary conversation we often use the word *ego* to refer to a person's arrogance and self-satisfaction. "What an ego he has!" But in Western ego psychology, ego refers to diverse mental functions and activities (Valliant, 1993) such as: distinguishing inner from outer stimuli, accuracy of perception, reflection and all other aspects of mentalization as described above, judgment and discernment, prediction, regulation of impulses, affects and impulses, delaying gratification, and the ability to remember, concentrate, and manage stimulus. Another set of ego activities is the mind's capacity for synthetic and integrating functions, which includes its faculties of binding, unifying, creating, coordinating, and integrating experience and thought. The ego organizes and makes meaning out of an infinite number of perceptions, impressions, feelings, and emotions. Also considered as activities of the ego's synthetic function are the mind's ability to assimilate internal and external elements and reconcile conflicting ideas. Certain ego functions are recognized as *defenses* since they help preserve a coherent self-state and they act as a protective barrier against excessive external and internal stimuli. These include activities such as denial, projection, fantasy, dissociation, displacement, intellectualization, repression, reaction formation, suppression, sublimation, and altruism (Freud, 1937).

The quality of a person's ego functions establishes his or her character or personality style. In Western psychology, character or personality is seen as more or less healthy depending on its ability to adapt to the infinite number of internal and environmental conditions it encounters on a moment-by-moment basis. Consistent with the Buddhist perspective, this will depend on its openness and flexibility; its ability to go to pieces without falling apart (Epstein, 2001). Clearly, a healthy ego from the Western perspective is essential for progress along the Buddhist path.

The Fruits of Group Therapy and Contemplative Group Process

Yalom (1985) sees the potential results of group therapy as instilling hope, allowing for catharsis, and giving members a sense of universality and altruism. Ormont (1992) discusses numerous social benefits of group treatment. His emphasis on immediacy gives members the "opportunity for on-the-spot self definition... [and] the benefit of *in vivo* versus *in vitro* learning" (Ormont, 1992, p. 29). Members of Naropa's contemplative groups, like members in therapy groups such as Ormont's and others, witness and get feedback about their interpersonal patterns. This feedback may be diverse and the group member's knowledge that who one is often depends on who is being asked is reinforced. They learn more about the co-constructed nature of self. Also, these groups offer a relatively safe place to practice new behavior. Rules regarding confidentiality and socializing help establish boundaries that contain experience, giving greater opportunity for testing, experimentation, and practice. Although not a goal of Naropa's contemplative groups, with time these conditions may lead to character change.

To the extent that group therapy and contemplative group help develop the ego functions mentioned above, they dissolve the defensive ego cocoon that Chödrön (2006) describes. From a Buddhist perspective, these are positive changes in that the ego is rendered more open, available, malleable, and spacious. However, as Aronson (2004) aptly puts it, "to the extent that we get absorbed in the content of our minds and our mental associations, we lose focus on the fundamental changing nature of thoughts, feeling, and bodily phenomena and their lack of inherent existence" (p. 42). The inclination to create a solid sense-of-self, the challenge of listening, investigating, and articulating on the one hand, and on the other becoming seduced by the contents of our experience, seems ever present in contemplative group process and in traditional Buddhist meditation practices.

Contemplative group has many commonalities with Buddhist meditation. Practicing touch-and-go in this group helps to cultivate a mind which is tamer, has a stronger witness or observing ego, is less conflicted, discursive and speedy, and renders it a mind with greater capacity for presence. This experience heightens perceptions and increases recognition of the constructed and impermanent nature of experience, as well as of the spaciousness or emptiness of self and all phenomena. The process of shifting identifications with diverse aspects of self and others, together with open investigation and communication, helps develop greater patience and appreciation for oneself and others. The practice of mindfulness in both settings heightens awareness of one's inner experience, and interpersonal verbal exploration develops its context and meaning.

Conclusion

Although Naropa students identify numerous constructive personal changes resulting from this group practice, as with meditation practices, the emphasis is on the activity of practice and not on particular goals or outcomes. This attention to process rather than product helps group members soften and relax their personal aspirations and develop the paramitas, giving them a greater sense of what happens when their minds and hearts meet (Stern, 2004).

What is potentially dispelled through Buddhist practices, some types of psychotherapy, and contemplative group is the sense of solid self. Buddha's teachings and Freud's psychoanalytic psychology show us that we are not (only) who or what we think we are. By including efforts to know ultimate truth, Buddha's teachings go further than Freud's. However, any practice that leads toward this spaciousness can potentially offer "some tincture of the realization that one is making oneself up as one goes along" (Langan, 1999, p. 95), and help us ride the wave of life with deeper appreciation, responsibility, agility, and vitality.

References

Allen, J. (2006). Mentalizing in practice. In J. Allen & P. Fonagy (Eds.), *Handbook of mentalization-based treatment* (pp. 3-31). West Sussex, England: John Wiley & Sons, Ltd.

Allen, J. & Fonagy, P. Eds. (2006). *Handbook of mentalization-based treatment.* West Sussex, England: John Wiley & Sons, Ltd.

Aronson, H. (2004). *Buddhist practice on Western ground: Reconciling Eastern ideals and Western psychology.* Boston: Shambhala.

Batemen, A. & Fonagy, P. (2006). Mechanisms of change, mentalization-based treatment in borderline personality disorder. *Journal of Clinical Psychology, 62*(4), 411-430.

Bateman, A. & Fonagy, P. (2004). *Psychotherapy for borderline personality disorder: Mentalization based treatment.* Oxford: Oxford University Press.

Billow, R. (2004). Truth and falsity in group. *International Journal of Group Psychotherapy, 54*(3), 321-345.

Bion, W. R. (1967). *Second thoughts.* London: Heinemann.

Bion, W. R. (1977). Learning from experience. In *Seven servants: Four works.* New York: Aronson.

Burner, J. (1990). *Acts of meaning.* Cambridge, MA: Harvard University Press.

Chödrön, P. (1998). *Noble heart: The ground of bodhichitta practice.* [Cassette Series] Boulder, Colorado: Sounds True.

Chödrön, P. (2005). *No time to lose, a timely guide to the way of the bodhisattva.* Boston: Shambhala.

Chödrön, P. (2006). *When things fall apart, heart advice for difficult times.* [Cassette Series] Boulder, Colorado: Sounds True.

Coates, S. (2006). Forward. In J. Allen & P. Fonagy (Ed.), *Handbook of mentalization-based treatment* (pp. xv-xvii). West Sussex, England: John Wiley & Sons, Ltd.

Epstein, M. (1995). *Thoughts without a thinker.* New York: MJF Books.

Epstein, M. (2001). *Going to pieces without falling apart: A Buddhist perspective on wholeness.* New York: Broadway Books.

Fonagy, P., Gergely, G., Jurist, E. L. & Target, M (2002). *Affect regulation, mentalization, and the development of the self.* New York: Other Press.

Freud, A. (1937). *The ego and the mechanisms of defense.* London: Hogarth Press.

Freud, S. (1913). *On beginning the treatment, further recommendations on the technique of psycho-analysis* [Standard Edition, Vol. 12]. London: Hogarth Press. [Original work published in 1913]

Germer, D., Siegel, R., & Fulton, P. (Eds.). (2005). *Mindfulness and psychotherapy.* New York: Guilford.

Gunaratana, Bhante Henepola. (2001). *Eight mindful steps to happiness, walking the Buddha's path.* Boston: Wisdom Publications.

Hayes, S., Follette, V., & Linehan, M. (Eds.). (2004). *Mindfulness and acceptance, expanding the cognitive-behavioral tradition.* New York: Guilford.

Hunter, V. (1994). *Psychoanalysts talk.* New York: Guilford.

Karr, A. (2007) *Contemplating reality, a practitioner's guide to the view in Indo-Tibetan Buddhism.* Boston: Shambhala.

Langan, R. (1999). What on closer examination disappears. *The American Journal of Psychoanalysis, 59*(1), 87-96.

Langer, E. (1989). *Mindfulness.* Reading, MA: Addison-Wesley.

Langer, E. (1997). *The power of mindful learning.* Reading, MA: Addison-Wesley.

Morvay, Z. (1999). Horney, Zen, and the real self: theoretical and historical connections. *The American Journal of Psychoanalysis, 59*(1), 25-36.

Nimmanheminda, S., Kaklauskas, F. & Sell, B. (2003, August/September). Buddhist mindfulness practice in group therapy. *The Group Circle, The Newsletter of the American Group Psychotherapy Association,* 4-6.

Ormont, L. (1968). Group resistance and the therapeutic contract. *International Journal of Group Psychotherapy, 18*(1), 147-154.

Ormont, L. (1992). *The group therapy experience, from theory to practice.* New York: St. Martin's Press.

Ormont. L. (1993). Resolving resistances to immediacy in the group setting. *International Journal of Group Psychotherapy, 43* (4), 399-418.

Rahula, W. (1959). *What the Buddha taught.* New York: Grove Press.

Rubin, J. (1999). Close encounters of a new kind: Toward an integration of psychoanalysis and Buddhism. *American Journal of Psychoanalysis, 59* (1), 1-24.

Sakyong Mipham (2003). *Turning the mind into an ally.* New York: Penguin Putman Inc.

Segal, Z., Williams, F., & Teasdale, J. (Eds.). (2002). *Mindfulness-based cognitive therapy for depression, a new approach to preventing relapse.* New York: Guilford.

Siegel, D. (2007). *The mindful brain, reflection and attunement in the cultivation of well-being.* New York: W. W. Norton & Company.

Stern, D. (2004). *The present moment in psychotherapy and everyday life.* New York: W. W. Norton & Company.

Thompson, G. (2004). *The ethic of honesty, the fundamental rule of psychoanalysis.* New York: Rodopi.

Vaillant, G. (1993). *The wisdom of the ego.* Cambridge, Massachusetts: Harvard University Press.

Wegela, K. K. (1998). Touch and go in clinical practice: some implications of the view of intrinsic health for psychotherapy. *Journal of Contemplative Psychotherapy, 5,* 3-21.

Yalom, I. (1985). *The theory and practice of group psychotherapy* (3rd ed.). New York: Basic Books.

9

A Discipline of Inquisitiveness: The Body-Speech-Mind Approach to Contemplative Supervision[1]

Robert Walker

This chapter includes instructions for carrying out the body-speech-mind approach to clinical supervision, a practice that was first presented in 1987 (Rabin & Walker, 1987). This descriptive discipline is a kind of intuitive awareness, or space awareness, practice whose purpose is to bring the client, the client's world, and the therapeutic relationship (as experienced by the helping professional) vividly into the group supervisory situation. This presence, in turn, is used to directly facilitate working with energetic and conceptual obstacles, providing a basis for subsequent therapeutic interventions. This approach has been used in the training of students in the Masters of Arts program in Contemplative Psychotherapy at Naropa University, by Naropa graduates, and other therapists who have encountered and been inspired by this approach for over twenty years.

These instructions include clarifying the intention of the practice, awareness instructions for the group leader and group members who are facilitating the presentation, descriptive guidelines for the presenter, and practice guidelines for the supervisor and group members. The phenomenon of *exchange* (Luyton, 1985), the practice of *therapeutic resonance* (Silverberg, 1988), and related countertransference literature, how to work with obstacles in the practice and additional notes on the *mind* aspect of the presentation are also discussed.

Supervision offers an opportunity for both students and experienced health professionals to work with the various emotional, style-based, and conceptual obstacles that inhibit their clinical work. While not intended as a method of formulating treatment plans or choosing

---

[1] I am indebted to Dr. Farrell Silverberg for conversations which clarified many points and for his editorial assistance with this chapter, as well for the excellent editing work by Dr. MacAndrew Jack and Dr. Louis Hoffman. This chapter is excerpted from a longer paper, which contains a broader coverage of some important themes of this paper. This paper is available through the author.

interventions, the practice of the body-speech-mind descriptive discipline creates environments for having discussions that may lead to creative and accurate clinical decisions. This chapter concludes with a brief exploration of the relationship of this approach to ongoing contemplative education of health professionals and cites the importance of becoming aware of and discussing the world views and understandings of human path which have so great an effect upon the decision making process and clinical interventions of health professionals.

Start Where You Are. Practice Without Pretense.

A basic premise of the *body-speech-mind* descriptive discipline is that "it is possible to train ourselves to touch and be touched by the people we are serving and their worlds more directly" (Rabin & Walker, 1987, p. 146). Awareness practice rooted in the simplicity of experience is an important support for such discipline. A natural result of the practice, in the process of describing the client, is that a person "can become a living presence in the room" (p. 144). One could add here, not only do the client and the world of the client become available but, in particular, the health professional's relationship to the client and their world, along with the health professional's related experiences, feelings, and thoughts, also become vivid.

The assumption that underlies the need for such practice is that, without a direct experience of our own minds and without being open to others, relationships have no basis in reality. Without training in mindfulness and awareness, we could attempt to perform contemplative practices such as loving-kindness (*metta*, Salzberg & Zinn, 2004), or the practice of *tonglen* (exchanging ourselves for others; Chödrön, 2001b; Kongtrul, 2005; Shantideva, 2006; Trungpa, 1993), but find that we are so self-absorbed that our thoughts have little relation to whoever we are in relationship to. We may be too wrapped up in fantasies about ourselves to see clearly how we actually affect others, or too wrapped up in theoretical understandings (isolated from personal experience) to have an open, nonjudgmental experience of others. In such cases, both our personal paths and paths as helping professionals will have a poor foundation. Our out-of-touchness, could get in the way of communication and seeing ourselves and others clearly.

This is a significant reason that "the practice of mindfulness-awareness meditation... provides the context in which our clinical work takes place" (Rabin & Walker, 1987, p. 3). Being more in touch with our own being and that of others, beyond our wishful thinking, is one of the primary functions of mindfulness practices.

> From the Buddhist viewpoint, the study of theory is only a first step, and must be completed by training in the direct experience of mind itself, in oneself and others ... developed through the

9. A Discipline of Inquisitiveness

> practice of meditation, a first-hand observation of mind. (Trungpa, 1987, p. 3)

Therefore, some approach to having a direct, experiential way of working with mind is the ground of our work. Chögyam Trungpa (1987) further noted: "Western psychologists do seem intuitively to recognize the need for greater emphasis on the direct experience of mind. Perhaps this is what has led many psychologists to take an interest in Buddhism" (p. 5).

In many of his teachings on mindfulness practice and elsewhere, Trungpa (1974b; 1973/2002) emphasized the importance of seeing through pretense, and that such pretense can be a significant barrier to having a straightforward experience of ourselves and others. The human suffering of ego-process was presented by him as a kind of hypocrisy, always discontent, always grasping after some better way to be. In giving meditation instruction, that much initial theory was deemed to be necessary – pointing out the pain of ego-process, expressed as the workings of the eight consciousnesses (Mipham 2000b; Trungpa 1974a; 1975a), the five skandhas (Mipham, 2000b; Trungpa, 1975, 1973/2002), or the "three lords of materialism" (Trungpa, 1973/2002, pp. 5 &11).

Trungpa would often point to our attempts to use spiritual practice to create some blissful state of mind (spiritual materialism), or to confirm one's ideological, political, or moral correctness (psychological materialism, related to speech), or as an aspect of achieving physical comfort (physical materialism, related to body; Trungpa, 1973/2002). Likewise, in the therapy process, or the therapy supervision process, such materialism may arise as an obstacle. Within such aspirations one can see the rejection of or even hatred for our actual state of being, and the creation of suffering rather than the alleviation of suffering. This is not really in the spirit of the process of "making friends with ourselves," (Chödrön, 2002) a common descriptor of mindfulness practice (Chödrön, 1997; Mipham, 2003; Trungpa, 1974a).

Interestingly, this is in harmony with the psychoanalytic critique of meditation practice expressed by Freud and others (Epstein, 1990) as infantile, pathological, and bliss-driven. Such views, of course, stem from a misunderstanding of the purpose and context of the meditation practice presented here. Rather than a reaction to mindfulness practice itself, it seems to be a reaction to missteps made by some practitioners. Although the power that can be uncovered by calm abiding (shamatha) practice may be used selfishly, that power can serve a trained mind to be strong and clear enough to exchange oneself for others and to walk the warrior bodhisattva path of putting others before oneself (Mipham, 2003).

The basic attitude of being willing to sit down on one's meditation cushion, with all one's flaws and busy mind, and gradually settle down to earth, treating whatever arises to mind as just thought process, is crucial to the descriptive practice of body-speech-mind discipline. That kind of open mindedness creates an interpersonal environment within which the presentation can happen. The activity of description, in itself, can undercut tendencies to pigeonhole oneself (as a good or bad health professional) or the client (as a good or bad, promising or hopeless, worthwhile or less than worthy human being). We give ourselves the space to be with the client, that environment, and our relationship to that person, in as unbiased a way as possible. This cannot happen if we are overly tied up in psychological materialism, for example, making the treatment into a project of proving to ourselves or others what kind of people we are or what kind of theories we prefer.

Sakyong Mipham (2000a, 2003) frequently presents the first step of meditation practice as checking in with one's own motivation – not the motivation we would like to have, but how we actually are. That is what he calls the *outermost circle* or "gathering the mind" (Mipham, 2003, p. 59), the first step towards having a gathered, stable, clear, strong mind of calm abiding. Without that self-loving, humorous attitude of seeing one's actual starting point, which could be "it's all about me" (as Mipham [2005] cheerfully describes the common attitude of egocentricity), there is no ground for further practice.

Genuine beginnings matter and can be encountered at any stage of meditation practice. Pema Chödrön (1994), in her book *Start Where You Are,* also presented this foundational approach to practice. In the supervision discipline as well, inviting some atmosphere of humor and honesty while checking in on motivation is a crucial first step, without which the whole process may lack integrity or operate in an unnecessarily primitive way. These are addressed here in the context of initial instructions given to group members and the presenter, discussed later in this chapter.

The Body-Speech-Mind Discipline as an Intuitive Vipashyana Practice

While calm abiding (shamatha) practice functions as a foundation, the body-speech-mind descriptive discipline may be better understood as a kind of intuitive vipashyana practice, a space awareness practice, based on but not limited to calm abiding. Here, the practitioner is encouraged to tune in to the experience of environmental textures, energies, and space, both physical space and psychological space. Having settled down and opened up to one's own local, personal experience of body and emotions through calm abiding practice, it is more possible to lift one's gaze and appreciate an increasingly broader view of situations without the need for extreme self-consciousness. It is this environmental appreciation and sensitivity to the totality of perceptions, emotions, and energies that becomes the basis for clear verbal communication, as well as the practice of artistic disciplines (Kornman 2006; Trungpa 2004).

9. A Discipline of Inquisitiveness 179

Intuitive vipashyana can be understood as a certain kind of space awareness related to egolessness; related, in particular, to experiences where the textures and qualities of space become more available as the obsessive, largely subconscious activity of checking back on oneself in order to confirm one's personal existence is disempowered. As described by Trungpa (2004b), vipashyana practice is not the frenetic approach of a busy attention hopping from object to object or one that makes a big deal out of psychological obstacles. There is nothing to prove in vipashyana practice and no sense of goal. Rather, such practice is the result of a tamed mind and relaxed sense perceptions that are capable of taking in the totality of a situation in one shot, one panorama, and can use psychological obstacles as stepping stones for relating to an ever expanding experience of situations (Trungpa, 1995). The heedfulness or watchful awareness (*sheshin*, Tibetan) within calm abiding meditation could mature into a panoramic awareness that is not so much characterized by getting stuck in details as by a sense of *letting go*, an awareness that does not have to check back to the origin of that awareness.

As a technique, the presenter is asked to describe the client's body, environments, movement (the *body* aspect), language, energy, style of communication, qualities of relationships (the *speech* aspect), relation to thoughts, mental speed and patterns, horizons of possibility, biases, and approach to mental contents (the *mind* aspect). In the course of such description, the presenter's own body, speech, and mind may also be presented, to greater or lesser degrees. The supervisor and supervision group members, in turn, are instructed to support the presentation with their own discipline of inquisitiveness, asking questions to further *flesh out* the presenter's description, while also tuning in to their own experiences of physical and psychological space that are provoked by the presentation, sometimes reporting such experiences.

General Instructions for Performing
the Body-Speech-Mind Supervision Practice

Preparing the Group: First Clarify the Intention
In leading such a group based on this descriptive speech discipline, it is useful to start out by letting participants know that this is, in fact, a space awareness practice that all people in the room are expected to participate in, not just the presenter and the designated supervisor. Any practice is facilitated when the practitioners know what they are doing and why. The organizing principle of the presentation, for the group members, supervisor, and the presenter, is curiosity about that world (of the person or persons being described) and the presenter's relationship to that world. Clarifying this view, or study related to this, should be part of the basic instructions given to group members. In particular, the group members should be familiar with the body-speech-mind descriptive

guidelines that the presenter is following, such as those presented in this chapter.

Group members could be aware of this intention, and aware when a question or comment is *off task*. Such a shift from the group's intention should not be seen as arbitrary, but usually as some aspect of the difficulty of relating to the task at hand, the description of the subject, and the relevant relationships. As in calm abiding meditation, it is important to first be clear about one's motivation – both one's actual motivation and ideal motivation. In this case, it is important to clarify the intention up front, setting the stage for the performance of this discipline, just as a meditation practitioner, upon first sitting down, first *takes the temperature* of his or her motivation and remembers just why it would be a good idea to come back to the present moment (Mipham, 2003).

Instructions on Posture, Presence, and Balance of Awareness for Group Members and Group Leaders

Group participants could be encouraged to take a good posture and have a sense of relaxed, open awareness that extends not only to the presenter and the meaning of his or her words, but to the other members of the group as well. The presenter may be relatively more absorbed in and focused on the presentation, but still could work with space awareness as much as possible. The space awareness instruction for group members is neither to purely zero in on the presenter, nor to get lost in one's own reactions to the presentation, but to have a balanced awareness that includes the presenter, one's own emotions and thought processes, and the other group members.

This requires a somewhat relaxed, spacious attitude that is also capable of picking up on poignant details from time to time, whether they arise in the environment, as an aspect of the clinical presentation, or internally as feelings, thoughts, or sensations. The group participants who are not presenting should be aware of creating with their posture and attitude an open, awake atmosphere. Each individual in the group should project a definite sense of their own presence, which is a natural result of open awareness. It is the attentive, relaxed awareness of each group member that largely creates the quality of the space within which the presentation may take place.

Just as a master chef has an open awareness of his or her entire kitchen and is immediately aware if something is out of place, or if something is about to boil over, human beings who participate in groups can develop environmental awareness that also picks up on poignant details that arise internally or externally. One can be aware of others and at the same time be aware of one's own feelings and thoughts.

Fundamentally, there should be no difference in the space awareness practice of the supervisor and that of the group participants. All should basically have the same intention – to establish an open awareness that is sensitive to environmental textures and energies, the

9. A Discipline of Inquisitiveness

awareness of everyone in the room, as well as awareness of one's own sensations, feelings, and thoughts. Everyone in the room is facilitating the presentation.

Inquisitive Participation by Group Members and Group Leaders: Facilitating the Presenter's Body-Speech Mind Description

The most obvious way that group members and group leaders facilitate the presentation is by asking open questions that help the presenter deepen the description in process. In many groups, such questioning routinely happens after the presenter concludes one section of the presentation, such as the description of body. Such open questioning may be invited sooner if the presenter is *stuck*, or groping for words or feelings or for a more vivid picture.

Group members ask questions according to their curiosities. These queries are also descriptively oriented. The guideline for such questioning is to promote further description, along the same lines as the guidelines given to the presenter. Leading questions, by contrast, masquerade as open questions, but are really just types of interpretations, narrowing down the description according to the best guess of the questioner. A second way that group members and leaders may participate in the presentation is by tuning in to and sharing their own sensations, emotions, and thoughts that arise in response to the presentation. This will be discussed later in this article.

Guidelines for the Presenter

Description of Body.[2] Overall, the body description includes the physical description of the client, the client's environments, and how he or she moves through such environments. The physical description of the client may include his or her coloring, size, styles of dress, grooming, movement, and posture, as well as overall health and appearance. The literal shape of the client's body, head and neck, shoulders, torso, and legs, lines and curves, wrinkles, smile or frown, could be included. Posture includes not only a literal physical description, but also a sense of how the client holds him or herself in various situations. Is the client's posture fragile, collapsible, sturdy, or brittle? Is there any attitudinal posturing in the person's approach to meeting the world, such as rigidity or flaccidness? Could posture serve as a reminder of *wakefulness*, or heightened awareness, for the individual?

Small details can be included: perhaps the presenter notices the client's bitten fingernails or their smile. The presenter can also describe how he or she tends to hold their own body when with this client, and group members might notice the presenter's physical presence and

---

[2] Many of these guidelines for the body, speech, and mind descriptions are derived from instructions given in the Rabin and Walker (1987) article, especially the sections on body and speech.

comportment when making the presentation, along with taking note of their own physical presence and comportment in response to the presentation.

With respect to the description of the client's physical environment: Does he or she live alone or with other people? What are the surroundings like? What kind of car does the person drive? How does the client spend time vocationally and outside of work? Is there a schedule? Routines? Is scheduling loose or precise? Does the client pursue a physical discipline, such as a martial art or jogging? What does the person like to eat? What about his or her style of eating, food preparation, and table manners? How does the client inhabit the environment of the therapeutic situation, and how does the client orient himself spatially to others, including the presenter?

The history of the individual's experience with various body disciplines, the potential for those disciplines to promote wakefulness, and the possibility and appropriateness of those disciplines being revived or intensified at this stage in the client's life can also be explored. Body disciplines can be an important part of a person's *history of sanity* (Podvoll, 1983), and in this case are viewed in terms of opening or widening whatever possibilities the individual may have for experiencing wakefulness and wholesomeness in his or her present existence. Such thoughts may be taken up in more detail in the *mind* section of the presentation.

Description of Speech. During the presentation of the speech aspect, the communication between the client and therapist, and the client and his world, is highlighted. This can include verbal speech, communicative gestures, or abstract ways of talking about the energy exchange between the client, other people, and his or her environments. The basic metaphor for the speech aspect, borrowed from the discipline of mindfulness-awareness meditation, is that of the breath, which is a continuous medium of exchange between a person and the world. Breath, here, is considered in its dimension of one's feeling of being alive and the qualities that can be connected with that: liveliness or deadness; a sense of well-being or fear, anxiety, and insecurity. Breath can be shallow, deep, vigorous, or fragile; all of these have implications for one's communication and quality of energy. For that matter, communication itself can be said to have qualities of depth, shallowness, vigor, or fragility.

The description of speech may include a somewhat literal account of how the client speaks – the tone, modulation, and accent. Are there any particular words or phrases the client uses frequently? Are there characteristic gestures? Does speech flow? Is there space between words, or long pauses? Does the client express him or herself directly? Does he or she describe sounds, images, sensations, abstractions? Does the client stick to the point? Does the client forget what he just stated? What is his style of communication? Metaphor? Story? Clinical case history? What about the individual's diction, or pronunciation? Does the

9. A Discipline of Inquisitiveness

client hear himself, and does he seem to know how he sounds to others? Does he talk at you? Through you? Beyond you? With you? Does the communication style change in different circumstances? What is the melody of his or her voice? Do the ends of sentences go up or down in tone, or stay level?

With regard to the individual's emotional life, relationships, and other environmental exchanges, questions such as the following may be relevant: How does the client relate to other individuals? To groups? To animals? To money? To dreams and images? How does he or she express feelings? Who are the significant people in that person's life and what is communication like with them? What about the person's repertoire of moods and the situations in which each arises? Is there a feeling of confidence? In what contexts? Depression? In what contexts? What are characteristic emotional or energetic manifestations, and when do these arise?

Does the person carry any conviction that he can actually *say what he means and mean what he says*? Is the client able to complete her sentences or does she lose heart and trail off halfway through her thought? And what does it feel like for you to be with this person? What emotions are evoked in you when with that person in various states of mind? Which kinds of communication seem to be invited, and which kinds seem to be obstructed?

Just as the *body* part of the description is analogous to presenting the history of sanity of physical disciplines, here one may present a history of the fate of the client's compassionate strivings. What have been the results of their passion and compassion? How have others received them, now and in the past? The history of the client's compassion, just as the history of his physical disciplines, is not used as an analytic tool, but is examined with regard to its implications for the client's current relationships, including his or her relationship with the presenter. It is an opportunity for the entire supervision group to feel the possibilities for and obstructions to the client's passion and compassion, which are central to the discovery of path in any human life (see Podvoll, 1983). These topics may be taken up further in the mind section of the presentation.

As was the case at the end of the body part of the presentation, group members may further facilitate the presentation by asking questions designed to elicit further description.

Description of Mind. Mind is reflected and revealed through the body and speech. However, in presenting the mind dimension, it is the client's own thought processes and those of the presenter when with the client that is made the focal point. Is there a haunting lyric or basic obsession that continuously or frequently plays in the thought process of the client? Does the presenter have nagging little thought processes, aspirations, and fears that are provoked in the client's presence? Are there experiences of clarity, simplicity, nonfixation, brilliance, either of the client or the presenter in each other's presence (or some other context), and how are these accommodated (or not)? How is the client's concentration? Does their mind hop about or stay put?

The above questions, in a Buddhist context, may be seen as investigating the client's and presenter's style of ego-process, awareness, and mindfulness or lack of mindfulness. This can include different styles of grasping, hysterical mind, or stable and strong mind — brilliant mind experience that lives on the edge, or buffered mind experience that plays it safe with ideas and experiences.

The actual content of thoughts and how those thoughts are held may also be part of the mind presentation. Some examples of questions that may be appropriate to address during the mind phase of the presentation are: How does the client think? What kinds of things does the client think about? What kind of relationship does he or she have with logic? Does he or she tend to be analytical? Intuitive? Dogmatic? Flexible? Do thoughts come along with examples? Images? Lines of poetry? In holding an opinion, does it seem like the client is fighting for his or her life, or couldn't care less?

How does he or she relate with surprise? With pain? What makes his or her eyes light up? What is his or her mind-landscape like: bright, barren, crowded, spacious, red, black, fuzzy, clear? What is his or her relationship with health? With death? How does the client work with gaps in thought, doubt, and curiosity? Does the client make things up, or stick to the facts? Do you believe them? Do they believe you? Has the client made vows, promises to self or others, remembered or forgotten? Is there trust of self and/or others? How big or small is this world? What shrinks or expands that world? Does the client know about environmental or communicative situations that may tend to expand or contract his or her world view? What happens to your mind when you are with that person?

World-views and Versions of Reality

An important aspect of the mind part of the presentation is that mind includes thoughts and interpretations of reality, notions about what is possible with human life and what is not, and theories about how human development and path works. Confidence about whether there is such a thing as human development or path at all, for a particular person and situation, may also be included in the description of mind. As well, mind includes holistic feeling judgments, prejudices, and bigotries, as well as the ability (or inability) to accurately take the feeling temperature of a social situation, physical space, or aesthetic presentation in one experience.

Mind comes in different flavors and different styles, and there are many Buddhist and Western approaches that describe such styles. Naropa University students are trained in the Maitri Space Awareness practice (Gimian, 2003) and the sensitivity to textures, energies, and mind-styles that go along with such. They contemplate the five buddha family wisdoms and their related emotions; these should not be excluded

9. A Discipline of Inquisitiveness

from the body, speech, or mind section (as appropriate) of a presentation by those who have this sort of sensibility. Maitri space awareness practitioners, in gaining some understanding of their own responses to various energies, could rely upon these understandings to inform their clinical work.

The views and understandings of both clients and the health professionals who are working with them, and how they come into communication with each other or not, are crucial for any therapeutic process, and become part of the mind description in contemplative supervision. Clients possess their own theories of human development, some notion of their own path, and whether they bring these into awareness or not. It is ironic to consider that the act of pigeonholing and theorizing, which has been put aside in the descriptions of body and speech, re-emerges in the descriptive discipline at this point in the form of the theories about human nature and path that are held by the subject of the presentation, as well as those of the presenter, the supervisor, and the supervision group members. It is not helpful to ignore these or pretend we don't have them; they are part of the space of the supervision group, as well as the shared world of the client and therapist.

Both Fleischman (1988) and Silverberg (1988, 1990) discuss the importance of therapeutic interventions arising from a contemplative space, related to both the meditation practice of the therapist (expressed in his or her groundedness and openness) as well as the environments created by that therapist, both physically and by virtue of his or her very being. Silverberg (1990) said, "As therapists, our most important contribution to the healing of the patient is our ability to 'resonate' with and be with the patient in a truly accepting way" (p. 10). He also related the ability to both evoke and tolerate resonance to his meditation practice (Silverberg, 1988). Fleischman (1988) makes a similar point with respect to his therapeutic work: "My practice of vipassana meditation naturally extends an atmosphere charged with the awareness of change, loss, sorrow, re-emergence, and transformation" (p. 45).

However, that space related to the being of the therapist and supportive environments do not tell the whole story of what is required to do therapy, or to train therapists.

> Resonance alone is not sufficient to heal a patient. In addition, the skillful therapist participates in strategic activities which arise from the 'ground' of resonance... It may at first seem contradictory to use the openness and goal-lessness of resonance in a strategic fashion, however a skilled therapist can act spontaneously as well as strategically in the same moment. (Silverberg, 1988, p. 31)

In Fleischman's (1988) words: "It is important to emphasize that *anicca* (atmosphere of impermanence, Pali) is the ambiance that informs my work, but is not the work. Psychotherapy is a professional task of great complexity" (p. 46).

Acknowledging the importance of analytical approaches and theoretical understandings, the question arises: What discipline, set of disciplines, or therapeutic containers exists that can accommodate our intellectual understandings in awareness practice? How can such intellectual understandings themselves develop and mature? How could our understandings of reality contribute to some kind of shared path rather than a destructive force which becomes the basis for power struggles, prejudice, or just further confusion? How can we work with thoughts without trampling feelings or obscuring energetic experiences? How can working with intellect be an awareness practice?

One suggestion for supervision groups may be, in the process of articulating our understandings or world views or those of our clients, it is important to see them as views, thoughts and understandings, rather than as simply true or false. Views need to be given space and time, so that their implications can be explored so that assumptions on which they are based may be examined. If we are too rigidly attached to our views, or disdainful of alternative views, it is difficult to examine them for their value and meaning. It is important not to be too quick to embrace or discard views when introducing them into the space of a discussion. There are many techniques for investigating underlying approaches or for following assertions to their logical conclusions, and examining these in both Western and Buddhist traditions of logic and intellectual training (Kornman, 2006).

Seeing Thoughts *as* Thoughts, Rather Than Excluding Them

The willingness to see thoughts *as* thoughts is basic to mindfulness-awareness meditation. One uses the technique of *labeling* thoughts as thoughts before returning to the object of meditation (Trungpa, 1988). This is not the same as rejecting thoughts. Rather, the interdependence of objects of experience and experiencer, thoughts and thinker, is highlighted as part of the ever-changing, moment-by-moment, relentless process of creating the world and the self which is natural to dualistic mind.

In the Mahayana Buddhist teachings, making friends with this dreamlike reality is presented as the basis for exchanging oneself for others in meditation and postmeditation (Chödrön 2001b; Kongtrul 2005; Trungpa 1974b). In body-speech-mind supervision, befriending and giving voice to descriptions of dreamlike reality – whether that of the therapist, the patient, the group members, or all of the above – facilitates a grounded experience of exchange.

Participation, Timing, and Sharing Sensations, Feelings, and Thoughts

Working with emotions requires strength of mind, relaxed awareness, and some willingness to see thoughts as thoughts. For this reason, it is important that group members work consciously with space awareness practice in their basic participation. This is the container of stability, openness, and strength which holds the possibly wild and unowned energies of the supervision group.

Group members could take note of their feelings and thoughts in order to share them at some appropriate time in the presentation, and they should be encouraged to do so. The description of such experiences can become an enrichment of the situation. Statements as simple as "I have a lump in my throat," or "I feel a ball in my stomach" or "I don't trust the cousin," or even "for some reason, I really want to muss up your hair right now, you little scamp" may resonate with the supervisee and other group members in surprising ways. It is not unheard of for someone in the room to have experiences that are very much like those of the subject's sister, or father, or some other significant person in their world, or thoughts and feelings that the presenter holds but was unaware of until expressed by the group member.

However, in the complex dynamics of a room full of people, group members should usually simply abide with such experiences and be aware of how such experiences affect their own awareness. Note taking should be minimized because it cuts into the basic space awareness practice, but it is acceptable to occasionally jot down a few notes to facilitate later questioning that may further the descriptive process or to better recall feelings or thoughts that may be worth sharing later on. Having an ongoing sense of the other people in the room is crucial because it is the prime determinant of how and when one chooses to communicate, or whether one decides to speak at all.

This is the main reason that the group leader's and group members' awareness should include not only the presenter, but awareness of everyone in the room. One could take the attitude that the group members' various responses are also part of the presentation, which they are communicating constantly, whether they are speaking or not. At natural stopping points in the presentation, such as at the conclusion of the body description section of the presentation or the speech description section, or when the atmosphere in the room shifts, the group leader may choose to ask group members to report on their feelings, thoughts, sensations, and images that may be arising for them, not just at times of apparent crisis.

In a situation where one person is the designated presenter and there is a roomful of people full of openness, love, and curiosity poised to ask questions, the question of when to speak could be a touchy one. Worst case scenario would be the presenter being bombarded with questions, either all at once or rapid-fire, one after another, by a succession of helpful colleagues. It may be useful in such situations to restrict questioning or limit the number of questioners. Most groups adopt such approaches as a useful adjunct to the basic technique. However, relying completely on rules restricting the flow of speech could undermine this discipline as an awareness practice.

In any group (not just supervision groups), if the group members maintain awareness and some sense of nonverbal communication with each other, people who tend to talk too much naturally learn to listen more. Being more in touch with the others in the room and their signals, those who talk too much become more reticent. Curiosity about what others have to say could inspire a naturally talkative person to talk less. The reticent ones, in turn, may talk more because they can feel the attention of others inviting them to speak, that others are picking up on their cues, and are interested in what they may have to say. Many communication problems in groups can be addressed largely by encouraging group members to work with their awareness or simply reminding them to do so.

Exchange, Countertransference, and Obstacles in Contemplative Supervision

Most people have characteristic ways of losing awareness in a group setting. Some look down and implode, simply closing down. Some become agitated and break the descriptive form, suddenly stating their interpretation of the situation as fact, forgetting that such thoughts and feelings are just thoughts and feelings. Some become confused and disorganized, grasping onto rigid interpretations of the descriptive form and the body-speech-mind sequence with which presentations are supposed to take place. Others do the opposite: proliferate abstract imagery in such a way that mundane sensual details of description become completely lost. In any of these circumstances, whether the participant is imploding or exploding, narrowing down or spacing out, that participant's general awareness has usually been interrupted or become unbalanced. This could go along with feeling temporarily overwhelmed by feelings or thought processes, generally in response to the presentation.

When a painful or agitating experience is described by the supervisee (or even if it is not described so clearly, but there is some attempt at description), various intellectual and emotional responses of group members and the supervisor may ripple across the room, spoken or unspoken. Such concordant and complementary countertransferences (Racker in Silverberg, n.d., p.14) are acknowledged in modern psychoanalytic approaches as part of the therapeutic process and are accepted in a similar spirit in this context. Apart from painful or agitating experiences, subtle feeling and thought connections may also arise, as group members imaginatively identify with and arouse their curiosity about the relationship being described. Luyten (1985) called this phenomenon *exchange*, which for her was "that process by which we consciously or unconsciously experience another's state of mind, or they experience ours" (p. 45-46).

The various experiences of the group members are nearly always related to the presentation. Here (as in Luyten, 1985), the reality of such permeability is not taken as evidence of some *ego deficit*, but a choiceless, albeit challenging, aspect of human communication, when given an appropriate, supportive context. Such a context supports the possibility of abiding with feelings and thoughts, energies and textures, but does not necessarily clarify ownership of such experiences. This could be seen as threatening; however, developing the ability to abide in and relax with such experiences is one of the purposes of this supervisory practice.

Intellectual and emotional responses of group members and the supervisor to the presentation may include one or more styles of losing awareness or struggling with awareness, particularly if emotions which arise are agitating, painful, or embarrassing to the group members. In such a case, such sharing in an atmosphere of mindfulness and awareness may be particularly valuable. The *obstacle* could introduce some aspect of the subject being presented or the presenter's relationship to that subject that might not otherwise be easily available. In that way, group members' challenging emotional experiences can be included in the discipline of this practice as reflections of the relationship being presented, rather than breaking the therapeutic container or shifting to another topic.

Just as "the therapist's relaxation and lack of fixation is directly available to the client" (Luyton, 1985, p. 46), so, too the supervisor and supervision group's relaxation and lack of fixation. The supervision process, in allowing the therapist-client relationship to come to life in the room through the process of description, becomes available to the one being supervised. The vivid dream of the supervisory situation could then not only be the opportunity for exchange, but an opportunity for the actual practice of exchanging self for others, working with emotional and intellectual blockages which inhibit the therapeutic relationship. As well, the space could be opened up for a more intelligent discussion of possible therapeutic interventions or the timing of such interventions.

The Relation Between Intention and Technique: The Inseparability of Body, Speech, and Mind

It is common practice to pause at the end of each phase of the presentation, to thoroughly let one's attention and curiosity play on the body aspect of the presentation before moving on to speech, and to attend thoroughly to the speech aspect before moving on to mind (Rabin & Walker, 1987). The purpose of this is to slow down any tendency to rush through the presentation (skipping over painful, embarrassing, boring, or energized aspects of the descriptive process) and to encourage richness of description. Richness of description, in turn, tends to bring the subject and the relationship being presented more completely to life in that space.

However, there is room for variations in style among presenters and groups. In fact, the three aspects – body, speech, and mind – are not experientially discrete. The description of body already speaks, communicates, and implies energy. The form of body and the energy of space are always related to a particular mind, person, and relationship set. Separating these three aspects is just a technique, a potentially useful technique. However, technique serves us best if it is not allowed to get in the way of the basic intention, which is to evoke the person or persons being described and the presenter's relationship to them. Some presenters' communication or perceptual styles are too holistic in nature to easily separate out these aspects and may be given some latitude. It is important to mention this because of the potential to become too concerned about procedure and sequence, at the expense of the basic intent of this discipline.

There have been effective presentations that have skipped around among the three phases of the technique with no loss of heart or thoroughness. The important thing is to slow down, be as thorough as one can, and evoke the situation as well as one can. There is more than one way to do this. The group leader and group members can keep track of aspects of the presentation that may have been neglected even if the presenter does not conform completely to the standard sequence of body, speech, then mind.

Hollow Brilliance, Heartfelt Stammering

There have also been brilliant, almost literary, presentations using this technique that do not evoke the subject of the presentation at all, because the heart of the supervisee is somehow missing from the presentation. There can be great detail of description, but somehow a hollow, disconnected feeling of *something missing* arises. Such almost literary accomplishment may even feel as if the supervisee was merely biding time or fulfilling some externally imposed requirement which must be tolerated until it is time to unleash the *real work* of supervision: the diagnosing and pigeonholing of the subject and presenter, and developing the treatment plan based on such diagnosis. Any technique can be subverted if motivation is not clarified.

Such hollowness may be an aspect of the subject being presented, or the relationship to that subject, or it may reflect some confusion about the intention of the presentation by the presenter or supervision group. Whatever the case, when this sort of experience arises, it is sometimes useful to invite the presenter to talk about their *own* body, speech, and mind when in relationship to the subject being presented, and the quality of space and energy between the presenter and the subject. Shifting the emphasis of the description more to the relationship between presenter and subject or the experience of the presenter, with less emphasis on describing the subject as a kind of literary figure, may be useful.

On the other hand, there have also been stammering, seemingly inept descriptive presentations where the presenter could barely describe any sensual attributes of the subject of the presentation at all. Somehow, the presence of the subject was provoked anyway, along with some heartfelt feeling. In such cases, it is important to not lose faith in the descriptive discipline, continually inviting the presenter to place his or her awareness on the subject of the presentation and to continue to speak in the midst of whatever blankness or anxiety is arising. Group members may use whatever shards of description the presenter offers to form open questions, inviting the presenter to talk further, or to ask questions based on their own genuine curiosity. It is important, at such times, to be patient and not to hurry. Inviting group members or the presenter to describe bodily sensations or feelings that arise in response to the presentation may also lubricate the situation, bringing the presentation along. Heartfelt silence and attentive awareness may also be developmental. It is not useful to judge a developing presentation based on preconceived notions about the value of eloquence.

Conclusions:
A Vision of Contemplative Education

With respect to the process of supervising health professionals and our ongoing training as health professionals, our study of human development in both Buddhist and Western contexts and bringing them into open dialogue with each other is important. The Tibetan Buddhist teachings and Shambhala teachings have clear articulations of the nature of the spiritual and secular path as human beings, including a vision of the nature of being human, what is worth living for in life, an understanding of how we grow up and mature, and what it means to be an adult. They are not just a collection of techniques and practices. Study of the three or nine yanas (vehicles) of Tibetan Buddhism, of which there have been many fine presentations, is pertinent here (Dorje, 1988).

In a Western context, there are the developmental psychologies and assumptions about human development that are implicit and explicit in the various therapeutic techniques. Notions about what it means to be an adult, how both children and ourselves may change and develop, and what is possible or not possible for individuals with particular psychiatric diagnoses, can be drawn out of the variety of Western psychologies.

A truly contemplative psychology, or, for that matter, contemplative education, would not seek to necessarily integrate such views, mashing them into an undifferentiated whole, but rather provides the space and techniques for bringing them into conversation with each other, so that they could *spark*, so that something creative and culturally powerful could evolve. That was how Trungpa (2003) articulated his view of contemplative education at Naropa with respect to discussing how different traditions (in the quotation below, Hindu and Buddhist) could come together in dialogue:

> There is a particular philosophy at Naropa which is not so much trying to bring it together, like a spoonful of sugar in your lemonade so that it becomes more drinkable, but the point is more like a firework – not so much that each will fight with the other in the destructive sense, but that there is an enormous individualism in terms of the doctrines and teachings that are presented. All of them are valid but at the same time there is a meeting point which takes place in a spark.(p. 630)

Theoretical perspectives from different traditions – wherever we draw our understandings from — need to be brought into play as part of our decision making processes, our notions of path and treatment plan. If we do not do this in an aware manner, they will not go away; they will merely operate under the surface.

To some degree, bringing these into conversation with each other in a genuine way can occur in supervision. Such conversations can play a significant role, not only in the supervisory process, but as a dynamic approach to our ongoing training as health professionals and in our training curricula for students.

Techniques, including the variety of meditation practices, therapeutic approaches, and the body-speech-mind discipline presented in this chapter, are not *fix it* pills, but imply an ongoing process of learning and maturation of practitioners as their relationship to such practices deepens. Books such as this one could be part of an ongoing, joyful conversation which furthers such processes. The sparks that fly in this conversation could be the light and smell of our own developing wisdom, compassion, and effective action.

References

Chödrön, P. (1994). *Start where you are: A guide to compassionate living.* Boston: Shambhala.

Chödrön, P. (1997). *When things fall apart: Heart advice for difficult times.* Boston: Shambhala.

Chödrön, P. (2001a). *The places that scare you: A guide to fearlessness in difficult times.* Boston: Shambhala.

Chödrön, P. (2001b). *Tonglen: The path of transformation.* Halifax, Nova Scotia: Vajradhatu.

Chödrön, P. (2002). *Comfortable with uncertainty: 108 teachings.* Boston: Shambhala.
Dorje, L. (1988). Human development and the Tibetan Buddhist tradition. *Journal of Contemplative Psychotherapy, 5,* 71-82.
Epstein, M. (1988). Meditation and the dilemma of narcissism. *Journal of Contemplative Psychotherapy, 5,* 3-19.
Fleischman, P. R. (1988). Awareness of Anicca and the practice of psychotherapy. *Journal of Contemplative Psychotherapy, 5,* 43-52.
Gimian, C. R. (2003). Editor's Introduction to Volume Two. In C. R. Gimian (Ed.), *The collected works of Chögyam Trungpa* (pp. 9-34) Boston: Shambhala.
Kongtrül, J. (2005). *The great path of awakening: The classic guide to Lojong, a Tibetan Buddhist practice for cultivating the heart of compassion.* (K. McLeod, Trans.). Boston: Shambhala.
Kornman, R. (2006). *Prolegomena to a Theory of Contemplative Meditation*, A Lecture given at Naropa Institute on Practice Day, October 17, 2006. Retrieved November 17, 2007 from http://www.geocities.com/artemisgr.geo/prolegomena.htm
Luyton, M. F. (1985). Egolessness and the borderline experience. *Naropa Institute Journal of Psychology, 3,* 43-70.
Midal, F. (2004), *Chögyam Trungpa: His life and vision.* (I. Monk, Trans.). Boston: Shambhala.
Mipham, J. (2000a). *1999 seminary transcripts: Teaching from the Sutra tradition* (Book One). Halifax, Nova Scotia: Vajradhatu.
Mipham, J. (2000b). 1999 *Seminary transcripts: Teaching from the Sutra tradition* (Book Two). Halifax, Nova Scotia: Vajradhatu.
Mipham, J. (2003). *Turning the mind into an ally.* New York: Riverhead Books.
Mipham, J. (2005). *Ruling your world: Ancient strategies for modern life.* New York: Morgan Road Books.
Podvoll, E. (1983). The history of sanity in contemplative psychotherapy. *The Naropa Institute Journal of Psychology, 2,* 11-32.
Rabin, B. & Walker, R. (1987). A contemplative approach to clinical supervision. *Journal of Contemplative Psychotherapy, 4,* 135-149.
Salzberg, S, & Cabot-Zinn, J. (2004). *Lovingkindness: The revolutionary art of happiness.* . Boston: Shambhala.
Shantideva (2006). *The way of the Bodhisattva: A translation of the Bodhicharyavatara* (Rev. Ed; Padmakara Translation Group, Trans.) Boston: Shambhala.
Silverberg, F. R. (Forthcoming). Using indigenous ways of knowing in psychotherapy: The psycho-spiritual healer as mediator between two realms. In B. Tedlock (Ed.), *Healing medicine.*
Silverberg, F. R. (1988). Therapeutic resonance. *Journal of Contemplative Psychotherapy, 5,* 25-42.

Silverberg, F. R. (1990). Working with resistance. *Journal of Contemplative Psychotherapy, 7,* 21-33.
Trungpa, C. (1974a). *The 1973 seminary talks: Hinayana-Mahayana.* Halifax, Nova Scotia: Vajradhatu Publications
Trungpa, C. (1974b). *Training the mind,* Audio Seminar (given at Rocky Mountain Dharma Center, Red Feather Lakes, Colorado). Halifax, Nova Scotia Kalapa Recordings.
Trungpa, C. (1975a). *Glimpses of abhidharma: From a seminar on Buddhist psychology.* Boston: Shambhala.
Trungpa, C. (1987). The meeting of Buddhist and Western psychology. *Journal of Contemplative Psychotherapy,* 4, 3-14.
Trungpa, C. (1988). *Shambhala: The sacred path of the warrior* (C. R Gimian, Ed.). Boston: Shambhala.
Trungpa, C. (1991). *The heart of the Buddha* (J. L. Lief, Ed.), Boston: Shambhala.
Trungpa, C. (1993). *Training the mind and cultivating loving kindness.* Boston: Shambhala.
Trungpa, C. (1995). *The path is the goal. A basic handbook of Buddhist meditation,* (S. Chödzin, Ed.). Boston: Shambhala.
Trungpa, C. (2002). *Cutting through spiritual materialism.* Boston: Shambhala. (Original work published in 1973)
Trungpa, C. (2003). *The collected works of Chögyam Trungpa* (Vol. 2). Boston: Shambhala.
Trungpa, C. (2004). Dharma art. In J. L. Lief (Ed.), *The collected works of Chögyam Trungpa* (Vol. 7; pp. 1-162). Boston: Shambhala.

10

Maitri Space Awareness: Developing the Therapist Within

James Evans
Alexandra Shenpen
Patricia Townsend

> The way to change the world is not to get people to focus on changing external circumstances or even to modify their own behavior. Rather, they first need to examine how they experience the world.
> –Chogyam Trungpa (cited in Midal, 2004, p. 405).

Maitri Space Awareness training combines the wisdom of Eastern (especially Tibetan Buddhist) meditative disciplines and Western-therapeutic views. *Maitri* is a Sanskrit word that can be translated as *loving-kindness* (Jacerme, 2005). Within the context of psychotherapeutic work, maitri refers to a direct sympathy, warmth, and openness to one's immediate experience. It is a simple friendliness or ease with whatever arises.

The Master of Arts in Contemplative Psychotherapy (MACP) program at Naropa University seeks to uncover and create opportunities for students to experience maitri. Students develop maitri through various meditation practices, including Maitri Space Awareness practice. The introduction of Maitri Space Awareness practice within Naropa's MACP program broke new ground by offering students new ways to experientially work with their own states of mind in order to be of benefit to their clients. Edward Podvoll, one of the founders of the Contemplative Psychotherapy program at Naropa noted,

> The space awareness practice helps practitioners to develop more rapidly as therapists, because they have developed more insight into their own states of mind, and consequently do not fear any state of mind manifesting in self or others. Because these practitioners are fearless, they are not distracted or confused by their own emotions, thoughts, feelings, or wild states of mind; nor

are they distracted or confused by any particular state of mind that a client presents in therapy. (E. Podvoll, personal communication, April, 1982)

Evolution of Maitri Space Awareness

In the early 1970's, Buddhist teachers Chogyam Trungpa and Shunryu Suzuki discussed their experiences of teaching meditation in the West. One challenge encountered by both teachers was presenting effective meditation instruction for people suffering from instability of mind due to psychological and emotional distress. Suzuki and Trungpa suggested that a community be created, inclusive of students both ready to practice formal meditation and those who needed a different approach. To sit still and attend to the simplicity of body and breath in the moment is a precise, immediate experience that can be difficult for most beginning practitioners, and impossible for some individuals. Meditation practice "involves an intimate relationship with ourselves... purely getting into what we are, really examining our actual psychological process without being ashamed of it" (Trungpa, 1975, p. 56).

The Maitri Project Vision

Trungpa's consideration of how to benefit those with mental instability gave birth to the *Maitri Project*, a contemplative therapeutic community open to practitioners of all levels of mental stability. This idea would eventually evolve into a training community for psychotherapists. Initially, however, a mix of meditation-ready practitioners and those who were not able to practice formally attended the maitri communities.

The working basis of the Maitri Project was the view that everyone is fundamentally awake, but most people have lost touch with their innate sanity to varying degrees. Maitri communities were structured as nonhierarchical therapeutic environments without discriminations made between *therapists* and *patients*. Everyone would be approached as an equal community member living in an extremely ordinary domestic situation. The approach was to simplify daily living tasks and to ground people whose minds were too unbalanced to work with a basic meditation technique. The point of using the basic physical situations of food and living environment as a focus of attention was "to communicate with the unbalanced person so as to awaken him... [starting] on the basic level of survival... The person should have some feeling of instinctive simple communication" (Trungpa, 1975, p. 72). By helping people synchronize body and mind, it was hoped that they could discover their intrinsically healthy nature despite the complicated machinations of their current state of mind. The retreat format was meant to be of limited duration, with the goal that participants would return to their lives more truly engaged and with a greater capacity for contributing to others.

10. Maitri Space Awareness

Through dialogue with the early retreat participants, Trungpa realized that introducing simplicity of environment was not always enough for helping balance the experiences of people struggling with mental instability. He began exploring new techniques to increase the effectiveness of the therapeutic community. These concerns gave rise to Trungpa's implementation of Maitri Space Awareness postures within the retreat setting.

Development of the Maitri Practice and Postures

The Maitri Space Awareness practice evolved from Tibetan Vajrayana Buddhist teachings (Evans, 1993). These teachings were part of the Buddha's original treasury of teachings given in India in the 6th Century B.C. The basic approach of space awareness practice was traditionally used with advanced Vajrayana practitioners who, on long solitary retreats, might become caught in intensified states of mind. In Western terminology, some of these states of mind could be referred to as psychotic. In Buddhist Psychology, they are seen as extreme states in which one's self-experience becomes fixated. To encourage allegiance to a more fluid and transparent self-experience during long solitary retreats, space awareness practices were implemented.

Maitri Space Awareness practice was developed based on these traditional Tibetan yoga practices and explorations with Western students into the relationship between bodily configurations and states of mind. The postures that were developed for the practice heighten styles of cognition, emotion, and sensory awareness to provide practitioners familiarity with the workings of their mind. The postures tend to exaggerate whatever emotional states or cognitions are already occurring, such that they pop into awareness more clearly.

Five postures were developed to support awareness of the *five wisdoms* in Buddhist psychological and tantric models. The five wisdoms are considered the quintessence of the five elements of water, earth, fire, wind and space. The five wisdoms are said to give rise to all the inner and outer phenomena of the relative world. Marvin Casper pointed out that in speaking of his enlightenment the *Buddha* described his awareness as "clear, even, discriminating, unobstructed, and all-pervading" (Jacerme, 2005, p. 129). These terms are often used to describe the awakened experiences of the five energies. Their respective Sanskrit names are *vajra, ratna, padma, karma,* and *buddha*.

We can experience the energies in ourselves as flavors of compassionate openness, as neurotic confusion, or in their most fixated state, as psychosis. In Buddhist Psychology, compassion and struggle are seen as arising together, or co-emerging, not as separate polarities. They arise from within a basic openness or potentiality; similar to the way any kind of weather can arise in the sky. We all experience a mixture of emotional energies and tendencies. If we can apply nonjudgmental awareness to them, we can catch glimpses of contrast between our compassionate, awake potential and our limited struggling selves.

Taking maitri postures that evoke expressions of the five energies gives us the opportunity to become better acquainted with ourselves and the world around us. The postures are not particularly comfortable, making it difficult to dissociate or ignore emotions and thoughts that arise. This inescapability can encourage a different relationship with one's mental states; one based on openness, and not judgment or fear. Trungpa explained, "The very energies that trouble us become the forces we use for awakening and insight" (Lief, 2005, p. 276). Heightened emotional states can dramatically illuminate the undercurrents of thoughts and core beliefs that make up our daily mental landscape. Bringing awareness to these thoughts and beliefs can offer us a magnified view of the workings of our mind.

The First Maitri Communities

Trungpa envisioned that the ideal locations for Maitri communities would be natural, rich sensory environments, since such places tend to invite us into our senses and can bring contrast to the power of self-absorption. The hopes and fears of projections might be noticed for what they are and clear perception might have a chance to dawn. Vision and actuality, however, often take time to catch up with each other. The land donated for the first manifestation of the Maitri project was a very rural setting, near Elizabethtown in the Adirondacks of New York state. However, original participants noted that the land did not feel terribly healthy; it was lacking wildlife, had sparse, gloomy vegetation, no old-growth forests, and a half-burnt building that was habitable but needing reconstruction provided the main living quarters (T. Leontov, personal communication, August, 2007).

A shoestring operation of about twelve people comprised the core participants of the first retreat. They managed daily living tasks, such as cooking and cleaning, practiced meditation, and did the Maitri postures in any available, usable room—literally wherever there was an unbroken floor. The community worked hard at planting organic gardens, hand-removing insects, and reconstructing floors. The combination of mindfulness meditation, posture practice, and daily life activities were extremely powerful for bringing awareness to participants' experiences of their minds.

Soon, word spread that the community was open to people struggling with various intensities of experience. Some of the first guests who joined the Maitri community were in extreme psychotic states. Community members helped these individuals, who had very wild minds, take the maitri postures through physical touch. Some of these guests, otherwise, had little reference point for their bodies. These new participants added to the tensions in the group, rife with its own relational chemistry.

One of these community members, Alan Schwarz (personal communication, August, 2007), recalled how deeply the staff thought of their efforts as trying to be of service in what could often be a cauldron of emotions. Although not present at the retreat, Trungpa would be consulted for ways to help ground people, to synchronize mind and body. After clarifying how a person was *stuck* according to the five energies, he suggested approaching the *less stuck* aspects with the person, looking for workability, or diving right into the stuck point. The vision was hard to manifest, given the degrees of psychological instability of some of the participants and the limited resources. The use of Western medicine was explored, and a Western doctor, James Sacamono, was consulted and some visitors were eventually hospitalized.

This said, it was also noticed that the practice had an effect even on people caught in severe psychosis. One community member described this as "watching a person able to track mind, rather than mind just running wild" (T. Leontov, personal communication, August, 2007). When another participant asked Trungpa why the project was so important to him and interested him so much, he replied, "Because crazy people are so intelligent" (N. Craig, personal communication, August, 2007).

Maitri Room Design

During the first Maitri Project, Trungpa and students worked on designing rooms in which to do the maitri postures to further evoke different styles of emotion and perception. Room design was inspired by traditional Tibetan Buddhist teachings about how the environment impacts perception. It was thus both traditional and very experimental. A unique feature of the first Maitri community became a rustic building, roughly 20 foot by 30 foot with five rooms for practice. A room was built in each corner with the fifth standing in the center of the building.

Each room was vibrant, painted a single color corresponding to one of the five basic energies. They were slightly different in size and design. There was a fifteen foot tall green room with a window to the sky at the very top, a square yellow room with a large round window, a red room with a big rectangular window, a deep blue room, very narrow with tiny slits of windows, and a smaller off-white windowless room in the middle.

The rooms were taken apart and moved when the Maitri project received another parcel of donated land in Wingdale, New York in 1974. The new property was idyllic, situated at the confluence of two rivers at the end of a road. The land had a farmhouse and barn, which were converted for group retreats. The maitri building was reassembled in a lovely two acre meadow and the windows of the practice rooms looked out onto the landscape (today's rooms are not oriented to an outside view).

Maitri Training for Psychotherapy Students

In time, the staff at Wingdale decided that although the Maitri retreats ripened their compassion and understanding of emotional states, they did not yet have the training, expertise, and facilities to provide the level of help needed by the people who were drawn to their community. However, the basic ingredients of the Maitri Project had great fertility. The decision to end the Maitri Project as it existed led to its transformation into an innovative, significant, and powerful contribution to the training of psychotherapists when Trungpa asked Marvin Casper to think of a way to more effectively use the rooms and practice.

Maitri Space Awareness was changed to a training vehicle for Naropa students and Casper has taught the application in this form for over thirty years now. Students with a sense of adventure, and an interest in developing insight and compassion, soon went to Wingdale for three-month retreats as part of their efforts to understand their own minds and to be of benefit to others. In the late 1970's, the Wingdale property was sold. The funds were used to strengthen Naropa's departmental offerings, one of which was the newly formed Masters in Buddhist and Western Psychology (currently the MACP program).

A new location, then called Rocky Mountain Dharma Center (currently Shambhala Mountain Center), was chosen to continue the retreats with a special emphasis on Maitri Space Awareness training for psychotherapists. The current facility has two beautifully designed maitri practice pavilions and accommodates the training retreats for all MACP students. Over the years, the retreats changed in length from three months, to ten weeks, to the current format: a one-month retreat in the first and second years of the training program, followed by a one-week retreat in the final year.

MACP students encounter an especially fertile ground for self-reflection and the development of maitri within their yearly retreats since they move as a cohort throughout the training program, attending all classes and retreats as a group. The community aspect of this program challenges students to observe not only how they relate to their own states of mind, but also how they relate to other students throughout their shared three-year journey. This challenge is especially magnified in the no-escape situation of the month-long maitri retreats in the first and second years.

To settle the minds and hearts of participants, the first two weeks of these retreats require up to eight hours of daily sitting meditation. Instruction is given in bringing maitri to the flurry of mental and emotional states that arise while sitting silently on cushions for hours on end. Training awareness on the intensity and impermanence of these experiences helps set the stage for a heightened experience of the posture practices that follow in the last two weeks of the retreats. While

10. Maitri Space Awareness

the first two weeks utilize only functional talking, communication between classmates is encouraged in the last two weeks. The increased level of interaction helps students more fully experience how they relate to others when their emotional states are intensified by the Maitri Space Awareness practice. To help ground these experiences, sitting meditation sessions are also included in the last two weeks, although to a lesser extent.

Living in community together can rub the hearts of students pretty raw with tenderness, humor, heartache, irritation, and yearning—sometimes for escape, sometimes for true openness and connection. The power of the sitting practice to illuminate and undercut habitual constructs of self, combined with the way perceptions, emotions, and thinking patterns change from room to room, can open up uncertainty about what the *self* really is. Students can find themselves in each other's psychological shoes, behaving and perceiving themselves in unfamiliar modes. There can be moments of awareness such as: "Oh, that's why that person does that. I get it!" or, "Now I understand my difficulty in relating to so and so. This must be what it's like for them," along with less insightful moments and observations. Either way, the impermanence of emotional experience is continually highlighted through the combination of room and sitting practices.

Several nights of expressive arts, dancing, and skit performances also punctuate the retreats with playfulness, depth, and creativity, providing participants outlets for exploring their relationships to the five energies. These activities also allow students to see each other's uniqueness, the brilliant sanity, and the personal stuckness that arise with regard to their differing emotional states. Humor and creativity based in unconditional friendliness is a good antidote to taking oneself too seriously. Integration of knowledge and experience is often helped by poking gentle fun at the discoveries of the practices. Although students may notice the impulse to turn tail and run at some point during a maitri program, and indeed some do, it continues to be one of the most innovative ways of investigating the nature, functions, and phenomena of mind.

The Practice

> Wakefulness is actually very close to us. We are touching it all the time. (Trungpa, 1980, p. 4)

In Buddhist Psychology, we can describe the five wisdom energies as expressions of brilliant sanity. The wisdom and confusion of each are seen as two sides of the same coin, just as bitter and sweet are known in the context of each other. In Maitri Space Awareness practice, one can taste the bittersweet understanding of the differences between being awake and confused. This is how we cultivate maitri toward ourselves. It becomes clear that attempting to manipulate the energies often backfires, that one cannot contrive the wisdom qualities, and that genuine experiences of brilliant sanity comes when we open to our experience with curious and gentle awareness.

The Maitri Space Awareness technique is simple. In the colored room, one adopts an attitude of bare awareness, a relaxed alertness; neither clinging to nor rejecting moment-to-moment experience. Instructions to participants include being aware of one's body, the space around one's body, and the flow of one's sense perceptions. As attention to space is highlighted, thoughts and emotions that arise become highlighted as well. The practice is neither to reject nor follow them, just to notice whatever arises and come back to being present. One can easily become self-absorbed in thoughts and emotions, losing awareness of the room and one's body altogether. Therefore, each posture also has an aspect of physical discomfort, which tends to be a grounding element.

Forty-five minutes in the colored room is followed by fifteen minutes of *aimless wandering*. The instruction is to allow oneself time outdoors, to *notice what you notice*. Students are instructed to walk, look, and touch whatever is of interest without interacting with other people. The aimless wandering allows time to adjust to moving around in the world, while noticing any shifts in perception. The colored room is actually meant to be a catalyst for experiential shifts that extend beyond the practice session; and bare awareness is encouraged as students resume activities and interactions with the world outside the room.

Five Expressions of Brilliant Sanity

The transmission of teachings on Maitri Space Awareness is an oral and experiential tradition; incomplete, and possibly unhelpful, to attempt to summarize in written words. Maitri retreat participants are introduced to the energies through five individual talks presented by retreat staff members. The speakers offer an embodied manifestation of the energies as much as possible by presenting general information along with their individual take on how the energies appear. These talks are personal not only to the staff members presenting them, but also to the overall emotional climate of the retreat and the individual needs of students who are present. The Maitri talks are most powerfully experienced within a retreat setting where personal exploration of them will proceed through room practice.

In the spirit of offering the reader a flavor of these types of embodied presentations, the following section introduces the five clear and confused expressions of brilliant sanity through the use of poetic prose; it is meant to evoke some taste of the room practice itself without presenting a complete map. There are a multitude of written sources which can enrich and clarify this presentation, such as those in the reference list of this chapter. However, again, the best way to clarify it is through personal exploration and participation in a group retreat.

10. Maitri Space Awareness

Lastly, although it is tempting to categorize oneself and others with information included in presentations of the five wisdom energies, participants are continually reminded to not do so. Instead, they are instructed to use the information to help hone awareness on the energies as they arise within themselves and others. The intention of sharing this material is not to freeze those experiences further; rather, it is to highlight the colorful and workable impermanence of them. We are all made up of changing variations of the five expressions of brilliant sanity. Where we are most vulnerable is perhaps where our gifts lie. Hopefully, presentations of Maitri Space Awareness can lead to a greater awareness of our humanity, rather than a new psychological overlay. When we relax with ourselves, the dynamic mosaic of our colors can become flexible, beneficial to others and ourselves. Please allow yourself to both discover and let go as you read on, touching into the energetic qualities through the presentation of the atmosphere of the rooms, the associated seasons, and the human characteristics portrayed.

BLUE (Water Element, Mirrorlike Wisdom, *Vajra*)

Deep, sapphire blue narrow windows are scattered in a horizontally, precise abstract pattern in the *vajra* room. The walls, carpet, and ceiling are deep blue. The posture can be uncomfortable for the neck and headaches can occur. It can also feel as if the front of one's body has turned into sky.

This room is associated with the unmitigated sharpness and clarity of awareness, mirrorlike wisdom. Imagine a mountain lake in the depths of winter at dawn, completely still, the pure morning sky reflecting into its depths, rock by snowy rock appearing, gleaming in shiny black granite. Not a ripple distracts from the clarity. Frosted stalks of dried grasses and pine needles are so precisely seen in the water, as if drawn with a single hair. Everything reflected just as it is, beyond interpretation, penetrates directly to the heart, before ideas, concepts, or names begin to dilute the fresh, peaceful mountain air of mind.

In the mirrorlike wisdom of bare awareness, cognition is pure, effortless knowing; intellect is unfiltered by bias; perspective is wide open and fluid. In the everyday, this translates as not putting effort into at trying to figure things out. Rather, there is a stillness and ability to let things reflect into the mind, a trust and ease in seeing the bigger picture as well as the details. Mirrorlike wisdom is gifted in naturally picking up on the patterns in the world, spontaneous and accurate analysis where the *knower* does not get in the way of the *knowing*. This aspect of awareness can be visionary, seeing further because it is not stuck in what is already known. The natural allegiance is to truth, curiosity, discovery, illumination, clarity, thoroughly understanding all perspectives and bringing about peace.

When this open state of awareness contracts and loses

confidence in itself, a cloudiness and furrowed brow can occur. Because clarity is lost, there is irritability and the struggle to know. There is a sense of something being *wrong*, picking up on mistakes and faults, fixation on details, preoccupation with *getting it right*, and avoidance of being the *one who is wrong*. The natural clarity narrows into an attachment to perfection and an intolerance of seeming imperfections. One becomes impatient and judgmental of vagueness, uncertainty and imprecision. There is a preference for order and for things *making sense*. This can also become self-aggressive, claustrophobic, and alienating. Emotionally cut-off and distant, abstraction can become preferable to human company's unpredictable emotions. One feels either compelled to retreat to the seeming safety of logic, or to resurface for a good argument. The most accessible emotion is that of anger, ranging from icy-cold deepfreeze to hot metallic rage.

YELLOW (Earth Element, Wisdom of Equanimity, *Ratna*)

A radiant warm yellow suffuses the walls, ceiling, and carpeting of the *ratna* room. Two very large round windows are positioned on opposite walls. Despite knowing they are both round, one cannot see either in its full rotundity when lying beneath. Attention is given to the open fingers of the hands, which tend to curl up when one spaces out.

This room is associated with the rich abundance of the wisdom of equanimity. Imagine sitting in a garden ripe for harvest amongst golden stalks of ripe corn. The tomatoes are blood-red, bursting with juice and heavy with scent. Limbs groan on trees as luscious peaches ripen. Apples weigh and pull on their branches, falling easily to the ground, some spilling their seeds for different creatures to feast upon. A grape bursts its skin. The fruits lie about, careless of their half-eaten selves, offering whatever is left to fall apart and mingle with the earth. Across the path, the majestic oak and maple leaves are chocolate, magenta, persimmon, and scarlet.

Time is slow as the sun fills the canopy of air with the warm rich smells of dark soil, composting leaves and ripe fruit. Looking up through the colorful crisp fall leaves on branches, a rich brocade carpets the sky amidst cumulous clouds. Cares crumble into the honey thick air; thoughts meander where they will, growing moss, resting with generous doses of appreciation. An acorn is a crown jewel. Everything, effortlessly, is generous, and the richness does not seem to belong to anyone.

When the earth element is expressed in a person as the wisdom of equanimity, there is a quality of being settled and satisfied, which can be majestic. This energy has steadfastness, a fullness of seemingly effortless hospitality, which responds to what is needed. Resourceful and bountiful, one is nonetheless not impressed with oneself when at ease, needing neither praise nor gratitude. There is a trust and evenness, which goes beyond the changing conditions of one's life. An ample and undemanding sense of welcome is felt by others.

10. Maitri Space Awareness

Losing touch with this inherent quality leads to a sense of insecurity, or insubstantiality. One attempts to compensate by accumulating material or psychological wealth. One loses track of how much or how little is truly needed. Therefore, letting go becomes difficult. One tends to hang onto everything, at least as much as possible—afraid of having too little, or just not having enough. There is a tendency to display or hoard one's perceived wealth, collecting admiration and affirmation from others, or keeping the goodies for oneself. This can translate into any area of one's life. Marketing strategies target this vulnerability and make powerful use of it.

When we are not present to the richness within ourselves, and are distracted by this style of preoccupation, we become less able to clearly discern our own needs and those of others. When we clumsily try to recover a sense of contentment, grasping and fixation occur, undermining our attempts to feel better. The dilemma feeds on itself, ingenious in its ability to feel unsatisfied, or fixated upon running out of satisfaction. The preoccupation with never being or having enough can be quite dramatic; a tragic twist on our inherent richness.

RED (Fire Element, Discriminating Wisdom, *Padma*)

Not a deep red, nor a light red, the *padma* room seems luminous and glowing with color—hard to pin down the exact hue. One side has a large rectangular window, which is warm-red, almost orangey-red, the opposite wall a smaller one of the same hue. It can be easy to fall asleep in any of the Maitri rooms, but the posture in this one can be particularly conducive to a dreamy twilight nap.

This room is associated with the warmth and compassion of discriminating awareness. The fire element awakens the spring within winter. When the crisp white snow and crystals of ice are warmed by the sun, patches of earth show beneath the crusty drifts; and melting snow moistens the ground. Fiery rays penetrate and soften the frozen earth. Rivulets and streams create their own shapes in the snowdrifts, between rocks, in the earth itself. Running together, apart, wider, glistening, winding closer together, separating again, they moisten the land where they flow, gurgling, chuckling, roaring, trickling. We name them, "Little Trout," "Moon River," "Shimmering Sadie," sensing their personalities.

The promise of spring draws us outside, toward each other in a wider circle, rediscovering connections and possibilities as the days get longer. We can linger in the changing colors of the evening sky. We begin to imagine the pleasures of the growing season, with the air on our skin and the fragrances of flowers, trees and grasses. It is easy to stop and be captivated by the first crocus in its vibrant, brilliant purple cups, tender white translucent petals, or the radiant buttercup yellow nodding heads. There are so many different colors of green to appreciate, so many hues of pinks and whites, even within a single branch of apple-blossoms.

Empathic and intuitive, there is a natural connectedness and ease in the wisdom of discriminating awareness. Just as the color red and the brilliant evening sky stop and magnetize us, the qualities of life seem full of personality and character, inviting an unfolding world of metaphor and relationship. It all seems like a *happening* conversation. The interconnectedness and simultaneous uniqueness of all beings is readily apparent and appreciated. One tends to connect to the world by sensing and feeling it, loving the textures of nuance and metaphor. Emotions are highlighted and communicated readily. It is a world of tonality.

However, as a person falls asleep to the natural interconnectedness of being, she awakens into an effort to restore, hold onto, or manipulate the sense of connection, which has been lost. The sense of playfulness can become ungrounded, dangerous. Fire, gone out of control, can devour its surroundings, leaving charred bits of friendship in its wake, or heaps of lifeless ash. The warmth disappears; a lack of empathy and a withdrawal sets in. The embers sulk. Moods predominate. Natural appreciation and empathy become a confused need for, or rejection of, attention. Relationships become an engrossing push/pull merry-go-round. "Go away... but don't leave me alone." Interpersonal distance becomes confusing; confluence, a comfort and a threat. The sensitivity becomes tiring; and seems very personal.

GREEN (Wind Element, All-Accomplishing Wisdom, *Karma*)

The ceiling in the *karma* room seems taller than in the other rooms, with a slightly elevated square green window up above. Wherever you look in the room, it is a fresh spring green. However, with sustained gaze, it can become a very dark color, deep emerald to black. It helps to remember to blink.

This room is associated with the wind element wisdom of unimpeded action. The garden in midsummer is teeming with activity. The ecosystem is alive and humming with life. Each plant has its own timing, unrolling its leaves, yielding to wind and rain, gathering moisture from cool night air, and drooping slightly in midday heat to conserve strength for more motion and movement. Each plant has its own wisdom in accomplishing its growth pattern, relating to the changing elements, and becoming whatever is destined within its seed plan. Shoots have their own power, cracking their shells, putting down roots further into the soil, and pushing up their limbs against morsels of earth. Stretching toward the sun, they navigate around other stems and leaves, expressing their life force with vitality and freshness.

At the height of summer, hummingbirds hover and hesitate in midair. With whirring wings seemingly still, they sink their long beaks deep in the orange centers of trumpet vines, drawing forth beads of nectar to drink. The ants are a mass of moving crumbs streaming back into sandy heaps between chives and poppy mallow, helping each other drag larger pieces as if with one body. Grasshoppers wait for their moment to spring forth from long grasses, completely soaring, legs relaxed until landing on a nearby leaf. Tiny yellow and black garden snakes quietly slip between the rocks and curl up in smooth cracks. Each creature and plant has its natural function to accomplish, inseparable from the causes and conditions present, as the wind of life moves in a unifying direction. Dusk falls at the end of the busy day. The air cools. The sounds lessen. And then, a chorus of crickets marks the opening act of night.

The natural power of wind and the activity of life fulfilling itself are expressed within a person as responsive active compassion, which has no hesitation in meeting situations directly and as needed. As wisdom is not based in any internal pressure or need to prove oneself, there is an inherent quality of restfulness, like the eye of a storm. A person might be fulfilling many different purposes, but at the same time can feel peaceful, as if nothing is really happening. There is stillness in movement. Since the wisdom of all-accomplishing action is not self-referencing, others can feel inspired, energized and included in its wake.

When we are not fully awake to the unimpeded power of our own compassion, the energy becomes fragmented and loses sensitivity to timing, trust, and balance. The natural power of compassion instead competes to get things done, to get ahead. There is a kind of pushing, which generates paranoia and fear, both intrapersonally and interpersonally. The genuineness of offering one's energy sensibly where it is needed becomes self-serving in the distracted state, and there is a loss of contact and responsiveness to anything outside of one's purpose. Getting things done supercedes *how it gets done*. This can be alienating to others. This tone predominates in current Western culture. There is a constant impulse toward comparison; and the pain of envy occurs.

WHITE (Space Element, All-Encompassing Wisdom, *Buddha*)

Off-white, almost a light oatmeal color, with diffuse light in the ceiling window, one moves around in the *buddha* room, trying to adjust to the uncomfortable posture, gaze open, and not too far from the wall and floor.

Above and below mingle in the wisdom of all-encompassing space. The sky has no argument with the clouds as they appear and disappear, or the raindrops, the thunder, the lightning. There is room for the play of all elements in the vast unencumbered nature of space. Within this spacious sky of mind, a sense of wellbeing and simplicity arise. A quality of bare awareness prevails, an expression of nonaggression; simply being. Nothing extra, just awake. Nothing but awake. There is room for everything, room for all kinds of personalities, lots of room to just be oneself. People often appreciate being around this quality in others, or they might not even notice the spacious-style person is there. There is room for a lot of projection, as assumptions can flourish in the absence of much expression.

This spacious intelligence can fall asleep to itself, forgetting its openness. Partially reawakening into a clouded and anxious state, it becomes characterized by a sense of thickness or dullness. The awake aspect of mind becomes ignorance. The natural bent toward simplicity constricts itself into an allegiance to familiarity and a need to secure oneself. One becomes frightened of change and attempts to ignore it. Routine is reassuring and self-consciousness a recurring sensitivity. A kind of numbing is present, so clumsiness easily occurs. There can be big blind spots in sensing one's impact on others; whereas, feedback from others, if noticed, can be irritating and invasive, reinforcing the impulse to snuggle further into ignorance. The pain which occurs with the space element results from the domestication of space. This can be quite impenetrable. Because the capacity to ignore is so profound and clever, it produces an absorption that can be very painful and confusing to wake from.

The Therapist Within

Maitri Space Awareness practice combined with meditative insight helps us notice the patterns of our minds and recognize the missteps of perception that cause us to become seemingly disconnected from our own brilliant nature. We learn that when those missteps occur, we struggle unconsciously to recuperate the intrinsic well-being, which haunts us in its absence. We experience this disconnect through different styles of distraction and confusion, "when we distance ourselves from experience and drift into indirect experience—duality. These patterns are pale and painful imitations of our liberated energies" (Chogyam & Dechen, 1997, p. 75). The drift into duality causes us to become entangled in our senses and sense objects, including mental and emotional events, in such a way that we lose track of our brilliant sanity. We then try to recreate it through psychological strategies and attempts to manipulate the conditions of our lives. This dilemma can be described as "distracted being" (Chogyam & Dechen, 1997, p. 33).

As contemplative psychotherapists, we are trained to look kindly and unflinchingly into the details of our own distracted being, so that we can do so with our clients, bringing awareness to *how* their suffering occurs. We become skilled in clarifying the distinction between causes and conditions, our relationship to the causes and conditions, and where our aliveness disappears into the mix. Seeing these processes up close develops a ground of tremendous empathy. To do this, we have to personally be able to go beyond the pursuit of comfort. Midal (2004) pointed out, "The pursuit of comfort makes human beings incapable of realizing themselves as true human beings; and it makes it impossible to develop genuine discipline, which is the source of true joy" (p. 398).

Most of us have a hard time with our suffering and do not really know how to work with it. We tend not to really be sure where it begins or ends. We flip-flop between pinpointing what/who to blame and what/who to fix. Just like our clients, the focus of that can become aggression toward ourselves. Trungpa (1980) wrote, "The key point in overcoming aggression is to develop natural trust in yourself and in your environment, your world. In Buddhism, this trust in yourself is called maitri" (p. 146). When we do not have a disciplined and kind view of ourselves, we often do not relate directly with how we are stuck and our attempts to free ourselves are only temporary. As the conditions of our lives change, from pleasant to unpleasant to pleasant again, from inspiring to brutally painful, this struggle of happy and sad is heightened in endless personal tapestries.

Maitri Space Awareness practice acquaints us more intimately with the five most basic ways in which this plays out. Through bare awareness, the ways in which we become distant and embroiled in ourselves, although psychologically seductive, are seen to be as flimsy and as ready to fall apart as anything else made of causes and conditions. Although attempts to feel better express some basic intelligence, these attempts can become habitual patterns that get in our way, limiting vibrancy and creativity in our relationships and lives. We mature as we gain insight and learn how to let go of them, daring to be present without efforting or strategizing. Chung (1990) stated:

> A well integrated personality is essential to being a good psychotherapist... The more the psychotherapist expands his awareness, the clearer becomes the reality within and without him... If his awareness extends beyond the ego, his capabilities to see, to know, to deal with and to maintain reality grow to a great extent. (p.29)

Conclusion

The view in contemplative psychotherapy is utter confidence in brilliant sanity. Maitri Space Awareness practice accompanied by mindfulness-awareness meditation is a vehicle through which people can be re-introduced to the qualities of their own brilliant sanity, as well as to the living cataracts of the mind in which they fall asleep. Discovering the wholesomeness of who we are, while becoming more awake to and discerning of recognizable struggles flavoring everyday life, can help us not to mistake *distracted being* as the whole story. Genuine confidence, compassion, and resilience in our work with ourselves and other people can develop further.

Maitri Space Awareness practice helps to develop bravery in being present to a great range of suffering. It allows us to venture out of our comfort zones. Sensing the terrain of how someone inhabits *which elements* may give rise to the kind of presence and curiosity which a client feels met by. How much space, how much support, how much curiosity, appreciation, distance might someone need? How much room to just be? To feel understood? To feel cared about? Where is their courage most accessible? Where are their blind spots in their efforts to be happy? To feel included? Capable? Worthwhile? Where has their innate goodness gotten mixed up in their efforting? Through uncovering and developing our awareness by lying quietly in a colored room, we aspire to bring ourselves back to the rooms of our lives, noticing the ways in which we and others color space.

In a Buddhist prayer, *The Aspiration of Samantabhadra*, it is said that "the unceasing lucidity of awareness is five wisdoms of one nature" and the essence of that nature is selfless compassion (Ponlop, 2006, p. 74). By approaching clients' experience with kind awareness, Contemplative psychotherapists can get a sense of how clients orient themselves and can help them feel more at home with themselves. Trungpa (1975) noted,

> Different types of individuality originate from different types of basic energy. These are basic energies that misunderstood themselves, right at the beginning, and differentiated themselves from the basic ground. That basic ground is an open one, but the energies it contains are colorful... Our particular individual style with its particular energies runs through all the processes of psychological evolution... But this is not a hangup at all. It is our wealth. (pp. 82-83)

With maitri, contemplative psychotherapists appreciate the wealth of their own confusion as the ground for discovering the brilliant sanity of themselves and their clients.

References

Chogyam, N., & Dechen, K. (1997). *Spectrum of ecstasy: Embracing emotions as the path of inner tantra*. New York: ARO Books.

Chung, C. (1990). Psychotherapist and expansion of awareness. *Psychotherapy and Psychosomatics, 53*(4), 28-32.

Evans, J. (1993). Personal growth in maitri space awareness. UMI Dissertation Services, 1, 5-13. (UMI No. 9415608).

Jacerme, P. (2005). The need for place: Maitri Space Awareness. In F. Midal (Ed.), *Recalling Chogyam Trungpa* (pp. 273-287) Boston: Shambhala Publications.

Lief, J. (2005). Transforming psychology: the development of Maitri Space awareness practice. In F. Midal (Ed.), *Recalling Chogyam Trungpa* (pp. 273-287). Boston: Shambhala Publications.

Midal, F (2004). *Chogyam Trungpa: His life and vision*. Boston & London: Shambhala Publications.

Ponlop, D. (2006). *Penetrating wisdom: The aspiration of Samantabhadra*. New York: Snow Lion Publications.

Trungpa, C. (1975). *Glimpses of Abhidharma*. Boston: Prajna Press.

Trungpa, C. (1980). Becoming a full human being. *Naropa Institute Journal of Psychology, 1* (1), 4-20.

Trungpa, C. (2005). *The sanity we are born with* (C.R. Gimian, Ed.). Boston: Shambhala Publications.

11

The Body in Psychotherapy: Dancing with the Paradox

Zoë Avstreih

As a psychotherapist, dance/movement therapist, and contemplative practitioner, my work embodies the paradoxes of our human existence. My clients seek psychotherapy because they suffer and desire change or, they want things to be different than they are. However, from the Buddhist perspective, all true change begins with the acceptance of the present moment.

> The very structure of our personality will become the pathway for revealing the transpersonal nature of our being itself. Every pattern of our behavior, every nuance in our thought, is a window that can reveal unconditioned awareness. In Zen, they say that unconditioned awareness is entered through the gateless gateway. The gateway is gateless, not only because there's no gate, but also because the gateway is always exactly where we are. (Fenner, 2007, pp. 18-19)

On the relative level, human existence is seen through the lens of our conditioned mind and body. From this perspective, life is defined and limited by our genetic heritage, our constitution, and the life events that influence our development, our preferences, and our aversions. The quality of our life seems to depend on the conditions of our existence. Buddhism speaks of another level of existence or consciousness. It is often referred to as Buddha-nature, openness, no-mind, pure awareness, witness consciousness, primordial mind, and unconditioned awareness, to name a few (Fenner, 2007, pp. 4-5.). "Unconditioned awareness is a state of consciousness that contains, yet goes beyond, all forms or structure of experience. It's sometimes also called the *source consciousness* because it's *that* which everything appears to arise from and return to" (Fenner, 2007, p.9). In Buddhism, it is the awakening to the experience of unconditioned mind, witness consciousness that moves one closer to genuine freedom, a freedom that does not depend on the circumstances of one's conditioned life (Fenner, 2007).

In Buddhism, the experience of unconditioned awareness is called the ultimate medicine – that is, other types of healing –have limitations. They work for some people and not for others, and even then, only some of the time. Universally, the ultimate medicine is healing. Every mind touched by the experience of its unconditioned nature moves closer to the experience of genuine freedom, which is, after all, the ultimate healing. (Fenner, 2007, p. 17)

As a therapist whose roots are in the field of Dance/Movement Therapy, the body is the portal to pure awareness that calls me. *Authentic movement*, is a form of dance movement therapy named by one of the pioneering dance therapists, the late Mary Starks Whitehouse. This discipline continues to teach me about the paradoxical dance between the relative and the absolute. In this chapter, I address the intersection of psychotherapy and Buddhist thought, and its relationship to therapeutic presence. I also address the discipline of authentic movement as an embodied mindfulness awareness practice and its ability to cultivate the capacity of the therapist to become an *embodied witness*. The therapist, as embodied witness, remains open to the ever present dance between the relative and the absolute and embodies the capacity to provide a therapeutic container that honors both.

Authentic Movement: Origins and Theory

I found the practice of authentic movement, or more accurately it found me, at the time I was training as a Psychoanalyst and beginning to practice Zen meditation in the tradition with Seung Sahn, a Korean Zen Master. Dance/Movement Therapy, psychoanalytic training, meditation, and creative process met seamlessly in the practice of authentic movement. At the time, I had no name for the process that was emerging in my studio as the deepening of my own analysis and my meditation practice met in my body.

Authentic movement evolved for Mary Whitehouse from the intersection of her roots in dance and her own experience in Jungian analysis. Whitehouse originally called her work "Movement in Depth" (Frieder, cited in Pallaro, 2007, p. 35). It was a form of active imagination in movement, embodied dialogue between the *self* with a small 's' referring to the ego and the "Self" with a capital 'S' referring to the transpersonal aspect of one's being. Whitehouse used the word *authentic* as an adjective to describe particular movements which she felt were genuine, true for the mover in the moment, free from habitual and learned patterns. "Movement, to be experienced, has to be *found* in the body, not put on like a dress or coat" (Whitehouse, cited in Pallaro, 1999, p. 53). The quality of movement that Whitehouse called *authentic* emerged when the mover surrendered to the moment and allowed herself to be moved. The movement had a quality of immediacy and transparency.

My analytic training was Freudian and the movement work that was evolving for me was profoundly influenced by teachings of D. W. Winnicott, Christopher Bollas, and Heinz Kohut. Initially, the practice of authentic movement emerged in me as an embodied reflection of the therapeutic container as a *facilitating environment* (Winnicott, 1965). The practice of authentic movement defined by the container of mover and witness, and the relationship between them, provided a container or *holding environment* for the true self to emerge once again directly on the body level. Winnicott (1960) defined the true self as "the inherited potential which is experiencing a continuity of being and acquiring in its own way and its own speed a personal psychic reality and a personal body scheme" (p. 46).

Bollas, in his book *Forces of Destiny* (1989), elaborates on the emergence of the true self. According to Bollas:

> If we are to provide a theory for the true self, I think it is important to stress how this core self is the unique presence of being that each of us is: the idiom of our personality.... It is only a potential, however, because it depends upon maternal care for its evolution. As its gestural expressions and intersubjective claims are never free of the other's interpretation, it depends upon the mother's and father's facilitations. No human being, however, is only true self. Each inherited disposition meets up with the actual world and one of the outcomes of this dialectic between personality idiom and human culture is psychic life. (p.9)

The true self is birthed in the presence of another who does not interfere or impinge on the representation of the true self as it emerges into form. As Bollas (1989) says, "the true self must be true to itself" (p. 83). Like the early caregiver, the therapist "celebrates the true self through his affective response to its presence" (Bollas, 1989, p. 86).

Description of Authentic Movement

Authentic movement is a profoundly simple form in which a mover or movers are invited to move with eyes closed in the presence of a witness. One enters the practice first as a mover; the external witness creates a safe space for the mover to listen deeply and yield/surrender to sensation, impulse, image, feeling as it bubbles up into consciousness in the moment. As sensation and impulse emerge into consciousness and manifest in movement, the invisible becomes visible, the inaudible becomes audible, and the formless takes form. Held by the spacious, receptive, and non-interfering presence of the witness, the mover begins to allow the spontaneous creations of the true self to emerge. Often I will hear a mover say I feel like I am coming home, and indeed, I believe they are coming home to the body as a source of uncontrived, spontaneous movement; a simple representation of the true self.

Influenced by meditation practice, my experience and understanding of authentic movement continues to evolve beyond the traditional roots of Western psychology. Authentic movement as a practice stands with an integrity of its own. It is a practice that activates healing on multiple levels of one's being (Avstreih, 2007). Ultimately, it is a practice that acknowledges the still and moving body as a manifestation of the gateless gateway, a portal into awareness itself.

Fundamental to the discipline of authentic movement is the understanding that transformation must be rooted in the body. This means we begin right here, right now, in our body, in this moment. We are the path, life is the path; this understanding is the basis of Buddhist thought and practice. "From the Buddhist perspective, our spiritual journey begins here – with this very body and mind. Who we are now consists of these two; body and mind, and who we might become will also be expressed through body and mind." (Ponlop, 2004, p. 53)

Authentic Movement as a Mindfulness Awareness Practice

Authentic movement is an invitation to be with the truth of the moment as it arises in the body – no right, no wrong. It requires impeccable attention to impulse, sensation, image and feeling as it arises into awareness and sequences into movement visible or invisible to the outer witness. For both mover and witness, it is fundamentally a practice of mindfulness awareness. It provides an opportunity for the experience of direct embodied learning, moment-to-moment. Mindfulness is seeing directly, paying bare attention without judgment. Awareness is the spaciousness from which we see. The combination of mindfulness and awareness brings one into the present moment, able to see it as it is with precision, clarity, and spaciousness. As one deepens into the practice of authentic movement, first as mover and later as witness, one develops what in Buddhism is called *choiceless awareness,* the capacity to be present and welcoming to whatever arises (Avstreih, 2005).

Authentic Movement:
An Embodied Approach to Training Psychotherapists

I teach authentic movement as an embodied mindfulness awareness practice to graduate students studying to become therapists. Authentic movement is a practice that has a theoretical ground and unfolds in an inherent order. The practice is defined by the container of mover and witness, and the relationship between them. One begins the practice as a mover, moving with eyes closed in the presence of an external witness. The witness, like a therapist, initially holds the responsibility for consciousness by inviting the mover to yield to the embodied wisdom of sensation and impulse. Before one sits as witness to another, one must know through direct experience what it means to take up residence in this perishable form called body. Following are the words of a mover coming into the practice, coming into his body:

> My overall feeling of being a mover in the form of authentic movement is best described as raw, in the sense that being aware of the direct experience of my body and movement is so unfamiliar that it leaves me feeling sensitive, exposed, sometimes vulnerable, but always alive.
>
> About a year and a half ago I was diagnosed with Lyme disease. In treatment over the past year, I have dealt with and thought about my body constantly. Paradoxically, all this attention paid to my body has not brought a real experience of body. Instead, I have ignored my body out of fear of knowing the full toll of the disease.
>
> Through the practice of authentic movement, I have been learning to relate to my body in a deeper way. This particular journal entry of mine shows the beginning of the process:
>
> My movements are meant to soothe, soothe the pain that lies in my hips,
> My knees, my back, my shoulders, wrists, ankles –deep in my heart
> Seven years of disease coursing through me in outwardly silent pain
> My movements are meant to soothe, so I can contain the hurt, the burden
> Soothe the heart and soul and mind,
> Soothe my innards,
> Soothe my family, soothe my eyes, my face, my shoulders, my chest,
> Soothe my legs
>
> So I am tall, erect, open
> So I can face the world
>
> I recall, as a mover, lying on the floor, rocking my legs and hips in a soothing motion. I began sinking in and listening to the pain in my body, the pain I often try to ignore. It was the first time in a very long time that I was truly present with my body. And the effect of that was that I could feel myself on a deeper level, below the pain.

With his words, this mover demonstrates his willingness to be embodied, to be fully present in the moment. In his words, we see the emergence of the inner witness enabling him to be present with the pain and yet not identified with it.

The cultivation of the one's inner witness function creates a spacious field for the energy of old wounds to sequence through the body, without judgment or interference. As the inner witness develops, there comes a time when one is both ready and longing to sit as witness for others. Having been seen, there is a desire to see, to bear witness. The spaciousness of self-acceptance extends as an offering to others as compassion. To sit as witness is to practice the ideal of the bodhisattva, to dedicate awareness in the service of others. "Embodiment is integral to the bodhisattva ideal" (Fenner, 2003, p. 34).

The practice of learning to witness begins in dyads. One enters the practice first as a silent witness. As a witness, one is cultivating the capacity to witness another with clear, open receptive attention free from judgment. The witness is developing the ability to see the mover and simultaneously begin to note the sensations, impulses, images, emotions, and memories that arise internally as one sits as witness. As Adler (1999) states, "First, the witness is responsible for seeing her mover as well as her self. Second, the witness does not enact or engage in her own experience, she witnesses it" (p. 143). Like the discipline of meditation, the authentic movement cultivates the ability to remain grounded in direct experience. Slowly, one learns to speak as the witness. Initially she uses first person speech to protect the mover from projection. The witness speaks in service of the mover and begins to discern how to use one's inner experience in service of another, an essential component of therapeutic process.

The relationship between mover and witness is subtle and complex. Although the witness does not engage in her own experience, the inner mover remains alive and resonant, nurturing the ability to be empathically attuned with another and with the potential to experience another directly. As one student said, "I both see my mover and I am my mover. I see her crying; I hear her crying; I am also the one crying. For the first time, I truly understand what is meant by the term Bodhisattva. We are all connected." She sees with the eyes of compassion. Her words bring to mind the words of Santideva, the eighth century poetic and mystic. He speaks of enlightenment as the perfection of compassion. Santideva urges one to meditate on the "sameness of self and others (paratma-samata) or the 'transference of self and others'" (paratma-parivartana; Gimmello, 1983, p.69).

Gimmello continues,

> Primarily one should zealously cultivate the equality of other and the self. All joys and all sorrows are equal, and I am to guard them like my own.... So why should the body of another not be taken as

my own?... Whoever wishes to quickly rescue himself and another, should practice the supreme mystery: The exchanging of self and other. (Shantidavi, cited in Gimmello, 1983, p. 69).

When the illusionary boundaries between self and other dissolve, there is only compassionate seeing.

In the practice of authentic movement, the conditioned mind/body of both mover and witness is the pathway that reveals our true nature. Authentic movement explores the relationship between moving and being moved, seeing and being seen. It is a form that sees embodied consciousness as a portal to the direct experience of witness consciousness or unconditioned awareness. There are moments in the practice where the uncontrived gestures of the true self become only movement and stillness. There is no one moving, no one still, only movement arising from stillness and stillness settling out of movement.

Fenner (2007) uses the term *embodied transcendence* to describe the practice of cultivating unconditioned mind in the midst of everyday existence. This approach to healing is in line with the Dzochen and Mahamudra traditions in Buddhism (Fenner, 2007). As a teacher of authentic movement, I find the term embodied transcendence closely mirrors the process of authentic movement in which one cultivates the inner witness in the midst of movement both visible and invisible. Every nuance of our being "is a window that can reveal unconditioned awareness" (Fenner, 2007, p. 19), and yet, form can remain form as it opens to emptiness. Our unique individual journey does not disappear in unconditioned awareness; only the suffering disappears. The ability to remain rooted in the body in the midst of disquieting states and strong emotions is essential for a therapist; in fact it is the antidote to disassociation and *spiritual bypass* sometimes seen in spiritual communities.

As a therapist and as a teacher of those who aspire to become therapists, I dance within the co-existence of the relative and the absolute. It is in the form of authentic movement that I have come to know intimately the profound truth expressed in the Heart Sutra: "form is emptiness and emptiness is form" (Bodian, 2003, p.234). Paradoxically, I have also come to know, as Bodian (2003) states, "form doesn't cease to be form, even though it is empty, and emptiness doesn't cease to be empty, even though it's also form" (p. 234).

As a therapist and teacher of authentic movement, I bear witness to pain, suffering, remnants of trauma, and lack of early attunement that remain in the body/mind of those I witness, as well as the joys, victories, and feelings of well-being that emerge. I see all these manifestations of the dance of *human-being-ness* as I open moment to moment to rest in the spacious emptiness of awareness, while simultaneously bearing witness to both form and emptiness. I have had glimmers through direct experience that all suffering dissolves when one rests in pure awareness.

Nothing has to happen for everything to be different. In the discipline of authentic movement I am learning to dance and am teaching others to dance, with the paradox that, on the relative level, pain and suffering exist even as unconditioned mind remains untarnished. It is not simply that one has to be someone before they can be no one. After all, we are always simultaneously both.

Authentic movement has much to offer to the field of therapy and to the training of therapists. It develops the capacity for empathic attunement and a therapeutic presence that invites the representations of the true self. It supports and sustains the capacity of the therapist to embrace the quality of not knowing that creates the potential space to register and reflect the emerging personal idiom of the client (Bollas, 1989. p.62). As a practice, it also cultivates the ability to witness oneself while witnessing another; an essential therapeutic skill which enhances one's capacity to use the subtle somatic indications of transference and countertranserence that appear in the therapeutic relationship.

In authentic movement I can dance with paradox of *true self* and no-self, the relative and the absolute, with form and emptiness. There is no resolution to the paradox, only the dance. When we enter the experience of another, we dissolve the illusionary boundaries of separateness and that expression of compassion eases suffering. At the same time, we can rest in the wisdom that no amount of suffering or pain can "conceal the innate radiance of mind" (Tilopa, as cited in Fenner, 2007, p. 1). As Nisargadatta, the great Indian sage of the non-dual tradition said, "With Wisdom, I see that I am nothing; with love, I see that I am everything. And between these two, my life turns" (Nisargadatta, as cited in Fenner, 2007, p. 121). And between the two, as therapist, teacher, and human being, I continue to dance.

References

Adler, J. (1999). Who is the witness? A description of authentic movement. In P. Pallaro (Ed.), *Authentic movement: Essays by Mary Starks Whitehouse, Janet Adler and Joan Chodorow.* (pp. 141-159). Philadelphia: Jessica Kingsley Publishers.

Avstreih, Z. (2005).Authentic movement and Buddhism. *A Moving Journal. 13* (3), 8-10.

Avstreih, Z. (2007). Achieving body permanence: Authentic movement and the paradox of healing. In P. Pallaro (Ed.). *Authentic movement: Moving the body, moving the self, being moved.* (pp. 270 – 273). London & Philadelphia: Jessica Kingsley Publishers.

Bodian, S. (2003). Deconstructing the self: The uses of inquiry in Psychotherapy and spiritual practice. In J. Prendergast, P. Fenner & S. Krystal (Eds.). *The sacred mirror: Nondual wisdom and*

psychotherapy (pp. 229-248). St. Paul, Minnesota: Paragon House.
Bollas, C. (1989). *Forces of destiny: Psychoanalysis and human idiom.* Northvale, NJ & London: Jason Aronson Inc.
Ponlop, D. (2004, September). The wisdom of the body & the search for the self. *Shambhala Sun, 13*(1), 53-59.
Fenner, P. (2007). *Radiant mind: Awakening unconditioned awareness.* Boulder, CO: Sounds True.
Frieder, S. (2007). Reflections on Mary Starks Whitehouse. In P. Pallaro (Ed.). *Authentic movement: Moving the body, moving the self, being moved.* (pp. 35-44). London & Philadelphia: Jessica Kingsley Publishers.
Gimmello, R. M. (1983). Mysticism in its contexts. In S. Katz (Ed.), *Mysticism and religious traditions.* (pp. 61-88). Oxford: Oxford University Press.
Whitehouse, M. (1999). The tao of the body. In P. Pallaro (Ed.), *Authentic movement: Essays by Mary Starks Whitehouse, Janet Adler and Joan Chodorow.* (pp. 41-50). London & Philadelphia: Jessica Kingsley Publishers.
Whitehouse, M. (1999). Physical movement and personality. In P. Pallaro (Ed.), *Authentic movement: Essays by Mary Starks Whitehouse, Janet Adler and Joan Chodorow.* (pp. 51-57). London & Philadelphia: Jessica Kingsley Publishers.
Winnicott, D. W. (1965). The theory of the parent-infant relationship. *The maturational process and the facilitating environment* (pp. 37-55). London: Hogarth.Press.
Winnicott, D. W. (1971). *Playing and reality.* London: Tavistock.

Part 3: Fruition

12

Listening Beyond the Words: Working with Exchange

Karen Kissel Wegela

I was sitting in my office one day with James who was complaining about his wife, a regular client of mine. With her permission, he had come in to tell me his view of their marriage. "She's dirty. She doesn't take care of the house. She doesn't wash her hands above the wrist! How can I feel safe eating food she prepares?" His angry litany went on for many minutes.

As I sat listening to him I noticed that I was starting to feel some trembling in my chest and limbs. My thoughts were beginning to quicken and my palms started to sweat. I recognized that I was feeling a bit frightened and anxious. I was not aware of being frightened of this man; he did not seem at all threatening. Then, it occurred to me that perhaps it was James who was feeling frightened.

As I brought my attention to my own experience and simply let it be as it was, I noticed that not only did my own feelings of anxiety begin to settle down, but James, too, began to slow down and to relax a bit. Then, he began to talk about his own pain and fear. That incident was the first time I became aware of the phenomenon that we call *exchange* in contemplative psychotherapy.

In this chapter, I present the idea of exchange, our direct experience of another and how we, as psychotherapists, can work with it and with the obstacles we bring to experiencing it fully.

The View of Contemplative Psychotherapy

Perhaps it would be helpful to begin with some background and assumptions. Contemplative psychotherapy, as it has been presented at Naropa University since 1975, is the joining of Buddhist teachings and meditation practices with the practice of psychotherapy. The Buddhist tradition that underlies our approach is Tibetan, especially the Kagyü and Nyingma schools. The founder of Naropa and the inspiration for the then "Buddhist and Western Psychology" program was Chögyam Trungpa Rinpoche.

Trungpa Rinpoche coined the terms "brilliant sanity" (Board of Editors, 1980, p. 1) and "basic goodness" (Trungpa, 1983, p. 6) to refer to our inherently, unconditionally pure nature. In the Nyingma tradition, this would be called Rigpa (Tsoknyi, 1998, p. 46) and in some other traditions, it would be called Buddha Nature or *tathagatagarbha* (Maitreya, 1985). Whatever it is called, it points to our basic being as open, clear, and compassionate (Wegela, 1994). If we hold this view of brilliant sanity, then it has important implications for what we think we are doing as psychotherapists. Rather than trying to fix or change people, we are more interested in helping them reconnect to their inherent nature, their brilliant sanity. As contemplative psychotherapists, we are interested in supporting and cultivating sanity and are wary of reducing our clients to diagnostic labels.

Mindfulness-awareness sitting meditation is a key practice for contemplative psychotherapists. In the Tibetan tradition two phases of meditation are identified: taming the mind and training the mind (Karthar, 1992). In taming the mind, we develop some peace and stability through mindfulness practice. We learn to let the mind settle itself by focusing on one object, usually the breath. In training the mind, we examine the nature of mind itself. We cannot look closely at what the mind does unless we have learned to tame it first. In particular, we examine the notion of a self-existent self or ego. Buddhism teaches that we will not find anything that corresponds to such an ego. That is, there is no separate, solid, or permanent self. Instead of existing independently, we are interdependent.

Thich Nhat Hanh uses a wonderful metaphor to clarify our interdependent nature (Hanh, 1990). Just as a flower is made up of *non-flower elements*, such as rain, sunshine, and soil, we are made of *non-self elements*. There is no self to be found separate from our *inter-being* of the moment. Clinging to and cultivating such a nonexistent self is the source of our suffering, the source of psychopathology. It is also the obstacle to experiencing exchange, as is discussed below.

One of the most important contributions that mindfulness-awareness meditation practice has given to psychotherapy is training in the ability to be simply present with our clients. By training in being present with ourselves through waves of thoughts, emotions, and sensations, we learn to be present with others as well. Mindfulness is the ability to place the mind on an object and keep it there. As therapists, we stay present with ourselves and with our clients. We are able to track our experience moment to moment.

Years ago I attended a conference in Phoenix, Arizona, "The Evolution of Psychotherapy," with more than 5,000 participants. Again and again we heard the message that the ability to be present with clients was the single most important factor in successful psychotherapy. However, in 1985 it was not widely known that this ability need not be something only some few lucky people possessed. It was not yet generally

12. Listening Beyond the Words

recognized that mindfulness-awareness meditation can train just this seemingly elusive quality.

Through meditation practice we become more at home with ourselves and with our true situation. That is to say, not only do we train in being more present and *mindful*, but we also become more *aware* of the clarity and openness that we are. We discover what Trungpa Rinpoche called "panoramic awareness" (Trungpa, 1976, p. 4). The particular meditation practice he taught us, and which we in turn teach our students, is an eyes-open, senses-open, relatively formless sitting practice.

As a psychotherapist, my practice is to be mindful not only of what is occurring in the room with me and with my client, but also to be aware of the space within which that interaction is occurring. I have a sense of *holding the space* or being aware of the space. By *space* here I mean both the literal space of the room and also the space of mind itself. With each client I *listen deeply* to what arises in that space. It differs with each person. We could say that I actually am a different person with each client and in each moment. This is one implication of recognizing the nonexistence of ego as separate and permanent.

In the Contemplative Psychotherapy program we introduce our students to *Maitri Space Awareness* practice. Developed by Trungpa Rinpoche in anticipation of a healing community envisioned together with Suzuki Roshi, Maitri Space Awareness practice is done in five specially designed rooms of different shapes, colors, and having different configurations of windows and light, each evoking a particular *Buddha family energy*. In each room, the practitioner holds a particular posture for a period of time. It is beyond the scope of this chapter to go into detail about this practice, but let me describe one such room.[1] The Vajra room is dark blue with a high ceiling that slopes down from one side to the other. The windows are somewhat wide and narrow, and while holding a belly-down, arms-outstretched posture, the practitioner cannot get a clear view of any of them. This provokes, for most people, a sense of wanting to see, wanting to know. It may bring up a sense of anger or coldness. On the other hand, it may bring up what is known as *mirror-like wisdom,* a deep sense of clarity. Each room is associated with both a *neurotic* and an *enlightened* aspect. When people spend 45 minutes in the blue room or the green, red or yellow room, they usually come out in a different state of mind from what they had when they entered. The point here, though, is that simply lying in a colored room can profoundly affect our state of mind. This can happen because we are not solid, but are, instead, permeable. If we are so permeable in a simple blue room, how much more so are we when we sit with our clients in the intimate and intense relationship known as psychotherapy!

Another key concept is the idea of *maitri,* which the room practice helps to cultivate. Maitri, or loving-kindness, one of the "four

---

[1] See Chapter 10 for a more detailed discussion of Maitri Space Awareness.

immeasurables," is the wish for all beings to be happy (Karthar, 1992). Trungpa Rinpoche (1983) encouraged us to apply it first to ourselves as an antidote for the rampant self-aggression he saw in his Western students. The basic idea is that not only can we be present with all aspects of our experience, as we train to do in meditation, but we can also bring an attitude of unconditional friendliness and warmth to what we discover.

If our intention as contemplative psychotherapists is to help clients reconnect with their brilliant sanity, in practical terms, this often means helping them to develop mindfulness and maitri.

A final key point in contemplative psychotherapy is the primacy of the therapeutic relationship itself as a healing factor. Participating in a genuine relationship between human beings is what most helps our clients reconnect with their innate brilliant sanity. It is an antidote to the problem of ego, a belief in our separateness, our solidity, and our permanence. Through a genuine relationship over time we see that together we are something different from who we are apart: we are connected with each other; we affect each other; and we change with each other.

Exchange

There are many ways of helping our clients to develop mindfulness and maitri (Wegela, 1996). For example, we can help them discover their already existing mindfulness practices; we can help them transform mindlessness practices into mindfulness practices; we can teach them mindfulness directly in the context of psychotherapy; and we can offer them the direct experience of mindfulness and maitri through how we work with exchange. For the remainder of this chapter, we will focus on how we work with exchange and with the obstacles that inevitably arise in that work.

Exchange refers to our direct experience of another being. As in the example at the beginning of the paper, often we *pick up* feelings from our clients. Once we are sensitized to this possibility, we discover that we are exchanging with others much, if not all, of the time.

Just this week I was in a meeting with some colleagues. In the process of interviewing a prospective candidate for a faculty position, we were together creating a spontaneous poem. The task at hand was to say something that arose in the immediate moment. A few humorous lines had been said before I was called on to share some words. I waited in a state of not-knowing until something came: "Why, with so much humor, do I feel like weeping?" I was a bit bewildered by what I had said, but it was exactly how I felt in the moment, and I trusted it fit in somehow. A few minutes later, I found one of my colleagues had tears running down his face. I had not been aware of his sadness, yet here it was. "Was that you?" I asked, since he's very familiar with exchange. "Oh, yes." he replied.

12. Listening Beyond the Words

In his 8th century classic, the *Bodhicaryavatara*, Shantideva describes the practice of "that holy secret, the exchanging of self for others" (Shantideva, 1992, chapter 8, verse 120). This practice invites us to imagine a series of situations in which we exchange places with another person and by so doing cultivate *bodhichitta,* awakened heart or mind. We use a similar term and take inspiration from Santideva's method. However, exchange as I am discussing it here is actually quite different.

The most important point to note is that exchange refers to direct experience, not something we imagine. That is, experience that is not filtered through our habits or preferences, and most importantly, not filtered through concepts. Some years ago I asked Dzigar Kongtrul Rinpoche about the notion of exchange. He suggested first that it was most frequently experienced through the faculty of hearing (personal communication, November, 1992). He went on to say that our experience of exchange is distorted in the same way that we distort our other sense perceptions, through our habits of grasping, aversion, and ignorance. For this reason, it is essential that we always hold lightly and tentatively any beliefs we come up with based on what we think is exchange.

Our meditation practice, our supervision, or consultations with colleagues, and our experience as therapists can help inform us about whether what we are experiencing is actually exchange or whether it is some form of counter-transference. For simplicity's sake, I will suggest that counter-transference refers to the therapist's own issues, referenced to the therapist's own history, as opposed to experiences that arise directly with a client. Of course, many times our experience with a client is a combination of factors including exchange and our own reactions as well as counter-transference.

Let me offer an example to tease these apart a bit more. Let's say that I am in a room with a large, frightened man. He is speaking in a loud voice. As I sit with him, I feel what I would call fear. One aspect of my fear may be exchange with his fear. Another aspect may be my counter-transference: I may have a deep-seated fear of angry, large men. I may think he is angry. I may also simply have a response based neither on my own history nor on the exchange. For example, I may guess that he is angry based on the volume of his voice. He has not said he is angry, and I haven't experienced anger. When I check in with him, asking about what he is experiencing, he lets me know that he is scared and that he really hates being scared. There is some accuracy in the exchange and also some correct information about his anger in my simple response.

I have noticed a number of times that large men who are scared may be the object of others' fear, not because they are threatening anyone, but because others react to their experience of exchange. They feel fear and may assume this is a frightening person instead of a frightened one.

Sometimes we blame clients for being difficult, when what is actually difficult is staying present and exchanging with their painful states of mind. I have noticed that clients with a borderline personality disorder diagnosis often provoke this experience in us as therapists.

Exchange also differs from empathy. Empathy usually refers to what we imagine another person is feeling. To the extent that empathy is based on our imagination and thoughts, it is not our direct experience and so it is not the same as exchange. That being said, I believe that often psychotherapists who are experiencing exchange, but lack the language or concept for it, call it empathy.

Rollo May (1989) has actually described as empathy what I would call exchange in the following way:

> In empathy there is a nonverbal interchange of mood, belief, and attitude between doctor and patient, therapist and client, or any two people who have a significant relationship... If you go into a music shop and pluck one string of a violin, each of the other instruments in the store will resonate with sound. Similarly, human beings can resonate with each other to such an extent that they can exchange understanding at a subtle level. (pp. 108-109)

Farrell R. Silverberg (1988)[2] describes something similar which he calls *Therapeutic Resonance*. "To resonate with someone is to serve as a mirror for him, and to be so closely identified that you feel his experience" (p. 25).

Much more recently, some writers have pointed to the phenomenon we have called exchange, based on our understanding of Buddhist Psychology, but which they have come to by other paths. Gay Watson (in press), in her book, *Beyond Happiness*, highlights the theory of intersubjectivity which emphasizes the importance of mutuality, relationship, and intimacy in the normal development of a child. Drawing on Allan Schore, she says:

> Resonance, synchrony and affective transactions with other brains are necessary components of natural development. Previous paradigms using the model of the isolated brain are now seen to be inadequate to describe the process of development, or indeed, the process of repair. Intra-psychic models are not adequate: interpersonal ones are certainly necessary. As yet one can only speculate about transpersonal. Paradoxically, understanding of intersubjectivity gives foundation for a theoretical, even a dispassionate understanding of compassion. (p. 93)

---

[2] See also chapter 13, Resonance and Exchange iin Contemplative Psychtherapy by Silverberg.

12. Listening Beyond the Words

In her book, *The Emphatic Ground: Intersubjectivity and Nonduality in the Psychotherapeutic Process*, Judith Blackstone (2007) discusses the idea of "empathy in nondual consciousness" (p. 35) and contrasts it with other descriptions of empathy in which dualistic barriers between self and other are experienced. As she presents it,

> The empathic capacity that emerges with nondual realization is not a function either of imagination or entrainment. Rather, it is based on a transpersonal dimension of our senses, a facet of the subtle nondual ground. It is the ability to actually perceive the movement and qualities of another person's cognitions, emotions, and sensations within the internal space of that person's body. This sensitivity naturally occurs as the barriers that we have organized between ourselves and the world are dissolved. (p. 35)

Gay Watson (in press), drawing on current neuroscientific research, points to the notion of mirror neurons as a physiological basis for exchange:

> Neuroscientist V.S. Ramachandran who has carried out research into the existence of these neurons in the human brain, has suggested that this discovery will provide for psychology what the discovery of DNA did for biology. Most tellingly, from my perspective, is the fact that he has nicknamed them 'empathy' or better still, 'Dalai Lama' neurons, as they seemingly dissolve the barrier between self and other. (p. 27)

Here are some additional clinical examples of exchange. Once I had a woman client with whom I had a very difficult time. Unless I interrupted her, she would tell long tales that seemed to me to have no particular point to them. I often became distracted listening to her and I had a hard time remembering what she had said. I am usually very present with my clients, perhaps more so than anywhere else in my life, so I was intrigued by this experience. Finally, I realized that even my distraction might tell me something about her. I checked with her and she agreed that she did not feel very present. Soon after that, I had an odd sensation of dizziness. Having already established some ground that my experience was something of interest to both of us, I asked her if she knew anything about this dizzy feeling. "Oh, yes. That happens to me a lot." She went on to reveal for the first time that she had been the victim of sexual abuse as a child. She had always known it, but she had practiced pushing away any direct experience of emotion connected with it. Sometimes she would have that sensation of dizziness and know that she would have to work harder to keep the unwanted emotions at bay. Over time, in the context of the safety of our relationship, we began to explore those painful memories and feelings together.

Another client, Marie, told me about a recent visit with her father who is dying of cancer. As she spoke I noticed that I was starting to feel an aching softness in my chest and that tears were starting to well up in my eyes. Marie described what might have been the last time she would ever see her father alive. She said that she felt nothing *left over* with him and went on to describe how she said good-bye to him and wished him well. Our eyes met and there was a momentary acknowledgement of our shared sad tenderness.

What made this moment especially poignant was that Marie's father had sexually abused both her and at least two other members of her family. When I had met Marie some years earlier, she had cut off all contact with him. In our work together, she spent some years connecting with herself and with the fear and anger that she felt toward him. Now, we were both surprised to experience her tenderness and a sense of letting go.

I suggested that this unexpected feeling she was having might be called *forgiveness*. Without the moment of direct contact that I have just described, I would probably have been hesitant to bring up this idea. Now, though, it was clearly *in the room* and appropriate to explore. With relief, Marie agreed that forgiveness was exactly what she had been feeling, but that she did not know if that was actually all right to feel. She explained that her brother, for example, who was still very angry with Marie's father, would not be a person with whom she would want to disclose that experience. We talked about who else she could share this with, and identified several close friends to whom she could reveal this secret compassion she felt for her father.

Exchange Goes Both Ways

Since exchange is a naturally occurring phenomenon, based on our interdependent nature, it is by no means limited to the therapist's experience of the client. The client also exchanges with us. How we work with our own minds, on the spot, is of paramount importance to the healing that can occur. Sometimes in contemplative psychotherapy we talk about *mutual recovery*. Clearly, the therapist needs to be in *good shape*, but we are always learning from and benefiting from our clients.

Specifically, our aspiration is to bring mindfulness, awareness, maitri, and compassion to whatever experience arises in the space of psychotherapy. If a client tells me about a painful incident from her life, how I receive that account becomes available in the room. In other words, if I can bring brilliant sanity to whatever I feel, think or sense, then the client may exchange with it.

Trungpa Rinpoche (1985) wrote about something similar between a healer and a dying patient:

12. Listening Beyond the Words

> The healing relationship is a meeting of two minds... If you and the other person are open, some kind of dialogue can take place which is not forced. Communication occurs naturally because both are in the same situation. If the patient feels terrible, the healer picks up that sense of the patient's wretchedness: for a moment he feels more or less the same, as if he himself were sick. For a moment the two are not separate and a sense of authenticity takes place. From the patient's point of view, that is precisely what is needed: someone acknowledges his existence and the fact that he needs help very badly. Someone actually sees through his sickness. The healing process can then begin to take place in the patient's state of being, because he realizes that someone has communicated with him completely. There has been a mutual glimpse of common ground. The psychological underpinning of the sickness then begins to come apart, to dissolve. [p. 7]

A man I had worked with about five years ago returned recently to therapy. Eddie is now the father of two young sons and he is very interested in exploring memories and emotions that are arising connected with his own painful childhood. Growing up, he was told repeatedly, directly and indirectly, that he was worthless and bad. In our earlier work we had done a lot of exploration of his internalized stories about his *basic badness*.

In our work this past week, he revealed that he has always been very sensitive to exchange. He did not use those exact words, but he described how readily he picked up on how others felt. The exchange can get confused with his own projections and internal stories as well. He was comforted to hear that this was not something *wrong* with him, but simply a natural human capacity. He then went on to describe his experience of me and why he had come back into therapy with me.

Apparently, the first time we met he had gotten the impression that I thought there was nothing fundamentally wrong with him (This was true.). This was a shocking possibility to him. It was not only that he felt safe and not judged, he felt, in my presence, that he might actually be a good person. At some level, he suspected this was true and so he kept coming back. It is only now that he has the words for this, but he always had a feeling of his goodness when we worked together. I never said to him, "You have brilliant sanity; you are basically good," but he felt it in the exchange. Obviously, I had to actually feel this, not just think it was a nice idea, for it to be available in the exchange. In fact though, it is easy to see Eddie's goodness and compassionate heart.

Difficulties and Obstacles in Working with Exchange

The basic practice, then, of working with exchange is to bring mindfulness and maitri to our experience. Whatever arises can be joined with clarity and with warmth. Then those qualities may be experienced by the client through their exchange with us.

Difficulties in Exchange

The main difficulty in working with exchange is that it means opening ourselves to the painful feelings and experiences of others. It is all well and good to aspire to be compassionate and suffer together, but truly, it can be difficult. If I am not experiencing much in the way of exchange, then chances are I have somehow diluted how present I am allowing myself to be.

From the point of view of the Buddhist teachings on emptiness and non-ego, we can recognize that what we experience is not being held in any *real* self. In theory, we may know that. Our meditation practice, and bodhichitta practices, such as tonglen (see Chödrön, 1994, or Wegela, 1996), can help us deal with our hesitations in this area. Khenpo Tsultrim Gyatso Rinpoche, a senior Tibetan teacher, once told me in an interview that if one is going to study the teachings on emptiness, it is essential that one first study the teachings on the truth of suffering (personal communication, March, 1992). We cannot dismiss the gritty quality of suffering and pain by referring to emptiness, nor should we.

At the same time, through our meditation practices, we discover again and again that we can, in fact, be present with pain and suffering. We can open to the direct experience of whatever arises and recognize the stories and thoughts as just that. When we let go of discursive thoughts, we are left with just the energetic direct experience, whatever it is. This is yet another reason why sitting meditation is essential to the contemplative or Buddhist-inspired psychotherapist.

The other difficulty associated with exchange is *getting stuck in the exchange*. We may be afraid to open to the exchange because we are afraid we will not be able to get out of it again. One of my students was doing an internship one year, and she told me the following story. While it is not a precisely accurate description of exchange, it reflects the fearless willingness to experience all states of mind that we may cultivate in meditation practice. Her supervisor was advising her to work with her clients by imagining that there was a kind of un-crossable pit between them. They could talk across this space, but the student should be careful to keep on her side of this boundary. My student replied that her training suggested that not only should she not stay on her side, she should jump right into the pit along with her client.

The point here is that we do not have to be afraid of our own experience. Because of our meditation practice we develop confidence in our unconditional brilliant sanity. We can experience our experience. If we do not believe that is possible, how can we invite our clients to do so? As I mentioned earlier, we always hold tentatively our belief that what we are experiencing has come through exchange. In any case, though, once we are experiencing whatever it is, it is now ours. It is our experience wherever it came from, and we need to work with it as we would with any other.

Touch and Go

A useful tool for working with the exchange is *touch and go* (Wegela, 1988). In meditation practice, we can use touch and go as a way of briefly but completely touching or directly experiencing whatever arises: emotions, thoughts, sensations. Then, we allow them to go, we let them go. Often, with students, in order to learn how to practice touch and go, we practice the two mistaken ways to do it: *touch and grab* and *go and go*. In the former, we hang on to experience; in the latter, we barely notice it. Both are ways to avoid the ever-changing texture of our aliveness. Touch and go provides a good technique for working with what arises in the exchange as well.

When people feel *stuck in the exchange*, they experience some intensity through exchange and do not seem to be able to let it go. Meditation practice is one good way of working with this. On the cushion we can practice touching our experience and letting it go. Sometimes we are *stuck* only because we have not actually recognized what is going on. Sometimes, though, we need more than our meditation practice.

Working with Obstacles Through Body-Speech-Mind Practice

Another practice that has been developed in contemplative psychotherapy is called *body-speech-mind* practice (Rabin & Walker, 1987; Wegela, 1996).[3] It is a supervision or consultation practice used to work with the obstacles to exchange. Body-speech-mind is a group practice in which we *invite the client into the room* by describing, and not interpreting, the unique qualities of a particular client. The presenter describes the details of the client's body, speech (literally speech, but also relationships and emotions), and mind. Different people in the room pick up on different aspects of the presenter, the client and their mutual relationship. All the participants pay attention to their direct experience during the presentation and offer what they notice. A working assumption that has proven its usefulness over time is that everything that arises in the group's participants during the presentation is relevant to the clinical work being presented.

Rather than trying to categorize the client diagnostically, or in any other way, body-speech-mind practice highlights one unique individual at a time. As participants share their responses during the presentation,

---

[3] For a thorough description of body-speech-mind practice, see the updated version of Rabin and Walker's article that appears as chapter 9, *A Discipline of Inquisitiveness*.

different aspects and textures of the presenter's relationship with the client become illuminated. It can be a very rich experience in which the presenter's relationship to the client is clarified and deepened.

Conclusion

Working with the naturally occurring phenomenon of exchange provides therapists with a wealth of information about what is happening with clients and within their relationship with their clients. It is a kind of deep listening to all that arises within us and is a reflection of our essentially interdependent nature. Beyond providing us with information about the client, ourselves, and the relationship between us, the experience of exchange *is* the experience of the deep connection between client and therapist.

Mindfulness-awareness meditation provides us not only with a way to prepare ourselves to work with exchange, it also is a tool to help us deal with difficult experiences of exchange. Finally, though, our willingness to be fully present with our own and others' pain allows us, both therapists and clients, to recognize our shared *brilliant sanity*.

References

Blackstone, J. (2007). *The empathic ground: Intersubjectivity and nonduality in the psychotherapeutic process*. Albany, NY: State University of New York Press.

Board of Editors. (1980). Brilliant sanity. *Naropa Institute Journal of Psychology, 1*, 1.

Chödrön, P. (1994). *Start where you are: A guide to compassionate living*. Boston: Shambhala.

Hanh, T. N. (Speaker). (1990). The practice of mindfulness in psychotherapy (Cassette recording). Boulder, CO: Sounds True.

Karthar, K. (1992). *Dharma paths* (L. M. Roth, Ed.; N. Burkhar & C. Radha, Trans.). Ithaca, NY: Snow Lion.

Maitreya, A. & Asanga, A. (1985). *The ultimate mahayana treatise on the changeless continuity of the true nature* (2nd edition; K. Holmes & K. Holmes, Trans). Scotland: Karma Drubgyud Darjay Ling (Karma Kagyü Trust).

May, R. (1989). The empathic relationship: A foundation of healing. In R. Carlson & B. Shield (Eds.), *Healers on healing* (pp. 108-110). Los Angeles, CA: Jeremy P Tarcher.

Rabin, B. & Walter, R. (1987). A contemplative approach to clinical supervision. *Journal of Contemplative Psychotherapy, 4*, 135-149.

Shantideva. (1992). *A guide to the bodhisattva's way of life* (S. Batchelor, Trans.). Dharamsala, India: Library of Tibetan Works and Archives. (Original work from the 8th century)

Trungpa, C. (1976). *The myth of freedom and the way of meditation.* Berkeley, CA: Shambhala.

Trungpa, C. (1983). Creating an environment of sanity. *Naropa Institute Journal of Psychology, 2,* 1-10.

Trungpa, C. (1985). Acknowledging death as the common ground of healing. *Journal of Contemplative Psychotherapy, 3,* 3-10.

Tsoknyi, D. (1998). *Carefree dignity: Discourses on training in the nature of mind.* (K. Moran, Ed.; E. P. Kunsang & M. B. Schmidt, Trans.). Boudhanath, Nepal: Rangjung Yeshe.

Watson, G. (In press). *Beyond happiness.* London: Karnac Books.

Wegela, K. K. (1988). "Touch and go" in clinical practice: Some implications of the view of intrinsic health for psychotherapy, *Journal of Contemplative Psychotherapy, 5,* 3-23.

Wegela, K. K. (1994). Contemplative psychotherapy: A path to uncovering brilliant sanity. *Journal of Contemplative Psychotherapy, 9,* 27-51.

Wegela, K. K. (1996). *How to be a help instead of a nuisance: Practical approaches to giving support, service and encouragement to others.* Boston: Shambhala.

13

Resonance and Exchange in Contemplative Psychotherapy

Farrell Silverberg

Our prime purpose in this life is to help others.
– Tenzin Gyatso, The 14th Dalai Lama

Psychotherapy and Buddhism: Flowers of the Same Garden

One way to look at the vehicle to healing in psychotherapy is as a certain and identifiable resonance between therapist and patient; one that may be sensed only unconsciously by the patient, but is sensed consciously by the therapist. For many therapists, such a connection has palpable meaning, but it comes and goes with waves increasing and decreasing in intensity. From a Buddhist perspective, that deeper connectedness to the patient is always there and accessible, it is only our access to it that waxes and wanes giving the illusion that there are times of deep connection and times of surface interaction. Ryokan (1977) said, "If we gain something, it was there from the beginning. If we lose anything, it is hidden nearby" (p.48).

The term *therapeutic resonance* (Silverberg, 1988) applies to those moments, minutes, or hours during which the therapist is fully aware of such reverberation and intentionally remains open and calm in the face of it – welcoming it. For those of us therapists who work in this way, there is a sense that when this connection is accessed, the deeper and more profound work of the therapeutic process is taking place.

The Mahayana practices of Buddhism and the empathic practices within psychotherapy are both flowers of the same garden. The psychotherapist who is committed to the well being of his or her patients and the Buddhist practitioner who is committed to being of compassionate service to others are both on the same path of commitment to relieve suffering. Both are using themselves as the instrument and compassion as the vehicle.

Therapeutic Resonance

To create a receptive ground for connecting with the patient's experience, the therapist is in a better position if he or she creates an "inner silence" (Izutsu, 1975, p. 3) for each patient that allows that patient's experience to come into awareness.

Although Buddhist meditation training is one possible way to gain the inner clarity and strength to practice patient and calm tolerance, *abiding* with all the experiences that may occur in providing the atmosphere for psychotherapy, it is not the only way to so develop. Bringing the patience and tolerance resulting from a deep training analysis to one's clinical work, and obtaining supervision while practicing, is another possible way.

Therapeutic resonance is a way that therapists open to and connect with the patient's experience and it can be defined as:

(1) the capacity to quietly absorb, reverberate with and contain the patient's experience;
(2) the capacity to intentionally welcome being this reflection of the patient, no matter how uncomfortable or disquieting; and,
(3) the awareness that this process is occurring.

According to Silverberg (1988),

> Therapeutic resonance is the vehicle to healing. Resonance is a way of "being with" another person and expressing fundamental receptivity and openness to that person. To resonate with someone is to serve as a mirror for him or her, and to be so closely identified that you feel that person's experience. Resonance is rooted in the stance of quiet attention, with minimal resistance of value judgment about its nature. (p. 25)

Through the process of resonance it becomes possible for the information in the emotional-experiential field of one person to be perceived and experienced within the emotional-experiential field of another person through some as-yet-undiscovered means of transmission, absorption, and compassionate exchange. The means of that transmission, absorption, and exchange may involve or rely upon the nature of or access to the greater interconnectedness between us all that operates parallel to our day to day consciousness or within which our ordinary perceptions take place. The experiences absorbed and contained are welcomed with the intention of co-experiencing another person's suffering for the sake of the patient's well being. Openness to being a container for these experiences is a disciplined practice that can be cultivated over time and training.

13. Resonance & Exchange

Therapeutic resonance is a psychotherapeutic application of the Tibetan Buddhist Mahayana practice of the "exchange of self for other" (Kongtrul, 1987, p. 6). Access to the experience of another person can be seen as a highly developed, cultivated, and possibly transcendent form of compassion that goes beyond the ordinary reality of one individual relating to another individual separated by the bodily containers in which we reside. The mechanism that permits such co-experiencing within the emotional-experiential field of another person remains undiscovered amongst medical model practitioners, although it is still an object of study. Most recently in the pursuit of discovering the mechanism of empathy, scientists have looked towards the activity of *mirror neurons* (Gallese, Eagle, & Mignone, 2007).

Rather than look to a neurobiological explanation within us, it is possible that the operating mechanism in such an exchange may utilize some matrix of interconnectedness that exists between and around us. It may well employ an experiential but non-material soup that Channapatna Shamasundar (1999) considered the interface of the experiential fields between us all – an interconnectedness of all beings. Meredith Luyten (1985) suggests that such an exchange is "not a therapeutic technique, but a constantly recurring moment in which the distinction between self and other flickers" (p. 45). This vehicle, which permits access to a deeper way of knowing, comes with a sense of awe that there may exist something greater than perception, cognition, and ordinary communication.

Despite the great soaring architecture of methods, techniques, and psychotherapy literature that abounds, there may be, underneath it all, a very simple and direct access to the bridge of helpfulness between ourselves and others. In a sense, therapeutic resonance can be seen as a *functional spirituality* that, although sprung from Buddhist practice, need not be bound to any particular spiritual path and one which can be commingled with any psychotherapy technique.

Giving Health and Taking Suffering

Yeshi Donden (1983), in discussing the role of the Tibetan physician, stated that the healer "contemplates that all the darkness, all the shadows, all the sickness of the patient are being absorbed by oneself and all of the light rays are being emanated to the patient" (p. 26). Donden's words summarize the Buddhist practice of Tonglen. Tonglen means "giving" (Tong) and "taking" (len) and there are many traditions and training practices of this giving/taking practice in Buddhism (Tharchin, 1999). For instance, in the Lojong lineage tradition, one can visualize this exchange of taking the suffering of another upon oneself and then giving some of one's own inner peace in its place (Tharchin, 1999).

The practice is not limited to the time spent meditating about Tonglen on the cushion, but, when the practitioner is ready, it is then carried into all activities. Khen Rinpoche warned, however, that Tonglen is not for the novice (Tharchin, 1999). Even if the novice sincerely wants to give well being and take suffering, it is advised that an advanced level of practice must be attained first (Tharchin, 1999). Likewise, it is preferable if the psychotherapist who intends to practice the taking on of suffering that occurs in the resonance is not a novice, otherwise there may be a danger of being adversely or prolongedly impacted by the exchange.

For those therapists who naturally open their hearts and begin to practice exchange without realizing it or before they have developed the strength and peace of mind to do so with impunity, supervision is required. Supervision becomes a place where the resonances that remain active in the therapist and continue on beyond the time frame of the session can be processed in order to give the therapist relief and to orient the therapist towards a more aware view of the patient and the exchange process in the future.

For the beginning therapist who has a great proportion of natural empathy, or raw compassion, repeated and prolonged supervision may be required to help remove emotional or other toxins experienced in an exchange from his or her system. Additionally, contemplative supervision practices, such as the *body, speech, mind practice* developed by Bonnie Rabin and Robert Walker (1987), invite fuller experience of the patient and create support for the therapist to experience the associated resonances.[1]

Karen Kissel Wegela (1988) discussed the phenomena of getting "stuck in the exchange" (p. 9) that results from not moving towards the pain fully and in holding back. Whereas moving fully into the suffering along with the patient leads to a relaxing of grasp on the experience, paradoxically, the experience becomes *grasped* and prolonged if trying to protect oneself against the experience (p. 19).

Pema Chödrön (1994) explains that,

> The basic message of the lojong teachings is that if it's painful, you can learn to hold your seat and move closer to that pain. Reverse the usual pattern, which is to split, to escape. Go against the grain and hold your seat. Lojong introduces a different attitude towards unwanted stuff: if it's painful, you become willing not just to endure it but also to let it awaken your heart and soften you. You learn to embrace it. (p. 7)

Such embracing in the practice of psychotherapy means to rise above the patient-therapist dyad and taking a meta-perspective on the transference-countertransference interchange.

---

[1] See chapter 8 for a more detailed discussion of body, speech, mind practice.

Cultivating Compassion

While meditation and Buddhist practice can foster the ability to *befriend* others in a compassionate way, this is not the only way to go from raw empathy to cultivated compassion. Supervisees who study the therapeutic resonance as a secular form of *calm abiding* awareness practice, without obtaining meditation training, find that they too can develop their strength and inner peace from self development work via paths of their own choosing.

Still, the cultivation of compassion in Buddhist training is so central that it seems only common sense to harness the millennia of development of Mahayana practice and include it in the training of cultivated compassion for psychotherapists. As Wallace (2005) asserts,

> The first task in the Buddhist cultivation of compassion is to develop a sense of equality between oneself and others in terms of the nature of suffering and the common desire to be free of it. The extension of the field of one's concern beyond oneself, to include all other beings, in fact brings a greater burden of suffering upon one's own shoulders. (p. 97)

Beyond Resonance: Sending Health

Amongst the more difficult experiences encountered in resonance with our patients are those of helplessness, failure, and vulnerability. Yet, since we are opening ourselves to the experiences of our patients, what choice do we have when our intention is to connect with them other than to feel profound helplessness, failure, and vulnerability at times? The hopeless patient has no reason to believe that either through his or her own devices or through psychotherapy treatment, their situation will become adequately livable, never mind enjoyable. Soon this hopelessness spreads to the therapy itself and when the patient's hopelessness has touched the treatment, the therapy too may be experienced as a potential failure and unable to be of help. The patient feels that he or she is failing and that the therapy is failing, and that therefore their despair is an unchangeable fact. This is when the therapist can go beyond resonance and give of his or her health in the exchange of self for other.

At such times, simply resonating with the despair, although required to help the patient feel companioned and supported, may not be enough. Something of the therapist's own path and health may be required to *send* out in the resonance as well. While resonating with the hopelessness and despair the therapist can bring to mind his or her own hope for the patient and send, either in the tone or in speaking the message that, "as long as one of us still has hope for you, then there is hope."

What we can bring to the treatment, that the patient is without, is our hope. Our hope can be based upon our past experience in helping others out of despair and possibly, based on our own experiences of having been helped out of despair ourselves. We know that it is possible. For instance, I had one patient who had been terribly physically abused and humiliated by her father during her early and middle childhood years. This patient was a very good person who helped many people as a vocational therapist, but she felt worthless and so deeply and permanently damaged that she felt that any contentment or personal happiness was beyond her reach. She was profoundly depressed and hopeless. She constantly wished and prayed that she would die through some accidental means such as from an overdose of the narcotic pain killers she frequently took to numb herself. She had little life outside of her job, avoided all social contact, and assured herself that she could never have children of her own since she was too mentally ill to raise them.

Her first months of psychotherapy were spent hardly talking. She arrived, sank to the floor next to the couch in my office, and slumped down, silently, for long periods of time. Occasionally, she would report an event or complain of her torment, but mostly she was silent and the suffering in her silence was deep. I would say something once in a while, but mostly remained silent and felt the deep despair along with her for the time she was in my office.

Her fear was palpable each time she entered my office, and in sensing it I always moved several feet away from her path as she went to seat herself. Eventually, in trembling and hardly audible tones, she began sharing about her childhood and the beatings, tortures, and humiliations she suffered, as well as the many times she nearly died at her brutal father's hands. She was convinced and attempted to convince me as well that he had damaged her so badly emotionally that, although she loved children, she would never have a *normal* family life or any comfort in her existence. In her opinion, it would be better if she died.

In listening to her over a long period of time I was filled, alternately, with deep sadness and feelings of protectiveness and anger, including thoughts of wanting to die. Although her depression and drug use diminished over this time, she still reported feeling hopeless and that someone *normal* like me, with a marriage and children, could never understand her. She felt that the therapy was a waste of time for both of us and there was no use going on.

I contained the resonance of despair and depression and infused it into the times I spoke. But she was such a gentle person it was difficult to imagine how to infuse any anger at her persecutor into the treatment without frightening her. It occurred to me, time and time again, that infusing hope from my own path was required. As I had been through similar experiences as this patient during my own childhood, I knew in a real way that the damage caused by these horrors does not have to doom one from enjoying sanity and a loving and rewarding family life. I knew that

13. Resonance & Exchange

it is possible to overcome the depths of despair from my own case and the cases of many who had been through my office before.

In response to hearing about an incident that occurred when the patient was eight and was attacked with a knife, I began by saying "With father's like ours, who were such animals..." Curious, of course, the patient asked about my experiences and my path to health and gradually hopefulness became more of a reality in the treatment room than before.

Paul Fleischman (1988) talks about the importance of a psychotherapist's ability to attune to *anicca* – a sense of the transience of all things – characterized by the "dual atmosphere of loss and renewal" (p. 50). My patient's progress, as she allowed herself to open up into this anicca atmosphere, continued steadily. Her depression waned; she reported that her depression was minimal and that there were some weeks that went by during which she was not depressed at all. She is now in a relationship and has begun to talk in her sessions about the future possibility of having children. She now says she wants to live.

Since I happen to have suffered and surmounted what many of our patients have gone through, I can use that past suffering to "perform the function of a spiritual friend" as recommended by Jamgong Kongtrul (1987, p. 45). I appreciate having had this past history in that it serves the treatment work with patients. There are many ways that a therapist can draw upon his or her own spiritual friends, humanity, and path to better resonate, bring hope, and *send* health in the exchange with the patient.

What of other cases wherein the contemplative psychotherapist is exposed to the extremes of resonance? If a patient is feeling ultimately despairing and suicidal, does the therapist who resonates have to feel suicidal? Potentially, yes. If we can contain that feeling as a result of our self-work, our calm-abiding meditation work, and in our own time in psychotherapies or training analyses, then the answer is yes! If suicidality is the resonance, then that is what we will feel in the exchange. Sharing this burden with the patient, who will sense on some level the companioning, lessens a sense of isolation and ultimately might reduce the suicide risk and be healing in and of itself.

Part of the definition of therapeutic resonance is that the psychotherapist voluntarily welcomes into himself or herself the painful and suffering experiences of the patient if that is what is contained in the resonance. Kongtrul (1987) advised that such adverse experiences need not frighten us, nor do we have to avoid them:

> By using adverse conditions, you can gather the accumulations, clear away obscurations, be reminded of dharma, and derive benefit from your understanding. There is no need to be frightened of visions and hallucinations associated with gods or devils or of the trouble that demons cause. Because they help to increase your faith and virtue, they are emanations of your guru or

of buddhas... Sickness clears away all the evil and obscurations gathered from time without beginning. When suffering comes, if you look at just what is, it arises as emptiness. However much you suffer, the suffering is just the dance of what is. (pp. 45-46)

Countertransference

Psychoanalysis, as a profession, seems divided about whether the incorporation of compassionate connection with the patient, sometimes seen as countertransference, is helpful or harmful to the healing process. Although there are a few schools of psychoanalytic thought that still discourage having strong feelings and experiences when with a patient, empathic experiences, even if categorized as countertransference, are increasingly seen as something with which we can and should work.

Experiencing such painful states, so long as it is used in the service of understanding the patient's problem, is not the taboo activity that Freud believed contaminated the treatment. Instead, in Modern Psychoanalysis (Spotnitz, 1969), for instance, it is a desirable, even necessary experience that the therapist must have in the process of treatment. Additionally, in *relational psychoanalysis*, countertransference is understood as a "form through which the therapist tries to reach the client" (DeYoung, 2003, p. 149).

The psychoanalytic work of Heinrich Racker (1968) can be seen as having posited, or as verging on positing, a system of empathic countertransference, although not referred to as such. Racker's ideas about countertransference move away from the view of countertransference as a problem. When the patient's transference (experiencing the therapy relationship as if it were the same as a past significant relationship) becomes activated, it brings with it a certain set of thoughts, feelings, and style of interaction with the therapist. When the therapist becomes the recipient of this transferred set of experiences, he or she has reactions to it – countertransference. Racker's ideas moved towards seeing certain therapist countertransferences as reflecting something *objective* about the patient (Ormont, 1970).

Racker (1968) discussed two modes of therapist empathic reaction: concordant and complementary. *Concordant* countertransferences allow the therapist to experience something akin to the patient's experience and *complementary* countertransferences allow the therapist to experience something akin to what it may have been like to be some *other* object in the patient's past or in that patient's intrapsychic reality. In much of psychoanalysis, while such phenomenon may be accepted as part of therapeutic process, there is little in the way of explanation offered as to the mechanism by which such experiences take place. Additionally, there is a dearth of discussion of how to cultivate the therapist's ability to access such experiences.

Luyten (1985) points out,

> There is no equivalent term in the psychological literature for the experience of exchange. "Empathy," "intuition" and "parallel process" are terms frequently and loosely used to describe aspects of exchange, but in their usage all fall short of any acknowledgement of egolessness as the ground of communication. Always there is an assumption of separate minds. (p. 46)

Taming Wild Resonance

If, before we are born, we are of the same fabric, and after we are born we are still of the same fabric but our minds construct walls and we become deluded about our degree of separateness, and after we die we are again reabsorbed back into that same fabric – why not have the capacity to absorb and contain each other's experiences? This raises the problem that Freud cautioned us against in his article on *Wild Psychoanalysis* (1957b) and could lead to conducting treatment based on the therapist's countertransferential imaginings about the patient rather than in relation to that patient. The more experiential evidence is included in the treatment process, the more potential may exist for such wildness. Many would say that therapeutic resonance and exchange is just such soft data and all the more subject to subjectiveness.

Possibly there is a middle way through this dilemma; that the experience can be thought of as being the patient's experience or a close reflection thereof, but only after some confirming empirical evidence has been gathered from the session content of other information. By incorporating such a check and balance, we can be more assured that the treatment is really about the patient and not about our illusions or subjective countertransferences. The idea of self-checking is also consistent with the Mahayana training advice given by Kongtrul (1987) regarding the practice of exchange of self for other:

> You must find freedom from disturbing emotions and ego-clinging by constantly examining and investigating your course of experience. Therefore, turn your attention to an object that gives rise to disturbing emotions. Examine carefully whether they arise or not. If they do arise, apply remedies vigorously. Again, look at ego clinging to see what it is like. If it appears that no ego-clinging is present, examine it again in reference to an object of attachment or aversion. If ego-cherishing then arises, immediately stop it with the remedy of exchanging yourself for others (p.40).

For all practitioners of psychotherapy, contemplative or not, there is much to be said for using evidence from each individual treatment to confirm or disconfirm what we experience and believe while conducting treatment. Such testing is consistent with what has been called individualized evidence-based practice (Persons, Davidson, & Tompkins, 2001). For instance, in a therapy session with a patient I had been seeing for some time, I was struck by a strong urge to be more giving. As the session progressed, this feeling distilled into the impulse to give the patient a small print of a Japanese woodcut that I had been carrying in my appointment book for some weeks.

Following the principle that such information was to be evaluated and not taken as an instruction to act in any way, I studied the feeling to see if it was at all quasi-empirically related to anything the patient was discussing that day, but saw no connection. The same experience overtook me in the following session and still there was no clarity. Usually, with such a strong experience, evidence of a resonance presented itself with the patients session content or report of life events that permitted me to consider how to infuse the resonance into intervention, but no such evidence presented itself this time. In the absence of confirmation that this was resonant information, and considering the possibility that it might be a *wild* resonance, I practiced calm-abiding restraint and contained but studied the impulse as in the practice of zazen and limited my "activity to the smallest extent" (Suzuki, 1970, p. 75).

Finally, in the session after that, it all became clear when the patient entered and handed me a rolled-up sheet of rice paper stating that he had been intending to give me this piece of artwork for a few weeks. I opened the paper to find a woodcut print. It seemed now that my desire to give may have been a resonance and an experience of exchange about his desire to give. My restraint allowed his process to go to completion and there was, in retrospect, some wisdom in awaiting some empirical evidence before infusing any intervention with the giving impulse rather than allow untamed or wild resonance into the treatment.

Transforming Resonance

For the most part, what we are asked to absorb in the process of exchange of self for other entails pain and suffering, profound hopelessness, debilitating lethargy, fragmented confusion, burning anxiety, or even strong and seductive impulses to end one's suffering by ending one's life. In more advanced and esoteric spiritual practices, such as Tantra or Vajrayana, such disturbing emotions are transformed into a form of wisdom.

> Thus hatred is sublimated into mirror-like primordial wisdom, pride into the primordial wisdom of equality, attachment into the primordial wisdom of discernment, jealousy into the primordial wisdom of accomplishment, and delusion into the primordial wisdom of the absolute nature of reality. (Wallace, 2005, pp. 100-101)

13. Resonance & Exchange

A more advanced resonance practice that may be uncomfortable for the therapist and require additional fortitude is to sit with a disquieting resonance throughout a session or throughout many sessions with a patient until that resonance transforms and can be helpfully infused into the treatment. For instance, I had a session with a patient who had been working in another city for two years. During this time we kept in contact by telephone but did not see each other. During this time he experienced a significant personal loss. His older sister, with whom he had been very close, died after a short battle with pancreatic cancer which had only been diagnosed a few months earlier.

When he returned to Philadelphia and we had our first in-person session in a long while, he talked about experiencing "loneliness in the room" that he felt was coming from me or my office. Indeed, I, too, sensed a very distinct loneliness and a very hollow quietness that felt unsettling. He moved to the psychoanalytic couch where we had conducted many of his sessions in the past and I could no longer see his face. He spoke in halting cadence, mentioned his sister and was quiet for periods of time. Then he fell into complete silence. The hollow loneliness continued to pervade the room, everything felt cold and empty.

Sometimes when a patient is quiet and the room is cold it is good to talk and warm them up. This time, however, I felt that something was on the verge or the edge and I remained silent. I did not have the worry that I sometimes have, that the patient would suffer badly during the silence. After a few minutes, I noticed myself feeling terribly sad, tearing up, and eventually crying softly, just a little bit. At that same moment I noticed that the feeling of loneliness in the room, that was so palpable to both the patient and me only a few minutes earlier, seemed to disappear. At that same moment, the patient sat up from the couch and was looking down. Then he turned towards me and I could see the tears streaming down his face.

On his way out he touched my shoulder and I touched his. He said it was good to see me and I said it was good to see him. And it was. Without much content, this particular session touched some deep pain and moved it somewhat, through the vehicle of resonance and not much more in this instance.

Sometimes just the therapist's calm abiding of this access without much in the way of technique can also be helpful for a patient. For instance, a supervisee of mine told me that she was feeling lost, confused, and out-of-touch with herself during one of the initial sessions with a new patient. My supervisee felt worried during the entire session and the confusion was making her feel incompetent. She questioned whether she was helping the patient even though she felt she was providing some support. Finally, her patient ended the session by reporting that she had been feeling very lost, confused, and out-of-touch for some time but this session made her "feel better." My supervisee realized that this was an example of how simply resonating, and not doing much more, helped the patient feel understood and relieved.

Is One-ness Progressive or Regressive?

If we accept much of traditional psychoanalytic doctrine, we might have to consider such oneness with the patient as a sign of regression rather than enlightenment. Ever since Freud first alluded to a feeling of melding with the "oceanic state" (Freud, 1957a) there has been derision cast upon such experiences. Barry Magid (2000) states that psychoanalytic attempts to discuss oneness have inevitably, "tried to fit oneness experiences into some pre-existing psychoanalytic schema, often resulting in the conclusion that "oneness" must involve some sort of regressed state, some kind of primitive loss of differentiation between self and other" (p. 515). For instance, Hanley (1984) states that,

> Merger experiences in themselves can scarcely be therapeutic in so far as they involve regression both of instinctual organization and ego structures to their most primitive forms. The intense elation they can release is not an effective emotion for any practical life purpose nor could it be utilized, even if it were, by an ego that has become unified, purified and paralyzed. It is an escape from intrapsychic conflict rather than a resolution of it" (pg. 244).

It seems that one of the least derisive of the *oneness as regression* theories is espoused by Cohen (2007) who takes the viewpoint that though the product of a regression, the capacity for oneness is based on a memory of original "gestational" unity with the womb of the mother and such a memory allows for empathy with others.

Still, all of these viewpoints are contrary to the resonant exchange point of view. The naysayers will argue that there is nothing oceanic actually going on in the present reality at the moment of the resonance. But why not consider that there may well be something oceanic going on in the psychotherapy treatment that connects patient and therapist in the same field, and this interconnectedness can be increasingly cultivated as a disciplined practice and used for helping the patient?

Magid (2000), in just such a positive reframing of "oneness" as a reflection of how things are, not how things were, takes the position that we are indeed interconnected:

> Perhaps it is finally time for psychoanalysis to stop thinking that experiencing "oneness" means momentarily returning to the way things once were and to recognize that it means seeing things as they are. Dualism, fundamentally a defensive, fantasized attempt

to split off the self from a world of potential suffering, represents a developmental failure. (p. 519).

Rather than seeing the ability to approach patients in this resonant way as a form of regression, it may be that such a capacity along with maintaining the structure of the psychotherapy work is an expression of what Magid (2000) sees as "true developmental maturity" (p. 519).

Applied Resonance: Inhabited and Uninhabited Interventions

I have come to think that in psychotherapy there are two distinct modes for delivering any intervention: with or without the infusion of resonance. I refer to these two modes as interventions delivered in *inhabited* and *uninhabited* fashion. For instance, the subtle emulations of a joining, mirroring, or reflecting technique can be delivered either inhabited by experiences gleaned in the resonance or based instead only on the content and observed tone or cadence. In the inhabited case, it is a technique that is informed by and infused with elements from the resonant exchange and in the uninhabited case; it is technique that is guided by ordinary reality observations only.

Through the experience of resonance, the therapist can sense what it may be like to be the patient. A small trace of that accessed knowledge can be intentionally infused into the therapist's tone of voice or into the content of the words being spoken to the patient – reinforcing that the patient is being understood.

> Such an intervention gives the patient a sense that he is not suffering alone and unnoticed and an opportunity for relief from defensiveness. For the patient who is hesitant, beaten-down, weakened, and isolated, this intervention can have the effect of a transfusion. (Silverberg, 1988, p. 34)

It is near impossible, unless either therapist or patient is quite capable of total dissociation, to completely hide a resonance from a patient. Yet, until the therapist is ready to infuse the resonance back into the treatment atmosphere when it is consistent with the psychotherapy process, it is important to keep the resonance in the container of the therapist and under wraps if at all possible. Sometimes, however, it is just not possible to do so and at those moments when expression cannot be curtailed (as in the case of crying I discussed earlier), remaining conservative but trusting in the process is the only choice.

Adding the element of habitation to intervention makes those interventions, and thereby the treatment process, freer from cookbook application. Instead it is informed and infused by the resonance of the present moment, a moment that, if fully experienced, contains also the past. As Gargiulo (2006) noted, this moment in history becomes salient, not only the precedent events which help determine this present moment.

Those of us who are called to be therapists, or even psychoanalysts, may, by definition, hear that voice that is listened to "with the third ear" as Reik (1949, p. 125) noted. But to make that element part of the formula that pulls the entire treatment paradigm into the present moment to accompany this singular patient requires inhabiting, as fully as possible, each intervention. As psychotherapists, we are not required by our training or the techniques we learn to operate the treatment from this more interconnected ground. The techniques of psychotherapy can be performed without being in touch with the resonant flow and even without having empathic alignment with the patient. By relying only on intellect and emotions that are not cultivated from the deeper connections, it is possible to conduct a valuable and helpful psychotherapy or an analysis.

However, with that more strategic mode of operation is it possible to conduct a freeing treatment outcome for the patient? Or, is an infusion of resonance required to do more than replace the patient's old unhealthy patterns with new healthier but equally determined patterns? With resonance, it seems to me, there is a chance of an opening into the therapy work so that the patient's heretofore inaccessible *black box* of conditioning that constrained his or her true nature becomes fluid, accessible, and returns to being *in process* rather than frozen and experienced as solidified into a terrible and interminable punishment. Psychoanalysts might think of this access as the ability to bring into the transference interaction those deep and damaged aspects of character otherwise kept defended so that a deeper repair can ensue.

Without the contributions of cultivated compassion and resonant exchange to the treatment, I doubt whether such a breadth and texture of healing can be brought into the process. The limitation of more technically based work might well halt the process at symptomatic relief without nearing a more transformative rebirth. This does not mean that the practice of psychotherapy and psychoanalysis in general is empty of a resonant core. But, certainly, with an intentional and disciplined effort to cultivate resonance and infuse it into interventions, therapists are more likely to practice resonant exchange therapeutically and consistently (Silverberg, 1999).

Dong Shik Rhee (1991) stated that elements brought to the therapy situation by the psychotherapist "bring Spring to the patient who is frozen, who is shivering in a frozen land" (p. 379). Resonance, I propose, is that aspect in the psychotherapy interchange that, beyond bringing symptomatic relief and functional improvements, works on a more profound level to *bring Spring* to the patient.

Those who are more familiar with the shorter term and single-mindedly symptom relief focused treatments are sometimes befuddled as to why a patient might choose to continue treatment after the

13. Resonance & Exchange

symptomatic relief is achieved and stabilized. But, it is for this very reason – in order to become unfrozen and grow in the renewed Spring of one's life, to deepen one's befriending of oneself, and increase the capacity to have deeply connected and mutually fulfilling relationships with others and meaningful work in the world.

If resonance could very well be the most important element of the treatment, why, then, in our usual psychotherapy training, is this one of the elements that takes a back seat to theory and technique? I am not aware of any state psychology or social work licensing exam or any psychiatry board testing that examines whether the candidate for licensure can resonate with the patient's experience, or where tester and examinee may, for instance, cry together over a mutually felt grief or loss. But, as we know, information about diagnosis, treatment strategies, and psychodynamics is more unremarkably tolerable, easier in a way, and more amenable to *quantification* and scoring.

Compassion is Not Psychotherapy and Psychotherapy is Not Compassion

I have found that the two forms, inner core of resonance and outer casing of analytic technique, work together well. Just as meditation practice has a certain form that brings about a better container for developing the capacity for experience within (certain posture, certain breathing, and certain mind practices), so, too, psychoanalysts, cognitive behavioral therapists, and others have chosen techniques and dependable ways of structuring the session so it can be a similar container. It is important to be clear that cultivated compassion is not the practice of psychotherapy but can possibly infuse the practice of psychotherapy with a more deeply healing and profoundly informative component. Likewise, developing skill in the techniques of psychotherapy can offer the person who has cultivated his or her compassion additional means with which to enact compassionate work and reduce the suffering of others.

Realistically speaking, even advanced Buddhist practitioners, having achieved a very high state of cultivated compassion, but lacking in psychotherapy experience or training, would have no more likelihood of success conducting a psychotherapy treatment than they would performing an intracranial neurosurgery operation. Although closely related in practice and stemming from the same root, compassion is not psychotherapy and psychotherapy is not compassion. As I mentioned in a previous writing,

> The practice of psychotherapy as a healing art involves the development of two capacities in the therapist. One is the capacity to resonate in response to the patient. The second is the development of technical therapy skill to the point of intuitive mastery. (Silverberg, 1988, p. 25)

Beyond Mindfulness Techniques

That the techniques of *mindfulness* have increasingly been applied in psychotherapy methods is good in that mindful awareness is helpful to many people and for many reasons (Germer, Siegel, & Fulton, 2005). Yet, simply applying or teaching these techniques as an adjunct to psychotherapy technique can be likened to taking and using some leaves from the tree of Buddhism ignoring the deeply rooted aspects.

It is in the roots of that tree of Buddhism, after all, that the power lies. Those roots, as I discussed thus far, are not far from our human experience as compassionate beings who are committed to helping others. At the core of contemplative psychotherapy practice is the ability to sustain a calm abiding, along with mindful and open discipline, while with our patients. This discipline may be initially nurtured through sitting meditation practice and befriending ourselves (Trungpa, 2005) in a way that brings the matured fruits of these efforts to practices of therapeutically befriending others. Or, such mindful openness may be the fruits of diligent personal development, initially through our own training, psychotherapy, or training analysis. Most of us who utilize an approach related to contemplative psychotherapy practice have taken both paths of self-work.

The practitioner who is in profound in-touchness with the deeper levels of connecting to others, and who is able to do so with minimal personal distortion, may be better able to apply psychotherapy techniques with respect, precision, and context-awareness. In bringing that calm abiding presence to the therapy encounter, there is a chance that an atmosphere fostering deeper healing will be more likely to arise.

Conclusions

Buddhism and psychotherapy are really not very far away from each other. They have common roots in compassion and common goals of helping to relieve suffering. When I first wrote about calling upon the application of the "exchanging oneself for others" (Kongtrul, 1987, p. 6) in the process of psychotherapy, it seemed to me that if this very Buddhist practice was infused into psychotherapy, it could foster a more deeply and more continuously helpful atmosphere for patients. One could think of Buddhism as one hand and psychotherapy as the other hand attached to the body of cultivated compassion. They both serve in a mixture of similar and different ways. Whether and how much of one or the other each individual practitioner brings to the therapy situation is a personal formula.

When I first wrote *Therapeutic Resonance* (Silverberg, 1988) twenty years ago, I did not realize that my interest in bringing one Buddhist practice of experiential exchange into the psychotherapeutic setting would become a path, a discipline, and a teaching orientation that would engage me for these last two decades. It will probably be my journey for as many more years as I am fortunate enough to have this life I am living.

When inhabiting psychotherapy with the hard won and calmly abided fruits of the resonant exchange in the present moment of treatment with the patient, it seems to me that the "true welfare" (Kalupahana, 1987, p. 51) – sad-attha – of the patient's health is served. It also seems that the path of the treatment momentum is provided with a certain stability that comes from the ground of the resonant exchange. "This quality is like the four legs of a horse, which make it stable and balanced... you are not riding an ordinary horse, you are riding windhorse." (Trungpa, 1984, p. 114).

The practice of resonance and exchange are not psychotherapy per se, nor are they Buddhism or a path to enlightenment for the practitioner, per se. But these experiences of cultivated compassion in the psychotherapy stream can serve to augment, inform, and helpfully infuse the practice of psychotherapy technique from any school of thought. The value of the years of training oneself and being trained in psychotherapy, meditation, or both, becomes crystal clear as so beautifully stated by Susan Flynn (2007): "When you know beyond a shadow of a shadow of a doubt, that every session – be it analysis or meditation – was past being well worth it" (p. 197).

Every moment in resonant exchange, in the process of carrying out well honed therapy skills and awareness skills for the sake of the patient, in the deepening of the vibrancy and the helping of patients to carry out their own life intentions, is past being well worth it.

References

Chödrön, P. (1994). *Start where you are: A guide to compassionate living.* Boston: Shambala.

Cohen, T. (2007, October). *Considering gestational life.* Paper presented at the International Federation for Psychoanalytic Education, Toronto, Canada.

DeYoung, P. A. (2003). *Relational psychotherapy: A primer.* New York: Brunner-Routledge.

Donden, Y. (1983). Tibetan medicine: Buddha wisdoms and the healing of mind and body (R. Thurman, Trans.). *The Journal of Traditional Acupuncture, 7*(2), 22-26.

Fleischman, P. R. (1988). Awareness of anicca and the practice of psychotherapy. *Journal of Contemplative Psychotherapy, 5,* 43-52.

Flynn, S. (2007). A transformational moment. In P. Cooper (Ed.), *Into the mountain stream: Psychotherapy and Buddhist experience.* New York: Jason Aronson.

Freud, S. (1957a). Civilization and its discontents. In J. Strachey (Ed. & Trans.), *Standard edition of the complete works of Sigmund Freud* (Vol. 21: pp. 57-46). London: Hogarth Press. (Original work published in 1930)

Freud, S. (1957b). Observations on 'wild' psycho-analysis. In J. Strachey (Ed. & Trans.), *Standard edition of the complete works of Sigmund Freud* (Vol. 11; pp. 221-227). London: Hogarth Press. (Original work published in 1910)

Gallese V., Eagle M.E., & Migone P. (2007). Intentional attunement: Mirror neurons and the neural underpinnings of interpersonal relations. *Journal of the American Psychoanalytic Association, 55*, 131-176.

Germer, C. K., Siegel, R. D., & Fulton, P. R. (Eds.). (2005). *Mindfulness and Psychotherapy.* New York: The Guilford Press.

Hanly, C. (1984). The search for oneness. [Review of the Book *The search for oneness*]. *International Review of Psycho-Analysis, 11*, 243-244.

Izutsu, T. (1975). *The interior and exterior in Zen Buddhism.* Dallas: Spring Publications.

Kalupahana, D. J. (1987). *The principles of Buddhist psychology.* Albany, NY: State University of New York Press.

Kongtrul, J. (1987). *The great path of awakening: An easily accessible introduction for ordinary people* (K. McLeod, Trans). Boston: Shambhala.

Luyten, M. F. (1985). Egolessness and the 'borderline' experience. *Naropa Institute Journal of Psychology, 3*, 45.

Magid, B. (2000). The couch and the cushion: Integrating Zen and psychoanalysis. *Journal of American Academy of Psychoanalysis, 28*, 513-526.

Ormont, L.R. (1970). The use of the objective countertransference to resolve group resistance. *Group Process*, 96-111.

Persons, J. B., Davidson, J., & Thompkins, M. A. (2001). *Essential components of cognitive-behavioral therapy for depression.* Washington, DC: American Psychological Association.

Rabin, B. & Walter, R. (1987). A contemplative approach to clinical supervision. *Journal of Contemplative Psychotherapy, 4*, 135-149.

Racker, H. (1968). *Transference and counter-transference.* New York: International Universities Press.

Reik, T. (1949). *Listening with the third ear.* New York: Farrar Strauss.

Rhee, D. S. (1991). The integration of East and West psychotherapy. In T. J. Choi (Ed.), *The Tao of psychotherapy: A festschrift in honor of Dr. Dong Shik Rhee on the occasion of his 70th birthday* (pp. 375-380). Tae Gu, South Korea: Lee Moon Publishing Company.

Ryokan. (1977). *One robe, one bowl: The zen poetry of Ryokan.* (J. Stevens, Trans.) New York: Weatherhill.

Shamasundar, C. (1999). Understanding empathy and related phenomena. *American Journal of Psychotherapy, 53* (2), 232-245.

Silverberg, F. (1988). Therapeutic resonance. *Journal of Contemplative Psychotherapy, 5,* 25-42.

Silverberg, F. (1999). Psychotherapy Training East and West. *Proceedings of the 1999 Scientific Conference of Korean Academy for Psychotherapy.* 45-69.

Spotnitz H. (1969). *Modern psychoanalysis of the schizophrenic patient: Theory of the technique.* New York: Grune & Stratton.

Suzuki, S. (1970). *Zen mind, beginner's mind.* New York: Weatherhill.

Trungpa, C. (1984). *Shambhala, sacred path of the warrior.* (C. R. Gimian, Ed.) Boston: Shambhala.

Trungpa, C. (2005). *The Sanity We are born with: A Buddhist approach to psychology.* (C. R. Gimian, Ed.). Boston & London: Shambhala.

Tharchin, S. K. L. (1999). *Achieving Bodhichitta.* Howell, NJ: Mahayana Sutra and Tantra Press.

Wallace, A. (2005). *Balancing the mind: A Tibetan Buddhist approach to refining attention.* Ithaca, NY: Snow Lion.

Wegela, K. K. (1988). "Touch and go" in clinical practice: Some implications of the view of intrinsic health for psychotherapy. *Journal of Contemplative Psychotherapy, 5,* 3-21.

14

Exploring Countertransference, Emptiness, and Joy in the Path of the Therapist

MacAndrew S. Jack
Abigail M. Lindemann[1]

This chapter will focus on the effects on the psychotherapist of practicing clinical work. In particular, it will examine the opening provided by a tender-hearted feeling engendered in the therapist as a result of exposure to clients' suffering. This tender-hearted feeling, in combination with an ongoing practice of attending to one's countertransference experiences with clients, often reveals experiences of what has been described in Buddhist literature as the emptiness of self and other. I will use personal examples centered around a period of my life during which tender-heartedness and emptiness broke into particular prominence for me. In addition to helping ease the suffering of our clients, I suggest that clinical work can become a valuable practice for the personal growth and development of the psychotherapist through a relaxation into this emptiness and opening to our interconnection with the world.

Countertransference and the Breaking Heart

As a clinical postdoctoral fellow at Beth Israel Hospital in Boston, I took the train to and from work. I was living south of the city and I had about an hour on the infamous subway lines of Boston each morning and evening. While my morning train rides consisted largely of having breakfast and reading, the return trips had a decidedly different flavor. They would often begin similarly to the rides in, with a good book in my hands, but in the evening I rarely made much headway with the reading. Instead, I would find the wave of the day crashing over me. The flood of emotions, reflections on encounters with clients, and discoveries about myself would pass through me and I would frequently have tears streaming down my face by the time I switched trains from the Green line to the Red line.

---

[1] This paper is a joint project of the two authors, however whenever the first-person is used, it refers to the experience of the first author.

Fortunately, the etiquette of train ridership seemed to be that no one paid much attention to each other on the train. My emotional washes were no more noteworthy to other riders than the tinny sounds leaking from the headphones in the ears of the teenage girl sitting next to me. In that environment, liberating in its spacious nonimpingement, I could allow myself to begin to experience simple sadness, trickles of raw overwhelm, and so many other resonances of the day. During this time I had been maintaining a daily meditation practice and learning about my capacity to experience a client's world. The exposure to the pain of clients' lives, combined with quite human limitations on my ability to reduce that pain and even, at times, my direct role in causing pain through misattunement and rupture, left me with a tender feeling that co-existed with my professional boundaries with clients.

Many of us, I venture, have at times felt the tender pangs of hurt in therapy and perhaps struggled with sorting out our involvement in the pain present in the therapeutic relationship. These feelings are especially noticeable in psychotherapy in which we are following our subjective experience for clues about the therapeutic relationship and the internal world of our clients. Whether it is called countertransference, projective identification, or as it is referred to in contemplative psychotherapy, *exchange*,[2] somehow, in the medium of the therapeutic relationship, we contact a web of emotional energy.

Steven Mitchell (2000) has characterized this web as a "fundamental, boundariless, affective level of experience... in which direct affective resonances emerge in interpersonal [relationship]" (p. 62). Through contact with this web, our clinical work has many effects on our lives. The broad category *countertransference* has often been used to describe the more immediate experiences of the therapist engendered by therapeutic encounters. In this chapter I will examine a few models of countertransference for explanations of this potentially useful *porosity* of our boundary with clients including Racker's classic types of countertransference, Ogden's projective identification, and Mitchell's interpretation of Loewald's primordial density. I will use the work of Loewald and Mitchell on this subject to form the basis of a critique of the ontological assumptions of separateness and relatedness.

Identifications and the Therapist's Empathic Vibrations

"To clarify better the concept of countertransference, one might start from the question of what happens, in general terms, in the analyst in his relationship with the patient" (Racker, 1957, p. 164). Racker postulated that "the intention to understand creates a certain predisposition to identify oneself with the analysand, which is the basis of comprehension" (p. 164). True to his understanding of the complex object world, Racker pointed out that these *identifications* with the client lead

---

[2] See Wegela, Chapter 12.

therapists to become identified not only with clients' self objects, but also with their internally-projected object world, or internalized *other* objects. Thus, Racker outlined a framework for understanding our countertransference experiences of the client's self-experience as well as the projected experiences of others in the client's object world like her father or loved one. Racker used the term *countertransference positions* to refer to the analyst's identifications with positions in the object world of the client. These identifications contain elements of the client's infantile situations and archaic objects as well as "provoke in the unconscious of the analyst infantile situations and an intensified vibration of archaic objects of his own" (Racker, 1957, p. 180).

Enlistment and Induction
Thomas Ogden (1993) further detailed the interactional field of client and therapist object worlds in his work on projective identification. Ogden's view of countertransference similarly suggests that the therapist is "enlisted as a participant in the externalization of the internal object relationship [of the client]" (p. 154). He also refers to therapist's responses to clients as often including an "induced identification with an aspect of the patient's ego... [which] represents a form of understanding of the patient that can be acquired no other way" (p. 154). As we participate in and observe these enlistments, we can understand our clients in a deeply personal way.

What is the nature of that inducement? Ogden (1993) offers an example of a patient who complained of being *contaminated* by his mother and, through refusing to bathe and leaving an odor in the room and on Ogden's chair, left Ogden with the feeling that he had "unwittingly been coerced into experiencing himself as the self-component of the internal relationship to the contaminating mother" (p. 154). This example offers a quite literal and concrete example of a client's enlistment of the therapist. In a more explicitly interpersonal example, Ogden (1982) describes an example of interactive inducement where he was crowded, through verbal bullying by his client, into feelings of shame and inadequacy.

For me, Racker's descriptions of my archaic objects being stirred up through my identifications with clients and Ogden's notion of becoming enlisted as a participant in order to more deeply understand the client, has brought a certain amount of clarity to my experience. Yet, at the same time, something has felt off about these narratives.

Affective Resonance and the Construction of Self and Other
Mitchell (2000) offers a different model of the nature of shared affective experiences from those of Ogden and Racker that complements their missing elements. Mitchell's view does not presume that an emotional experience begins in one separate person and crosses into another separate person. It is also not simply an emotional experience replicated through an interactional pattern designed to reproduce the

same experience in the other. Mitchell (2000) offers an integration of Loewald's (1980) concept of primal density, which suggests that we are always operating in multiple modes: in one mode we are parts of a universal web of emotional energy without boundaries, in another our minds use a form of secondary process to draw distinctions between self and other. According to Mitchell's (2000) *interactional hierarchy*, the mode of *affective permeability*, is consistent with Loewald's revision of primary process experience in which "powerful emotional experiences are registered in a fashion in which what *I* am feeling and what *you* are feeling are not sorted out independently, but rather form a unity" (p. 62). Mitchell draws on Loewald's view that the true *matter* of our psychic world consists of "experience in which there is no differentiation between inside and outside, self and other, actuality and fantasy, past and present" and that our attempts at these dichotomies "operate as an overlay, a parallel mode of organizing experience that accompanies and coexists with experiences generated by the original, primal unity" (p. 4).

Mitchell contextualizes this view of mind and its experiences in the development of psychoanalytic thought. In this development, the view of the mind has moved, along with parallel paradigmatic movements in the physical sciences from studying individualized atoms to complex and interrelated quantum models, from focus on individualized intrapsychic structures to selves definable only in a relational context. Rather than individual minds finding relationship, Mitchell (2000) postulates that it is the "interpenetrability of minds that makes individual mindedness possible in the first place" (p. xi). This view is also consistent with Bromberg's (2001) interpersonal model in which persons are definable only within the context of a system,

> based on a field theory paradigm. Each person is shaping the responsiveness of the other, including empathic responsiveness. There is no suggestion of an empathic therapist operating on a patient in need of empathy. Rather, the model is of an open system, changing, developing, enriching itself through a process of interpenetration. (p. 155)

The Willingness to be Used

This recognition of the interrelatedness of self and other can assist the therapist in understanding the ways in which clinical experiences so deeply reach us as therapists. If we are *tapping our common source*, so to speak, in our emotional experience, we do not need to be quite so on the defensive to insulate our experience in order to protect its unique integrity. This recognition can manifest in what Ogden (1993) highlights, using Winnicott's terms, as the therapist's "willingness to be used" as an aspect of a client's effective projective identification through "making oneself available to participate to some degree in this form of identification" (p. 155). Writing personally on his own experience as a therapist, Ogden (1982) outlines the necessity of his openness to the full range of his experiences in order for him to discover the projective identification which he may be defending against. Like Racker, Ogden suggests that the therapist's awareness of and curiosity about feelings of guilt, and the impulses to defend against objectionable feelings such as greed, anger, hopelessness, etc. are part of the pathway to the identification of and reintegration of these feelings back into the ego structure of the client (Ogden, 1982, 1993; Racker, 1957). What Ogden (1993) left less elaborated is the nature of the therapist's work with herself, the "considerable psychological work involved in the therapist's consciously and unconsciously integrating the roles imposed upon him with his larger, more reality-based sense of himself (in particular, his role as therapist)" (p. 155).

Working with Countertransference: Challenges and Paths

Clinging to Independence
I suggest that there are two significant challenges in this *psychological work*. One of the challenges to the therapist lies in the clinging to notions of independence and solidity in the clinical encounter, clinging to Mitchell's mode characterized by self-other configurations as if they are real and ignoring the reality of affective permeability. This not only takes a tremendous amount of energy, but it accentuates a sense of struggle for survival which adds a backdrop of anxiety and fear. Thus recognizing that our *self* is quite interpenetrated and relationally co-defined by the client's world allows the dissolving of those efforts, the freeing up of unconscious energy, and a dissipation of the associated anxiety and fear.

Unconditional Positive Regard
The second challenge posed in Ogden's description of the therapist's integration of the roles imposed on him with his larger view of himself lies in the therapist's conscious or unconscious mandates to be compassionate, thereby leaving many types of feelings out of the realm of *acceptable*. In many ways this can be understood in the context of what Carl Rogers (1957/2007) defined as *unconditional positive regard*. Rogers, the founder of the humanistic school of psychotherapy, saw therapy as a growth experience. He sought to express his experience of practicing psychotherapy through a theory that included the necessary and sufficient conditions of therapeutic personality change. One central condition Rogers identified was the therapist's ability to hold *unconditional positive regard*. Unconditional positive regard aims to invite the client to be who he or she actually is, no matter what that may be. For the therapist, it is "experiencing a positive, nonjudgemental, acceptant attitude" (Rogers, 1986, p. 198). The therapist cares for the client not in a possessive way, nor simply to satisfy the therapist's own needs, but

rather she cares in an open and accepting way. Although Rogers felt it was necessary that this condition of acceptance and warmth for the client continued over a long period of time, he acknowledged that it occurred in the therapeutic relationship only in a varying degree on a continuum. His hypothesis was that the greater degree to which the therapist holds the client in unconditional positive regard, the more constructive change will occur in the client (Rogers, 1957/2007).

Lovingkindness and Friendliness

The profundity of unconditional positive regard's contribution to psychotherapy is evident in the discussion of its implications still ongoing in the literature of psychotherapeutic practice today, fifty years after Rogers introduced his theory into the field (e.g., Ackerman et al., 2001; Gelso, 2007; Norcross, 2003). However, this notion did not originate with Rogers or any Western psychology; it has roots in the perennial emphasis on compassion. In the Contemplative Psychotherapy program at Naropa University, a foundation of the training is teachings on *maitri*, a several thousand year old Buddhist notion connoting an attitude of loving kindness and acceptance towards all aspects of our experience. "The word for loving-kindness in Sanskrit is *maitri* or *metta* in Pali, which is related to the word for *friend*. A prosaic translation for this word is simply 'friendliness'" (Wallace, 1999, p. 87). Karen Kissel Wegela (1996), a key contributor to the field of contemplative psychotherapy, offers this straightforward suggestion on the role of unconditional friendliness in working with one's direct experience: "unconditional friendliness is looking at our experience with the same kind of honesty that we hope to show a genuine friend" (p. 66). Elaborating on this honesty in the context of maitri, she further sates that "maitri is about seeing clearly and letting be" (p. 64).

Rogers (1957/2007) believed that unconditional positive regard, this personal quality of compassion and friendliness essential to psychotherapeutic change, must "be acquired through experiential training" which he acknowledged "may be, but usually is not, a part of professional training" (p. 246). How does the therapist prepare for the challenges confronted in reconnecting with unconditional positive regard in the face of conditioned reactions that may occur in clinical work, including the infantile and archaic responses that Racker and Ogden highlighted as the especially troublesome aspects of countertransference?

Paths for Cultivating Maitri in the Therapist

The Contemplative Psychotherapy training program at Naropa University, drawing from the Buddhist and Shambhala traditions, identifies paths for moving more deeply along the continuum toward full acceptance of ourselves and others, including our *uncompassionate* experiences in therapy. One such path includes cultivating maitri, an awareness practice that is an essential part of a practice of sitting meditation. It involves, fundamentally, acts of recognition of the moment to moment activities of our mind, combined with acceptance of the actuality of these recognitions. A practice of sitting meditation cultivates this recognition and acceptance and we connect with an unconditional sense of well-being; we are less thrown by whatever arises on the cushion, with clients, and in our daily lives. This unconditional well-being is further facilitated through teachings on maitri which remind us of the attitude of friendliness and teachings which remind us that our brilliantly sane nature is marked by clarity, openness, and warmth.

Maitri itself is not a technique, however. It begins as a concept to be learned and becomes an essential view to be experienced and cultivated. If, as therapists, we can have maitri for our own and our clients' experiences, we are providing them with an experience of unconditional acceptance that they, in turn, might begin to have for themselves. Trungpa Rinpoche (1983) comments:

> Maitri can actually be cultivated in yourself, and in other people; you can cultivate gentleness and warmth. When you express kindness to others, then they in turn begin to find natural warmth within themselves. So the Buddhist approach to working with people - especially those who have been brought up in bad environments - is to provide a gentle, accommodating environment for therapy and teaching. (p. 4)

As a therapist, having loving kindness for oneself might manifest in viewing our countertransference responses with openness and non-judgment. It is possible, for instance, to bring this attitude of friendliness toward any feelings of judgment or hostility that arise in us toward our clients. The ideal of holding unconditional positive regard for our clients at all times in every situation would be impossible, as Roger's acknowledges. So instead of being discouraged about not meeting this ideal, we can be honest with ourselves and bring kindness to our experience. Rather than getting distracted by efforts to defend against our reactions to the client that do not fit this ideal of unconditional positive regard, we can allow them, accept our imperfection, and continue to be open and integrate our moment to moment experiences with the client as the next moment arises. In fact, many of these judgmental or hostile reactions may be important information about the client's experiences, although we cannot necessarily assume that their origins are other than our own.

The Vastness of the Experiential Field

As a post-doc on the train, it was not simply a matter of identifying my countertransference reactions and allowing my imperfections. I was finding that allowing a sustained honesty about my reactions broadened my sense of what I was capable of experiencing and desiring. I felt more depth of sadness, more profound fear, more destabilizing overwhelm through my work with my clients. I found myself with murderous rage toward perpetrators of abuse toward my clients. I wished to receive and to provide the softest of caressing.

Vulnerability

Combined with this sense of increased emotional range, I also experienced a greater degree of tenderness and vulnerability which I carried physically and emotionally. Here the psychoanalytic literature offered a mixed picture of support for my experience. In the days of Freud, clinical work took place from the distance of medical and scientific objectivity. Freud was more at home describing the structure and function of a *patient's* psychopathology than commenting on the challenges of the therapist's vulnerability. Years later, Roy Schafer would address, however obliquely, the vulnerability of the therapist. Schafer (1983) outlined the many ways that the ability of the therapist to empathize with clients is aided by the protected position of the therapist, including the asymmetrical investment and exposure of the therapist and the therapist's exemption from social norms of immediate responsiveness, allowing more carefully formulated responses. Yet, in some way, I think Shafer was also referring to therapists' need to be reminded of their protection.

Cheeseburgers and Clinical Gifts

When I consider the intimacy and vulnerability of clinical work, I am reminded of a case conference when I was in my doctoral program at Temple University in Philadelphia. Presenting at this case conference was a psychoanalyst from New York City. Although I do not remember his name, I remember his description of the intimacy of clinical work and of the ways that our clients need to get close to us and have an effect on us. He spoke of the ways that, while we may be quite boundaried and professional with clients, we are also inviting them into our psychic house. We are welcoming them as visitors to our emotional living room and they often take us up on the offer. The analyst extended the metaphor, suggesting that while in our house, our clients will want to make themselves at home, and will do things like leave cheeseburgers under the cushions of our couch.

For some reason the image of my client's cheeseburgers under the cushions of my couch has remained and served as an absurd version of the emotional and experiential wake left in my life by my interactions with clients. At some level, Schafer, too, may have been speaking of the risk that as therapists we will find, buried in the cushions of our experience, gifts left by our interactions with clients. What are these cheeseburgers, anyway?

In my experience, one of the *whoppers* I have found is a dissolving of my illusion of ultimate separateness from the world. As I sat with clients at Beth Israel, however, I was often aware of my impulse to draw a line between me and them. I used markers to differentiate myself, markers like the clipboard that I held under my arm or diagnostic categories that I could write into a case report. As a result of my meditation practice, I could also see the basic anxiety beneath my use of markers. I could recognize the activity of my mind splitting away from the intensity of the experiences with my clients.

Caring and Powerlessness

So what is the nature of this basic anxiety, this vulnerability that perhaps Schafer's comments were intended to assuage? However multifaceted the answer, I would suggest that one basis of the vulnerability lies within the experience of actually caring about our clients. We develop compassion for them and out of this a desire manifests to help ease their suffering. This compassion, combined with the often painfully obvious limitations on our ability to make the pain of our clients go away, or sometimes even to reduce it in a meaningful way, can result in a particular kind of broken hearted feeling. All the good intention, desire, and efforting we can manifest is not enough to *save* or *fix* anyone.

As a post-doc, I experienced the sheer powerlessness of being unable to remove the legacy of abuse that had been exacted on my clients (Harrison, 1994). The work was especially powerful with some clients. One of these clients was a refugee from a country which had experienced a horribly violent civil war. He was caught in this civil war during his early adolescence and forced into a bloody and chaotic prison work camp. At one point he was able to escape through killing a guard when he was alone with him at the edge of the jungle. This began another long and terrifying journey for him as he tried to rescue the rest of his family members from other prison camps while living in the lethally dangerous jungle. I was profoundly affected by the seemingly endless and truly life threatening situations in which he had found himself. I often felt that I was in a basic life and death struggle for my emotional and psychological integrity when listening to his stories. Through all of this, he continued to carry the guilt of having killed another human being. My powerlessness to change these life events, to take away the guilt that he carried, overwhelmed me; I wanted to remove it in whatever way I could and this was impossible. I learned to surrender to the unfolding narrative of his life as he told it in the present and accept the heartbreaking tragedy, the rawness of the violence and his powerful will to survive. I felt it physically as a profound tenderness in my chest, a soreness and fullness.

Tender-Heartedness and Contemplative Practice

Yoga and Bodhichitta

Another way that I was working with my life at the time involved a regular yoga practice. This yoga both exacerbated and freed up some of the physical correlates of my clinical work through sequences of asanas like backbends and shoulder openings designed to release physical and energetic armoring in the chest. During those practices I felt a concentration of many of the feelings of vulnerability, powerlessness, and compassion, and the space of these practices helped me to accommodate and integrate these feelings into my life.

Through my studies of Buddhism I came to understand the tender-hearted feeling as *bodhichitta*. Chögyam Trungpa (1988) describes bodhichitta as our sore, tender spot. He suggests that when you connect with this place and "open your eyes to the rest of the world, you feel tremendous sadness" (p. 45). Bodhichitta is defined as "awakened heart" and it refers generally to an "intense desire to alleviate suffering" (Chödrön, 2005, p. xiii). This innate quality is the ground of our shared humanity. According to Chögyam Trungpa (1999), the sense of woundedness runs to our core:

> There is also an inner wound, which is called tathagatagharba, or Buddha nature. Tathagatagharba is like a heart that is sliced and bruised by wisdom and compassion. When the external wound and internal wound begin to meet and communicate, then we begin to realize that our whole being is made out of one complete sore spot altogether [and] that vulnerability is called compassion. (p. 120)

Recognizing Emptiness and Joy

So while I carried this soreness, this desire to help my clients, the dissolving of the illusion of separateness was being further accelerated. A supervisor of mine had suggested a technique to me for connecting with clients in my personal empathic experience. With repeated use, this technique provided me with a deeper connection and recognition of similarity between myself and my clients. The technique she offered consisted of two simple questions. The first: "what experiences have you had that are similar to what the client is feeling?" This question allowed me to deeply plumb my memories and awareness for what were sometimes remote corners of my own life in order to connect with the more radical experiences my clients were bringing. The second: "under what conditions might you feel the same way as the client?" This question further allowed me to step outside of the particular life circumstances that I have found myself in, to recognize how utterly understandable my clients' sometimes bizarre or extreme behavior and reactions were to me. Another way to say this is that I recognized my capacities to feel in all the ways that my clients were feeling.

The net result of an ongoing practice of asking and answering these questions for myself continued to wear down the effectiveness of my efforts to separate myself from my clients. While remaining differentiated from my clients à la Mitchell's mode of self-other

14. Countertransference, Emptiness, & Joy

configurations, I was recognizing myself in my clients and my clients in myself with increasing ease. This brought, along with the deepening tenderness and vulnerability, a profound joy of recognition of more of myself, both through my countertransference as well as through my affective resonances with my clients.

In some circumstances this may sound like a destabilizing loss of identity. The subjective experience was far from it. On the one hand, I felt quite intact and able to continue to operate in the differentiated mode where I was the therapist; I had a life independent from the client and I was an expression of a different history and set of causes and conditions than my clients. On the other hand, my experiences were again supported by what I was learning in my Buddhist studies, in this case, teachings on emptiness.

A central tenet in Buddhism is that the absolute nature of reality is beyond and without truly separate, individualized entities. Although this is a teaching that a meditation practitioner may experience more directly, it is also supported philosophically by the written and oral teachings on emptiness. In fact, from a Buddhist view, the source of our suffering lies in our erroneous clinging to a belief in a solid, separate, unchanging self or ego. If we work with our minds and see through the walls of ego, we can see beyond this prison of isolation and experience ourselves as inextricably connected to all beings and therefore able to experience directly the joy and suffering of others. This experience of interconnection, beyond the bounds of ego, brings us in touch with the emptiness of self and other.

The term *bodhichitta* can also refer to this experience of emptiness. The longing and yearning aspect is called relative bodhichitta and it encompasses the aspiration to ease the suffering of all beings, or in the context of therapy, to ease the suffering of our clients. On an absolute level, bodhichitta is non-conceptual wisdom: not just the aspiration, but the realization of egolessness or emptiness. Emptiness is, from the Buddhist view, the true nature of all phenomena (Gyamtso, 2001).

Buddhism teaches that this innate wisdom is always there. We might feel distant from it, but the possibility of contacting our limitless compassion for others is present in every moment. As human beings, we often construct barriers to keep us from fully experiencing pain, both our own and others. Similarly, as therapists we are taught appropriate boundaries are important. However, through a softening of my constructed barriers against contacting my clients' pain, combined with my meditation practice and Buddhist study, I came to what I have understood to be an ongoing direct experience of the emptiness of self and other as distinct entities. As a result, I learned about an experiential landscape far more vast than I had known. Working with clients, I felt I was being given the gift of repeated opportunities to become familiar with this experience.

More than the products of grief and melancholia, the tears on my cheeks as I sat on the train were often out of overflowing gratitude for these opportunities of deeper connection with the world. This release of suffering was possible through resting in emptiness of self and other, through giving up the struggle to deny my interdependence.

Support on the Path

I doubt that this type of experience is uncommon for psychotherapists exploring the intimacy of clinical work. The tender-hearted feeling and the moments of allowing the dissolving of self and other in the relationship can be important entry points for psychotherapists. While this opening can lead to alarm and anxious efforts to re-establish our solidity and separation, it can also be a part of a practice of seeing the world as it is, beyond the constructed notions of isolation. Seeing the world as it is without such investment in isolation may also relieve conditions which can lead to burnout or compassion fatigue. With appropriate conceptual support of the opportunities of moments of emptiness, the therapist can potentially see positive *side effects* of clinical work which can become integrated into one's spiritual path. With the support of contemplative practice, this integration can take a deeper root.

In addition to the yoga practices mentioned above, there are two other practices on my path as a therapist that I have found extremely helpful and would like to offer for consideration as a support to anyone working with human suffering. One is the simple but profound practice of shamatha-vipashyana meditation. Shamatha, which means "dwelling in peace" (Trungpa, 2005, p. 17), allows us to become intimately familiar with the workings of our minds. As we sit and watch our thoughts, we become aware of the whole, the spacious totality and objects within it. This awareness is vipashyana. "Once we have been inspired by the precision of shamatha and the wakefulness of vipashyana, we find that there is room... we can develop a sense of relaxation and release from torment–from this-and-that altogether" (Trungpa, 1999, p. 122).

The practice of shamatha has contributed significantly to developing awareness of my reactions and countertransferences. The vipashyana aspect has provided a sense of freedom; in this space I am more able to make conscious choices about how I respond to my clients rather than feeling so claustrophobically consumed with the immediacy of the latest impulses. In addition, this combined practice offers a direct experience of impermanence as we watch our thoughts arise and dissolve over and over again. In this way we can avoid thinking we are stuck with the residue of the day in any fixed or unchanging way.

A second useful tool for therapists that has aided me on my path is the practice of Tonglen. This tool can provide support in giving the therapist a way to work with the suffering of others. Tonglen is the practice of sending and taking that reverses the process of separating ourselves from both our own painful experiences and those of others, by turning toward our pain and cultivating love and compassion (Chödrön, 2001). In this practice, instead of viewing our experience of suffering as something to avoid or get rid of, we can use it to help us realize our connection with all beings who are suffering. It helps the therapist dissolve the barriers constructed to avoid feeling his basic vulnerability. This provides the therapist an opportunity to experience more fully both the joy and pain in life.

Tonglen is both a practice that can be used on the spot during a therapy session and a step by step process practiced on the cushion that can serve as a tool for the therapist in working with their experience of suffering involved in directly contacting the feelings of their clients. The practice often begins with flashing on a sense of absolute bodhichitta, the vast, nondual, true nature of mind. One can then cultivate her innate capacity to be with whatever arises by moving toward pain, confusion, and regret, breathing it in and then on the outbreath sending compassion, openness, and brilliant sanity.[3]

Conclusion

Being in a therapeutic relationship, especially if one is involved in many at a time, provides the therapist again and again with experiences of egolessness. I suggest that as therapists who are open to our clients we often contact a broader range of emotional experience and many of these experiences are filled with more intensity than we are used to in our everyday lives outside the office. How we make meaning out of these experiences is often dependent on our models of self-care, but also our models of self in the first place. With a metapsychology like that of Buddhist psychology, one based on non-ego or emptiness, we can be supported in the recognition of the opportunities that clinical work provides to see the vastness of our true nature more clearly. We can allow our tender, soreness of heart. We can be encouraged to experiment with integrating our physical and emotional experiences of brokenhearted interconnection through yoga, with letting go of a fixed sense of identity in our practice of psychotherapy and through contemplative practices like shamatha-vipashyana and Tonglen. As a result, we can allow a nourishing contact with the luminosity and pregnant possibilities of our experience and discover the joys that emerge.

It is my hope that readers will recognize themselves in the material of this chapter and perhaps elements of this chapter in themselves. I hope that this writing offers encouragement and increased clarity of the promise in what can be experienced as troubling aspects of working with so much suffering. May we all find nourishing cheeseburgers.

---

[3] For a more in-depth resource on Tonglen refer to Pema Chödrön's book *Tonglen: The path of transformation*.

References

Ackerman, S. J., Benjamin, L. S., Beutler, L. E., Gelso, C. J., Goldfriend, M. R., Hill, C., et al. (2001). Empirically supported therapy relationships: Conclusions and recommendations of the Division 29 Task Force. *Psychotherapy: Theory, Research, Practice, and Training, 38*(4), 345-356.

Bromberg, P. M. (2001). *Standing in the spaces: Essays on clinical process, trauma, and dissociation.* Hillsdale, NJ: The Analytic Press.

Chödrön, P. (2005). *No time to lose.* Boston: Shambhala Publications.

Chödrön, P. (2001). *Tonglen: The path of transformation.* Halifax, Nova Scotia: Vajradhatu Publications.

Gelso, C. J. (2007). Special section: Reasessing Rogers' conditions of change [Special Issue]. *Psychotherapy: Theory, Research, Practice, and Training, 44*(3).

Gyamtso, T. (2001). *Progressive stages of meditation on emptiness.* Aukland: Zhyisil Chokyi Ghatsal Publications.

Harrison, G. (1994). *In the lap of the Buddha.* Boston: Shambhala.

Loewald, H. (1980). *Papers on psychoanalysis.* New Haven, CT: Yale University Press.

Mitchell, S. A. (2000). *Relationality: From attachment to intersubjectivity.* Hillsdale, NJ: The Analytic Press.

Norcross, J. (Ed.). (2003). *Psychotherapy relationships that work: Therapist contributions and responsiveness to patient needs.* New York: Oxford University Press.

Ogden, T. H. (1982). *Projective identification and psychotherapeutic technique.* New York: Aronson.

Ogden, T.H. (1993). *The matrix of the mind: Object relations and the psychoanalytic dialogue.* New York: Aronson.

Racker, H. (1988). The meanings and uses of countertransference. In B. Wolstein (Ed.), *Essential papers on countertransference* (pp. 158-201). New York: New York University Press.

Rogers, C. R. (1986). Client centered therapy. In I. L. Kutash & A. Wolf (Eds.), *Psychotherapists casebook: Therapy and technique in practice* (pp. 197-208). San Francisco: Jossey Bass.

Rogers, C. R. (2007). The necessary and sufficient conditions for therapeutic personality change. *Psychotherapy: Theory, Research, Practice, Training, 44(3),* 240-248. (Reprinted from *Journal of Consulting Psychology, 21* (2), 96-103, 1957).

Schafer, R. (1983). *The analytic attitude.* New York: Basic Books.

Trungpa, C. (1983). Creating an environment of sanity. *Naropa Institute Journal of Psychology, 1,* 1-10.

Trungpa, C. (1988). *Shambhala: The sacred path of the warrior.* Boston: Shambhala.

Trungpa, C. (1999). *The essential Chogyam Trungpa* (C. R. Gimian, Ed.). Bosten Shambhala.
Trungpa, C. (2005). *The sanity we are born with: A Buddhist approach to psychology.* Boston: Shambhala.
Wallace, A. (1999). *The four immeasurables: Cultivating a boundless heart.* Ithaca: Snow Lion Publications.
Wegela, K. K. (1996). *How to be a help instead of a nuisance.* Boston: Shambhala Publications.

15

Windhorse Therapy: Creating Environments that Arouse the Energy of Health and Sanity

Charles Knapp

The Windhorse therapy process is a unique multilayered and comprehensive treatment approach for people with a wide variety of mental health recovery needs. In this approach, *an individually tailored therapy environment is created for each client, addressing his or her needs in a whole-person manner.* This approach includes, whenever possible, the voice and needs of the client's family.

Windhorse therapy is based on understandings of the fundamental nature of human intelligence and the energy required to recover from mental disturbances. With this foundation, it incorporates a combination of ordinary common sense, considerable experience with the treatment process, and applied psychotherapy.

The term *windhorse* refers to a type of energy that is naturally positive, confident, and uplifted, and, according to the Buddhist tradition, fundamental to human beings. Our individual connection to this energy can wax and wane depending on what's happening in our environment and inside our self. Windhorse energy can be deliberately roused and when it is strong one feels confident that life is workable. Windhorse was chosen as the name of this therapy because sufficient windhorse energy is essential in order for people to recover from trauma, mental illness, and difficult problems (Trungpa, 1999).

The following example is a snapshot of how Windhorse therapy works. A client lives in a house or apartment with a housemate who is part of the treatment team. Their relationship is similar to that of roommates. There are a number of clinicians on the team who spend time with the client on a regular basis, sometimes doing one or more shifts per day. The time is spent doing a variety of activities, from keeping the house in order, to helping him or her be more involved in the community. These activities are elements of an individually tailored environment to help the client live in an ordinary way with healthy relationships and meaningful pursuits. The client may be employed, see friends and family, and be part of the normal community. The schedule usually includes meeting with a psychotherapist and with a psychiatrist, if medications are used. Treatment also includes a system of various meetings with the staff, client, and, when possible, his or her family members. The purpose of these meetings is to keep the therapy, household and treatment team coordinated and up-to-date. Treatments usually last from six months to two years.

Historical Roots and Evolution

The Windhorse Project, as it was originally called, developed during the early 1980s through the teachings of Chögyam Trungpa and the atmosphere he created at Naropa Institute, which he founded. Many distinguished and accomplished people were drawn to Trungpa and his influence invariably had the effect of helping these leaders see their respective disciplines in a new light and larger context. Buddhist scholars, poets, dancers, musicians, and many involved in the field of psychology found their experience teaching and/or studying at Naropa not just enlivening, but as revolutionizing the way they saw their work or art.

The late Edward Podvoll, who had had a distinguished career as director of psychiatry at the inpatient psychiatric hospital Chestnut Lodge, was one of these people. Through years of inpatient psychiatric work, Podvoll understood its benefits and deficits. That knowledge, coupled with a developing contemplative perspective, led him to consider other ways of treating people in extreme mental states. In 1981, with the help of Trungpa and a group of committed students, Podvoll founded the Windhorse Project (Podvoll, 2003).

Windhorse therapy was originally designed only for individuals with acute mental disturbances and currently many of its treatments are for people with schizophrenia, schizoaffective disorder, bipolar disorder, and major depression. However, over time, Windhorse therapy has been effective in treating milder forms of mood disorders, substance abuse and addictions, eating disorders, autism, head injuries, and issues of old age.

Therapeutic Foundations of Windhorse Therapy

Three Principles

Windhorse clinicians understand the healing process as being based on three principles. The first principle is: *All human beings are fundamentally sane and healthy.* As Trungpa (2005) states, "Mental confusion exists and functions in a secondary position to one's basic health" (p. 160). This first principle is not about just adopting an optimistic attitude toward human beings. Confidence in basic sanity is a direct experience that results from the clinicians' contemplative discipline, which will be elaborated on in the next section.

The second principle of the Windhorse therapy process is: *Because human beings are inseparable from their environments* (Epstein, 1999), *if a healthy treatment environment is created, then clients will have a greater probability of recovery.* As we will see, creating tailored healing environments is the core therapeutic methodology of Windhorse therapy.

The third principle of Windhorse therapy is: *The client's recovery is a process of discovering and synchronizing with their fundamental health and sanity* (Trungpa, 2005). As our clinical results show, the client gains health, skills for his or her particular life needs, confidence, and independence as this discovery and synchronization takes place and stabilizes. Windhorse clinicians recognize *recovery* as a significant, stable, and heartening increase in *Windhorse* energy.

A thoroughly trained Windhorse clinician has a confident and practical understanding of each core principle, along with therapeutic expertise for treating specific psychological disorders.

Contemplative Training

The innovations of Windhorse therapy are founded in the practice of a contemplative tradition. Whatever its form, contemplative discipline invites a progressively more intimate relationship with one's own mind and life in a fresh, moment-to-moment way (Trungpa, 2005). For our purposes, it is important to note that a typical individual's contemplative path follows the basic pattern of a typical process of mental health recovery. This parallel has great implications for the design of Windhorse environments and for how a client's recovery process is understood, nurtured, and achieved (Epstein, 1999).

One's contemplative path often begins with the distinct sense that something is not right with the way one's life is going. For some individuals, a safe, simple, and attractive method to interrupt this repetitive confusion is to adopt a contemplative practice such as meditation, tai chi, or yoga. Most Windhorse clinicians have experience with the contemplative practice of Buddhist/Shambhala meditation. This is a discipline of attending to or watching one's state of mind without judgment. It can be done in formal meditation practice and also informally in the midst of ordinary activity as clinicians go about their day (Mipham, 2003).

To begin, one learns to tolerate how it feels to be aware in the present moment and how it feels to be with whatever is going on in one's life without self-conscious judgment. Over time, one becomes less carried away by strong positive or negative thoughts and feelings. As one's mind becomes more settled, clarity and awareness develop. With this comes vivid insight, or *islands of clarity*, as this experience is referred to in Windhorse therapy (DiGiacamo & Herrick, 2007).

Tolerating and appreciating insight is a basic life skill essential to any process of recovery. As a typical contemplative path progresses, healthy self-love begins. This is called *maitri* in the Buddhist tradition (Chödrön, 1997). Maitri is the experience of one's own basic intelligence, warmth, compassion, and good intentions. It is the brilliant capacity to love and forgive oneself for not living up to unrealistic expectations that can cause so much suffering and self-aggression. This tradition considers healthy self-love to be a basic life energy and the experience of maitri is frequently a turning point in the path of recovery.

In the contemplative process, one also discovers a naturally confident energy; *Windhorse* can be used in the service of countering hopelessness, depression, and the mindless repetition of habitual patterns. In contemplation, as in recovery, the more we see our lives and ourselves clearly, the more we have a sense of which actions and thoughts lead to a harmonious life and which lead to suffering and unnecessary confusion. Making skillful choices and rousing the confidence to implement them emerges as a discipline. In Windhorse therapy we refer to this discipline as having an *allegiance to sanity* (Podvoll, 2003). With the recognition that there is a choice between actions that lead to more or less sanity and then with the discipline to implement those choices, one feels that recovery from a confused state is not only possible, but likely.

A thoroughly trained Windhorse clinician has direct experience of the process described above. One result of this contemplative foundation is the clinician's personal conviction that being synchronized with one's basic sanity and health is possible for all human beings. This is not academic knowledge but lived experience.

As our contemplative path develops, it becomes apparent how much we effect and are effected by our friends, family, household, and the way we are in the world. We see clearly that as individuals we are inseparable from the powerful effect of our environment. This insight has had a significant influence on the methodology of Windhorse treatment environments. We recognize that our clinical work with a person's specific mental health and life issues is inseparable from how we *treat* the person's environment in order to promote recovery.

We also know there is no end point in contemplation, a point after which we cease having problems or suffering. Instead, what we gain through this practice are tools for working with whatever comes up in life. Synchronization with our fundamental sanity and health becomes a way of life in relationship to ourselves, our friends and family, and our environment as a whole. Fundamentally, we have not become something different; we have become a more integrated and harmonious version of who we basically are. This is also how *recovery* is defined in the Windhorse therapy process: The client develops a way of living that is synchronized with their fundamental health and sanity.

Recovery Environment
Windhorse therapy can appropriately be conducted by a small number of clinicians, using the same fundamental view as a fully developed team. However, in order to illustrate the assembling and operation of a recovery environment, the following discussions will be about fully developed teams.

15. Windhorse Therapy

To clarify the therapeutic methodology of *treating* the client's environments, Windhorse therapy defines environment as having three aspects: body, speech, and mind (Rabin & Walker, 1987). Very simply, *body* has to do with a person's body, dress, and any aspect of the immediate physical world. This includes home, food, exercise, drugs and alcohol, and the use of money. *Speech* is about communication with the world, emotions, creativity, and relationships. *Mind* has to do with thinking, attitudes toward self and others, spirituality, and schedule.

When a Windhorse therapist initially meets with someone who is struggling with mental health and life issues, it is very common to see the following type of situation. On the *body* level the person's home is very disorganized, dirty, and uninviting. The person is not eating regularly or nutritionally, not exercising, not going out for walks or fresh air, and not doing their laundry. He or she typically has problems with money and finances – has no sense of budget, is bouncing checks, is over spending – all of which produces significant stress for the client and family. The abuse of drugs and alcohol is often a contributing factor to this disarray.

On the *speech* level, communication is often very strained. If the primary client is a dependent son or daughter, he or she may be angry and frustrated around issues of separation and self sufficiency, yet the parents may be the only reliable people in his or her life. The client and his or her parents may love one another, but there are many unresolved problems, and anxiety and fear make a normal conversation impossible or very unlikely. It is also common for this person to be socially isolated, and what friends he or she has may have a variety of problems themselves, which sometimes creates further difficulties.

On the *mind* level, the client may have previously had a creative and meaningful intellectual life, but is presently cut off from former disciplines, activities, and any feelings of success and confidence they may have afforded. There may be insufficient meaningful activity such as work or school and the client's schedule has become very irregular. Such conditions lead to feelings of alienation and self aggression. For the sensitive person, and so many of these people are profoundly sensitive, the intricately interconnected and self-sustaining problems of this environment create hopelessness. When conditions have evolved to this stage, Windhorse energy is deflated and there is little loving kindness toward one's self or other. When a person feels this bad, they believe they *are* bad. The client in this condition and their family has no sense of how to begin the recovery process. The Windhorse model maintains that in order to interrupt the various destructive cycles and compounding feedback loops of such a predicament it is most effective to work with all aspects of the client's life concurrently. By creating individually tailored recovery environments, the unique strengths and difficulties of each client and family can be simultaneously held and engaged (Almaas, 1998).

When a Windhorse recovery environment is created, the focus is on forming a very specific arrangement of elements and relationships, which will be discussed in the next section. The treatment process has stages - beginning, middle and end, and we attempt to create an environment with optimal boundaries that are permeable yet containing between the client and his or her world. This environment is a comprehensively coordinated organization of *body*, *speech*, and *mind*, comprised of the physical setting of the treatment, the people and relationships, therapeutic methodologies, schedules, and awareness. Influenced by the Buddhist concept of *mandala*, the Windhorse recovery environment is defined as a total environment, association, *orderly chaos*, or *gestalt* (Trungpa, 2003). In practice, a recovery environment functions as a compensatory, external organizing entity.

In many ways, families naturally work this way. If a family member has a challenging life situation, for instance a woman has a baby, it is very hard during the first few weeks for the mother to be able to shop, cook, clean house, and take care of all the baby's needs. There is a good chance the mother's sleep is disrupted and there is simply not enough energy to do the tasks of life. It is very common under these circumstances for partners to take time off from work in order to make sure that everything in the life of the mother and child can be accomplished as necessary. Other family members may also help out. In this case the mother and the baby are the focus, but anyone who is helping out will do their best to help in a balanced way so they themselves don't lose their health in the process. Like a Windhorse recovery environment, this family system is compensating for a change that has occurred and there is a sense that this is a transitional phase.

Therapeutic Elements and Roles

In order to create a compensatory recovery environment, a team is created made up of the clinicians, the client, and whenever possible, the family. These people work in a complementary system of roles, each carrying out a range of functions and therapeutic activities that develop, maintain, evolve, and *are* a large part of the environment. The cohesion and communication of this, gestalt, or *whole person system* is carried out within the household, the meetings, and the relationships of the team.

Clinician Roles

Most of the direct clinical contact in Windhorse therapy is performed by a *basic attender*. He or she will usually have two shifts per week, generally two to three hours in length. The *team leader* is the primary coordinator and a major participant in the direct clinical contact. He or she oversees the day-to-day flow of activity for the team as well as being a sturdy, dependable, and knowledgeable reference point in the life of the client.

The *housemate's* job has two primary functions. The first is simply to live, with good boundaries, in the therapeutic household and support

15. Windhorse Therapy

the functioning of a normal and uplifted domestic setting. The second is to be in relationship with the client in that ordinary and earthy way that tends to occur when people share a home.

A *psychiatrist* is often part of a recovery environment as frequently our clients are using medications. Some psychiatrists may be doing only medication management, so their involvement with the team is minimal. Others, particularly those with whom we have worked over years, can be a critical part of the treatment management. As is most often the case, when a client enters Windhorse treatment they are able to be on less medication, and their needs change over time. We find that the psychiatrist has a more subtle knowledge of the client and his/her needs if they are an integrated part of the team structure.

The *psychotherapist*, who usually meets with the client once or twice a week, is looking for the intelligence and patterns that reside below and within the often-confused behaviors of the client. He or she learns this through the work done in sessions with the client as well as through experience in meetings where the housemate, basic attenders, team leader, and psychiatrist describe their client contact. Likewise, the insights about the client that the psychotherapist provides during meetings helps inform the entire clinical team.

The *team supervisor* oversees the dynamics and patterns of the team as the treatment progresses, often working with the family as they make their own recovery journey. The team supervisor also has a key role in creating *visualization* for the team and the entire Windhorse therapy plan, while holding the overall activity of the recovery environment in his or her awareness.

Basic Attendance

As a highly flexible and innovative clinical practice, basic attendance is the most active, apparent, and principle therapeutic activity in a Windhorse recovery environment. Influenced by the Buddhist practice of being attentive or simply watching the mind without judgment in the midst of everyday activity, basic attendance is: *Being actively and with helpful intention in relationship with someone in the broad spectrum of his or her life activities, in order to promote the synchronization of body, speech, and mind, and connection to his or her fundamental health* (Podvoll, 2003). The activities of the person in this role range from being with a client in the ordinary domestic activity of a household, doing artwork, signing up for classes, looking for employment, or simply having time to relax and play. The work of basic attendance may look very simple to the untrained eye, but a seemingly simple task for the client, such as cooking a meal, can stimulate a powerful profusion of conflicting thoughts, emotions, and growth frontiers. It can take a great deal of skill and sensitivity on the part of the basic attender to create a safe and successful experience.

The Therapist-Friend Relationship

In most psychotherapeutic disciplines, therapy occurs in an office. For some roles in a Windhorse recovery environment, the formality and boundaries that are a normal part of how most psychotherapy operates would seem altogether unnatural and stiff. In fact, the basic attenders intentionally acknowledge and cultivate client relationships that are part friendship and part therapist. With this in mind, basic attenders are carefully chosen to match a client's interests, deficits, and diagnosis, with an eye toward whether they might actually like one another (Podvoll, 2003).

The therapist–friend relationship has a number of benefits within the recovery environment. First, it can make basic attendance more relaxing and fun, much more like normal life than therapy. Secondly, many of our clients have had a very difficult time forming treatment alliances. For these people, having clinicians who share at least a slight mutual attraction as friends may make it possible to join and stay in treatment. Similar to ordinary friendships, as the therapist-friend relationship develops, it is common for shared interests to *jump-start* dormant passions and interests in the client's life. Thirdly, it opens up the possibility of being able to bring the client into the team member's household. Whenever appropriate and in well-considered measure, a Windhorse clinician will often invite a client into the world of their family and home. This can provide a powerful experience of acceptance and role modeling for the client as he or she enters the home and relationships of the therapist-friend.

Mutual Recovery

A therapeutic element related to the therapist-friend relationship is called mutual recovery (Podvoll, 1990). As Trungpa (2003) stated in the root text on Windhorse therapy, *Creating Environments of Sanity,* "you don't just regard psychology as a J.O.B." (p. 551). This means that the Windhorse clinician aspires to conduct his or her professional work in fundamentally the same way that he or she lives life. This training promotes a sense of inclusion of everything in one's personal discipline, a *sacred world* orientation (Hayward & Hayward, 1999), to borrow a Buddhist concept, where *sacred* does not mean precious or rare, but what reminds one of basic sanity and goodness. Since everything is included in one's view of how to live and work with life, then relationship with the client and his or her recovery environment is naturally part of this. Instead of "I'm well, you are sick, and I'm going to fix you," there is a sense that we are in this together and we all are working on our humanity. With this attitude, a Windhorse environment tends to produce growth and *recovery* not only for the clients, but for the clinicians as well. Also, it can be enormously heartening to some clients to see their therapists growing as people as a result of being with them.

Meetings

In a recovery environment, meetings play a critical role. There are a variety of meetings and all are designed with complementary functions to enhance the communication, cohesion, synchronization, and awareness of the team, the client, and the family. Of the types of meetings generally conducted in the course of Windhorse therapy, these four, the *house meeting*, the *supervision meeting*, the *team meeting*, and the *family meeting*, have the most central roles (Fortuna, 1994).

Attended by the team leader, client, housemate, and held in the home on a once a week basis, the *house meeting* supports the operation of the therapeutic household. Helping the client and the housemate work with relationship and communication is a large part of the work of this meeting.

The *supervision meeting* is held at an office, usually on an every other week basis in alternation with the team meeting. The entire team, except the client and family, attends. These meetings typically have a relaxed but precise focus, often with good humor. Aside from issues of recovery environment coordination, this meeting is a place where the team can freely discuss the experience of his or her work and develop further understanding of the treatment issues. While checking-in, we encourage clinicians to take risks with saying whatever he or she is thinking and feeling, as it is so often the odd and even embarrassing experiences that are most informative for how the client is doing, the next steps the therapy may need to take, and how to best care for the health of the entire team.

The clinicians and the client attend the *team meeting*. When possible, it is held in the client's home. Because of this, the team is very careful to tailor the meeting to the client's needs and sensitivity. Some clients can comfortably participate with those involved being relatively direct and forthcoming in their communication. Others need more emotional insulation and a less stressful meeting environment. Some clients can not, or will not, participate for some time. A team meeting is a holding environment that allows the client and clinicians to be comfortable, but also sustains enough tension to produce therapeutic work.

The *family meeting* includes whatever combination of client and family is most relevant to the recovery process, along with the clinician or clinicians who specifically work with them. As family circumstances and their readiness for therapy have so much variation, these meetings are carefully tailored in their form and frequency (Miklowitz & Goldstein, 1997).

Meeting Dynamics

The mind and speech dynamics in meetings are remarkably energetic, complex, often subtle, and at other times not. They generate a wide range of feeling experiences. For those who are paying attention, a wealth of information about how the client is doing and what is going on altogether in the recovery environment is available.

The Phenomenon of Split-Transferences. Over time, we have come to recognize that each team member establishes very different and individual relationships with the client. It is obvious that this should happen, but the observed implication is that as the client relates to each therapist-friend, a different part of the client's mind is engaged and revealed through the relationship. Often when an individual therapist works with a client, a transference develops. In this case, when one client is working with a team of clinicians, transferences often develop unique to each clinician, which we refer to as *split-transferences* (Goldberg Unger, 1978). After a time of working together, through the process of split-transferences, the clinicians frequently take on identifiable family system roles. We see the roles of siblings and parents most often, as over time the client's and family's dilemmas tend to be inhabited by the team.

Through these split-transferences we often see elements of the client's mind come forth, maybe only briefly, of which they, or we, have not previously been aware. As each clinician – with their individual relationship with the client representing an aspect of the client's mind and personality as a split transference – comes together in a meeting with the other split transferences, *the client's whole mind* is now in the room and able to be more aware of itself than it may otherwise be. As this happens, there is a chance for us to see what sorts of tensions and dynamics might be activated. For example, we could see what roles or tensions in the transferential world are particularly irritated at that time.

It is important to highlight that Windhorse therapists do not pigeonhole themselves into fixed transferential roles. They are also very careful not to invest their feelings with too much meaning when split-transferences become vivid, as they have the potential to calcify into conflicting, treatment destructive sub-groups. An example of this occurred recently for a young woman client who experienced her father as distant, punitive, prone to demanding too much of her, and insensitive to her desire to have a psychological treatment that was non-traditional. In contrast, she experienced her mother as very nurturing, always protective, and generally willing to protect her from her father. In her treatment, the psychotherapist transferentially became her mother and the psychiatrist became her father, even though they were of the opposite gender. The psychotherapist found himself to be suspicious and resentful of the motivations of the "medical model, overly stuffy and arrogant psychiatrist" who wanted to impose herself on the client without really understanding who she was. The psychiatrist perceived the psychotherapist as a "spineless enabler." Through contact at meetings it did not take long for us to catch on to what was causing these feelings, and the psychotherapist and the psychiatrist maintained their collegial relationship of mutual trust. This experience gave insight into the potency of the split in the family, which had previously not been very apparent.

There was truth to the family split, as well as exaggeration on the part of the client as to how black and white the situation was. Over time we helped the family become less polarized and helped the client see her parents in less good and bad terms.

The Phenomenon of Exchange. The atmosphere of mind of the recovery environment is created by all people involved. This occurs through a process referred to as *exchange* (Podvoll, 2003). The presence of one's mind does not just exist within our cranium; it can be felt by others. Most Windhorse clinicians can remember the experience of noticing how their mind feels and works differently around different people. For example, with some they might feel more competitive or less sure of themselves. With others, they might think more clearly. The process of exchange is that mixing of mind that happens when people are together (Goleman, 2006). For example, during a meeting, a team member has a mental or physical experience and it may be completely impossible to know its source. But if he or she is sufficiently aware, through the practice of being clear and attentive to the mind atmosphere of the recovery environment, he or she will notice patterns that appear unmistakably specific to that particular situation.

The phenomenon of exchange is often a subtle experience, with maybe only minor variations of how one might normally think or feel in a meeting. For example, with one client in particular, when I was in her supervision meeting my mind tended to be unusually clear. Whatever I was thinking about displayed itself in much more detail than usual. It felt like what I imagine having a very high IQ would be like. That quality of mind I experienced was a sane aspect of the frighteningly intense and complex mind of this person. With this same person, as a group we would often be trying to control her in unreasonable ways, which was what she frequently tried to do to us as her treatment team. The mind element is too fluid to make such experiences of exchange completely reliable, but the ephemeral reality of experience and insight triggered during Windhorse meetings offer highly valuable knowledge about the client and the team.

One particular aspect of exchange in a meeting can look similar to the example already mentioned in split-transferences where clinicians appear polarized. In the case of polarized feeling states that seem to arise from exchange, the polarized individuals may not have any identifiable transferential roles. A vivid example of this phenomenon occurred with a treatment that had been ongoing for several years. We could see that the client was struggling to take risks with new behaviors. These behaviors would potentially have made her feel much better in many ways, but she would have had to raise her commitment to responsibility and accountability to a higher level. As her hesitation was discussed in supervision meetings, we identified some extreme feeling poles among the clinicians. Two of the poles were particularly clear: one represented the client's strong desire to progress to a higher level of functioning and the other represented her self criticism and condemnation of being hopelessly incapable of such growth.

This is a gentle way of stating that the two individual clinicians who held opposing views felt like they hated each other. I was the person who held the view that the client was capable of taking the next steps and my colleague and friend of many years, whom I had great respect for, felt the very opposite. As these feelings escalated, for weeks I really hated to even look at my fellow clinician; it felt injurious and insulting. I wanted her off the team because it seemed to me she was damaging my client who had so much potential for growth. She, on the other hand, thought I was being reckless to encourage the client to attempt such growth steps, irresponsibly setting her up for failure, which could produce long-term damage to her confidence and self-esteem. She wanted me off the team as well. No one else on the team of about 10 clinicians was feeling anything like what she and I were experiencing. When we finally recognized that we had been holding these polarities, we were relieved that we understood what was going on and that our friendship of many years was not on the rocks. We also were stunned and heartbroken by the vicious, murderous intensity of the struggle our client was having between her progressive and regressive impulses.

As with split-transferences, the information that exchange can produce has the potential for very positive effects on the treatment or equally destructive effects if the team is not aware and paying attention to this aspect of group mind.

The Phenomenon of Group Windhorse. The team often shows up for meetings having done a lot of individual work since the last gathering. Some may be feeling isolated and road weary. The basic attenders, team leader, psychotherapist, housemates, team supervisor and psychiatrist have all had their experience of client and family, and of each other. Clients and family members likewise have had to deal with the team members and with each other. Feelings have developed, questions have come up, and perhaps a troubling observation needs to be discussed with the group. Intense emotional energy may have arisen for some. In the various meetings the team has a chance to hear and feel what is going on with each other and to explore personal experiences during the work. Split-transferences may appear, exchange experience may be there, and a significant task for the group is to help everyone describe their experience. Once again, no matter how negative, painful, or hopeless it might sound, the team members need to feel heard and be connected to the whole. From there, the team tries to make sense of feelings and experiences as they relate to the developing understanding of the recovery environment, the client, and this unique shared path of recovery. Once the team members feel heard and connected to the whole, feelings are not experienced as being quite so solid, and people tend to relax. With relaxation and clarity often comes the experience of heightened compassion and the arousal of Windhorse energy in the group (Gaviotas,

1998). This phenomenon of *Group Windhorse* is an experience of certain qualities of mind being heightened – upliftedness, confidence, compassion, and the absence of fixation of particular thoughts or feelings. Windhorse clinicians recognize this experience and it is directed back to the client and family in our individual contacts after the staff-only meetings. In the meetings involving the client and family, everyone is participating in this heightened positive atmosphere of mind, which promotes Windhouse energy. Through *meeting practice*, confident life energy is strengthened in the team and the entire recovery environment is effected positively.

Case Study

Julie was a 27 year-old woman whom Windhorse worked with for about two years. Five years prior to our first meeting she had experienced her first manic episode. She had been hospitalized seven times while maintaining that she did not need psychological treatment. What was different about her current hospitalization was that for the first time she said she was tired of being "thrown in the hospital" and wanted some help. The hospital staff and doctors thought Windhorse Community Services could be a good resource and her mother called us.

I spoke with her mother, Beth, who was in a guardedly hopeful state of mind, but also heartbroken, bewildered, and exhausted. As she had never heard Julie say she needed treatment, this was stunning. She had been hoping for years that Julie would say this and follow through with getting help. Beth was almost afraid of this little ray of hope and the thought that "I might be finally getting my daughter back." While being careful not to create false hope, I described the Windhorse approach, which made great sense to Beth. We agreed that I should go to the hospital to meet Julie.

Julie was a petite person, about 5 feet 4 inches tall and around 115 pounds, but she looked physically strong. She had a pleasant face and the ruddy, fair complexion of someone who had spent a lot of time outdoors. Our initial meeting in the hospital did not last long as she immediately told me that her mother had described what Windhorse does and that it sounded fine to her, "just to get everyone off my back." She said she really did not need treatment but would agree to work with us for six months. It felt like she was commanding me to listen, not interrupt, and not to make eye contact or say anything that would put her on the spot. I complied with her "commands," and asked her if it would be "okay" if I started introducing her to potential team members while she was in the hospital and she said a bit dismissively, "of course." She reported no preference for men or women on the team and that anything I needed to know her mother could tell me. She then impatiently asked if we were done with our meeting.

Although she was outwardly a bit hostile, I found her quite likable. I could see it was unspeakably difficult being in her situation and thought she did a good job of getting to the point and taking care of herself. I left with the impression that Julie was terrified, feeling completely vulnerable, and making a tremendously courageous effort to try something different in her life.

Once someone agrees to work with Windhorse, an assessment is conducted in order to know what kind of recovery environment is needed. The assessing clinicians explore what the life and mental health issues are and what type and size of treatment the client and family will need. We pay particular attention to understanding the client's and family's history of sanity, as that is a key component to establishing a successful recovery environment (Podvoll, 2003).

From all we could gather, Julie had grown up quite normally as an intelligent and creative person. She had begun to experience mood instability late in high school, at times needing to withdraw a bit from her usual lively flow of activity, seeming depressed with lower energy. Once in college, Julie continued to do well in all areas, but her mood irregularity became more pronounced. Sleeping was often difficult and it was harder for her to keep an energetic schedule. Her art became more brilliant and subtly expressive, but she also did less of it. She tried medications for a brief period, but rapid weight gain and unimpressive results convinced her that they weren't worth the trouble and she stopped. In the meantime, Beth and Julie's father were in the midst of a fairly amicable divorce, which resulted in Julie's father moving out of state and essentially out of her life.

After a heroic struggle to stay in school and with her life situation significantly deteriorated, she finally graduated from college. Shortly after, Beth visited her and immediately knew that something was terribly wrong. Julie was talking in a rapid and pressured way, was very irritable, and was speaking in an urgent manner about what sounded like Christian mysticism. Her apartment looked like someone had ransacked it and it appeared that Julie might not have been sleeping for a while as her bed was now under many layers of oddly arranged artistic creations that appeared to constitute a shrine. When Beth urged her to see her old psychiatrist again, Julie stormed out of the apartment and recklessly drove off. She was picked up later that day by the police and was taken to a psychiatric hospital on a mental health hold. Thus began the cycle that would become her life for the next five years: brief periods of stability interrupted by involuntary hospitalizations, medications, weight gain, "stupidity," occasional jobs that were hard to cope with, no friends, and no meaning,

The consensus of the assessment was that at least during the initial stages of treatment Julie needed a fully developed team with two shifts per day. This level of contact is considered high by Windhorse standards and we recognized that it could be overwhelming to Julie, but we also sensed that she needed a very solid structure to be safe. The contacts would be relatively brief, an hour and a half in the morning, to help her get breakfast and organize the day, and another shift at around 6:00 to 8:00 to get dinner and to make the transition from the day to evening. Framing the day in this manner, the contact was also designed to help stabilize Julie's sleep cycle, i.e., being awake during the day and sleeping at night. As Julie was committing to taking her medications, she would handle them herself. We tried to collaborate with her around this plan, but she was not interested in the details of what we would all do. She just said, "I'll do whatever for six months."

The immediate work at hand was to create the recovery environment. John was chosen to be Julie's psychotherapist and a woman named Sandy was selected as the team leader. Both were very experienced Windhorse clinicians with strong expertise in bipolar disorders. Because Julie was quite intelligent and had a severe and deadly mood disorder with psychosis, we knew the team also needed skilled basic attenders with experience in bipolar disorder. We wanted them to be in their late 20's or early 30's and we recognized that the team needed a gender balance. Fortunately, such candidates were available, and after the first interviews, Julie accepted them all. The team had three women basic attenders and two men. There was also a woman housemate available whom Julie really liked. Rounding out the team was a psychiatrist with extensive Windhorse experience, and me in the role of team supervisor. With the team selected, we were ready to gather for the first supervision meeting in order to assemble the schedule and create a vision for the beginning phase of the journey we were about to take.

As the treatment began, Julie's terse guardedness with me was in stark contrast to how she spoke in one-on-one situations with John, the therapist, and with Sandy, the team leader. She related to them as if they were her students and she was a spiritual teacher. She was a little formal, tolerant, and "patient" with how distracted they were by mundane life activity. At any given opportunity, she would teach about the spiritual aspects of life, relationships, the universe, and anything at hand that had inspired her. She would let John and Sandy do their work, and she would cooperate and teach them when she could. She related to the basic attenders in a similar manner.

The scheduled contact began when Julie was still in the hospital and shortly after she was discharged the schedule began in full. A good deal of the early shift activity, especially for the team leader and the time with Donna, the housemate, was spent finding an apartment and shopping for furnishings. Of anyone on the team, she seemed to feel the most relaxed with Donna. This was the least professionally oriented relationship she had with the team, and they often were just in the house together in a quiet way. They both enjoyed working together to make a comfortable home and she did very little teaching with Donna.

Julie settled into the basic attendance schedule in what appeared to be a surprisingly un-conflicted manner. She was on time for shifts, did not seem to get particularly close to people, still did a lot of teaching, and tended to be pretty organized about how the time was spent. She would typically use shift time to do errands, get coffee, take a walk, or organize her art studio. However, her psychotherapy sessions, which were once a week, were rapidly becoming less comfortable for her and John. They would meet in his office, and she began to be either completely silent, or show the same kind of guardedness she had with me during our initial contacts. When she did talk to John it was mostly in order to teach.

For our family meetings, we decided that in the beginning, we would meet at least every two weeks, but that of course Beth could call me as needed. Julie declined to be part of the early family meetings to begin with, although she spoke with her mother several times per week.

Things were going well for a beginning phase. Her sleep was getting into a more normal day-night rhythm, relationships were maturing, and she was eating in what appeared to be a normal manner. She was also beginning to swim as a way of getting into shape again, and she would spend a lot of time during the day walking around town.

In the supervision meetings some basic attenders expressed feeling useless and irritated. The shifts felt like a waste of time. My own experience was almost always one of vigilance. Despite how smoothly many aspects of the treatment were going, I felt like we were constantly on the verge of something dangerous happening, some disaster. We were also able to easily see what a lovely person Julie was, and her good heartedness showed in many ways. Even her teaching felt like a generous offering to us. It had a touch of a psychotic flavor, but we could see that she really cared about what she was saying. We all really liked her and sensed she had been, and continued to be, in a terrible life predicament.

The team meetings were held at her house. These were generally not very comfortable: a difficult variation on a basic attendance shift, with Julie needing to keep the relationships at a safe distance. The house meetings, also held at the home, were more comfortable and productive as they focused on details of running the home with Donna.

Julie continued showing up for every shift, but as time passed she was beginning to let it be known that we were all nice enough people, but quite useless as therapists, especially John. There were many sessions where they would just sit with a lot of silence. A little teaching would happen and then Julie would tell John what a waste of time therapy was. She did not need therapy and John was a lousy therapist anyway. As tense, guarded communication, and dissatisfaction mounted, a transition to the middle phase of treatment appeared to be underway.

One morning Julie did not want to get out of bed. Her polite demeanor had been slowly changing over the previous month and she had stopped teaching. This morning she looked withdrawn and terrified and seemed to be really suffering as if it was difficult for her to breathe. She spent the morning in bed but seemed to appreciate the quiet company of the basic attender, who brought her tea and food and read a book while Julie laid there not wanting to talk. Later in the day she had a therapy session with John and, surprisingly, she seemed interested in seeing him. At the beginning of the therapy session she was quiet, but her presence had a different feeling about it. Instead of angry and guarded, she appeared completely vulnerable and fearful, very uneasy. Finally, in a quiet tone, she said, "I can't believe this is who I am." Then in a steady and measured flow of words, she described how horrible it had been over the last five years to see life as she thought it would be completely washed down the drain. She could not count on herself and nobody else could count on her, except to do something crazy, destructive, and stupid. She had wanted to ignore it, but the mania kept coming back. She wanted to leave everything, but the police kept bringing her back. Now she was here and having more awareness than she wanted, and John, after having survived so much of her anger, felt like the safest person to be with, at least for right now. Because of the depression, the insight of what she had lost, and no sense of a way out of her horror, she saw no realistic option other than to kill herself. She had no immediate plan, but she promised that if she tried again, she would be successful. It was clear to John that she meant it.

    John quietly listened to her. When she appeared to be done speaking, he said that he was glad she came in that day. The simplicity of his listening and the genuine communication that he was glad to be with her went straight to her immediate experience. She was feeling utterly lonely and unlovable, cut off from everyone, unspeakably afraid, and out of control in a world without allies. She cried for most of the rest of the session until John took her home. Once there, Sandy joined Julie and John to talk about what was going on. After credibly agreeing to not hurt herself, they all thought it was best to increase Julie's shift support for at least the next week. As we had expected her to get depressed at some point and thought this was likely to be a positive development, no medication changes were indicated.

    Waking up to who you are and how your life has been is a critical part of the recovery process. Stated succinctly by Trungpa (1983), "Earth is good" (p. 555). This dramatic shift in Julie's awareness was very sudden, which can create a dangerous mental state for many people. It can be extremely difficult to tolerate the sudden and acute awareness of such a disturbing predicament. Often, a person needs to diminish their awareness through re-cultivating psychosis, finding other ways of being defended, or by killing him- or herself. Julie, however, was able to tolerate this experience and to use it as a reference point throughout the rest of her Windhorse treatment. It was very striking to her that the team did not shy away from the painful intensity of her emotional state, but actually seemed to appreciate her even more. Julie's awakening was a dramatic example of an *island of clarity*, an insight that interrupts confusion and helps one become oriented to the reality and potential sanity of the here-and-now.

Julie's first shifts with each clinician after this breakthrough were a little awkward. She was embarrassed that people had seen her act the way she had and was very grateful that everyone stood by her. It seemed to her that we had more confidence in her than she had in herself. It appeared to us that she no longer wanted to die, but instead was genuinely connecting with energy and passion to be physically active and to resume her artwork.

This middle phase felt like an unleashing of Julie's pent-up desire to have a normal life again. If that were simply a matter of her taking medications and having some therapy to help her recover from five years of life trauma, we could have ended the team. But since she had experienced radically unstable moods for such a long time, it took Julie about a year and a half to get her moods and the persecutory voices that came along with them, to settle. During this period, Julie would enthusiastically work on getting started with any number of activities, for example, doing art, beginning to look for work, and getting involved with organized sports. However, it was very difficult for her to establish continuity and momentum as frequently hypomania would reduce her ability to concentrate and tolerate people. Or she might get depressed and simply not feel like doing anything. As hard as it was for her to be patient with her mood cycling, it was encouraging when she had that realization that she became more stable and closer to her normal mood baseline, the quieter and, at times, non-existent her inner voices became.

Despite the relentless grind of setbacks, Julie continued to get clearer about what she valued in her life and to pursue re-engaging activities that reflected them. Volleyball and tennis, first with the team members and later with the city's Parks and Recreation leagues, became great opportunities to get her weight down to what she felt was a comfortable place. She then had more energy and felt more like her competent self. These activities also helped her to meet new people outside the Windhorse team.

A major part of the work of the team over the middle phase became helping her to learn, as John put it, "the care and feeding of Julie." She essentially had to learn that how she engaged with her physical world, how she related to people, how she worked with meaningful activities, and how she worked with her thinking, had a profound effect on whether her moods were more or less stable. She learned that how she slept had an effect on how she ate and that her relationship world impacted how she ate and slept, and that her thinking was related to everything. She was patient and hard working. As tedious and frustrating as this process felt, she was fundamentally inspired, knowing she had a path out of her previous life predicament. She was beginning to have more maitri toward herself and her strengthened windhorse energy was beginning to produce the confidence that she was not a bad and hopeless failure of a person. She felt better, more alive and like herself again.

15. Windhorse Therapy

As time went on, Julie was clearly becoming a peer to the rest of us on the team and she did not hesitate to confront us on our blind spots. For instance, she felt that for all our "nice" attitudes about the *therapist-friend* relationship, she often found us to be arrogant, as psychotherapists can be, about the fact that *she* was the *client* and we were the *mature professionals* who have their lives together. As uncomfortable as this was at times, we also appreciated the piercing accuracy of her observations and her confidence to speak directly to us. Our team meetings were now almost always lively, sometimes intense, as we were all holding back much less. That shift in honesty with the team was the outer reflection of a shift in her interest and capacity to be more honest with herself. She was gaining strength in unflinchingly identifying which of her actions and thoughts led to more confusion and suffering, and which to more health and harmony in her life. It was clear that her *allegiance to sanity* was becoming a reliable reference point.

Julie never felt compelled to be an ongoing part of the family meeting as the tension between her and her mother seemed to resolve through their informal contacts. Between the infrequent face-to-face meetings we had with Julie and Beth, and Beth's more frequent phone conversations and visits, they did manage to establish a much more natural relationship tone and distance for a mother and her adult daughter. This was largely possible because Julie was being *held* by the recovery environment. She was healthier and Beth was not induced into so much vigilance and protection. Beth could treat her more like a mother and not as a caretaker. Also, in a parallel process with Julie, Beth's confidence in Julie's recovery was strengthening. She was very appreciative of how the team was being helpful to Julie and could see the lessening of her dependence on the compensatory nature of the team as her health became more resilient.

Eighteen months into her process with Windhorse, Julie's schedule had been reduced to four basic attendance shifts, one psychotherapy session a week, one meal per week, and grocery shopping. Julie still attended all the regular meetings, but with fewer shifts we were able to reduce the number of basic attenders she needed.

There was one more significant life development that occurred in this phase that should not have been a surprise. Once Julie was more confident in her ability to be in complex social environments outside the team, she found a local church to attend. It was a progressive Christian church that practiced meditation and centering prayer. Besides participating in many social activities and making some healthy friendships, she began a daily meditation practice.

The end phase of Julie's Windhorse treatment was brief and it began with an argument. Her brother, Bob, was coming to town for a visit and this seemed like an opportunity to have him join a family meeting. Julie really liked that idea. Her life was in a much better place. She was physically healthier, her moods were more stable, and her inner voices had almost entirely disappeared. She had also taken over most of the organizing of her life that the team had previously done. Julie continued to work on relationships both in and out of the team in a wonderfully direct and honest way and she had learned for the first time how to live with someone her age in relative harmony and to be close with them at the same time.

Once we all had settled into the family meeting, her brother said in a heartfelt way how amazed he was to see her having such a good life. Hearing this, Julie exploded, "You think this is my life! I'm in treatment and have paid friends! Don't try to make me feel good because I've learned to tie my shoes and you've got your life so together."

Bob was stunned. He was glad that Julie was doing as well as she was and had tried to express this. She accepted his apology and over the next hour and a half they were able to resolve the immediate tension between them. It was hard for Julie to hear that Bob's initial compliment had come from his recognition that her illness had diminished almost all his confidence that she would ever live a normal life again. He felt that she might not even survive. He had not meant to be condescending, although he understood how she had experienced it that way.

Something that was particularly meaningful to Julie was the insight that both Beth and Bob had when Julie became angry and essentially declared that she would not settle for half a life. They agreed, "It feels like we've got our Julie back." Significantly, we all noticed that Julie did not experience any mood instability from this very intense emotional experience as she previously might have. She, too, was very surprised by this and later said, "This showed me that I was ready to leave treatment."

In the next week's team meeting she announced that she was leaving the team in a month. She had been researching colleges where she could get a master's degree in physical education and had found one that she liked in a small city out of Colorado, about an hour from where her father lived. School would be starting in nine months and she wanted to move there, get her life established, and apply to school. Once there she would also look for a psychiatrist and a psychotherapist to continue the work she had done with us. She expressed appreciation for all we had done together: "I think you actually saved my life." However, she also said she was tired of having training wheels and paid friends, and needed to get on with her life. "I think I've learned the care and feeding and thinking of Julie, and have a good toolbox for when things come up that I need to deal with." Once she finished talking, she seemed to glow with a quiet resolve, confidence, and a bit of defiance.

To say we were stunned was an understatement. Also, we knew this was absolutely the right thing for her to do. But *we* were not ready to have her leave. We had a more graduated plan for the eventual team reduction and how we could continue to see her for years to come. We really liked her. We wanted to feel appreciated and valued. As is usually the case in the life of a family, artificial or not, emancipation is not how the parents planned it. Also, as is usually the case with a successful treatment, recovery is almost always more intelligent than the clinician imagines and certainly not in your control. John was the first to say something, and much like once before, he said something simple, "This sounds really right." Others expressed support.

The last month went by quickly while we said our goodbyes and packed up the house. Julie was busy making plans and saying goodbye to friends. Without a lot of sentimentality, she ended with us as individuals, as part of the group, and as the host of a lovely going away party. Then she was gone.

In summary, this case shows the compensatory recovery environment in action. Julie entered treatment in a highly disturbed state, in which she was not able to care for herself and had no sense of how to get back to meaningful and recognizable life. In a very real way, Julie's recovery began as she became part of a recovery environment that allowed her to have a life that functioned, because it functioned in a comprehensive and synchronized manner with her and her mother fully integrated into it. Simultaneously, the recovery environment provided specific and integrated psychological treatment that identified and interrupted confusion-producing life patterns and behaviors, helped establish new ones based on health, and over time stabilized those new behaviors.

In the beginning of Julie's treatment, we saw her explore whether she could trust the team. She knew that she needed to do something different or die, either literally or to herself as she knew herself to be. As with so many people who are in her predicament, it is easier to stop clinging to unhealthy defensive behavior patterns once in a gentle environment.

The middle phase began with Julie appreciating and learning to tolerate the difficult, life-changing insight she had. She became more fearless and attentive to the islands of clarity that she had previously avoided. She was also continuing to live as an integral part of a sane environment. This was a world with good *body* and domestic practices and *speech* elements of strong and healthy relationships. The *mind* element included rhythms that tended to support the harmony of the total environment and adaptable intelligence and awareness. By herself, and in the varieties of dyadic and group Windhorse relationships, the practice of waking up to her sanity and developing confidence in her path of recovery became a compelling and lived experience, not unlike the contemplative training and life experience of the Windhorse clinicians.

As Julie grew healthier and more independent, we collaboratively reduced the structure of the environment. This reduced its compensatory effect, and Julie progressively lived a less protected and more normally engaged life at a more comfortable relational distance from her mother. With solid skills around working with her mood stability, with confidence in her health, and the knowledge that she was on a resilient recovery path,

Julie left treatment. By then, she had internalized a treasure of healthy experience gained from being part of the recovery environment.

Conclusion

After 26 years and hundreds of treatments, a lot has been learned about Windhorse therapy. It is a highly adaptable form of psychological treatment that is effective with a wide variety of complex mental health and life problems. Windhorse creates compensatory recovery environments that range in size from being quite small to being like small towns. Not everyone needs or wants this type of treatment, but for many who choose it, it is exactly what is needed. It works for the client, it works for the family, and it works for the team itself. Those of us who have been fortunate enough to do this work find each team in its own way to be a health promoting and clarifying experience for our personal growth as human beings and as clinicians. A significant reason for this is the ability to raise individual and collective windhorse, which promotes staying committed, learning, and being confident in each person's possibility of recovery and growth, including the clinician's.

We also know, based on our personal contemplative experience as well as from conducting treatments, that Windhorse therapy is based on a powerful combination. It connects the fundamental health of a human being, which is naturally inclined toward recovery, with cutting edge treatments for the psychological disorders, in a highly adaptable recovery environment. This makes Windhorse therapy particularly effective for complex, difficult to treat conditions, while having tremendous potential to evolve and be ever more relevant in the future.

References

Almaas, A. H. (1998). *Facets of unity.* Boston: Shambhala Publications.
Chödrön, P. (1997). *When things fall apart.* Boston: Shambhala Publications.
DiGiacamo, A. M. & Herrick, M. (2007). *Beyond psychiatry: The windhorse project.* Berlin: Peer Lehman Publishing.
Epstein, M. (1999). *Going to pieces without falling apart.* New York: Broadway Books.
Gaviotas, A. W. (1998). *A village to reinvent the world.* New York: Chelsea Green Publishing.
Goldberg Unger, J. (1978). Working with the split transference. *Modern Psychoanalysis, 3*(2), 217-232.
Goleman, D. (2006). *Social intelligence: The new science of human relationships.* New York: Bantam Dell Publications.
Fortuna, J. (1994). The windhorse project: Recovering from psychosis at home. *Journal of Contemplative Psychotherapy. 9,* 73-96.

Hayward, J. & Hayward, K. (1999). *Sacred world* (2nd Ed). Boston: Shambhala Publications.
Miklowitz, D. J. & Goldstein, M. J. (1997). *Bipolar disorder: A family focused treatment approach.* New York: Guilford Press.
Mipham, J. (2003). *Turning the mind into an ally.* New York: River Head Books.
Podvoll, E. (2003). *Recovering sanity.* Boston: Shambhala Publications.
Rabin, B. & Walker, R. (1987). A contemporary approach to clinical supervision. *Journal of Contemplative Psychotherapy, 9*, 135-146.
Trungpa, C. (1999). *Great eastern sun.* Boston: Shambhala Publications.
Trungpa, C. (2003). *The collected works of Chögyam Trungpa* (Vol 2 & 6). Boston: Shambhala Publications,
Trungpa, C. (2005). *The sanity we're born with.* Boston: Shambhala Publications.

16

Contemplative Psychotherapy: Integrating Western Psychology and Eastern Philosophy[1]

Kyle Thomas Darnall

In recent years, *mindfulness-based practices* (MBP) have drawn considerable attention from the psychology community. Meditation and relaxation techniques are common elements of many therapeutic interventions and have become so accepted that they can be found in general treatment planning publications (e.g., Johnson, 1997). In a recent literature survey, Walsh and Shapiro (2006) stated that meditation has become "one of the most enduring, widespread and researched of all psychotherapeutic methods" (p. 227). Mindfulness-Based Cognitive Therapy (MBCT; Segal, Teasdale, & Williams, 2002) was developed as a method of preventing depressive relapse in formerly depressed clients. Dialectical Behavioral Therapy (DBT; Linehan, 1993) has demonstrated effectiveness in reducing the suicidal and parasuicidal behaviors of individuals with borderline personality disorder. Mindfulness-Based Stress Reduction (MBSR; Kabat-Zinn, 2003) has repeatedly demonstrated that it can increase the quality of life and reduce levels of pain for individuals with chronic health problems. Additional research has begun to explore the change factors associated with MBP interventions. Fennell (in press) has operationalized mindfulness as "metacognitive awareness (acceptance of the idea that thoughts, assumptions and beliefs are mental events and processes rather than objective truths)" (p. 1). This notion of metacognitive awareness and acceptance has been elaborated on by Hayes and colleagues (1999; see also Hayes, Follette, & Linehan, 2004). The developing trend of mindfulness and metacognitive awareness in the behavioral traditions suggests that the form of problematic cognitions is not as relevant as their function (Hayes, 2004). The efficacy of MBCT intervention for depressed individuals (Ma & Teasdale, 2004; Segal et al.,2002; Teasdale et al., 2002; Williams, Teasdale, Segal & Soulsby, 2000) and DBT for individuals with borderline personality disorder (Linehan, 1993) speaks to the importance of this trend toward

---

[1] This chapter was originally published in *The Behavior Therapist*, Volume 30, October, 2007.

integration of MBPs into contemporary empirically based psychotherapies.

The process of integrating Western psychological concepts with Eastern meditative philosophies has been rife with misunderstanding and some loss of the depth for both traditions and what they have to offer each other (Walsh & Shapiro, 2006). In part, this may be due to empirical investigations supporting the efficacy of mindfulness-based treatment interventions without a thorough theoretical understanding of mindfulness and its mechanisms of change (Baer, 2003; Shapiro, 2006). Until recently, the psychological community lacked a comprehensive, operationalized measure of mindfulness that would facilitate further investigations. Using a recently developed, multifaceted mindfulness questionnaire, Baer (2006) reported that mindfulness is composed of four primary factors: "describe, act with awareness, nonjudge, and nonreact" (p. 42).

Contemporary behavior therapies such as Acceptance and Commitment Therapy (ACT; Hayes et al., 1999), DBT, MBCT, and MBSR have all either overtly or covertly emphasized the development of mindfulness through various methods. The purpose of the present chapter is to expose readers to a form of psychotherapy, contemplative psychotherapy (CP), which has been taught at Naropa University and is a synthesis of Buddhist and Western psychology. The CP model and associated training may be of benefit as an integration proceeds. This chapter will present key facets of the CP model, supporting evidence from the contemporary behavior therapies and a brief summary of limitations.

CP and the Nature of Suffering

Although CP is a synthesis of Buddhist and Western psychology (Wegela,1996), it is grounded in principles of Buddhist phenomenology and asserts that suffering is ubiquitous, suffering is caused by attachment, there is a method to the cessation of suffering, and the method consists of contextual changes in behavior and cognitive restructuring (Hayes, 2002; Kumar, 2002; Robins, 2002) that are achieved through "right understanding, right thought, right speech, right action, right livelihood, right effort, right mindfulness, and right concentration" (Robins, 2002, p. 52). De Silva (2002) notes that this strategy toward the amelioration of the symptomology associated with suffering predates cognitive and behavioral interventions in Western psychology but can be conceptualized as "systematic use of rewards and punishments; fear reduction by graded exposure; modeling; self-monitoring; stimulus control; overt and covert aversion; use of family members for implementing a behavioral-change programme; and specific techniques, including distraction and overexposure, for unwanted intrusive cognitions" (p. 116). It should be noted that cognition is defined as "those subjective experiences that one can know or become aware of" (Toneatto,

2002, p. 73) and that this should be distinguished from cogitative or cogitation so often emphasized in many CBT interventions. "Thus, cognition can include all emotion, mood, feeling, discursive thinking, imagery, memory, dreaming, sensory perception, and somatic sensation" (Toneatto, 2002, p. 73). This operational definition is an important departure from traditional CBT and becomes an integral element of the meta-cognitive processes of decentering involved in MBCT, ACT, MBSR, CP, and DBT. Using Toneatto's operational definition of cognition, meta-cognition entails a conscious awareness of all experience and phenomena that are known or can be brought to awareness.

From the Buddhist perspective, to live is to suffer. How then can there be a cessation of suffering? In Buddhism, the suffering that is targeted is not the suffering of life but "the flavor of attachment in a world of change" (Low, 2000, p. 252). We suffer because we do not get what we want; but we do get what we do not want. At its heart, suffering originates from a dualistic perspective (Hayes, 2002). According to Kumar, "Suffering is generated by the mental tendency toward essentialism," which "refers to the assumption of a discrete, fixed self and identity, independent of external environmental influences or internal physical processes" (2000, p. 41). He continues by asserting that the belief in a fixed self necessitates the belief in a fixed other. This dichotomization of experience extends to the "polarization of thoughts, emotions, and experiences as attractive or aversive" (Kumar, p. 41). Where Western psychology has emphasized self-efficacy and the individuation of the individual, Eastern perspectives have stressed an understanding of the self in context. From Batesonian and dialectical perspectives, the only way to understand phenomena is to consider those phenomena within the context of all the circular interactions relevant to them. Cybernetic epistemology and dialectic philosophy further postulate that to draw a distinction, to create a separation, is actually to articulate a contextual relationship (Flemons, 1991; Linehan, 1993). Suffering is caused when relationship to context is lost and the individual begins to believe that distinctions and separations are literal and real.

> The individual, being absorbed in their own view of themselves, finds no gap in the world to enter, no way of speaking or connecting. And the world, other people, seem to present nothing but demands, criticism, shaming perceptions and so forth and so has to be resisted. (Low, 2000, p. 251)

Buddhism puts forward that there is no real, discreet, and permanent self. Instead, phenomena interdependently co-originate from an infinitely complex and interconnected network of cause and effect (Kumar, 2002; Robins, 2002). "From the perspective of Buddhist dialectics, all phenomena, ranging from feelings to physical structures, are temporary confluences of multiple influences" (Kumar, 2002, p. 41).

Meta-Cognitive Awareness and Decentering as Mechanisms of Change

Suffering is often maintained through the use of overlearned, habitual responses to stimuli, both behaviorally and cognitively. In the CP model, this is accomplished through the utilization of passion, aggression, and ignorance in the service of the ego to avoid the experience of impermanence and the attempt to maintain a separate sense of self. Passion is utilized to cling to pleasurable phenomena; aggression is used to avoid aversive experience; and ignorance is practiced when confronted by the nature of an impermanent self. Buddhist psychology assumes that suffering arises from ignorance of the interdependent nature of phenomena and that it is possible for humans to decrease their ignorance by increasing their moment-to-moment awareness, thereby experiencing the interconnectedness and nondual nature of existence (Wegela, 1996). For CP and the third-wave behavioral therapies the treatment target becomes increasing metacognitive awareness.

In exploring the mechanisms of change in cognitive therapy (CT) for depression and in the creation of a depression relapse-prevention treatment, Segal et al. (2002) observed that previous cognitive models have focused on the content of dysfunctional thoughts and further hypothesized that the central factor is the decentering which occurs through the successful process and implementation of CT and CBT (Orsillo, Roemer, Block Lerner, & Tull, 2004). Decentering is the development of metacognitive awareness, an ability to observe one's cognitive process without discursive judgment, which enables successful cognitive restructuring. Consistent with the CBT model of anxiety maintenance (Foa & Kozak, 1986; McGlynn & Lawer, 2000; Newman, 2000; Tsao & Craske, 2000), Segal et al. (2002) suggested that avoidance of depressive cognitions does not lead to avoidance of depressive symptoms, but may instead contribute to the frequency, duration, and intensity of relapse episodes, in part because the individual does not habituate to the experience of temporary depressive thoughts. Building on the theoretical and empirically supported model of MBSR, MBCT for depression was designed to provide a psychoeducational framework for depression and specifically target the development of metacognitive awareness. Further research has supported this by suggesting that utilization of thought-observation and acceptance is more successful than thought suppression in the management of intrusive thoughts, which can trigger depressive episodes (Marcks & Woods, in press).

Hayes (2004) notes that the third-wave therapies have abandoned an exclusive commitment to first-order change, and have significantly broadened the scope of change by incorporating contextualistic assumptions and experiential or indirect strategies. He describes an underlying premise of ACT as avoiding the cognitive fusion and associated suffering experienced when a presenting problem or chief complaint remains the focus of attention in therapeutic interventions. Hayes suggests that it is akin to asking the client to not think about chocolate cake, noting that the minute the individual attempts to not think of chocolate cake, they have. Any attempt to think of something else in order to stop thinking about chocolate cake fails because chocolate cake is again evoked. When a specific pathology becomes the focus of therapeutic interventions, the associated experiences and cognitive processes associated are reinforced by the shift in metacognitive awareness toward the pathology (Hayes et al., 1999; Hayes, 2002). While ACT incorporates many elements of traditional CBT into its model, a central feature is cognitive defusion, which targets the context of thoughts rather than the content (Masuda, Hayes, Sackett, & Twohig, 2004). In this manner, thoughts are not labeled as dysfunctional or maladaptive cognitions. Through the development of metacognitive awareness, the individual begins to accept a thought as a thought and recognizes the meaning he or she has attached to such. This process is believed to facilitate cognitive restructuring and behavioral hypothesis testing necessary for change.

According to the present analysis, third wave behavioral therapies such as ACT and MBCT promote the development of metacognitive awareness and facilitate the process of decentering, enabling the individual to engage in successful cognitive restructuring and behavioral hypothesis testing (Hayes, 2004; Segal et al., 2002; Segal et al., 2004). CP views mindfulness similarly. Mindfulness is paying attention, in a particular way, without discursive judgment (Kabat-Zinn, 1990; Wegela, 1996). Mindfulness practice facilitates the development of an *observer-self*, one in which thoughts are seen as thoughts, judgments are seen as judgments, and experiences are seen as experiences. Mindfulness has often been associated with traditional practices, such as sitting meditation, yoga, Zen tea ceremonies, or martial arts. All these practices can facilitate a state of mindfulness; however, mindfulness can also be experienced while doing the dishes, eating, walking, and daily living (Hanh, 1975). CP also describes another state: mindlessness. This state is often associated with adherence to passion, aggression, and ignorance. However, as Toneatto's (2002) definition of cognitions suggests, a mindlessness practice can become a mindfulness practice by shifting one's attentional state to the context in which the practice is utilized (Wegela, 1996).

CP Assumptions and Dialectical Experience

The CP model assumes three marks of existence: impermanence, egolessness, and suffering (Wegela, 1996). CP asserts that when exposed to these realities, individuals first experience a *sense of shock*, which is followed by uncertainty as the individual attempts to make sense of the new phenomena and incorporate these into their current *cognitive maps*. The individual then either accepts the new experience and adjusts his or her cognitive maps or ignores the disconfirmatory information and maintains existing behavioral responses, cognitive maps, and attributional systems. This cycle of shock, uncertainty, and conviction represents the human capacity to be aware of and acknowledge the three marks of existence. It also implies the potential for an individual to *wake up* or become *enlightened* about perpetual attempts to grasp, push away, or ignore phenomena in an attempt to maintain a sense of permanence, a separate self, and avoid pain. In CP, this underlying human potential is referred to as Brilliant Sanity and in Buddhist psychology as Buddha nature or intrinsic health.

CP states that Brilliant Sanity is expressed through five primary phenomenological dialectics (Wegela, 1996), which can be best understood through a thesis, antithesis, and synthesis model.

CP asserts that an experience of claustrophobia or lack of boundaries is an expression of the human capacity to be accommodating; poverty and gluttony are expressions of an appreciation for the richness of experience; confusion and conviction are expressions of clear perception, etc. Viewed in this manner, sanity can be found through the neurosis (Wegela, 1996).

Thesis	Synthesis	Antithesis
Claustrophobia	Accommodation/ Spaciousness	Boundariless
Poverty	Appreciation for the Richness of Life	Gluttony
Confusion	Clarity of Perspective	Convictions
Loneliness	Compassionate Relationship	Passionate Grasping
Lack of Initiative	Effective Action, Skillful Means	Frantic Activity

CP Interventions

CP is similar to the third-wave behavioral therapies in its indirect approach to change. Neuroses are seen as expressions of an individual's intrinsic health and are not necessarily to be directly ameliorated: Mindlessness practices can potentially become mindfulness practices. An integral element to the CP intervention process is modeling. The CP training program places primary emphasis on the development of the therapist. In addition to traditional didactic education, the program requires regular training in a body discipline (e.g., Aikido, Tai Chi, or Yoga), daily meditation practice, and regular meditation retreats. A specific retreat is designed to trigger and amplify the experience of the thesis and antithesis elements of the dialectics identified above. The overarching goals of these practices are for the therapist to become intimately familiar with the thesis, antithesis, and synthesis; to allow this familiarity to inform the intervention; and to model the synthesis while exploring the dialectical experience.

Limitations of CP

With a basis in Buddhist psychology, many of the underlying constructs and phenomenological assumptions are foreign to most Westerners. The very notion that psychological health (operationally defined in CP as an experience of space, relationship, clarity of perspective, appreciation for the richness of experience, and effective action) is present unconditionally and is actually expressed through neurosis appears to contradict medical models that suggest that health is obtained when symptoms are reduced. I have heard individuals state that to accept that suffering is ubiquitous is pessimistic. Paradoxically, CP practitioners and Buddhists would contend that to accept suffering is the first step to begin experiencing joy, pleasure, and compassion for others. This can be a difficult concept for clients to accept because they often present in distress, looking for a therapist to facilitate the amelioration of such.

Unfortunately, while rich on philosophy, CP is lean on specific interventions, treatment protocols based on client presentation, empirical investigation, and validation. However, it should be noted that while Western psychology has pursued a nomothetic, quantitative approach, many Eastern traditions have followed a more ideographic, qualitative method. This may, in part, reflect the cultural differences between these two traditions. There may also be methodological difficulties in operationalizing the underlying constructs within CP. As the third-wave behavioral strategies continue to evolve, the investigation of such may prove beneficial in the exploration of indirect change mechanisms and operationalizing constructs that have previously eluded clear definitions and presented confounding variables.

References

Baer, R. A. (2003). Mindfulness training as a clinical intervention: A conceptual and empirical review. *Clinical Psychology Science and Practice, 10*, 125-143.

Baer, R. A., Smith, G. T., Hopkins, J., Krietemeyer, J., Toney, L. (2006). Using self-report assessment methods to explore facets of mindfulness. *Assessment, 13,* 27-45.

de Silva, P. (2002). Buddhism and counseling. In S. Palmer (Ed.) *Multicultural Counseling: A Reader* (pp. 114-118). Thousand Oaks: Sage.

Fennell, M. J. V. (in press). Depression, low self-esteem and mindfulness. *Behavior Research and Therapy.*

Flemons, D. G. (1991). *Completing distinctions: Interweaving the ideas of Gregory Bateson and Taoism into a unique approach to therapy.* Boston: Shambhala.

Foa, E. B. & Kozak, M. J. (1986). Emotional processing of fear: Exposure to corrective information. *Psychological Bulletin, 99,* 20-35.

Hanh, T. N. (1975). *The miracle of mindfulness.* Boston: Beacon Press.

Hayes, S. C. (2002). Buddhism and acceptance and commitment therapy. *Cognitive and Behavior Practice, 9,* 58-66.

Hayes, S. C. (2004). Acceptance and commitment therapy and the new behavior therapies: Mindfulness, acceptance, and relationship. In S. C. Hayes, V. M. Follette & M. M. Linehan (Eds.), *Mindfulness and acceptance: Expanding the cognitive-behavioral tradition* (pp. 1-29). New York: Guilford Press.

Hayes, S. C., Follette, V. M., & Linehan, M. M. (Eds.). (2004). *Mindfulness and acceptance: Expanding the cognitive-behavioral tradition.* New York: Guilford Press.

Hayes, S. C., Strosahl, K. D. & Wilson, K. G. (1999). *Acceptance and commitment therapy: An experiential approach to behavior change.* New York: Guilford Press.

Johnson, S. L. (1997). *Therapist's guide to clinical intervention: The 1-2-3's of treatment planning.* San Diego: Academic Press.

Kabat-Zinn, J. (1991). *Full catastrophe living: Using the wisdom of your body and mind to face stress, pain and illness.* New York: Dell.

Kabat-Zinn, J. (2003). Mindfulness-based interventions in context: Past, present, and future. *Clinical Psychology: Science and Practice, 10,* 144-156.

Kumar, S. M. (2002). An introduction to Buddhism for the cognitive-behavioral therapist. *Cognitive and Behavioral Practice, 9,* 40-43.

Linehan, M. M. (1993). *Cognitive-behavioral treatment of borderline personality disorder.* New York: Guilford Press.

Low, J. (2000). The structures of suffering: Tibetan Buddhist and cognitive analytic approaches. In S. Batchelor & G. Watson (Eds.) *The psychology of awakening: Buddhism, science and our day-to-day lives* (pp. 250-270). York Beach, ME: Weiser Books.

Ma, S. H. & Teasdale, J. D. (2004). Mindfulnessbased cognitive therapy for depression: Replication and exploration of differential relapse prevention effects. *Journal of Consulting and Clinical Psychology, 72,* 31-40.

Marcks, B. A. & Woods, D. W. (in press). A comparison of thought suppression to an acceptance- based technique in the management of personal intrusive thoughts: A controlled evaluation. *Behavior Research and Therapy.*

Masuda, A., Hayes, S. C., Sackett, C. F. & Twohig, M. P. (2004). Cognitive defusion and self-relevant negative thoughts: Examining the impact of a ninety year old technique. *Behavior Research and Therapy, 42*, 477-485.

McGlynn, F. D. & Lawer, S. R. (2000). Specific phobia. In M. Hersen and M. Biaggio (Eds.), *Effective brief therapies* (pp. 79-98). San Diego: Academic Press.

Newman, M. G. (2000). Generalized anxiety disorder. In M. Hersen & M. Biaggio (Eds.), *Effective brief therapies* (pp. 157-178). San Diego: Academic Press.

Orsillo, S. M., Roemer, L., Block Lerner, J. & Tull, M. T. (2004). Acceptance, mindfulness, and cognitive-behavioral therapy: Comparisons, contrasts, and application to anxiety. In S. C. Hayes, V. M. Follette and M. M. Linehan (Eds.), *Mindfulness and acceptance: Expanding the cognitive-behavioral tradition* (pp. 66-95). New York: Guilford Press.

Robins, C. J. (2002). Zen principles and mindfulness practices in dialectical behavior therapy. *Cognitive and Behavioral Practice, 9*, 50-57.

Segal, Z., Williams, M., & Teasdale, J. (2002). *Mindfulness-based cognitive therapy for depression: A new approach to preventing relapse.* New York: Guilford Press.

Segal, Z., Williams, M. & Teasdale, J. (2004). Mindfulness-based cognitive therapy: Theoretical rationale and empirical status. In S.C. Hayes, V. M. Follette & M. M. Linehan (Eds.), *Mindfulness and acceptance: Expanding the cognitive-behavioral tradition* (pp. 45-65). New York: Guilford Press.

Teasdale, J. D., Moore, R. G., Hayhurst, H., Pope, M., Williams, S., & Segal, Z. V. (2002). Metacognitive awareness and prevention of relapse of depression: Empirical evidence. *Consulting and Clinical Psychology, 70*, 275-287.

Shapiro, S. L., Carlson, L. E, Astin, J. A., & Freedman, B. (2006). Mechanisms of mindfulness. *Journal of Clinical Psychology, 62*, 373-386.

Toneatto, T. (2002). A metacognitive therapy for anxiety disorders: Buddhist psychology applied. *Cognitive and Behavioral Practice, 9*, 72-78.

Tsao, J. C. I. & Craske, M. G. (2000). Panic disorder. In M. Hersen & M. Biaggio (Eds.), *Effective brief therapies: A clinician's guide* (pp. 63-78). San Diego: Academic Press.

Walsh, R., & Shapiro, S. L. (2006). The meeting of meditative disciplines and western psychology: A mutually enriching dialogue. *American Psychologist, 61*, 227-239.

Wegela, K. K. (1996). *How to be a help instead of a nuisance: Practical approaches to giving support service and encouragement to others*. Boston: Shambhala.

Williams, J. M. G., Teasdale, J. D., Segal, Z. V. & Soulsby, J. (2000). Mindfulness-based cognitive therapy reduces overgeneral autobiographical memory in formerly depressed patients. *Journal of Abnormal Psychology, 109*, 150-155.

17

Mothering in the Moment: Explorations on Mindfulness in Mothering and Therapeutic Experiences[1]

Elizabeth A. Olson
Helena Unger
Francis J. Kaklauskas
Letitia E. Swann

> Just as the mother at the risk of life,
> Loves and protects her son.
> So let the monk cultivate this boundless love
> To all that live in the whole universe...
> When he lives with perfect insight won,
> He surely comes no more to any womb.
> — The Buddha[2]

Since becoming a mother seventeen months ago, my life has expansively changed. I was surprised to discover that the last six years of my life spent completing my clinical psychology doctorate with an emphasis on children and families had only marginally prepared me for my new role as a mother. While in the past I had desired a regular schedule, an organized house, and clothing without stains, I have adjusted to the many ways that my life has changed. Becoming a mother has challenged me to tolerate more intensive stimulation. My meditation practice has helped me to accept and be present with my new life as it is. My former morning meditation practice has changed into a ritual of changing diapers, nursing, and building block towers on the floor with my son. While the time spent on my formal meditation practice has temporarily

---

[1] This paper uses the first person perspective as a means of connecting personally with the reader. The experiences expressed in the first person pronoun *I* represent the combination of similar experiences of the all of the authors, but most specifically those of Elizabeth Olson.

[2] Pali verse attributed to the Buddha from the Theravadin tradition. Cited from *The First Buddhist Women: Translations and Commentaries on the Therigatha* (1991) by Susan Murcott. Berkeley: Parallax.

decreased, my opportunities for mindful living have increased. As I rock my son when he is crying, I follow my breath and practice meditation-in-action to be with him in a calm, compassionate manner that will allow him to relax and sleep. My walking meditation happens now in the middle of the night, as I walk in slow circles around the living room feeling the wool rug on my bare feet and my son breathing in my arms.

When I put him to sleep and rest next to him, I find myself contemplating the teachings of being a mother. The experience of impermanence is with me every moment these days as each moment brings new rewards and challenges. One second my son dances and spins in the living room, and the next moment he trips, bangs his knees and cries. I have a better understanding of the ways that parents, including the Buddha's parents, wish that they could protect their children from suffering. I have had to accept that despite my love and tireless effort, my son will not go through his life without pain, discomfort, and confusion.

In my experience as a psychotherapist, I find myself feeling similarly with my clients as I do with my son. I notice that many of my interventions with clients are designed to give them feelings that I also want my son to have. These include the ability to feel joy, connect with others, and find meaning, as well as the ability to constructively tolerate frustration, anger, disappointment, and inevitable suffering.

A recent client, who I have been working with for the last two years, comes to mind. She has made significant changes in her life and continues to do so. This client is much more comfortable feeling her emotions freely without judging herself. She has developed a capacity to talk freely in the sessions, mindfully noticing and putting words to her impulses, thoughts, feelings, and sensations. Recently, she moved to a new city and has been developing her ideas regarding the career that she wants to pursue. Yet, she has struggled to find employment that matches her interests. During this transitional phase in her life, she has felt lonely, empty, discouraged, and somewhat hopeless. She struggles with the impulse of wanting to give up her pursuit of the employment that she wants.

In the current absence of daily routine and disconnection from her previous community, she felt alone. She described her thoughts as being magnified and consuming; she was more aware than ever of her hyper-critical, aggressive thoughts that she directs toward herself when she feels stressed. She resonated with the idea that, at times, it is as though she is in a cave on a forced meditation retreat. In sessions, she practiced mindfulness by attuning to her thoughts and feelings, even though she found it painful and difficult to do so in moments. She was learning to be more aware of her negative introjects, studying how she judges herself and how she wants to avoid the part of her that criticizes herself harshly. As she remained with the process of observing and describing the painful feelings and the negative thoughts that she has the impulse to push away, she developed a stronger capacity to tolerate the stress without allowing

17. Mothering the Moment 311

it to influence her as deeply. Even though outwardly she continued to struggle with finding the employment that she wants, inwardly she was developing a stronger capacity to accept her feelings without acting on impulses. My hope for her is that the capacity to mindfully tolerate the difficult feelings with equanimity will translate into her being persistent and patient as she pursues her career interests.

I notice that I want to provide a safe structure, a facilitating environment, for the client to feel comfortable to grow and change as she wants (Winnicott, 1963). I encourage her to talk freely, to notice her inhibitions to talk, to problem solve the obstacles that prevent her from having what she wants in her life, and to be an advocate on her own behalf. In our sessions, we both practice mindfulness. I practice mindfulness to study the impulses, thoughts and feelings that I experience with this client so that I am genuinely influenced and guided by her in the treatment. She practices mindfulness by observing and nonjudgmentally describing her thoughts, feelings, impulses, and sensations in my presence. Mindfulness creates opportunities for the treatment to generalize to other parts of her life. If she can speak comfortably and collaboratively with me, expressing a wide range of feelings in this relationship, then she can do so with others. If she can help me to help her get what she wants from the treatment, then she will likely be encouraged to manifest what she wants in her life.

Mindfulness

The practice of mindfulness may include sitting meditation, walking meditation, and conscious observation and description of daily activities (Gyatso, 2005; Linehan, 1993; Trungpa, 1976). Practicing mindfulness supports the brain to become more emotionally regulated and generally more optimistic (Siegal, 2007). Many scholars and teachers believe that the *Satipatthāna-sutta, the setting-up of mindfulness*, is perhaps the most important discourse given by the Buddha (Rahula, 1974). In this text, meditation is not seen as an activity separate from life, but connected with our daily activities, our thoughts and emotions, and our interactions with others (Gyatso, 2005; Rahula, 1974).

From the earliest known Buddhist texts, the Pali word *sati* and the Sanskrit word *smti* are usually translated into English as mindfulness. Sati and smti do not imply a passive position, but are understood as an engaged activity, the action of being mindful. Mindfulness is pre-symbolic and occurs underneath or before our cognitive and affective relationships with phenomena (Guranatana, 2001). Mindfulness is the foundation for meditation (Naht Hahn, 1975).

In most forms of Buddhism, a student usually begins meditation practice with shamata (Sanskrit) or the awareness of in and out breathing (Trungpa, 2005). Shamata encourages the foundation for a calm and receptive mind. When one's thoughts wonder, one brings attention back to the breath. The four foundations of mindfulness are used to develop one's awareness of the body, feelings, mental states, and objects of thoughts. Trungpa (2005) suggested that this practice "triggers an entirely new state of consciousness and brings us back automatically to mindfulness of breathing or a general sense of being" (p. 35), and this presence of mind "implies a process of intelligent alertness" (p. 36). Depending on the tradition and the instruction of the teacher, contemplation of the four foundations of mindfulness can be done during meditation and/or as part of post meditation study that could be viewed as meditation-in-action. Post meditation is actually still meditation: the experience of sitting on the cushion is generalized into the details of one's whole life.

Mindfulness practice assists mothers to be present and aware of thoughts, feelings, moods, and physical sensations. Thich Naht Hanh (1975) suggested that,

> mindfulness is at the same time a means and an end, the seed and the fruit. When we practice mindfulness in order to build up concentration, mindfulness is a seed. But mindfulness itself is the life of awareness: the presence of mindfulness means the presence of life and therefore mindfulness is also the fruit. Mindfulness frees us of forgetfulness and dispersion and makes it possible to live fully each minute of life. Mindfulness enables us to live. (pp. 14-15)

Mindfulness helps mothers more effectively attune to their children. If mothers engage in mindfulness practice, they will be more likely to modulate their emotional experiences and help their children be emotionally modulated as well. The transmission of compassion and equanimity from psychotherapist to client and mother to child occurs through the process of attunement, purposeful misattunement, and the repair of purposeful misattunements.

The process of mindfully mothering an infant parallels the experience of conducting psychotherapy. As Winnicott indicated, the mothering experience likely reflects many aspects of psychotherapy:

> My thesis is that what we do in therapy is to attempt to imitate the natural process that characterizes the behavior of any mother of her own infant. If I am right, it is the mother-infant couple that can teach us the basic principles on which we may base our therapeutic work. (as cited in Margolis, 1987, pp. 163-164)

In effective psychotherapy, the psychotherapist becomes attuned to the needs of the client. Attunement means to be attentive and mindful of the physiological, emotional, and cognitive processes occurring for the other in the relationship. In parenting, the mother creates an environment that

17. Mothering the Moment

provides optimal levels of stimulation: the mother does not overstimulate or understimulate the child. In clinical work, the psychotherapist modulates the intensity of the treatment to help the client experience emotional regulation. Mindfulness allows interactions to occur that prevent impingement or neglect, thus creating optimal levels of stimulation.

A contemplative approach to psychotherapy means that the psychotherapist practices awareness of the present moment for the purpose of creating genuine and compassionate responses that elicit the client's experience of basic goodness (Trungpa, 1987). In a sense, basic goodness involves choosing not to judge self or others in terms of being bad or good, but rather to be open and willing to develop more understanding of one's experience. Immediacy, being attuned to and present in the moment, is a fundamental component of contemplative psychotherapy that is born from mindfulness practice. Trungpa Rinpoche (1987) suggested that,

> The Buddhist viewpoint emphasizes the impermanence and the transitoriness of things. The past is gone, and the future has not yet happened, so we work with what is here: the present situation.... A fresh living situation is actually taking place all the time, on the spot. (p. 13)

Attuned responses, generated by mindfulness, offer an environment that engenders individuals to have new experiences, fresh insights, and a sense of aliveness that contributes to creative exploration. In addition, mindfulness practice increases the capacity to tolerate a wide range of feelings. The ability to tolerate emotions without clinging to judgment genuinely teaches individuals to feel more comfortable with emotional experiences and engenders a sense of freedom to respond to difficult situations spontaneously and with ease.

Tolerating Feelings as a Mother and Transmitting Emotional Regulation

The foundation for emotional regulation and secure attachment between a mother and her child stems from the mother's capacity to adapt and attune to her child's maturational needs. Mindfulness practice supports the mother's ability to tolerate her emotions so that she accurately interprets her child's internal states. The more accurately a mother can sense her child's internal process, the more likely she will respond well to his needs for love, care, boundaries, attention, and nurturance. Siegel (2007) suggested that,

> When relationships between parent and child are attuned, a child is able to feel felt by a caregiver and has a sense of stability in the present moment. During that here-and-now interaction, the child

> feels good, connected, and loved. The child's internal world is seen with clarity by the parent, and the parent comes to resonate with the child's state. This is attunement. (p. 27)

Mindfulness practice gives the mother a fundamental ability to attune with her child emotionally and mentally so that she can enjoy the loving times and so that she can effectively manage the challenging and more difficult times that arise as well.

Projective Identification

The mothering experience involves many challenges. Mothers and psychotherapists are susceptible to absorbing a wide range of the infant's and the client's emotions, many of which may be very difficult to tolerate. These overwhelming feelings may include the unexpectedly sudden and powerful manifestation of aggressive, anxious, and guilty emotions. Melanie Klein (1975) identified an early defensive response that infants use to manage primitive emotional states as *projective identification*. Projective identification may be understood as a defense that an infant uses to manage emotions that are overwhelming to his limited ability to digest aggressive and anxious states. The infant becomes overwhelmed with emotions and unconsciously projects these feelings into the mothering parent to hold and metabolize for him:

> Much of the hatred against parts of the self is now directed towards the mother. This leads to a particular form of identification which establishes the prototype of an aggressive object-relation. I suggest for these processes the term 'projective identification.' When projection is mainly derived from the infant's impulse to harm or to control the mother, he feels her to be a persecutor... as far as the ego is concerned the excessive splitting off and expelling into the outer world of parts of itself considerably weakens it. (Klein, 1975 p. 8)

The mothering parent and the psychotherapist must be able to tolerate and process the noxious emotions that are projected onto them in order to provide a regulated response.

Klein (1975) also indicated that projective identification may not be limited only to negative emotions. An infant uses a mother and a client uses a psychotherapist as the container of the self for both positive and negative self experiences until an individual is capable of containing these emotional states autonomously,

> It is, however, not only the bad parts of the self which are expelled and projected, but also the good parts of the self... The projection of good feelings and good parts of the self into the mother is

essential for the infant's ability to develop good object-relations and to integrate his ego. (pp. 8-9)

Projective identification serves as a container for the infant's undigestible emotions, positive or negative. This emotional containment allows the infant to develop a coherent, integrated sense of self. A difficulty regarding projective identification is that often, since it is an unconscious process, the recipient is unaware of the identification with these feelings and imagines that the aggressive, anxious, jealous, guilty emotions belong to them rather than to the infant or the client.

If the mothering parent is mindful and conscious of projective identification, the feelings can be digested effectively and tolerated so that the infant and the client may be protected from feelings that would be potentially disorganizing and dysregulating. The mother takes on the difficult emotions in order to function as a regulating mechanism for the baby who is not ready to regulate these feelings on his own, "the primary caregiver, acts as an external psychobiological regulator of the *experience-dependent* growth of the infant's nervous system" (Schore, 2003a, p. 5). If a mother is unable to tolerate and metabolize these feelings, she may become dysregulated by the emotions and be unable to serve as a regulating function for the baby. This dysregulation on the mother's part may create dysregulation and disorganization for the infant; subsequently, the infant may become overwhelmed with aggressive and anxious impulses and have little ability to manage these feelings. This experience may result in ongoing situations where the child is easily triggered by stressors and has minimal internal insulation to protect him from the difficulties encountered in the environment. Without containment and regulation, an infant is exposed to potentially damaging states of dysregulation that may evolve into characterlogical, habitual patterns for responding to distress.

Emotional Regulation

The power of the emotions involved with mothering can be overwhelming at times, causing many mothers to feel anxious, hostile, and distressed. Many of the feelings that mothers contain are generated from the ejected and projected feelings of the infant. These feelings might be difficult for mothers to tolerate and digest. Yet, the mother's skillful ability to tolerate and metabolize the infant's unpleasant, negative affective states supports the healthy development of her child. Schore (2003a), in address this, summarizes Demos and Kaplan: "Infant research now suggests that the baby becomes attached to the modulating caregiver who expands opportunities for positive affect and minimizes negative affect" (p. 8). For many mothers, affective states are more easily modulated when they incorporate moments of mindfulness into their daily activities. In addition to cultivating mindfulness, avenues to physically and emotionally discharge the projected affective states may be useful as well, such as exercise, writing, supervision, personal treatment, and talking with friends.

The critical issue for mothering is that the infant's ability to regulate emotional states depends on the mother's ability to stay regulated and to effectively manage the intensity of the feelings. The mother serves as a buffer to provide discrimination regarding levels of stimulation. The result of a mother modulating these affective states is that the infant develops the capacity to tolerate feelings in relation to others and learns to repair emotional and relational disruptions that may occur,

> If attachment is interactive synchrony, stress is defined as an *asynchrony* in an interactional sequence, and, following this, a period of reestablished *synchrony* allows for stress recovery. The mother and infant thus dyadically negotiate a stressful state transition. Infant resilience emerges from the child and parent's transitioning from positive to negative and back to positive affect. Again, the key is the caregiver's capacity to monitor and regulate her own arousal levels. (Schore, 2003a, p. 77)

As the mother provides the child with an emotionally modulated, holding environment (Winnicott, 1960), the child develops an internal sense for managing emotional states effectively with others. The early object relationship with the mother likely provides the foundation for how the child will regulate emotional intensity in relationships through out his life.

The Good Enough Mother

D. W. Winnicott (1958, 1960, 1971) provided a bridge for many Western Buddhist therapists. His idea that the psychotherapy process parallels the mother-child dyad in which each interconnects with the others' psychic world is in line with contemplative psychotherapy. The mother and psychotherapist must stay aware of the child or client's developmental needs and avoid *idiot compassion*, compassion that is born out of self-interest but that appears superficially to be "generous and impersonal" (Trungpa, 1994, p. 29) to further the maturational process. Winnicott (1971) suggested that attuned relationships involve participants that are sensitive, fluid, changing, comfortable with aloneness, yet interconnected. In his view, normal childhood development consisted of a series of transitions that move the child from completely bonded with the mother towards individuation.

Winnicott (1960) suggested that when a baby is first born, the baby does not exist as an individual. He only identified the baby within the context of the *nursing couple*, as a unit with the mother. In a departure from Melanie Klein's work, Winnicott was the first theoretician within the British Psychoanalytic Society to emphasize the importance of the

17. Mothering the Moment

facilitating environment (1960). Winnicott viewed the facilitating environment as a holding container, provided by the mothering one that adapts to meet the infant's maturational needs.

Winnicott (1960) referred to *the holding phase* as the container for the infant's experience of *absolute dependence*. He suggested that healthy development constituted a human being's ability to differentiate and become fully independent; however, he indicated that this was an ongoing lifelong process. In the initial stage of infancy, he proposed that the infant experiences a state of *Not Me* (1960). This Not Me state requires that the infant have no experience of self and that the infant be unintegrated. The infant experiences bare awareness with no sense of self or other. When my son was first born, he was vulnerable, open and easily molded into his surrounding environment: a shoulder, arms, or his crib. He appeared to be living fully in the pre-skandha world: basic ground, basic awareness (Trungpa, 2005), or bare awareness (Winnicott, 1971). During this phase, the infant is entirely dependent upon the mother's ability to adapt to the infant's needs. The mother must meet the needs of the infant in an attuned, knowing manner to create synchrony in the nursing couple. From the Buddhist view, dependence is actually interdependence, viewed only from the subjective discrete point of view. In fact, there is a dance between mother and child, moments of attunement and misattunement.

Winnicott (1958) described the mother during this time as having a *maternal preoccupation* with her infant. I know that during the first three months of my son's life, I experienced this preoccupation as my awareness of the world shrunk into a dyad. During those months, it was difficult to find time to shower, to do laundry, and sometimes even to eat. I was highly preoccupied with being with my baby and responding attentively to his needs. Mainly we rocked, nursed, and slept as a nursing couple. The outside world was difficult to engage during that time as I felt consumed with caring for his early maturational needs.

During the state of *relative dependence*, the infant begins to experience the sense of *I Am* and begins to separate from the mother. Winnicott (1960) indicated that at this time, the infant experiences himself or herself as a separate object from the mother and begins to realize that he or she is dependent on the mother. Inevitably, the mother creates "minor failures in adaptation" that cause her to become the *good enough mother* (p. 87). As the mother fails to provide total adaptation to the child's needs, the child experiences anger, aggression, and a sense of omnipotence. The infant, experiencing himself and his mother as discrete, becomes angry at her for not meeting his needs.

Winnicott (1960) argued that the infant may use the anger, if channeled constructively, to strive toward living and creating. He did not associate this anger with a destructive drive. Rather, he believed that tolerance for aggression fueled the infant forward in life. The infant learns that he can signal the mother to meet his needs. This creates a sense of omnipotence, the sense that he created the breast that appears to feed him; however, Winnicott indicated that if the mother does not create minor failures in adaptation, the infant cannot experience anger at the object and subsequently, does not experience the self as omnipotent. If the mother is remiss in creating minor failures of adaptation to the infant's needs, in other words if the mother over-gratifies the infant, Winnicott indicated that the child could experience the offering of the breast as an impingement in the environment.

> Often the child's growing up corresponds quite accurately with the mother's resumption of her own independence, and you would agree that a mother who cannot gradually fail in this matter of sensitive adaptation is failing in another sense; she is failing (because of her own immaturity or her own anxieties) to give her infant reasons for anger. (Winnicott, 1963, p. 87)

Winnicott (1963) indicated that impingements were healthy as long as the mother was good enough at meeting her infant's environmental needs. If the mother created impingements that interfered with the child's development, these impingements were identified as dangerous: "Negatively speaking, severe early deprivation or impingement shatters the infant's global or basic trust and consequently obstructs the infant's constitutional capacities that organize body-me-caregiver representations into a relatively coherent self-structure" (as cited in LaMothe, 2000, p. 359). This brings to light the unnecessary debate between having a functioning self as seen in self psychology with the skills of impulse control, reality testing, and problems solving (Bocknek, 1992; Hartmann, 1939; Kohut, 1977) and the Buddhist idea of egolessness. In fact both exist: a Western relative self that organizes each unique, human experience and the Buddhist view of the absence of a separate, unconditioned ego. The relative self creates forms to endure the uneasiness and uncertainty of groundless, yet interconnected, experience. As a mother, I have been pulled into the relative view, perhaps in conjunction with my son's development of both Western and Eastern ideas of ego. A good enough mother inevitably has to support the development of both forms of ego, for it appears to me that my son must function in the relative as a base from which to experience the absolute.

The good enough mother is not overly attuned all the time; if the mother tries to be perfectly attuned and therefore, extremely permissive with a child, this may result in overstimulation and overgratification. The good enough mother creates a safe environment that allows the child to explore. She provides enough experiences of attunement so that the child is able to depend on her for support in becoming regulated. This mother provides more positive than negative experiences, but as the child matures, she fails to meet her child's needs some of the time.

My son and I were in a toy store the other day and I heard a mother asking her two year old son if they could leave the store to go grocery shopping. The two year old replied, "No." The mother responded with, "Well, do you think we could go grocery shopping soon?" This is an example of an impingement because the mother is overgratifying her child and allowing him to have more omnipotence than is appropriate. A purposefully misattuned response to the child and a *minor failure of adaptation* would be, "We are going to the grocery store and I know that this is hard for you. Maybe you could play with a toy on the way over to the store." The parent would still be validating her child's feelings and offering him an alternative, regulating activity, while also taking care of her own needs.

Parents might engage in impingements throughout the child's development, sometimes into adolescence and even adulthood. The transition from adolescence to young adulthood is an extremely challenging time. I am providing family therapy with a young adult and her mother as they navigate this transitional time. In the mother's family, historically, her parents encouraged her to be dependent on them for financial and emotional support. This mother has successfully tolerated her impulses when she feels induced to become overly involved in her daughter's life financially or emotionally. She has been intentionally aware and mindful of her impulses to engage in historical, transgenerational repetitions that would interfere with her daughter's independent growth. The mother has tolerated her grief regarding the loss of her daughter's dependence on her. The daughter has since successfully secured employment and is managing her own financial responsibilities very well. Although the daughter struggled to secure employment and make the leap toward independence, she did so nevertheless. In this case, the mother avoided creating reenactments that would impinge on her daughter's current maturational needs.

Winnicott (1958) addressed the issue of reparation as a vital component to the infant's development. He indicated that the child's tolerance of aggression and rage toward the mother for not meeting his needs immediately was important in the development of concern for others, "In ego-id terms the sense of guilt is very little more than anxiety with a special quality, anxiety felt because of the conflict between love and hate. Guilt-sense implies tolerance of ambivalence" (p. 16). He stated that the child and the mother experience hate for each other. Through learning that the infant can ruthlessly hate his mother and have fantasies of annihilation that do not ultimately destroy her, he learns to tolerate his aggression. Through tolerance of aggression, Winnicott indicated that the child learns to create reparative experiences in relationship.

> At what is called the depressive position the infant is not so much dependent on the mother's simple ability to hold a baby, which was her characteristic at the earlier stages, as on her ability to

> hold the infant-care situation over a period of time during which the infant may go through complex experiences. If time is given – a few hours maybe – the infant is able to work through the results of an instinctual experience. The mother being still here, is able to be ready to receive and to understand if the infant has the natural impulse to give or to repair... Gradually as the infant finds out that the mother survives and accepts the restitutive gesture, so the infant becomes able to accept responsibility for the total fantasy of the full instinctual impulse that was previously ruthless. (1958, p. 23)

This reparative experience teaches the child to have guilt; therefore, Winnicott indicated that if the child experiences guilt, he experiences concern for others and develops a sense of morality and empathy. From the Buddhist perspective, the reparative experience can be seen as a fresh start, a dropping of storyline. Through being in the moment with attunement, the mother and child can move forward, with the child learning the essential tasks of empathy and compassion towards others.

Schore (2003a) suggested that during the second year of life, the mother provides socialization experiences that induce feelings of shame in the toddler. Schore stated, "Shame represents this rapid state transition from a preexisting positive state to a negative state" (p. 17). The toddler's experience of shame teaches the child how to interact empathically and respectfully in interactions with others. Schore proposed that the mother teaches the child through limit setting and feedback designed to regulate excitement states that may be experienced by the toddler as a misattunement. The primary concern regarding this interactional misattunement is that the mother is able to help the child recover emotionally from the shame, to shift from the negative emotional state back to a more positive affective state. Schore stated,

> In this essential pattern of 'disruption and repair,' the 'good enough' caregiver who induces a stress response in her infant through misattunement, reinvokes in a timely fashion her psychobiologically attuned regulation of the infant's negative affect state that she has triggered. (p. 19)

In order for the mother to provide this repair to the relational disruption, the mother must be able to communicate emotionally to the child that she can tolerate his or her rageful feelings and negative affective states. She must give the child the feeling that she can withstand the expression of negative affective states without retaliation. The mother emotionally communicates her ability to tolerate the child's wide range of affective states by staying regulated and responsive to the child's needs as well as by validating the child's emotional experience. This provides the child with the ability to tolerate what arises for him or her; it teaches the child to be with relative reality as it is.

At the 2007 American Group Psychotherapy Conference, Una McCluskey discussed the importance of *purposeful misattunements* in a workshop titled, "Identifying the Instinctive Behavioral Attachment Systems." Purposeful misattunements are used by the mother to increase or decrease emotional arousal. Schore (2003) addressed a similar idea when he discussed the method that mothers use to socialize children in the second year of life by misattuning to their excitement states and inducing feelings of shame. For example, now that my son is coordinated and strong enough to walk and chase our family dog, he can catch the dog grab his hair and pull very hard. My son enjoys this behavior; however, he is not seeing this enjoyment mirrored back in my facial expression. Instead, he likely sees a look of disgust and concern on my face while he is also hearing that this behavior is unacceptable because it hurts our dog. My negative affect is a purposeful misattunement that I use to communicate to him what is considered unacceptable behavior.

In terms of absolute dependence, Winnicott (1960) viewed the infant's ego as unintegrated; in terms of relative dependence, Winnicott indicated that the process of ego integration occurs as the infant develops the capacity for *I Am* experiences while learning to tolerate ambivalence toward the mothering one. The infant learns to tolerate ambivalence by experiencing the environmental mother as present and attuned even while the infant is enraged with the object mother. The mothering one does not act reactively against the child by denying environmental needs punitively, but rather can hold the environment while being hated ruthlessly. This allows for the process of reparation to occur and for the infant to tolerate feelings of hate without internalizing the feelings against the self.

The final phase of Winnicott's (1960) developmental approach was known as *towards independence*. Winnicott thought that the towards independence phase was the process toward maturity. Ideally, human beings become better ego integrated and the process of intellectual development is refined. Winnicott suggested that no one ever reaches a state of total individuation, but rather progresses toward states of interconnection, openness to the experience of others, fluidity, and impermanence. Through the development of a mature Western ego, one is better able to understand and tolerate the Buddhist view of the progression toward the absence of ego.

Tolerating Aloneness and the Facilitating Environment
Winnicott (1958) suggested that the capacity to be alone in the presence of another is a critical component of the development of emotional maturity. Winnicott (1963) proposed that the mother creates a facilitating environment for the child when she is able to adapt to the child's maturational needs. One of these needs within the overall

facilitating environment, according to Winnicott (1958), is for the mother to attend to the child while at the same time leaving the infant alone to experience his or her impulses,

> The individual who has the capacity to be alone is constantly able to rediscover the personal impulse, and the personal impulse is not wasted because the state of being alone is something which (though paradoxically) always implies that someone else is there. (p. 34)

Winnicott suggested that in a healthy facilitating environment, a child will ingest the mother's protective, nurturing, and attuned presence and be able to always have the sense that she is with him or her, even when she is not there physically. The child is capable of discovering his or her own personal impulses, and therefore a sense of an autonomous self, when feeling safe enough and regulated enough to manage his or her environment. The child will be able to manage his or her environment more easily after digesting the *introjected mother*.

Creating a facilitating environment for my seventeen month old son means that I engage with him in what Winnicott (1958) referred to as only minor failures to adaptation. Mindfulness assists me in being aware of my impulses instead of repetitively reacting to them. If I can tolerate my own experience of aloneness, I am comfortable enough with allowing my son to have his own internal and external experiences. Epstein (1998), referring to Winnicott, stated that,

> [The mother] must also be able to leave her child alone. This leaving alone does not mean ignoring, nor does it necessarily mean physically, or literally, looking away. An infant, after all, has to be attended to almost constantly. Leaving alone means allowing a child to have her own experience, whether alone or when feeding, bathing, or being held. When suspended in the matrix of the parent-child relationship, a child is free to explore, to venture into new territory, both within herself and without. This freedom to explore while held within the safety net of the parent's benign presence develops into the capacity to be alone. (pp. 17-18)

Creating a facilitating environment for my son means that I make responsive choices, instead of reacting from habitual thinking, feeling, or behavioral patterns. I use mindfulness to avoid unconsciously discharging my fears and worries through interactions with him that might interfere with his development.

Sometimes, I find myself worrying that I am not attuned enough or present enough with my son. I worry that because I work hard during the week and my son is with a babysitter, I am not a good enough mother. Mostly, though, I feel comforted by the idea of the good enough mother. I feel comforted that I do not need to be perfectly attuned to my son at all times and that some misattunement, or failure on my part, actually helps him develop stress tolerance. I am mindful with myself, when I worry, that it is not in his best interest for me to be overly gratifying and never frustrating. The important message that I take from Winnicott (1958) is that if my son was consistently learning to react to a pattern of failures on my part, then I would be truly failing him. Sometimes when I am feeling distressed, I soothe and regulate myself with these understandings that help me be present with how my life is, which is sometimes quite stressful, knowing that I am capable of constructing a facilitating environment that is good enough for my son's maturational needs.

    I am a beginner as a mother and therefore, I practice a willingness to be open to the experience of beginner's mind (Suzuki, 1970). Suzuki Roshi proposed that, "If your mind is empty, it is always ready for anything; it is open to everything. In the beginner's mind there are many possibilities; in the expert's mind there are few" (p. 21). This willingness to be in beginner's mind allows me to spontaneously and creatively meet my son's needs based on my intuitive, internal sense instead of on influences outside of me that may be viewed as expert. Following my internal sense and responding to him from beginner's mind allows me to be true to his experience so that I am attuned and capable of repairing misattunements based on his individual developmental needs. Motherhood means *polishing the tile*. Suzuki explained this idea in the retelling of the story of the teacher Nangaku and his student Baso:

> Nangaku asked, "What are you doing?" "I am practicing Zazen," Baso replied. "Why are you practicing Zazen?" "I want to attain enlightenment; I want to be a Buddha," the disciple said... So Nangaku picked up a tile and started to polish it. Baso asked, "What are you doing?" "I want to make this tile into a jewel," Nangaku said. "How is it possible to make a tile into a jewel?' Baso asked. "How is it possible to become a Buddha by practicing zazen" Nangaku replied.... "There is no Buddhahood besides your ordinary mind. When the cart does not go, which do you whip the cart or the horse?" (p. 80-81)

Being a mother or being a psychotherapist means whipping the horse, or working on oneself. I polish my tile of motherhood and my tile of psychotherapist. I realize that it is unnecessary to expect my son or my clients to become jewels. Whatever I do has the opportunity to be Zazen. Whether I am changing diapers or asking open ended questions, it is only through bringing awareness to each task, being open minded, and non-attached to expectations that I move along the path. In polishing the tile, I practice being a good enough mother.

Mindfulness and Mothering

As a mother, mindfulness practice has been helpful, although difficult to cultivate at times. Mindfulness practice assists me in being aware of my instincts and my intuition while also teaching me to let go of worries and fears regarding the future. Sometimes, I find myself feeling attached to ideas or fantasies that I have regarding future struggles or difficulties that take me out of the moment. I can feel a palpable difference in the quality of our bond when I am distracted by cooking dinner, straightening the house, or taking a phone call versus when I am just being with him.

The experience of just being with my son means that I follow him in his play. He guides me in the moment to respond playfully to whatever we might be doing together. When I am just being with him, our play tends to lack structure. We engage with ease. We are relaxed and all of our interactions flow from one state into another. He moves from one activity to the next and I respond to his exploration of opening and closing, finding shapes and colors, playing music, singing and dancing, and all sorts of imaginative games that we create together. He shifts into and out of various emotional states that include laughing, crying from a fall or a separation from someone he is close to, startle responses from a loud sound or a stranger approaching him too quickly, frustration at wanting to have or do something that he is not allowed to have or do, and intensely focusing on his current exploration. If I get attached to something that he has moved on from, our synchronicity is broken.

Practicing mindfulness helps me track disruptions in the interactions and allows me to reconnect with my son; however, mindfulness practice is not easy to do when feeling tired, distracted by something work related, making dinner, talking with my husband, and generally attending to the daily needs of myself, my family, and my house. Multitasking, the bane of most women and a basic component to managing day to day responsibilities, breaks the moment to moment connection. I notice that when I am distracted with the many tasks required of daily functioning as a working mother, I find myself feeling painfully separated from myself and my son.

Mindfulness practice allows me to be aware of this separation and assists me in being able to tolerate the feelings that arise while reconnecting with myself and my son. When I say that mindfulness is not always easy for me to cultivate, I mean that practicing mindfulness takes focus, attentiveness, and time. If I am feeling rushed due to a lack of time to prepare dinner or get out of the house in the morning, it is not easy to relax, be present in the moment, and follow the flow of my son's play. I have a friend whose Buddhist teacher insisted that she make time in her day for a formal sitting practice. She was a single mother of two children and simply could not do it. The teacher continued to press her to make time and told her she was resisting her practice; however, the reality of the woman's day made it impossible at that time in her life to do a formal practice. Instead, she found ways to weave the practice into the moments while she was interacting with her children, doing the dishes, transporting her kids, and making dinner. I have had a similar experience to my friend.

The majority of my mindfulness practice is meditation-in-action. I am noticing and being with the emotions and thoughts that arise as I go throughout my day; sitting with a client, feeding my son, and welcoming my husband home after a work day. It is hard not to resort to my habitual, repetition compulsions, particularly when I am sleep deprived and struggling over worries and day to day stressors. A dialectical behavior therapy skill that I use frequently is *turning the mind* (Linehan, 2000). In each moment that I am aware of, I practice turning my mind so that I am conscious of what is happening inside of me and in my environment. In this way, my daily responsibilities become the opportunities to practice moment to moment mindfulness.

I find that when I stay in the moment, it helps not only in my interactions with my son, but also with my husband and my clients. A good friend came for a visit recently and stayed with my family. It was a chaotic time in our day to day lives as my husband and I were balancing work, time together as a family, and maintaining the household responsibilities. She commented that she imagined that it would be easy to discharge the tensions that we take in from caring for our son on each other. This comment resonated with me as I think that many of the disagreements that my husband and I have stem from tensions that we are holding as parents. This reminded me of the importance of being mindful with my whole family, not only my son. I think that the projective identifications that my husband and I take in may be discharged on each other sometimes. We must remain aware of how we are metabolizing our aggressive and hostile feelings. When I am capable of being mindful, I am conscious of the ways that I am discharging my tension and I make choices regarding how I want to respond to everyone in my environment.

Practicing mindfulness also assists me in being more comfortable in my experience of aloneness (Trungpa, 1976). Mindfulness results in me being more aware of my fears, my sadness, and my painful attachments. Becoming a mother increased my sense of vulnerability regarding aloneness and the importance of letting go of a false hope for control. A friend of mine became a mother several years before me; I remember her saying that mothering created the strongest feelings of vulnerability that she had ever felt. Becoming attached to fears and vulnerabilities has the potential to interfere with allowing my son to develop, what Winnicott (1958) referred to as, the child's *capacity to be alone*.

As a mother, I practice effectively managing my anxieties, worries, and fears that often stem from my fear of being alone. The ways that I have created enmeshments, meaning ways that I lose myself in my husband or my son, become apparent in the places where I interfere with my husband's personal choices or my son's personal choices. The more that I can be conscious of staying with myself by being true to my feelings, even if I am annoyed, worried, or saddened by something that they might do, the more I can give them the freedom to be who they are and do what they want to do. When I am acting from enmeshment and attachment, I am trying to get them to do what I want because of some cognitive judgment or anxiety I am feeling.

For example, a friend of mine has a son who plays baseball. She talked about how she struggles with what she wants him to do: take the game seriously, play his hardest so that he does his best for the team, and really engage in the games and practices. Her son on the other hand, wants to play baseball, but he does not really care if he wins or loses. He is most comfortable enjoying himself with his friends, laughing, and joking around. He does not take the game that seriously. For my friend to disengage from an enmeshment with him, she has to choose to accept her emotions genuinely as her own without trying to influence how he decides to play. In my view, personal choices encompass any behaviors, thoughts, or choices that do not cause danger or are not destructive for others. Being mindful assists me when I am stuck on trying to influence another's behavior instead of taking responsibility for myself and caring for myself.

Psychotherapy and Contemplative Considerations

Objective Countertransference

Psychotherapists may share similar feelings with mothers given that objective countertransference, exchange, and projective identification cause psychotherapists to absorb intense and challenging emotions. Objective countertransference occurs when a psychotherapist is induced either into a client's emotional experience (concordant) or into the emotional experience that others in a client's life experience in relation to him (complimentary; Racker, 1968; Zeisel, 2007). This means that a psychotherapist may be induced into feelings that others experience when interacting with a client. Usually, countertransference involves some form of a repetition compulsion that is reenacted in the transferential relationship. A repetition compulsion arises when the client unconsciously recreates early object relational interactions with the desire to experience a sense of resolution and potentially a progressive response to old, painful and uncomfortable feelings. Often, the compulsion to repeat generates the old, habitual reactions rather than the new experiences that are sought after.

The Dalia Lama (Gyatso, 2005) described a similar repetition: "Buddhism teaches that we actually conspire in the causes and conditions that create our unhappiness and are often reluctant to engage in activities that could lead to more long-lasting happiness" (p. 148). In the transferential relationship, the repetition compulsion is often unconsciously reenacted by the therapist and the client leading to the reoccurrence of painful, early experiences,

> The therapist who misattunes and is subsequently unable to recorrect will thus project the unregulated state back, further stressing the working alliance. The patient who receives an unmodulated stressful communication now becomes, as a repetition of his/her early history, further psychophysiologically dysregulated by the misattuning object. (Schore, 2003b, p. 86)

If a psychotherapist is unable to be conscious of the induction to create a transferential reenactment, then the client is at risk for being further damaged by the repetition of an old experience.

Trunga Rinpoche (2005) suggested that habitual patterns can be easily loosened and shifted if one can be attentive to the present moment and the immediacy of interactions. He proposed that,

> you can let go of your habitual patterns and then when you let go, you genuinely let go. You do not recreate or rebuild another shell immediately afterward. Once you let go you do not just start all over again. Egolessness is having the trust to not rebuild again at all, and experiencing the psychological healthiness and freshness that goes with not rebuilding. (p. 11)

Consistent mindfulness practice on the psychotherapist's part provides a nonjudgmental, compassionate holding environment for the client to gain comfort with sensing habitual patterns. As the client develops the capacity to sense the habitual patterns, the client may also become more at ease with letting go of the attachments to these habitual ways of reacting. New responses to chronic patterns can occur in the therapeutic relationship when the psychotherapist engages in interactive immediacy. For fresh, immediate experiences to occur in the transference, the psychotherapist is mindful of the unconscious patterns and responds differently than the original objects by relating cooperatively with spontaneous, progressive, and emotional communications.

Progressive Emotional Communication

Spotnitz (2004), the father of Modern Psychoanalysis, implied that the psychoanalyst's use of emotional communications in the transferential relationship "[helps] the patient talk progressively, rather than repetitively" (p. 180). In essence, Spotnitz's treatment approach supports the psychoanalyst's use of emotional communications that speak directly to the unconscious. These emotional communications help clients work through resistances so that they may choose to engage in new behaviors and new relational approaches. Both the psychoanalyst and the client engage in progressive emotional communication. The psychoanalyst uses emotional communications that offer new responses to the client's unconscious, habitually reactive behaviors so that the client may engage in progressive communications; in other words, the client begins to speak a new language. When the client engages in progressive communications, the client is responding rather than only unconsciously reacting in habitual manners.

Since a client's resistance to progressive communication tends to be unconscious, the most effective treatment approaches are those that relate directly with the client's unconscious and immediate experience. The use of classical psychoanalytic interpretations will likely be least effective in assisting the resolution of resistances since interpretations access the logical and insight oriented, more conscious parts of the client's brain (Schore, 2003b). Winnicott (1963) implied that interpretations could be experienced by clients as impingements that interfere with progress. In order to access the unconscious, implicit, and more emotionally driven parts of the brain, the modern psychoanalyst engages the client through emotional communications that speak directly to the unconscious. The modern psychoanalyst attunes to the emotions induced by the client to sense the responses that will synchronize with the client's maturational needs. In *Just Say Everything: A Festschrift in Honor of Hyman Spotnitz*, a contributor, Harold Davis (1991), stated,

> So the degree to which Dr. Spotnitz shocks and surprises us is a direct measure of how much new information he is giving us about our unconscious thoughts and feelings. Of course this is what all analysts are supposed to be able to do – interpret the unconscious. But the way Dr. Spotnitz does this has a special impact because he makes his interpretations in the direct language of the unconscious. (p. 89)

Direct communication with the unconscious involves a dialogue between the psychoanalyst's right brain and the client's right brain. For these direct communications to be truly helpful, the psychoanalyst is mindful of the genuine feelings induced by this client and responds to the client spontaneously in the moment.

In my training analysis, my modern psychoanalyst has engaged in many spontaneous interactions that shocked and struck my unconscious, implicit, right brain experience. One experience stands out as particularly shocking. After a few years into treatment, my analyst asked me a question. My response was, "I don't know." She subsequently stated in an angry tone, "I don't know means 'Go to hell.'" She mobilized the anger that was being enacted silently by my not talking. This intervention helped me continue to talk in new ways. My psychoanalyst's emotional communication encouraged me to work through a resistance to not talking progressively. She got me talking and engaging in new treatment experiences.

Egolessness

Trungpa Rinpoche's (1987) description of the movement towards the state of egolessness correlates to the experience of progressive communication. Progressive emotional communications are spontaneous, genuine responses made by a psychotherapist that stem from objective countertransferential feelings, exchange, and projective identifications generated by immediacy in interactions. Trungpa indicated that, "Egolessness... lets the whole process of working with others be genuine and generous and free form" (p. 12). The psychotherapist practices knowing the habitual patterns of her mind so that she frees herself from these storylines. She can discriminate between what is a habitual reaction and what is new. In Buddhism, ego refers to the constricted view of self and others that forms through multiple conditions, such as one's life experiences. Winnicott (1960) used ego differently to refer to the development of an integrated self sense. These views are actually complimentary: one must first develop an integrated healthy ego in order to tolerate letting go without fragmenting into a psychotic or dysregulated state (personal communication, Danon Henri Roshi, December 21st, 2002). Egolessness does not mean the absence of a regulating self system, but rather the ability to exist beyond it.

Cultivating egolessness through meditation gives rise to compassion and supports the process of psychotherapy (Trungpa, 1987). If a psychotherapist offers a truly compassionate presence, then she creates a therapeutic environment that allows a client to be kind and open to his experiences as well. This nonjudgmental openness promotes a sense of freedom to explore and understand whatever arises genuinely in the treatment. Egolessness serves as a conduit for a psychotherapist to spontaneously generate progressive emotional communications in a therapeutic relationship. Egolessness allows a psychotherapist to be nonjudmentally receptive to the unconscious communications from a client that may inform a psychotherapist about how to respond most effectively in the moment. Progressive communications are effective responses because these communications help to shift a client out of habitual patterns and into new, fresh experiences that are based in the present rather than the past.

Psychotherapists benefit greatly from being mindful and aware of the multifaceted ways that clients induce emotions in the moment. These emotional inductions inform the psychotherapist about the client's early object relationships and how the client experienced these care givers. The problem for psychotherapists is not that inductions and countertransferential reactions occur; the problem for psychotherapists is that these reactions occur unconsciously. Mindfulness of these emotional inductions allows psychotherapists to ingest the feelings consciously in order to feed the feelings back to clients in ways that create new experiences. Supervision, one's own treatment, and a contemplative practice support the likelihood that a clinician will respond consciously, curiously, and compassionately in the transferential relationship.

Egolessness relates to this process in that the more conscious, a psychotherapist is, the less likely she will respond from an ego-oriented position. Trungpa (1987) proposed that,

> You can not have genuine sympathy with ego because that would mean that your sympathy would be accompanied by some kind of defense mechanisms. For example, you might try to refer everything back to your own territory when you work with someone, if your own ego is at stake. Ego interferes with direct communication, which is obviously essential to the therapeutic process. (p. 12)

Ego might also interfere with progressive communication. When clinician's react from an ego oriented state to the client's emotional inductions, a psychotherapist places both herself and her clients at risk for potentially damaging reenactments to occur.

Exchange

Exchange was mentioned earlier as a conduit for the psychotherapist to experience the client's emotions. Exchange differs from projective identification and objective countertransference in that exchange is a process that is going on in all interactions, beyond only transferential relationships, and involves a two way communication. The concept of exchange is grounded in the experience of oneness or interconnectedness. Karen Kissel Wegela (1996) suggested that,

> Exchange is not a technique, but a natural process. We all experience moments in which the distinction between self and other gets blurred… it is the sign of our basic connectedness. Exchange seems to happen whether we know about it or not. If we know about it, we can recognize it and make use of it in order to be of benefit to others. (p. 128)

A psychotherapist exchanges with the client while the client exchanges with the psychotherapist simultaneously. Given that exchange is ongoing, the psychotherapist has the potential to influence the client with compassion and basic goodness by offering an aware, nonjudgmental presence into the therapeutic relationship.

Mindfulness and Psychotherapy

In *The Mindful Brain*, Siegel (2007) suggested that the experience of mindfulness exists within brain states. He proposed that a mindful brain state is conducive for the process of attuned interconnecting and intrarelating. He indicated that executive brain functioning enters a state of *receptive awareness* when the brain is regulated emotionally. The receptive awareness state reflects a mind that is calm, open, nonjudgmental, and capable of being fully present with whatever arises:

> people can engage a more intentional state of mindful awareness in which they can be purposefully receptive, open to whatever arises in the moment. In this reflective state they can choose to engage their autobiographical memory stores, inviting whatever comes into awareness to come fully: Sensations, images, feelings, thoughts. In a mindful state we can SIFT through the mind's rim with intention and openness, ready to sort through anything that comes into our awareness. (Siegel, 2007, p. 133)

Siegel implied that if the client is mindfully present as they process past and current emotional states, the content that is being explored will be alive and experienced wholly in that moment. He stated that, "The healing that emerges with this reflective form of memory and narrative integration from a mindful exploration is deeply liberating" (p. 133). If the psychotherapist practices being intentionally aware of the process, this may support the client to experience immediacy as they process memories, life events, and past and current emotional encounters.

Mindfulness practice also assists the psychotherapist to be less impulsive and more able to inhibit reactions that might create damaging reenactments in the transference. Siegel (2007) suggested that mindfulness practice inhibits impulsivity. He stated, "In mindful awareness we can transition from being reactive to becoming receptive" (p. 127). The psychotherapist tracks her internal process without judging. Judgment interferes with understanding. If the psychotherapist is receptive to whatever arises in the treatment and is nonreactive to this process, the psychotherapist will develop a better understanding of who her client is and what her client's maturational needs are. If the psychotherapist becomes impulsive and unconsciously discharges unwanted thoughts, feelings and impulses, this may collude with the client's induction toward creating problematic reenactments. With a contemplative psychotherapy approach, the psychotherapist is receptive to who the client is as a whole person in the moment and responds with thoughtfulness and genuine emotion as the guides for intervention.

Conclusion

Attunement is a basic, foundational component of forming meaningful relationships. The mother attunes to her child's maturational needs by sensing who the child is from moment to moment and by providing a holding environment that matches her child's developmental states. The psychotherapist attunes to her client by sensing the client's emotional and mental states and by consciously and nonjudgmentally observing her own internal process. The psychotherapist's internal process guides her to better understand the nature of the client's internal experiences, his impulses, and his repetitions with others in his life.

Mindfulness practice provides a conduit for attunement to occur. The practice of mindfulness encourages the mother and the psychotherapist to become more comfortable with internal emotional, mental, and physical states that allows the mother and the psychotherapist to be more present and genuinely available with the child and the client. Attunement leads to the formation of emotional regulation and secure attachments. Emotionally regulated children are capable of modulating intense affective states and responding resiliently to stressful situations (Schore, 2003b). The ability to modulate internal emotional states encourages the process of connecting with others in meaningful, stable, satisfying, and reciprocal relationships.

In a sense, mindfulness practice sustains the process of becoming emotionally mature and individuated while also engendering a deeper, underlying connection with the self and others. To borrow from the work of Suzuki Roshi (1970), to view the mother and child, or psychotherapist and client, as *one* is the wrong understanding and to view them as *two* is also the wrong view. We are alone, but through mindfulness realize that we are connected.

References

Bocknek, G. (1992). *Ego and self in weekly psychotherapy.* New York: International Universities Press.

Davis, H. L. (1991). Harold L. Davis. In Sheftel, S. (Ed.), *Just say everything: A festschrift in honor of Hyman Spotnitz* (pp. 87-89). New York: Association for Modern Psychoanalysis.

Epstein, M. (1998). *Going to pieces without falling apart: A Buddhist perspective on wholeness.* New York: Broadway Books.

Gunaratana, B. H. (2001). *Eight mindful steps to happiness, walking the Buddha's path.* Boston: Wisdom Publications.

Gyatso, T. (2005). *The universe in a single atom.* New York: Morgan Road Books.

Gyatso, T. (2006). *The essential Gyatso: His important teachings.* New York: Penguin Press.

Hanh, T. N. (1975). *The miracle of mindfulness: An introduction to the practice of meditation.* Boston: Beacon Press.

Hartmann, H. (1939). *Ego psychology and the problem of adaptation.* New York: International Universities Press.

Klein, M. (1975). *The writings of Melanie Klein* (Volume III: Envy and gratitude and other works). New York: The Free Press.

Kohut, H. (1977). *The restoration of the self.* New York: International Universities Press.

LaMothe, R. (2000). The birth of reality: Psychoanalytic developmental considerations. *American Journal of Psychotherapy, 54* (3), 355-370.

Linehan, M. M. (1993). *Skills training manual for treating borderline personality disorder.* New York: The Guilford Press.

Margolis, B. (1987). Treatment and transition: Observations on modern pscyhoanalysis. *Modern Psychoanalysis, 12* (2), 163-177.

McCluskey, U. (2007, February). *Identifying the instinctive behavioral attachment systems.* Paper presented at the 64th meeting of the American Group Psychotherapy Association, Austin, TX.

Racker, H. (1968). *Transference and counter-transference.* New York: International Universities Press.

Rahula, W. (1974). *What the Buddha taught.* New York: Grove Weidenfeld.

Schore, A. N. (2003a). *Affect dysregulation and disorders of the self.* New York: W.W. Norton and Company.

Schore, A. N. (2003b). *Affect regulation and the repair of the self.* New York: W.W. Norton and Company.

Siegel, D. J. (2007). *The mindful brain: Reflection and attunement in the cultivation of well-being.* New York: W. W. Norton and Company.

Spotnitz, H. (2004). *Modern psychoanalysis of the schizophrenic patient: Theory of the technique.* New York: YBK Publishers.

Suzuki, S. (1970). *Zen mind, beginner's mind: Informal talks on Zen meditation and practice.* Boston: Weatherhill.

Trungpa, C. (1976). *The myth of freedom and the way of meditation.* Berkeley: Shambala.

Trungpa, C. (1987). The meeting of Buddhist and western psychology. *Journal of Contemplative Psychotherapy, 4,* 3-14.

Trungpa, C. (1994). *Illusion's game: The life and teaching of Naropa.* Boston: Shambhala.

Trungpa, C. (2005). *The sanity we are born with: A Buddhist approach to psychology.* Boston: Shambhala.

Wegela, K. K. (1996). *How to be a help instead of a nuisance: Practical approaches to giving support, service, and encouragement to others.* Boston: Shambala.

Winnicott, D. W. (1958). The capacity to be alone. In *D.W. Winniccott, The maturational processes and the facilitating environment* (pp. 29-36). New York: International Universities Press.

Winnicott, D. W. (1960). The theory of the parent-infant relationship. In *D. W. Winniccott, The maturational processes and the facilitating environment* (pp. 37-55). New York: International Universities Press.

Winnicott, D. W. (1963). A theory of psychiatric disorder. In *D.W. Winniccott, The maturational processes and the facilitating environment (pp. 230-241].* New York: International Universities Press.

Winnicott, D. W. (1971). *Playing and reality.* Middlesex, England: Penguin.
Zeisel, E. (Febuary, 2007). *The role of the therapist's theory on the development of group culture.* Paper presented at the 64th meeting of the American Group Psychotherapy Association, Austin, TX.

Part 4:
Talks

18

From Eros to Enlightenment[1]

Mark Epstein

My introduction to the teachings of the Buddha came during the summer of 1974 at Naropa Institute where I traveled between my junior and senior years of college. I was drawn to Naropa by the collection of celebrated faculty who seemed to represent the tail-end of the counterculture movement of the 1960s, a healthy mix of artists, poets, spiritual teachers, and personalities. I was looking for a topic for my senior thesis in psychology and already had the nascent notion that I might be able to write about Buddhist psychology although I knew very little about it. I approached classes at Naropa the way I had approached learning at other institutions: I took notes, listened to the teachers, and did my best to do my homework. While I learned a great deal, the actual practice of meditation was difficult for me to get a handle on.

I received help from some unexpected quarters, however. My roommates, assigned to me at random by Naropa, were a set of twins from Long Island who were early exponents of herbal remedies, naturopathy, and alternative medicine. Long before Andrew Weil had popularized any of this, my roommates were already amassing knowledge and information. Their bible was the book *Back to Eden* (Kloss, 1974). They looked askance at much of what was going on at Naropa that summer. They had disdain for the egos on parade in the name of egolessness and, after a while, they began to make early morning trips to Denver's wholesale fruit and vegetable market to load up on supplies. They watched me going from class to class trying to master meditation, occasionally chuckling to each other, until finally one of the twins pulled three oranges from a crate and offered to teach me to juggle. I was hooked and practiced until I could keep three oranges in the air with relative ease. Then I noticed something. My mind was still but awake; relaxed yet alert; effortlessly entered into the *way*. Meditation was suddenly alive for me and I began to listen to all of the words about it with new ears.

---

[1] Originally presented as paper at the *Buddhism and Psychotherapy Conference: Celebrating Thirty Years of Contemplative Psychotherapy* at Naropa University in May, 2006

Unintergration

Much later, as part of my training as a psychotherapist, I came upon the work of D. W. Winnicott. I was introduced to Winnicott by a psychoanalyst friend of mine, Emmanuel Ghent, a psychiatrist/musician who lived close to me in downtown New York. Mannie got in touch with me after I published an article in the *International Review of Psychoanalysis* about how Freud had partially misjudged meditation in his formulation of the oceanic feeling. Freud had corresponded with the French poet Romain Rolland, a devoted student of Ramakrishna and Vivekananda, about the origins of religious feelings. Rolland wrote of a feeling of oneness, of connection, and Freud responded that he could not find such a feeling within himself but that it must have its origins in the early experience of the infant at the breast. He called this the oceanic feeling and this formulation became the standard psychoanalytic interpretation for mystical experience: a return to primitive narcissism. I felt that Freud was on to something, that meditation *could* create limitless feelings evocative of such early union, but that he was unaware of the deeper purpose of Buddhist meditation: the analysis and investigation of the seemingly solid self. Psychoanalysts might want to investigate these practices, too, I wrote.

Mannie got in touch with me shortly after this article appeared and asked me if I knew the work of Winnicott. I was familiar with an article or two but I was no scholar. He gently urged a new biography of him by Adam Phillips upon me and I became entranced. Winnicott wrote about the places where childhood experience, artistic inspiration, and emotional and spiritual feelings overlapped. He wrote movingly about what he called *unintegration*, a state that he distinguished from both integration and disintegration, a state in which the infant or child feels secure enough to let themselves go, confident of the parents' non-intrusive but non-abandoning background presence. In the state of unintegration, as described by Winnicott, the child relaxes the need to keep the self together but does not fall apart. This creates a different way of being, a kind of lying fallow, in which thoughts, feelings, sensations, and memories can wash through the body/mind unobstructed. In reading about unintegration, I remembered at once my juggling experience at Naropa. I also remembered how, at my first intensive meditation retreats, I had the profound experience while sitting of coming home to myself. Meditation seemed to be another route into unintegration, a way of recovering an essential, if often overlooked, natural resource, one that is often sacrificed in childhood. There *was* something oceanic in the feeling, but it was not the bliss of union, precisely, as Freud had conjectured. The Zen scholar, D. T. Suzuki (1960), once described it as a "royally magnificent aloneness" (p. 30) in which one feels connected to all things. It is a state of deep subjectivity in which the self can keep opening to itself as part and parcel of the world from which it springs. It is an open state that makes more openings possible. Rather than the oneness of the infant at the breast, the closest metaphor seemed to me to be the mutual resonance of heightened erotic intimacy.

Desire

As I became more immersed in the Western Buddhist world while beginning my training as a doctor and psychiatrist, one of the things that struck me most pointedly in my exploration of the interface of Buddhism and psychotherapy was how confused people on both sides of the aisle seemed to be about desire. This struck me as odd because of how relevant the imagery of erotic union seemed to be to both disciplines. Yet on the psychoanalytic side, the emphasis was primarily on the value of accepting and mediating unacceptable impulses. As important as this can be, it neglected the connection to higher states of consciousness that erotic desire can bring. On the Buddhist side, the conventional approach was the oft-repeated phrase, "The cause of suffering is desire—to stop suffering you must stop desire." This also seemed to neglect the link between desire and spiritual experience—the need for *unintegration* as so beautifully described by Winnicott.

In exploring this issue more, I found that the conventional understanding of the place of desire in Buddhist thought—"The cause of suffering is desire—to stop suffering, you must stop desire"– did not ring true to my own experience. There are a number of reasons for this.

First, I believe that this is a mistranslation of the phrase the Buddha used in describing his Noble Truths. In his First Noble Truth, he did declare that there is *duhkha*. Suffering is a reasonable translation, although something on the order of "life is tinged with a sense of pervasive dissatisfaction," might come closer to describing his vision. The cause he gives in the Second Noble Truth is *tanha*, which can be translated as *thirst* or *craving* or *clinging*, words or concepts that, upon investigation, mean something other than what we think of as desire. In the Fourth Noble Truth, the Buddha lays out a scenario for release in which many aspects of desire are, in fact, maintained.

Secondly, the cause of my own suffering was clearly not desire, it was a feeling of estrangement from desire; more of a fear of what could happen if I surrendered to it, a fear of embarrassment, of falling apart, or of becoming out of control. As I have worked as a therapist I have seen that this relationship to desire is widespread. Trying to eliminate it plays into the defense—it does not help solve the problem. Pushing desire away brings to mind Freud's famous phrase, *the return of the repressed*. Or it connotes a French phrase one of my patients quoted to me, "Chassez le naturel, il revient au gallop." Chase away the natural, and it comes back at a gallop.

Thirdly, coming of age in a community whose members were besotted with Buddhism allowed me to see, early on, what happens when people try to be more spiritual than they really are, when they try to act a part instead of letting it emerge out of their practice. Trying to go out to eat as a group, for instance, became an exercise in *having no preferences*.

"You decide," someone would say.

"It really doesn't matter," another would respond.

People were easily taken advantage of when this ideology was running things. The surrender of meditation became confused with submission to powerful teachers or gurus and people's judgment became confused.

Finally, I have come to understand that the disengagement that Buddhism promotes through its meditative practices is not the end-point but is only a means of promoting a deeper, fuller, richer engagement with life. Dogen's famous phrase:

> To study Buddhism is to study the self.
> To study the self is to forget the self.
> To forget the self is to become intimate with all things," is one way of putting it.

Another wonderful teacher, Sri Nisargadatta, put it this way: "The problem is not desire," he would say, "The problem is that your desires are too small" (quote from Epstein, 2005, p. 8).

To give an example of how desire can be used to wake up the mind, listen to Jack Kornfield, one of my own Buddhist teachers, talk about his experiences in long-term retreat in a monastery in Thailand.

> In my earliest practice as a celibate monk I had long bouts of lust and images of sexual fantasy. My teacher said to name them, which I did. But they often repeated. 'Accept this?' I thought. 'But then they'll never stop.' But still I tried it. Over days and weeks these thoughts became even stronger. Eventually, I decided to expand my awareness to see what other feelings were present. To my surprise I found a deep well of loneliness almost every time the fantasies arose. It wasn't all lust, it was loneliness, and the sexual images were ways of seeking comfort and closeness. But they kept arising. Then I noticed how hard it was to let myself feel the loneliness. I hated it; I resisted it. Only when I accepted this very resistance and gently held it in compassion did it begin to subside. By expanding my attention, I learned that much of my sexuality had little to do with lust, and as I brought an acceptance to the feeling of loneliness, the compulsive quality of the fantasies gradually diminished.
>
> How is this done in practice? The loneliness I encountered that was giving rise to sexual fantasies can be an example. It returned often and painfully even though I named it and

felt it with care. Loneliness has been one of my deepest sources of pain for as long as I can remember. I am a twin, and sometimes I think I got my brother to come along in the womb so I could have some company.... As the loneliness continued to arise, I brought more careful attention to where it was held. Mostly it felt centered in my stomach.... I asked myself what beliefs and attitudes I held about it. The story that came out sounded like a child who says, 'There is something insufficient and wrong with me and I will always be rejected.' It was this belief, along with the attendant feelings, that I had identified with and contracted around.

As each of these layers opened in awareness, the pain gradually eased, the feelings softened, and the fire subsided. As I continued to feel into the center of the loneliness, I seemed to sense a hole or space in my belly that the pain had closed around. I named this central hole softly and felt its deep hunger, longing, and emptiness. Then I let it open as much as it wanted, instead of closing around it as I had done for so many years. As I did, it got bigger and softer and all the vibrations around it became very fine. The hole changed to open space and its hungry quality shifted. Though it was empty, it became more like clear empty space. Gradually this filled more of my body, and with it a sense of light and fulfillment arose. I was filled with a sense of ease and profound contentment and peace. Resting in this open space, the whole notion of rejection and insufficiency was totally unnecessary. I could see that all of it—the loneliness, pain, sadness, thoughts of rejection—was a contraction of my body and mind based on the frightened and very limited sense of myself that I had carried for a long time. I could even see with compassion the scenes and conditions that generated it. But here, resting in the spaciousness and wholeness, I knew it was not true. And while the pain of loneliness has certainly come again in my life, I now know for certain it is not who I am. I have learned that its beliefs and contractions are based on fear and that underlying it all is a genuine wholeness and well-being that is our true nature. (Kornfield, 1993, pp. 108-110)

The Buddha's Self-Analysis

Jack's discovery of his true nature by tracking loneliness through his desire brings to mind an event from the Buddha's own life that also speaks to the importance of an open and accepting attitude toward all the qualities of our being. The story is the only one from the Buddha's life to involve a childhood memory, and so, as a psychotherapist, I am particularly interested in its meaning. The Buddha, at the time of this memory, was pursuing ascetic practices with a vengeance. In a way, he was at the opposite end of the spectrum from Jack in his monastery looking at his lust. The Buddha, before his enlightenment, tried to eradicate from his psyche all traces of impurities. He fasted, deprived himself of sleep and shelter, and perfected all of the yogic austerities of his day. Like a modern-day anorexic, he found power through self-abnegation. At the height of this pursuit, he had a memory, one that is recorded as the turning point in the Buddha's spiritual trajectory, the memory that led him directly to the Middle Path, the way between indulgence and deprivation. The Buddha remembered himself as a young boy sitting under a rose-apple tree watching his father plow in the fields. It was a beautiful day, the wind stirring the leaves on the branches above him, and the young boy was filled with a sense of well-being. To my mind, it was a kind of Winnicottian moment: the boy's father was present but not too present, supportive but at a distance, allowing the child to relax into the surroundings and into himself. He was suffused with joy. But the Buddha, remembering this, noticed that he was afraid.

"Why should I be afraid of this?" he asked himself. He proceeded to analyze, in the best Freudian way. What the Buddha discovered was that he was afraid of the joy that was intrinsic to his being, the joy that he first encountered under the rose-apple tree. It frightened him because it was so clearly outside of his control. It seemed to come from nowhere and it was bigger than he was. It had the potential to overwhelm, to make him disappear. But surrendering more fully into this joy, the Buddha realized that there was no inherent reason for fear. Perhaps there was even something of the liberation he was seeking in the experience. It had certainly caught him by surprise, and such an event is always worth looking at. He saw that if he was interested in exploring it further, he would need to eat something: his body was simply too rundown to support the feeling for very long. He decided to accept some nourishment. Having done so, he proceeded to the fabled Bodhi tree where he sat down and found his enlightenment. It is said that five ascetics who were the Buddha's companions during this period were disgusted with him after witnessing this event. They thought he had gone soft, lost his way, and given up his rigor. They treated him the way we might feel about someone suddenly going into therapy to embrace their inner child. They turned away and left him to proceed on his own.

The Buddha's embrace of a joy intrinsic to his being flies in the face of the conventional view of Buddhism as world or pleasure denying (see Epstein, 2001). It speaks, instead, of the Buddha's view of the entire world, the entire range of mental and emotional experience, as potentially enlightening and, in fact, as already free. The Buddha's ascetic colleagues treated his embrace of joy the way many Buddhists today treat desire. They look down on it as something unnecessary, something trivial, something polluting, or something unwholesome. They ignore erotic desire's capacity to illuminate the nature of self and other and, in particular, its ability to put us back in touch with that state that I discovered while juggling, the state that Winnicott called *unintegration*, where the need to be *someone* drops away and experience opens up, where self and other lose the usual object status that we unconsciously give them.

Erotic Union

Unintegration is the central, sacred, linking state between meditation and therapy. While it can be thought of as an intrapsychic phenomenon, in which a solitary individual relaxes into the play of their own minds without identifying exclusively with the observing ego, it can also be thought about interpersonally. In the intersubjective view, unintegration is either the means by which one person enters into a reciprocal, mutual relationship with another or the fruit of a successful such encounter. Kernberg (1995) describes this beautifully as follows:

> There is an intrinsic contradiction in the combination of... two crucial features of sexual love:... the constant awareness of the indissoluble separateness of individuals, on the one hand, and the sense of transcendence, of becoming one with the loved person, on the other. The separateness results in loneliness and longing and fear for the frailty of all relations; transcendence in the couple's union brings about the sense of oneness with the world, of permanence and new creation. Loneliness, we might say, is a prerequisite for transcendence.
> To remain within the boundaries of the self while transcending them in identification with the loved object is an exciting, moving, and yet painful condition of love. The Mexican poet Octavio Paz (1974) has expressed this aspect of love with an almost overwhelming conciseness, stating that love is the point of intersection between desire and reality. Love, he says, reveals reality to desire and creates the transition from the erotic object to the beloved person. This revelation is almost always painful because the beloved presents himself or herself simultaneously as a body which can be penetrated and a consciousness which is impenetrable. Love is the revelation of the other person's freedom. The contradictory nature of love is that desire aspires to be fulfilled by the destruction of the desired object, and love discovers that this object is indestructible and cannot be substituted. (pp. 43-44)

Erotic union is more complicated than a simple state of merger in which self and other are conflated. While there may be desire for just such a disappearance of self or other—this is the *destructive* drive that Kernberg refers to—the actual experience is much more nuanced. Self and other open to each other in a mutually enhancing unintegration that reveals the fluidity of the self while affirming its ultimate unknowability.

Proust (1923/1966) revealed something of the same sentiment in his description of a tender and intimate moment.

> "I might caress her," he wrote, "pass my hand slowly over her, but, just as if I had been handling a stone which encloses the salt of immemorial oceans or the light of a star, I felt I was touching no more than the sealed envelope of a person who inwardly reached to infinity." (pp. 248-249)

The Third

There was something in the way mind opened up to itself while juggling at Naropa that is similar to what is described in these passages. It has seemed to me that psychotherapy might function in a similar kind of way under the influence of Buddhism—as a kind of high-wire act, a balancing, that offers a window into a state of mind in which the usual dichotomies of subject and object, me and you, separation and union, sacred and profane, acceptable and unacceptable or wholesome and unwholesome are no longer structuring our realities. The psychoanalyst Jessica Benjamin, picking up where Winnicott left off, has written about how the psychotherapeutic encounter can create an intermediate state in which just this kind of experience becomes possible, a state that she calls *thirdness*.

> For a few years now I have been thinking and writing about thirdness both as a mental function and an intersubjective state, the position that turns the opposition of dichotomies into tensions, spaces, possibilities for creative dissonance and harmony. My image of thirdness is based on a musical metaphor, an image of two or more people following a score, not one they have already read but one that reveals itself only as they go along. Indeed, as they play their notes, the score is being written, becoming what it is, realizing itself. This image is meant to capture the intersubjective process by which two people cocreate or follow a pattern, an interaction in which neither person leads and neither simply reacts. In the space of thirdness, as Winnicott (1971) said of transitional experience, it is unclear whether truth is invented or discovered....In other words, we try to be both observers and participants, to overcome a split between doing and thinking...
>
> Can I find a way to link thirdness and integration with... surrender, with the letting go of ego, with the immersion or subjective awareness I have been talking about? As I think we aim for in analysis... there is a point when the split between self-consciousness and subjective awareness is momentarily suspended. Thus, surrender, or the point of thirdness, can be seen as transcending the split between immersion and self-

consciousness. That is, thirdness can allow self-consciousness in without having it impinge, or wreck, the attention to the object. That is where the Big Energy enters, in the open space of the third. (Benjamin, 2005, p. 197)

This *Big Energy* is akin to the Buddhist unconscious, to the joy that the young Buddha remembered under the rose-apple tree. When this energy breaks through, as it unexpectedly can when conditions are right, it makes us question, as it did the Buddha himself, "Why am I so afraid of this pleasure?" Psychotherapy is our version of the rose-apple tree, another place where this energy can enter and where our fears of it can be addressed.

References

Benjamin, J. (2005). From many into one: Attention, energy, and the containing of multitudes. *Psychoanalytic Dialogues, 15* (2), 185-201.

Epstein, M. (2001). *Going on being.* Boston: Wisdom.

Epstein, M. (2005). *Open to desire.* New York: Broadway.

Kernberg, O. (1995). *Love relations.* New Haven, NJ: Yale University Press.

Kloss, J. (1974). *Back to Eden.* New York: Lifeline Books.

Kornfield, J. (1993). *A path with heart.* New York: Bantam.

Proust, M. (1966). *Remembrance of things past* (Vol. 5: The captive; C. K. Scott-Moncrieff, Trans.). London: Chatto & Windus. (Original work published in 1923)

Suzuki, D. T. (1960). Lectures on Zen Buddhism. In E. Fromm, D. T. Suzuki, & R. DeMartino (Eds.), *Zen Buddhism and psychoanalysis* (pp. 1-76). New York: Harper.

19

Psychoanalysis and Buddhism: Paths of Disappointment

Robert Unger

I'd like to begin with a vignette. A little over 20 years ago, Rangjung Rigpe Dorje, the 16th Galwang Karmapa, head of the Karma Kagu lineage of Tibetan Buddhism, and thought by many to be next in importance to the Dali Lama in Buddhist culture, lay dying of cancer in a Chicago hospital. He is said to have refused pain killers, yet he astonished his nurses with his presence, kindness, and compassion (Goldstein, 2003). Just as he died, his attendants reported that his last words were, "Nothing happens." In this chapter, I'd like to discuss the relevance of this simple statement through personal experience. I entered the field of psychoanalysis with the highest of hopes. It was the end of the exciting 1960s, I was in my early 20s, was new to New York, and was determined to shed a constrained, self-conscious identity. Although at the time I was in another occupation, psychoanalysis seemed like a natural fit for me and, after a couple of years of analysis, I entered social work school, psychoanalytic training, and faced the future with new excitement and optimism.

The years rolled on and, although my schooling seemed to be progressing quite well and my analysis—conducted by a brilliant, exciting, and charismatic analyst—was always interesting, I still found myself uttering a familiar refrain. It took a variety of forms, but its essence was something like this: "Sometime, after some more analysis, I'll be as smart as my analyst," or "a better athlete," or "a more desirable lover." What these statements had in common was the notion of my becoming more *something* than I was in the present—internally a combination of more confident, more relaxed, and more accomplished, and externally more revered by others. Given that the content of these fantasies varied, I was not aware that the core thought was being endlessly repeated.

After about ten years, my personal and professional circumstances called into question the validity of this path and I retreated from the psychoanalytic world. It was at roughly this same time that I was introduced to Tibetan Buddhism and meditation practice. That path began to make much more sense to me than psychoanalysis and my allegiance shifted. I left analytic work altogether, moved to a meditation center in

Colorado, and became a committed Buddhist practitioner. Eventually, I returned to psychoanalytic work, but I continued my meditation practice and my involvement in the Buddhist community in Boulder.

After several years of meditation practice I began to notice an all too familiar refrain creeping into my meditation. Once again, I found myself thinking that if I continued to meditate, "sometime, after more meditation, I'll become as smart as my meditation instructor," or "a better athlete," or "a more desirable lover," and so on. I eventually realized that I had returned to my former wishful thinking. Although the content of the thoughts and fantasies typically referenced the future, I had learned a fundamental lesson in analysis—as Freud (1923/1989) noted, whatever thoughts and fantasies were occurring in the room were of the present. In Buddhism, I had also learned that whatever arises in the mind has the nature of nowness (Trungpa, 2004).

It was clearly time to explore what information these hopes and fantasies of the future provided about the present. I concluded that fantasizing myself in a different position, state of mind, or circumstance implied that I was less than satisfied with my present state of mind, emotion, and being. And that implied some state of disappointment. Furthermore, I realized that over time, neither psychoanalysis nor Buddhist meditation had offered any particular cure for disappointment. I was spending just as much time fantasizing about the future now as I had when I began following the paths of analysis and meditation. It was hard to acknowledge that it had taken so many years to understand and face this seemingly simple truth.

I decided that it might be useful to view disappointment in context of Freud's pleasure principle (Freud, 1920/1961). We know that it is natural to seek and imagine situations that might result in greater comfort or in reduced internal tension, with the classic example being that of a person stuck on a desert island who fantasizes about a good meal. From the time a baby cries to express its response to discomforts such as being hungry, wet, or cold and a parent responds with the appropriate remedy, humans learn to fantasize about the things that will make them comfortable or reduce their internal tension. As we mature, this process increases greatly in complexity and subtleness. Society provides events and circumstances that raise our anxiety and tension while simultaneously promising remedies that can reduce it. In a materially focused culture such as ours, we are bombarded with information about a variety of products and activities that will allegedly make us more comfortable. The increase in ambient stimulation and tension in society over the past 50 to 100 years has been much greater than the human body's ability to acclimate to it, spurring a new urgency for securing relief. As the ambient level of tension rises, that tension becomes manifest in a variety of symptoms and behaviors. People tend to embrace activities or products that promise relief, from buying material goods to turning to alcohol, legal and illegal drugs, exercise, and perhaps even psychotherapy or meditation. In fact, mainstream psychotherapy is moving strongly toward a focus on symptom relief as its primary objective.

The dilemma is that if these panaceas provide any relief at all, it is usually transitory. In an article in *The New York Times* entitled "The Futile Pursuit of Happiness," Jon Gertner (2003) describes research conducted by a group of psychologists and economists in the area of affective forecasting—the notion that virtually all of the decisions we make are based on our prediction of the emotional consequences of those events. The research showed that we are not very good emotional forecasters. What we imagine will make us happy probably will not make us as happy as we had imagined and the effects will be short-lived. In an article in *Psychology Today*, titled "Great Expectations," Polly Shulman (2004) emphasized something most of us know from experience—that the *ideal mate* does not exist. This notion is usually some projection of what we *think* will make us content. Writings espousing these notions seem to be appearing more frequently of late, perhaps a natural response to the increasing emphasis on comfort and relief in the culture.

So, if we do not pursue an external solution to our internal state of dissatisfaction or disappointment, what alternatives do we have? What happens if, as in psychoanalysis or Buddhist meditation, we are directed to study our own internal states, moment by moment? What seems to come into focus is a state of disappointment that may initially be experienced as hunger, fear, anxiety, tension, loss, sadness, or some other distressing feeling. In a culture largely driven by promises of solutions to uncomfortable states, it is deeply frustrating to spend years in analysis or a meditation practice only to discover, in the words of the 16th Karmapa, that *nothing happens.*

Why engage in such often expensive and time-consuming yet disappointing activities? Here we might turn to the notion of addiction as it becomes more widespread in the culture. Although it is common to think of addiction in material terms, the list of other kinds of addictive behaviors, such as sexual addiction, exercise addiction, relationship addiction, and so on is growing. To break free of any form of addiction, one must go through a withdrawal process that can be both painful and lengthy. Recent neuropsychological research has supported the enduring Freudian concept of repetition compulsion, as it has become apparent that addictive processes are woven into our brains from our experiences (Siegal, 2007).

In fact, the cinematic experience in our present culture clearly reflects the overwhelming availability of diverse, intense stimulative forces. Which of you readers has been to a movie lately and not felt bombarded by the emotionally explosive excess of the trailers for coming attractions, never mind the movie you came to see? Few among us can imagine life without cell phones, computers, television, and other modern electronic stimulants that did not exist a short time ago. No sooner do we purchase one of these technological wonders than it becomes obsolete, with the next generation of gadgets providing even more complex stimulation. In a very interesting and entertaining book titled *Faster: The Acceleration of Just About Everything,* James Gleick (2000) describes more than thirty areas of stimulation that have seen exponential acceleration in recent years.

When considering life without the everyday stimulants we have come to take for granted, it is instructive to monitor our emotions when one of these agents of stimulation is suddenly unavailable to us. Think about how you feel when the phone does not work, the TV breaks, the power goes out, a friend cancels an appointment, or another source of stimulation is withdrawn. We might say that we are disappointed, but physiologically or emotionally what we experience might actually be akin to withdrawal. Rather than accept the unexpectedly empty space or time in our lives, our need for constant stimulation often leads us to quickly find an alternative source. We might decide to head out for a neighborhood bar, call someone else, or maybe go to a movie. The experience of disappointment or withdrawal is very hard to tolerate. Today, in too many cases, our culture defines the uncomfortable experience of disappointment or withdrawal with a diagnostic label such as depression or anxiety—diseases that need to be cured. Large corporations make a great deal of money creating medicines to *cure* these uniquely modern ailments.

It can be helpful to take a step back and study the internal state created by a culture that provides and supports a rapidly increasing level of stimulation. In those moments when we are not engaged in stimulating activities—which are frequently moments of disappointment or withdrawal—what is actually occurring internally? That is, when we are not focused on participating in environments of stimulation or reducing the discomfort caused by lost stimulation, what happens when we find ourselves doing nothing? We must face the possibly extreme discomfort of merely experiencing our internal state with no explanation or solution to it.

This introspective activity is not well-supported in our society. Addiction loves company. I think of a patient of mine who in his 30s had been a heavy social drinker since his teens. After receiving his third DUI three years ago, he came to me with a resolve to stop drinking. He has been sober since, but he is astonished at the persistent efforts of his friends to get him to return to drinking. The media continually promises health, wealth, relief, and happiness to those who adopt stimulating/addictive activities. People who choose to abstain are often thought of as square, not cool, old-fashioned, boring, or timid.

Given this environment of stimulation, what occurs when we chose to engage in psychoanalysis or Buddhist meditation? In the mainstream culture of psychotherapy today, now that the practice of advertising therapeutic services has become accepted, promises of comfort abound—make an appointment and get relief from depression, fix

19. Psychoanalysis & Buddhism

your marriage, or improve your sexual functioning. It is hardly surprising that someone would enter psychotherapy with the expectation that this activity is going to make him or her feel better. The increasing popularity of so-called *evidenced-based approaches* pressures therapists to relieve a patient's symptoms right away. Similarly, the popularization of Eastern religions in our culture has also come with promises of peace and happiness, relief from whatever state of dissatisfaction or disappointment you may be struggling with.

But what really happens in psychoanalysis? Once the initial stimulation of entering analysis and gaining the exclusive attention of the analyst recedes, we know that what we term the *transference neurosis* develops—that is, the patient's fundamental intrapsychic and interpersonal repetitions emerge and he or she is likely to experience frustration because nothing is happening. The patient's impulse to leave or to find some way to stimulate the analyst increases. During this period, the patient might be said to be experiencing withdrawal or disappointment as his or her fantasies of relief or fulfillment go unanswered, particularly if the analyst remains an essentially neutral, investigative object. If the analyst is successful in helping the patient put hopes, wishes, and fantasies into words and then to describe their underlying emotional experience in the present, the patient might be able to learn how to tolerate the momentary, ongoing experience of disappointment or *nothing happening*.

Likewise, in Buddhist-oriented awareness meditation, fascination with one's thoughts begins to recede once the endless patterns of hope, fear, and expectation are recognized. Frustration, boredom, anxiety, and physical discomfort emerge in the moment, while meditating, as one realizes that nothing is, in fact, happening and nothing will. How disappointing!

In analysis and meditation, once outside stimulation has been minimized, one's own internal state of stimulation moves to the foreground of awareness. Accustomed to denying this reality through fantasy or action, we find this to be a most uncomfortable state. With little identifiable context, it might be experienced as disappointment, withdrawal, anxiety, or depression. I recall a conversation I had with my wizened meditation instructor shortly after beginning to meditate. I was telling him how terrific I thought meditation was. He commented ruefully, "Wait until you discover that it's not so terrific."

When considering the ramifications of disappointment in psychoanalysis, perhaps the most important variable to consider is countertransference. All analysts are acquainted with the subtleties and vicissitudes of countertransference, as a response to induction from the patient as well as to forces emanating from our own unresolved conflicts. The induction of disappointment from the patient is perhaps one of the most difficult manifestations of countertransference to tolerate. Most of us want to feel helpful to our patients, to witness progress, to alleviate suffering. A disappointed patient induces equally uncomfortable feelings of disappointment in the analyst. In addition, because today's culture of psychotherapy places so much emphasis on measurable, definable progress and symptom relief, an analyst's professional sense of self is challenged by patients who induce disappointment. Given these circumstances, it is inevitable that an analyst will feel the impulse to act in ways that will relieve disappointment in the patient, and by extension, in him- or herself. Even our most genuine attempts at understanding, our most brilliant, insightful, and accurate interpretations can be unconscious attempts to alleviate our own feelings of disappointment and anxiety by injecting *progress* into the treatment.

If it is true that psychoanalysis and Buddhism are, in fact, *paths of disappointment*, why walk those paths at all? One alleged reason for Freud's unpopularity was his so-called pessimism, his notion that in the best of worlds, psychoanalysis could only help people come to terms with the arduousness of daily living (Freud, 1905/2000). The fundamental tenet of Buddhism is impermanence (Trungpa, 1976), the obvious implication being that at best, we might prepare for our own impermanence or death. So if psychoanalysis and Buddhism might merely help people live an ordinary life and prepare for the inevitability of death, why bother?

In context of everyday life, the less able we are to tolerate disappointment—or withdrawal from constant stimulation, as I have focused on in this paper—the more dependent we are on external sources of stimulation and fantasies of accomplishments, rewards, or relief to distract us from immediate internal and perceptual experiences. Because external sources of stimulation are forever transitory and impossible to control, anxiety is inevitable. Therefore, we waste considerable energy trying to solve the inevitable and ever-present experience of disappointment.

If instead, through psychoanalysis or Buddhist meditation, we become more acclimated to and familiar with our own immediate state of disappointment, several things may become possible. As dependence on hope, solutions, and external sources of stimulation or distraction recedes, we may be able to experience a sense of freedom and true independence. We can learn to live with, and fully experience, the negative emotions of fear, sadness, frustration, loss, yearning, and so on. In familiar psychological terminology, this might mean that we could learn to accept and appreciate ourselves for who we are: neurosis, defenses, and all. We might be able to tolerate anxiety and intense emotional states, become familiar with our own minds, and become less reactive to the ups and downs of others.

Disappointment would become just one part of the total experience of being alive. This might be akin to what we think of as true individuation or a healthy ego. We would begin to see that this state of being is actually universal, and that could foster genuine connectedness to and compassion for others.

References

Freud, S. (2000). *Three essays on the theory of sexuality* (J. Strachey, Trans.). New York: Basic Books (Original work published in 1905).

Freud, S. (1989). *The ego and the id* (J. Strachey, Trans.). New York: Norton. (Original work published in 1923).

Freud, S. (1961). *Beyond the pleasure principle* (J. Strachey, Trans.). New York: Norton. (Original work published in 1920)

Freud, S. (1957). Instincts and their vicissitudes. In J. Strachey (Ed. & Trans.), *The standard edition of the complete psychological works of Sigmund Freud* (Vol. 14; 109-140). London: Hogarth Press. (Original work published in 1915).

Gertner, J. (2003, September 7). The futile pursuit of happiness in *New York Times*, 45ff.

Gleick, J. (2000). *Faster: The acceleration of just about everything*. London: Vintage.

Goldstein, J (2003). *One Dharma: An emerging western Buddhism*. New York:Harper Collins.

Siegel, D.J. (2007). *The mindful brain: Reflection and attunement in the cultivation of well-being*. New York: W. W. Norton.

Shulman, P. (2004). Great expectations. *Psychology Today, 2,* 32-42.

Trungpa, C. (1976). *The myth of freedom and the way of meditation*. Berkeley, CA: Shambhala.

Trungpa, C (2004). *The collected works of Chogyam Truungpa* (Vol. 5: Crazy Wisdom; Carolyn Gimian, Ed.). Boston: Shambala.

20

Psychotherapy and the Paramitas: Walking the Bodhisattva's Path[1]

Lauren Casalino

Grief Ushers in the Aspiration to Become a Bodhisattva

My father died when I was 15. *The Three Marks of Existence* in Buddhism, which characterize human experience, became vividly real to me. I was experiencing impermanence, the first mark, in one of its most shattering manifestations, the loss of someone I loved. The second mark, suffering, is born from attachment and aversion, and at fifteen, due to my attachment to my father and my aversion to my experience of his death, my suffering was prolonged and profound. The third Mark of Existence, egolessness, made itself apparent in my complete loss of a sense of who I was, of what my life was. Such was my disorientation that I could walk down the street where I had lived all my life without knowing where I was.

My father's death led to a complete collapse of my belief in life and love, and suicidal thoughts brought my own commitment to living into question. I vowed that if I chose to live, if I discovered anew how to love and laugh, I would accompany others in their passages through excruciating states of emotional, mental, and physical experience.

Years later, when Buddhist practice and teachings had taken root in my life, I realized that without knowing it at the time, I had taken the Bodhisattva Vow. Bodhisattvas are, in the Mahayana tradition of Buddhism, individuals who strive to develop wisdom and compassion in order to help all other living beings to also do so, thus bringing to an end everyone's endless re-birth into suffering. Bodhisattvas make a vow to strive to let go of the harmful and delusional ways of relating, which come with attachment and aggression and ignorance.

I knew that if I had any chance of fulfilling this aspiration to be of help to others, I needed to work with my own tendencies toward depression, rage, and all the other destructive emotions and thoughts I had accumulated. This necessity had been brought home to me by fights between my idealistic older brother and my mother. My brother was

---

[1] Chapter adapted from a talk given at Naropa University, June, 2006, Boulder, Colorado.

dedicating his life to the non-violent protest of the Vietnam war while my mother was doing her best to raise four children. My brother felt it to be immoral to pay income taxes which were being used to support the war and to purchase flowers while people were being killed. My mother was law abiding and wished to preserve the beauty of flowers on a Thanksgiving table, even if people were killing each other elsewhere. While not physical, their fights seemed anything but non-violent, given the hurt and anger they caused within the family. They made me realize I needed to work with my own rage if I were ever to be an instrument of peace on the earth.

Deep down I knew that I was a loving person, but that loving nature did not necessarily manifest in my daily life. Even at the still relatively young age of 24, my failures to love seemed legion, ranging from horn honking at an inept driver, to the concise and cutting statement with which I ended a love affair. I would act and then I would feel ashamed of myself. Yes, I wanted to be the kind of person who left the grocery clerk with a small smile on their face from our brief and anonymous interaction, but how did that desire hold up in the face of being in a time crunch to get to work and finding the clerk to be bumblingly slow? All too often, my impatience and irritation were more apparent than whatever understanding and kindness I might feel towards the clerk's confused and tense state. If I were ever to help myself, no less others (the Bodhisattva Vow still floating around in my consciousness), I somehow needed a way to not simply sink into despair or rage in the face of my and others' cruel and ignorant acts with each other. I needed a way to work with whatever arose in my mind and my emotions so that those very thoughts and feelings could be skillfully used to increase my own awareness and compassion. I needed a way which would bring that workability, along with whatever awareness and compassion I could manifest, to others despair, rage, and confusion. I needed a way to work with my own discomfort, with whatever reactions might arise within myself when with another, so that I might truly be able to accompany them through their own suffering. As Jakusho Kwong noted, I needed a path; "not to go from here to there, but to go from here to here" (as cited in Welwood, 1990, p. 11).

Buddhist Study and Practices Offer a Path toward Becoming a Bodhisattva

I was an aspiring Bodhisattva without a path to the realization of my aspirations. I began to study Buddhism, which offers me a resonant description of the nature of human life and of the workings of the human mind. I began to meditate and I have found that meditation practice is the tool that I need to help me work with suffering. I enrolled in the MA Psychology: Contemplative Psychotherapy program at Naropa University in Boulder, Colorado. The program holds at its core the ancient Buddhist knowledge that human beings are innately good and that all human experience is workable. Thoughts and feelings are not seen as problematic, as something to be denied or eradicated, but rather as the basis of our life itself. Students are trained in developing their capacity for awareness and compassion in order to relate sanely with any energy, thus fostering our capacity to enter into healing relationships. A path had formed, one which I continue to walk in a variety of ways in my life and, specifically, through the practice of contemplative psychotherapy.

The Paramitas and Walking the Path of the Bodhisattva
in Psychotherapeutic Relationship

The paramitas provide a framework in which to detail my view and experience of how psychotherapy can be practiced as the path of the Bodhisattva. Paramita is often translated as *Perfection* and refers to the development of qualities of being which purify negativity and lead to the development of wisdom and compassion. Their practice supports Bodhisattvas in their aspiration to help others cease their engagement in the cycle of suffering. Sometimes they are called *transcendent virtues*, where what is being transcended is how one gets in the way of one's own innate sanity.

The first paramita is generosity. In the therapeutic setting I understand this to involve two things. First, is a basic sense of hospitality towards one's clients; I try to create this atmosphere through providing an inviting physical environment which offers a safe container. Drinking water is available, tissues are within reach, and sounds will not be overheard outside the office.

I then try to offer a sense of welcome through my own presence. I wish to convey the feeling that here, with me, clients can experience their lives and be witnessed and supported in doing so. I am guided in how I might help a client welcome or turn away from their own experience by remembering how I was treated in numerous episodes of fainting in my earlier years. Each time I came back to consciousness after a faint I was quite sensitive to the energy of whomever was responding to me. With some people I was neither jostled out of where I had been nor left alone in where I was. They seemed to act as midwives holding me in a peaceful birth into the present moment. With others, whose own fears or desires for me were antithetical to my own at the time, fading back into unconsciousness, perhaps the equivalent to habitual patterns in the psychotherapeutic setting, seemed the most desirable choice. Drawing from these experiences, with clients I am as conscious as possible of my eye contact, my posture and movements, the tone of my voice, the usage of words, and all of my thoughts and feelings which underlie those behaviors. I shape who and how I am in the moment to be as welcoming as I can be with my clients.

The second thing I think of as involved in the practice of generosity is what Farrell Silverberg calls *therapeutic resonance*. In Silverberg's (1988) words,

> Therapeutic resonance is the vehicle to healing. Resonance is a way of "being with" another person and expressing fundamental receptivity and openness to that person. To resonate with someone is to serve as a mirror for him, and to be so closely identified that you feel his experience. Resonance is rooted in a stance of quiet attention, with minimal resistance or value judgment about its nature." (p. 25)

Recently, a client of mine, David,[2] was telling me about having to choose whether or not to sign medical papers which would allow doctors to perform a life-sustaining procedure on his aged father, whose quality of life was seriously compromised. I felt a sort of panic, a clenching of the muscles of my body, a rising of sadness from my heart into the backs of my eyes. I felt alone and nearly breathless. I noticed all this, and continued to hold my attention on David, whose speed of speech had hastened and become somewhat breathless. He spoke of the terror he felt when presented with that decision and began to cry.

As I remained present with the experience in the room, David was able to both talk more about the difficult thoughts he was going through as well as to express more of the difficult emotions. Although the complexities of human relationship do not lend themselves well to hard fact, I felt quite sure at the end of this session that through my resonance with him he had felt understood and accompanied in his pain and that he was leaving the office somewhat unburdened and ready to face what was next.

The second paramita is discipline. It involves providing a sense of security for the client, a sense that "I'm here for you to return to." That sense can be provided in a practical way through the way one structures sessions, holds boundaries of time and payment, and works with cancellations and re-scheduling. It could include the way the therapist takes vacations and the provision of back-up support. In a psychological sense, one uses one's own discipline of returning time and time again to the present moment, with the intention not of fulfilling one's own needs but with the intention of being of service to the client.

More years than I could keep track of, in my quest to answer my own undeniable imperative to be a mother, I found myself working with two clients, Isabelle and Karen, who had unwanted pregnancies and were leaning towards abortion. I wanted to be the mother of those babies. There was nothing in my life I wanted more than a baby, nor had there

---

[2] All client names are fictional.

ever been anything I had wanted so much in my life; this wanting was no fly-by-night fantasy but had persisted for several years.

It had trumped all other desires. This desire to be a mother had made me willing to be a single mother. Then, when a relationship formed, it made me willing to give up that relationship if parenting was not in his future. It had made me venture into a labyrinth of medical procedures, a realm I have spent the entirety of my life avoiding. The desire to be a mother had occasioned me to take a mental tour of the world in consideration of what country I might go to for adopting a child. It was the only reason, other than some catastrophe, that I could imagine for depleting a substantial portion of my savings. All this is to say I really wanted to be the mother of those children! Although for complex reasons I had chosen not to go the full medical infertility route, there was virtually nothing I was stopping at in my pursuit of having a child.

Was my relationship with Isabelle and Karen going to become another arena in which I pursued my own undeniable need? The answer was no. Although I considered many times if it would be helpful for them to know that I would be willing to adopt their baby, I always came up with the internal reply that it would not be and so I never voiced my desire. I was in a relationship in which I was the therapist, and the women who were pregnant in front of me were my clients. They were engaged in a painful process of having to decide how to relate with an unwanted pregnancy. Walking the path of the Bodhisattva as a psychotherapist clearly meant helping them to explore their thoughts, feelings, choices, and supporting them to act in the way that was truest for their lives. Although I have and do and expect I always will receive much in non-material gifts from my clients, the intention I hold as a therapist is to be of benefit to my clients. Corollary to that intention is that the relationship is in no way about satisfying my needs, though that may nevertheless happen. Isabelle and Karen did choose to abort; I have since become the mother of a four year old boy.

The third paramita is often called Patience and contains the sense of an unconditional confidence in awakened mind. Practicing patience requires the therapist to allow for transference and the playing out of projections without taking a distanced stance of judging or diagnosing the client during the time that they are caught up in transference/projections. Being alert to the possible sanity in a client's manifestations and being present and curious are what is called for here. Trusting in the process, and in the ultimate benefit of bringing awareness and compassion to what is occurring is of great importance.

I have a client, Trevor, who has been adept at thwarting whatever need of mine to be helpful that sneaks into my work. Not infrequently, I have left our time together feeling like there is a hole in my stomach, like I am somehow a very bad person. I have enough knowledge of Trevor's past to know that he must sometimes feel like a very bad person. I have no idea whether he has the experience of a hole in his stomach, although I do know that he has stomach problems. I have returned time and time again to our sessions, questioning in between our meetings whether there is any worth for him in our relationship and whether I have the *stomach* to keep going. Over the course of years, now, the frequency with which I leave the session with a "hole in my stomach" has greatly diminished. Trevor has opened up to me more and more, and I see a relaxation, humor, and warmth that were largely masked earlier. Practicing patience allowed for this unfolding of Trevor's sanity.

The fourth paramita is often translated as exertion. Here, the therapist is working with their own tendencies to fall sway to the forces of attraction, repulsion, and ignorance, thereby distorting their ability to be in a healing relationship. These forces need to be brought into awareness and consciously held so that they are not unconsciously and destructively running the relationship. Exertion is meant to help us be present with our own experience and to see our own tendencies to solidify, diminish, and control experience so that we are able to open yet again to ours and the client's experience, as it is ever-changing.

Four and a half years ago I flew to the East Coast to be with my hospitalized mother. She had just undergone a leg amputation and needed to have another one. She had lived on her own for the 20 odd years since I had left home, maintaining her dignity, and her ability to care for herself. Although she spent three days a week at the hospital receiving dialysis, underwent a quadruple bypass surgery, as well as countless other traumatic medical events, she continued to care for herself and feel gratitude for her life. When I arrived at the hospital she was in an active process of considering whether or not to continue dialysis. She was deciding if it was her time to die.

Many and intense were the thoughts and feelings I had about this choice, but it seemed to me that I could best express my deep love for my mother, my gratitude for all that she had been for me, by honoring and supporting whatever choice she made. When she did make her choice to die, she asked for my help in the form of bringing her bananas, oranges, and chocolate. That evening, I fulfilled her request. She and I both knew that far from being treats for her, these foods were poisons, since they increased potassium levels and led to paralysis of the heart and death in people who, like my mother, were in kidney failure. Although I still mourn the absence of her physical presence in my life, the peace, love, clarity, and connection which were her state of being in the last twelve days of her life leave me no doubt that she made the right decision for herself. Exertion was required on my part to rouse the necessary trust and acceptance to support her, my own grief notwithstanding.

The fifth paramita, meditation, involves the coming back and opening of the heart, further and further. One extends one's availability, one's openness, one's patience. All of human experience can be talked about, held together, in the therapeutic setting.

I worked with a client, Susan, whose hygiene was terrible and who added to the smell of being around her by smoking cigarettes. Susan would go off into long diatribes with whomever she was hearing speaking to her in her head. On those occasions when she spoke directly to me, it was often to repeat the same stories I had already heard, or to request that I get rid of the voices, which I had continuously proven myself unable to do. Repulsion, boredom, frustration, and inadequacy dominated my experience while with her. Disembodiment reigned. Yet, over the years, I was able to enter into Susan's world more and more, swirling around in conversations that seemed to untwist and travel on the breeze like puffs of smoke. She looked me in the eyes more often. We laughed together a lot. I came to feel love for her. She still repulsed me. But clearly, we had a relationship, one that at least for short periods of times gave Susan some relief from the tormenting voices. Without meditation practice, which has so many effects on how one perceives, relates, and is open to the unknown, I doubt I could have traveled so far into her world, given how alien and repulsive it was to me.

The sixth paramita, wisdom, involves holding an understanding of what causes suffering and what leads to the cessation of suffering. The Four Noble Truths map the origination and path to cessation of suffering in detail. Wisdom involves actively working, in the moment within the therapeutic relationship, with impermanence, egolessness, and suffering: the Three Marks of Existence. It means relating fully and directly to the present moment, present experience, the *isness* of the client, while also allowing for new ways of seeing and of being.

I had a client named Diane who was good at putting herself down. Together, we worked so that she was able to hear herself putting herself down and to simply notice, rather than believe in, the thoughts and emotions which arose when she got into putting herself down. Diane began to see herself in a more positive light and developed her ability to disengage from how she created her own suffering. She, too, wanted to be a mother and was having difficulty conceiving. Together, we engaged in the balancing act of not ignoring or giving up what most matters to her while not ruining the life she did have through unanswered desire. Each day a new balancing was required. Because Diane is still alive, this continues. Hopefully, the understanding she has of what creates suffering and of what leads to its cessation continues to support her in finding her balance.

As Trungpa (1999) stated,

> When you experience your wisdom and the power of things as they are, together, as one, then you have access to tremendous vision and power in the world. You find that you are inherently connected to your own being. That is discovering magic. (p. 24)

There is a Buddhist tale that describes the ways in which dogs and lions react to a thrown stick. Dogs run after the stick. Lion's run to the place from which it was tossed, to the source of the tossing. Once one has experientially understood the truth of the Four Noble Truths and has utilized the tool of meditation to become more able to observe, rather than be caught up in the processes of mind, one becomes more able to act like the lion. Instead of chasing momentary satisfaction, one goes to the source of what is. One becomes a warrior of the heart, answering time and time again the call to be of help, the imperative to develop the wisdom and compassion to do so, the courage to have one's heart broken again and again and still return to and sustain the aspiration and effort necessary to walk the Bodhisattva's Path.

Conclusions

The roots of suffering are deeply embedded in our ways of living. Human relationship is complex. Pulling up the roots of suffering through human relationship is the work of therapy. A journey through the pain of the past and the hopes and fears for the future must sometimes be undertaken in order to live fully in the present. But this journey is not one of remembering what was, or of trying to control what is and what will be. It is a leap into the unknown, into the ever-changing reality of the present moment.

The Four Noble Truths provide a map to suffering and its cessation while the Three Marks of Existence help us situate our human experience as the journey's landscape unfolds. Relationship can offer the heart connection and helping hand which makes pulling up the roots of suffering more possible and worthwhile. It takes courage to move through heartbreak and perseverance to continue to believe in and work to develop awareness and compassion. Accompaniment can be ever so helpful. It is almost as if therapist and client begin to dance with each other through life's journey. The practice of the six paramitas supports the therapist in resting in the quiet before the music starts and then listening with our whole selves to be one with the music. A connection with space and boundless potentialities and the realization of interdependence make for attuned dance partners. The therapeutic relationship becomes a dancing journey of presence and truth, flow and connection.

I believe that the lifelong endeavor to cultivate wisdom and compassion within ourselves, coupled with the intention to be of service, can be a potent force in addressing the many ills on this planet. May it stop warfare. May we cease to suffer and may all beings be happy. In the Dalai Lama's (1999) words: "Compassion and love are not mere luxuries. As the source both of inner and external peace, they are fundamental to the continued survival of our species" (p. 130).

References

Gyatso, T. (1999). *Ethics for the new millennium*. New York: Riverhead Books.

Welwood, J. (1990). *Journey of the heart*. New York: HarperCollins Publishers.

Silverberg, F. R. (1988). Therapeutic resonance. *Journal of Contemplative Psychotherapy, 5,* 25-42.

Trungpa, C. (1999). *The essential Chogyam Trungpa*. Boston, Shambhala Publications.

21

A Personal Journey with Buddhist Psychotherapy[1]

Verónica Guzmán with Silvia Hast

Contemplative psychotherapy has provided me with both personal and professional life lessons. If not for my practice of this tradition, I would not have taken on this project of giving this talk or allowing for it to be published. This is one of those situations in my life that I basically try to avoid and that, in fact, I have always avoided. Like most people, from the perspective of our habitual ways of relating with mostly everything, we do not want to be put in situations where we are vulnerable or afraid, and even less do we want others to realize that we are feeling scared. Perhaps this is a bit strange for me to be up here telling you about all this, but as an introduction, it is what shows best a contemplative approach to our emotions, thoughts, and life in general.

To give you a taste, from a contemplative approach we could say something like this: "If you are afraid of making mistakes, allow yourself to make mistakes more frequently. If you fear failure, fail more often. Whatever you are afraid of, relate to it more frequently."

This is not to say that the contemplative approach has a masochistic flavor. It is different from the familiar reasoning that whatever we fear we should confront, engage in battle, and overcome. Rather, from this perspective, the point is to learn to acknowledge and relate with anything that comes up in our experience with openness, clarity, and warmth (Trungpa, 1976).

Opening ourselves to recognize whatever experience we may have, whether we like it or not, allows us to look at it with clarity: its form, texture, color, and taste. We invite it to come in so that we can know what it is and we receive it with warmth and interest to see how we can journey further with it. The issue is not only how can we handle and control all that happens to us, but rather how can we listen to and learn from everything that arises. This can be very challenging, especially if what arises in our experience is something very difficult, something scary, or painful.

---

[1] Paper presented at the Second Humanistic and Transpersonal Meeting, Santiago, Chile. November, 2005.

So here I am before you and my fear is right by my side. Since as much as I would have liked to, I could not get rid of it, and since I do not really have much clarity about what it is that I am so afraid of, the only thing left was to invite it to accompany me in this experience and let it show me whatever it has to present. It is an opportunity. I can really see and know its face firsthand in this particular situation that I usually try so hard to avoid. If I can stay with it, then it is probable that during my presentation you will also be able to see its face. Then we all will be able to share this part of the experience rather than me spending all my energy hopefully trying to keep it from showing up and you wasting your energy in critical judgments about what is obvious, but not acknowledged.

From this experience, we can begin to talk specifically about the overall theme of this conference, which is suffering. Buddhism and Western psychology have in common their concern for human suffering and their desire to relieve it. However, when we study Western psychology or when we see what is taught at Universities, we rarely hear the word *suffering*. Of course, we hear about pathology, neurosis, and psychosis. Beyond that, the rest of our experience is seen as the normal, albeit often painful, realities of life. These painful realities are precisely what Buddhism refers to as suffering, that painful experience that all human beings share. Some embrace it as part of their daily lives and relate to it in a sane way, but most of us spend our lives struggling against it because we would like for it not to exist. Others go to the other extreme and are even attached to it.

What makes somebody go to a psychologist if it is not that he or she is somehow suffering and is looking for help to get rid of it? Clearly it is getting rid of suffering that we are after. I do not think anybody has ever come to me searching for guidance to learn how to relate with suffering. Most clients seek out counselors to learn how to change the way they are or the way others are, rather than learning how to relate with themselves or with others just as they are. That motivation itself is one of the principal sources of suffering (Trungpa, 1973).

Within the Buddhist perspective, the approach from the beginning is less aggressive with oneself and others. The main theme is to learn how to relate with any experience that arises in life, including unavoidable suffering. Understanding that suffering is part of our lives and seeing where it comes from is what eventually allows it to diminish or cease. This allows us to find a path to make this cessation of suffering possible. Rather than judging and parceling out blame, we are capable of intensely living each moment of our experience. When we begin to do that, we can better understand the context of what arises, discover its origin, and learn how to truly release it. We can do all this with the Buddhist spirit of much kindness and a good dose of humor.

Before we go further exploring how to relate with suffering, how to relate with who we are, and how to relate with reality as it is, I want to clarify the methodology through which Buddhist tradition obtains its

21. Buddhist Psychotherapy

wisdom and knowledge. Chogyam Trungpa (2005), a Tibetan meditation master, said when he came to the West that Buddhism would find its expression in the West in the form of psychology. He also said that the objective of studying Buddhism is not really to learn about Buddhism, rather it is to learn about ourselves so that we can *liberate ourselves* or go beyond the limits of *our selves* as we usually define them.

Buddhism comes from knowledge accumulated over 2,500 years by people who sat down and practiced meditation, a technique that allows the direct observation of the nature of the mind and of reality. In this sense, it is a theory that has emerged from practice and from direct experience.

If we look at Western history, originally the object of study of psychology was the mind, the psyche (Zimbardo & Gerrig, 1999). Within the context where scientific positivism reigns and the scientific method is regarded as the only valid source of knowledge, psychology, as far back as Wundt in the 1880's, has tried to use introspection as a principal method to access a knowledge of the mind. Subjects have been trained to observe and describe their own experience. Nonetheless, this method has not been valued very highly because it is seen as too subjective. Discussions of the contested methodological approaches about how to train someone to observe and describe their own experience has often become more paramount than the findings of this personal approach. In today's empirically driven context, introspection is dismissed as an invalid source of knowledge.

To be considered as a valid science, psychology has had to fit with the contemporary scientific approaches such as double blind studies, matched groups, and rigorously operationalized treatment interventions. This forced psychological research into a direction away from the immediate and personal experiences of the research participants. First, the object to be studied has to be defined and then based on that definition a method has to be designed that allows access to measurement about the domain. Psychology has had to abandon its attempts to continue studying the mind itself and instead has placed behavior as the primary object of study. The mind per se has been left by the wayside, considered to be a kind of latent construct that is either of tertiary importance or beyond our reach.

Perhaps we could ponder more why it happened this way and think up fantasies of how things could have happened differently. If the West had known about meditation, this could have been the method that would have allowed psychotherapists to access knowledge about the mind and reality. This brings me to the necessity of specifying what I am referring to when I talk about meditation and the role that meditation plays in contemplative psychotherapy.

There are many different kinds of meditation and they are all valid in their own way. Nonetheless, meditation is very much in fashion these days and, as usual for us in the West, when something is in fashion, it is sold in many different packages with promises of all kinds of results. It becomes our newest and hottest object of consumption in our search for peace and happiness. In this context, meditation is a word used to describe the most diverse activities, many of which are really just types of relaxation exercises.

Many people report that at the end of a workshop they did "a meditation." If we ask of what it consisted, it turns out usually to be a relaxation exercise of some kind, providing a space to quiet down and enjoy a sense of well-being. It is a way of disconnecting from the earthly bounds and entering a space where we can shut out all those things that disturb us, make us uncomfortable, worried, sore, and scared, but that nonetheless is part of our daily lives. It is a notion of a kind of peace, where we can disconnect from all those things we want to eliminate from our experience, at least for awhile. Then we return to our hard realities.

Within the Buddhist tradition, meditation is a technique, a practice, a path of discipline that is characterized by the training of our attention and awareness. Through it, we learn how to become more fully present in every moment and at the same time more fully cognizant of who we are and what is going on around us moment to moment. As opposed to the caricature of chanting "Ohmm" and spacing out, we are being fully present in each instant with who we are and all that is happening in each instant. This signifies planting our feet firmly on the earth. From this perspective, meditation does not really have anything to do with reaching any exceptional states of consciousness, but rather it is about reducing all our unnecessary activities, simply being and observing our mind.

Within this quality of being mindful, the practice of meditation means embracing with kindness in the present moment *whatever arises*. This includes the whole spectrum of our experiences, be they pleasant, painful, or neutral. It includes those experiences that we want to stay, those we want to avoid or get rid of, and those we are indifferent about. It is like looking at our mind in a mirror and coming face to face with ourselves. We are looking directly at our habitual patterns and all the realities we have constructed about ourselves and about our situation, with our sources of suffering and happiness.

Now what specific role does meditation play in contemplative psychotherapy? Here there is another distinction we have to make. Meditation is the discipline the contemplative psychotherapist uses to train one's mind. The practice and study of Buddhist psychology offers the therapist, or anyone who practices it, an opportunity to familiarize themselves intimately with the sanity as well as the confusion within their own experience. Through practicing and studying meditation, one begins to feel more at home with the wide range of his or her own psychological experiences, to get to know them intimately, and learn to be able to stay with them as we accompany others in their own process.

Although we have tried for centuries to treat our body and our mind as separate phenomena, in fact, our body and our mind are constantly making an effort to synchronize with each other, and then to stay in synchronicity. Usually our habit is that our body is running after our mind, trying to keep up to wherever the mind is distracting itself. If we are sitting down reading, studying, or working, our mind gets distracted and remembers that it should call someone on the telephone. Then there goes our body looking for the phone. Soon we come back and sit down to read and very quickly our mind wanders away again, thinking how nice it would be to be eating something tasty. Once again there goes our body to the refrigerator. Over and over in that way, our mind continuously gets distracted in endlessly creative ways. By the end of the day, no wonder we are tired!

The body attempts to stay synchronized with the mind. For example, when the mind gets distracted with anxious thoughts, the body synchronizes activating the whole physiological repertoire associated with anxiety. If we have sad thoughts, the body follows and feels sad.

However, the body has two limitations. First, it cannot actually fly after the mind. If our minds could, we might all find ourselves flying right now towards a Caribbean island! Secondly, the body has no choice but to stay in the present. We cannot transport ourselves back to the past with our mind, nor can we journey into the future with our plans and expectations. Although it is obviously so, we do not often fully comprehend that the past has already happened and will not come back, and that the future will never arrive because when it does, it is the present, not the future. Therefore the only true reality that we have is the present moment. What we are doing in the practice of meditation is synchronizing our mind and body in the present moment. We are learning to move in the opposite direction of what we habitually do. During meditation we may inadvertently leave our body while literally sitting still in one place and then through awareness we bring our mind back again and again to where our body is. Our body is the continual reference point that is telling the mind where reality is. In this context, reality is the present moment, very simply, although it is always changing.

I would like to invite you to do a brief session of meditation with me so that you can know better what we are talking about when I say that meditation is a discipline for training a therapist. Many of you already may have had experience with different meditation practices. I would like to invite you to open to this particular way of meditating and see what happens. If we can share this experience together, that will give us a common ground to continue this dialogue further.

Instruction for the practice:

Body
- The posture is a straight back that is not leaning against the back of the chair. Your feet are on the floor parallel to each other with

hands on the thighs and the palms facing down. The head is aligned with the spinal column. Eyes are open with a relaxed focus about two meters in front and downwards.
- Connect with the sky above your head, the earth below your feet, and the space all around you.
- Feel the strength of your back and the vulnerability of your chest.
- Take your place between heaven and earth with dignity.
- Acknowledge who I am and how I feel today, here and now.

Mind
- Bring your attention to your breathing.
- When you realize that your mind has become distracted, label it thinking and return to the breath.

Although ideally now I could ask you what you have observed about your minds and how much are you really able to stay in the present moment, I think I can fairly safely guess what you would say. The majority of people relate more or less the same experiences. That one's attention doesn't stay with the breathing more than just a few seconds; that it is constantly returning to the past, planning about the future, making a list of the things that need to be done; and that often we are thinking of what we would rather be doing instead of what we are doing. Our minds are very well trained in the art of distraction. In fact, we think it is very efficient to be able to think of several things at the same time. We usually report that I just was not able to keep my mind on the breathing, as if it were *my* problem, although that is a commonly shared experience; we notice rather quickly that that's the way our minds work. If we observe carefully, we will see that we cannot really do more than one thing at a time with awareness.

We find that we are in the same position as a school teacher constantly asking, or even shouting at, our students to "Pay attention!" But if one does not train one's attention, how can anyone possibly do that? The mind of those students is the same as our own mind, constantly getting distracted; and we are the same as those teachers who constantly have to pull rabbits out of a hat to keep the attention of their students. Or better to say, we try to bring back their attention with something that catches their interest.

When we are the students and we have four exams in one week, while we are studying for one, we carry the other three in our minds as a preoccupation and we end up feeling exhausted with the sensation that we did not study for any of them very well. As we study for one, we are thinking of the others, although we know we cannot really study for all of them at the same time. We are just generating confusion and anxiety because of our inability to have our mind focused: to study one, let go of it, and then go on to the next topic. What also characterizes our students is that while they are studying they are distracted thinking about the parties they would rather be enjoying. Of course, if they do go partying, their minds are worrying at the party about the tests they should be studying for. We do not ever really do one thing or the other fully, but end up anxious and tired, which is a granted form of suffering, or that which we call *samsara*, the cycle of confusion that goes on endlessly.

In our daily lives, we can ask ourselves how many times we have really been washing the dishes when we were washing the dishes. Where is our mind when we are driving? When we are eating? And we can even go so far as to ask, where is our mind when we are making love? Not only is our mind habitually somewhere else, it is also as if we are walking around with a commentator inside our heads: that part of us which is always commenting about what is going on and takes us out of our direct experience. From the point of view of the practice of being mindful and aware, what is important here is not trying to ensure that the mind never wanders, but rather that we are able to bring it back to the present with greater ease and frequency.

It is important to keep in mind that the problem is not thinking per se, the problem is believing that our thoughts are, or are equivalent to, reality. When we make plans, it is easy to forget that it is a plan. Then when the reality does not go along with our plan, we get annoyed and frustrated; we look for whom to blame. When we expect something from another and then they do not meet our expectations, it is easier for us to get upset with them rather than see that we have created this whole scenario in our minds. Then based on our ideas, we end up believing that the situation has to be like that.

Since in our usual training as therapists we never have the opportunity to directly observe how our mind functions, it is easy for therapists to have the fantasy that when a client is telling us what is going on with them, our attention is completely attuned to listening to them and what they are saying. But if we observe more precisely, we see that our mind is continually wandering, coming back to listen for awhile, and then once again getting distracted. We are recalling what we were doing before the session, we think about what will happen afterwards, about what we should have said to our daughter before she left. We think of intelligent or helpful things to say to our client so that we can feel we are good therapists. We think about how truly boring what we are hearing seems to us. We think of so many different things and we do not even really notice we are doing it. As for what we don't really hear, we fill in the blanks in various ways, without very much awareness that we are doing so.

The ability to truly be present with the other has repeatedly been commented on as the most important gift a psychotherapist can offer a person who is suffering. This ability to be with others arises from developing the capacity to be with oneself in the present moment, no matter what mental state one might be experiencing, whether it involves intense emotions, confused thoughts, or tranquility and silence. This is asically the ability to stay present with oneself and relate with kindness to whatever arises.

In the practice of meditation, we are not trying to make our mind blank, nor are we particularly trying to avoid distractions. Instead we are learning how to bring the mind back to the present with more frequency. What do we observe when we look at ourselves in this mirror? We see all the things that prevent us from being in the present; we see how our mind functions. That is why it is not helpful to try to make the mind blank, because then we would not be able to see anything in the mirror, to see how our mind functions. When we undertake the simplest practice of just sitting and doing nothing other than breathe naturally and follow the breath's natural rhythms, we quickly observe how difficult it is for us to do something so simple. In a sense, we are working more with the obstacles rather than trying to achieve something; the path is the goal.

The contemplative therapist does not have his patients sit and meditate. Maybe in exceptional cases they would eventually suggest that. But more the point for the therapist is how to relate to the other with the vision that comes from their own practice of meditation. This bigger perspective arises from the experience of being mindful and aware rather than from some theory. For the contemplative therapist, Buddhism is not a theory to which one ascribes or believes in, but rather the result of his or her own experience of the practice of meditation as a valid source of knowledge. The theoretical aspect nurtures and complements that practice, but at no time does it ever replace it.

The fundamental root teaching of Buddhist psychology is the notion that although our basic wisdom may be temporarily covered over, it is nonetheless always there and we can cultivate it. Our mind is like the clear sky and our thoughts are like the clouds that temporarily cover it over. Nonetheless, the sky is always there. Our intrinsic well-being is characterized by openness, clarity, and warmth, although temporarily we walk around closed, confused and critical. With time and practice, students of Buddhist psychology develop the capacity to recognize the sanity in the midst of their most confused and convoluted mental states. Their journey is to nurture that sanity within themselves and in others.

What is it then that covers this health and basic sanity, this basic goodness or Buddha nature that we all have and only need to uncover? What gets in the way is basically resistance to what in Buddhism is called the Three Marks of Existence, or as Pema Chödrön (1994) refers to them, *the unavoidable facts of life*. These are suffering, impermanence, and the absence or insubstantiality of ego.

The First Inescapable Fact of Life is Suffering

Our physical body is characterized by its potential to feel pain when it is broken, torn, sick, and so on. Our emotional body is characterized by its potential to feel pain, hurt, and anger when we feel rejected, ignored, ashamed, and so on. This is part of what we are and is characteristic not only of us as human beings but of any sentient beings.

We can make here a principal distinction. On the one hand there is what is called *duhkha* in Sanskrit, which is the pain that is an unavoidable experience, direct and without commentary. This is different than the suffering that arises when we are not really present in our direct experience, but rather engrossed in our holding on or resisting in our never ending struggle against the present situation. In this second case, our conceptual mind has taken the place of our direct experience. Pain is pain; suffering arises from "I don't want to be in pain." We can make this distinction as well in our emotional response when we lose someone close to us. If someone close to us dies and we accept more easily their death, maybe it is because of their advanced age or because they have been sick and suffering a lot. We will feel a lot of sadness, but probably we will not suffer as such. On the other hand, if someone dies and with all our being we resist accepting their passing, maybe because they are so young, they had their whole life ahead of them; then the pain is transformed into suffering. In this example, is it the death of the other or is it our resistance to accepting this reality that is making us suffer?

Do you know anyone who has passed through this life without suffering in its more general sense, without going through a bad time in some way or other, without suffering in a physical or emotional way? If it is a fact that all human beings suffer during their lifetimes, would not it be better if we could accept that suffering is part of life? Instead of resisting that fact, we could learn how to relate with our suffering rather than going along always trying to avoid it, reject it, or feeling that when we suffer it is because something has gone wrong in our lives.

One of the principal sources of suffering is thinking that there is something basically wrong with us. We think that if we were different than how we are, everything would go well. Or that if the others were different than how they are, all would go well. Instead, think how it would be if we could really teach our children that life will not always be like they want it to be and that they are not to blame for that fact. How would our relationship with them be if we let them learn to relate with this reality rather than trying to protect them from the suffering that sooner or later they will surely encounter? Perhaps their lives and ours would be quite different.

Suffering is Based Upon Three Basic Emotions

We are constantly experiencing either *passion*, "I want what I don't have, and when I get it, I get very attached to it;" *aggression*, "I get what I don't want, and I reject it;" or *ignorance*, "I don't know what I want or don't want, and everything passes me by without touching me." These are the three basic emotions that generate our suffering.

We are constantly living between *hope* that others and the world will be like we want them to be and the *fear* that they will not really be that way. We are always trying to either reject or attach ourselves to something, thinking that this next time we will get the result we want.

Buddhism is based on what we could call *experiential realism*, the abandonment of the fantasy of how we think things should be or how we want them to be. Instead, it counsels us that we place ourselves in the vulnerable position of seeing how things really are and admitting how we really feel about them. Pleasure is pleasure and pain is pain. That is our direct experience, beyond hope and fear, rather than the scenarios we construct out of that experience. The present moment is a space of enormous vulnerability. We are not in control, we are not totally *on top of it*, and the world might touch us more than we might like. That place might involve pain, sadness, rage, happiness, in fact, everything!

I want to offer an example of this experiential realism that obviously does not come from the Buddha, but I think serves as a useful image. We are going to imagine that life is a chicken soup with peas. It has a little bit of everything in it: peas, potatoes, shredded carrots, onions, etc. When we are served up this bowl we did not particularly order ourselves, we immediately want to put aside one or more of the ingredients. Maybe this ingredient does not sit well with me. I tried it once and did not like it and I have never cared for it since. Maybe we just want the freedom to choose the ingredients we like and do not care for this particular mix that has been presented to us. Not this, not today. We like the chicken and the peas, but forget the carrots and potatoes. Or we like the peas, potatoes, carrots, and onions, but we do not like the dark pieces of chicken that have found their way into our soup. Or we just want the chicken by itself, no veggies. What we do not want is the whole chicken soup with peas. We never eat that mix of ingredients. Then we toss this aside into a convenient bag, along with all the other things in life we want to avoid. From time to time we toss in more things that we think are too mushy, too spicy, too old, or too odd. We carry this trash bag around with us wherever we go, knowing we are going to use it again and again. In this recurring process, we end up confining ourselves to the same familiar choices, the experiences that we reheat and eat again and again. Supposedly that keeps us safe, but in effect that also means we never allow ourselves to taste the flavor of today's soup just as it is, peas, carrots, and all. We never let ourselves taste life just as it is and then we complain life is such a routine!

To offer another example, if we observe carefully couples in relationship, what is most common is that each of them spends a great deal of time expecting that the other will be different than he or she is. If only they change, then we will be happy, and everything will go well. And our partner is thinking the same thing about us! There is a subtle and constant aggression here against the other and against our self. There is always something going awry with ourselves that we feel we need to improve and even more so there is something the other needs to correct. Our relationships are based on how we would like the other person to be, rather than on who they are and what is really happening today. Usually, we do not really consider what has been the past history of the other and our self. What are their and our true limitations, potentialities, good qualities, and defects?

To contemplate this situation accurately; to look at our self, others, and reality in a contemplative way, signifies moving towards it. We relate with the other person or situation just as it is, with openness, clarity, and warmth. This type of contemplation is not dependent on whether the person or situation is something I want or not right now. The more I try to deny a situation or try to change it or myself, the less I can see it or myself clearly. So we remain more stuck or unable to respond. We are constantly trying to manipulate reality. From a contemplative viewpoint, we should abandon all hope of manipulating a situation and relate with it just as it is; from there we will more clearly know what to do. Our action is the result of staying in the vulnerable space of the present moment. It is not a strategy of manipulation based on our fantasies of security.

When we put aside preferring one type of experience over another, preferring various kinds of good thoughts over bad ones, we are taking a break from the continual back and forth struggle of attachment or rejection. We are allowing a space to open in our self where we can see the nature of how our thoughts really are. This is when we might have some moments of understanding, of sympathy for our pain. We are beginning to relax with who we are; perhaps we are able even to laugh at ourselves and how seriously we take the dramas of our life!

Curiously, this is where we begin to change, or to say it more accurately, where change begins to happen. When we stop struggling and open a bit of space in our constant battle, when we can see our own direct experience with more kindness and smile a little, change occurs naturally.

The Second Unavoidable Fact of Life is Impermanence

We are constantly trying to hold on to some permanent point of reference. But since everything is always moving and changing, there does not exist any such reference point. This scares us a lot. We are left trapped in the illusion of security. Letting go of this illusion leaves us alone in the vulnerability of the present moment. At the same time this is the only way for us to discover freedom. If I am not manipulating reality in an effort to feel safe, I have the enormous liberty of opening myself to every experience, of letting the world touch me with all of its richness from moment to moment. Paradoxically, through letting go, there arises the great potential within the real world around us and within our own experience. If we do not run away by trying to escape from this moment of openness and vulnerability, many possibilities open up for us.

It is a common feeling that when things are going well for us, we want them to stay that way forever. Although if we imagine a kiss lasting for five hours, that would probably make us doubt the sanity of that wish! We try to clutch on to what we think of as positive and as soon as we have it, we begin to fear losing it; it becomes a source of suffering for us. Then when things are going badly, we want to avoid them, to escape this experience. Since that is not always possible that also becomes a source of suffering for us, especially since it is very difficult for us to distinguish between situations that are avoidable or only temporary obstacles, from those we cannot sidestep or get through quickly.

We have so much fear that things possibly might not work out the way we like that we come to expect negative experiences will arise for us and live in anxious anticipation of the danger of pain or failure. We are preoccupied and we do not know how to occupy ourselves with what is actually happening in any given present moment. On the other end of the spectrum, we often think it is better not to let ourselves be too happy when things are going well. We know better than to let ourselves get too attached and then find ourselves falling into a deep hole and hurt when things come to an end. In this flipside of our fear, instead of acknowledging the natural movements and rhythms of life, we feel we have done or are about to do something wrong. We feel guilty, that we are going to fail again. This also becomes a significant contributor to our suffering.

Then, at times, we so desperately want to get away from suffering when it arises that we lose the bigger perspective, and that suffering occupies all of our space. We are struggling so hard to get out of the black hole we find ourselves in that, in our desperate struggle, we have no idea of how to relate with it. We do not want to look at anything. We do not want to feel the pain that we are so afraid of feeling. We are so anxious to get out that we do not see that just behind us there is a stairway. It is always there as some other possibility if we give ourselves enough space to just stop, to stay with the pain and contemplate the situation, and to feel what is there to be felt. We can come to know ourselves anew in this place and discover what there is to learn from it.

The most extreme instance of our denial of impermanence is our denial of death. It is such a taboo in our culture that we do not even mention it. We fear if we do talk about it, we will be seen as harbingers of disaster. Have we ever thought to ask ourselves how we could and would live our lives if we never lost sight of the fact that we could die at any moment? We are not talking here about walking around with the specter of death hovering over our shoulder, nor are we particularly talking about what we would do if we knew we were going to die next week. It is more immediate than that. How would I live this present moment just where I am if this were the last moment of my life? Not only do we deny the ultimate reality of death, if we want to refer to it in that way, but also the relative moment to moment reality of death in the sense of the constant fluctuations of life. Every moment everything is dying and giving way to something new. We are so attached to what we have or do not have that we do not see the constant opportunities that change is offering us. Even beyond that, if we look at the reality of death without fear, that awareness of death can help us achieve greater clarity about our priorities in life and greater appreciation for the preciousness of each moment.

The Third Unavoidable Fact of Life is the Absence or Insubstantiality of Ego

That which relates to impermanence is what we call *me*. This is the basic ignorance of not wanting to see that this entity which we call *me* is nothing more than a construction we have made up about ourselves throughout our life's history. It is based on the image that others have shown us or that we have sculpted out of our own experiences. We believe that these definitions we have about ourselves are solid and continuous in time. We create them, we entrap ourselves in them, and we defend them fiercely before others. We are in a constant battle to maintain and expand our egos and this struggle is the root of our suffering.

The ego is not even the bad guy of this movie; if we see it that way then we find ourselves caught in another layer of struggle against it. That battle is just more of the same, another manifestation of the ego. As Trungpa Rinpoche (1973) put it, the way to proceed is that the ego can be worn out like the soles of our shoes. We only have to journey from suffering to liberation, through the path of being mindful and aware. It is not just our ideas of me that are of concern here; it is also our ideas of *mine*. If there is a jacket on the floor where everyone is walking, I can walk by it without the slightest upset until it dawns on me that, "Hey, that is my jacket." Then my whole relationship with that reality changes. We also are used to thinking about *my* husband or wife, *my* children, *my* family as if who they are and what they do exists only in constant reference to *me*, since they are part of what is mine.

Whether this *me* is on top of the world or depressed, shy or outgoing, equally it is a construction that we continue fueling, even if we do not like it, because it provides us with our identity. We believe that this recurring experience of ours, that which we relive again and again as habitual patterns of behavior that we keep tucked away in our memory banks since childhood, that "this is who I am." This is my nature and it is permanent. It makes me uniquely who I am, independent of others. This is the same *I* who often feels so frightened by the basic Buddhist premise that the ultimate reality is emptiness. However, that ultimate reality is not just some kind of empty space or a black hole; rather, it is a plenipotentiary space that allows me to see that I am more than that which I say or see about myself.

Can anyone really say that they are always solemn or charming, always introverted or extroverted, or any of those other categories that we call qualities or shortcomings? Maybe the most we can say honestly is that at times we are one way and at other times the other. It all depends on a complex network of interdependent factors. Then we are this and that as a manifestation; neither this nor that as our nature. It is much more fluid, interdependent, and full of possibilities than we usually acknowledge.

Hopefully we are now beginning to see that it is the resistance against these three marks of existence that generates our suffering. This points to what are called the First and Second Noble Truths that were the initial teachings of the Buddha after he achieved enlightenment. They are the truth of suffering and the truth of the origin of suffering. Once we realize these two basic truths, we can see that it is possible for this suffering to end, and that there is a path we can take to make that happen. These are the Third and Fourth Noble Truths: the cessation of suffering and the path.

We are not talking here about reforming or changing ourselves, or making ourselves better. Instead we are talking about learning to journey within confusion, chaos, aggression, passion, and ignorance. We can skillfully work with them to gradually liberate ourselves from their power over us. From this perspective, the path is the willingness to observe our mind and our experience so that we can see who we are and how we operate without judgment or blame. It is being willing to unmask our continual deceptions and manipulations. Our confusion and suffering will unravel themselves in a natural and organic way if we can stop our unnecessary struggles against them and instead embrace our experience in a compassionate and loving manner. We can open a space where our health and basic sanity can manifest, where we can express that which we really are. This is the accurate and natural path of healing and liberation.

Finally, with regards to a vision that a contemplative psychotherapist can train in and use in their work, I would like to add here that the Buddhist approach is an ecological vision of oneself. In the same way that a flower will end up as waste and waste will end up producing a flower, our neurosis can be transformed into wisdom. Neurosis and wisdom are made out of the same stuff. If we throw away our neurosis, we are throwing away the source of our wisdom. It is the same energy that can be used in different ways, and that can be used as the good earthy material we work with as we travel towards liberation.

In that light, the contemplative therapist discovers and deepens this vision upon which they will base their work, based on the practice of meditation and the study of Buddhist teachings. As I have said, the knowledge gathered arises from the practice itself. On that basis, one makes the journey as a therapist keeping clearly in mind that for the therapist, as well as the client, the path is the goal.

The contemplative therapist's journey has many interrelated, yet simple, characteristics (Wegela, 1994). Along this journey, one builds the capacity or is engaged in learning how to stay attentive to the other. We learn to be really able to listen, to be able to observe when our own mind becomes distracted, and then bring it back, staying present and aware of the experience of the other and oneself.

Contemplative therapists are able to recognize their own limitations so that we can better observe our own habitual patterns when confronted by others' emotions. As the path is never ending, one needs to continue contemplative practices to fully embrace and skillfully relate with whatever arises in our own experience and that of others without judgment and with openness, clarity, and warmth. Our experience of the nature of our mind as a clear, open sky allows us to relate to that same basic nature of the mind in others. Through the process of becoming comfortable with our own experiences, we are able to stay in the midst of the confusion, pain, and suffering of another person without needing to manipulate the situation. We have confidence in the health and basic sanity of ourselves and others, thus realizing that our common journey has more to do with uncovering inherent sanity rather than trying to become something different than what we are. We all can learn to live in each moment, even the most painful ones, in a healthy and sane way, with openness, clarity, and warmth.

We aim to open a space so that our clients basically feel accepted and accompanied on their own individual journies of discovering the particular qualities of each situation that arises and learning how to bring those experiences into their own path. We accompany the other in their path of transforming their confusion into wisdom, discovering sparks of wisdom in the middle of the most confused states.

We may suggest, too, that clients embark on a journey toward discovering who they really are, rather than looking for what about them needs to be changed. Through the therapeutic alliance, we look at how the person has manifested in distinct moments of their history and from there help them find the capacity to go beyond those solid and continuous definitions of their self. The goal is to learn from experience through being able to stay with any situation and contemplate its qualities, intensity, and texture without judgment; to learn to distinguish between direct experience and the interpretation of that experience; to listen to and get to know their own commentator; to check in with their physiological experience for insight and ground.

In some way, we are teaching meditation in action; that the person can learn to be mindful and aware of their actual concrete experiences in daily life. They can observe the thoughts that accompany their experiences: what they reject, what they grasp, and what they ignore. What happens when things change? They learn to observe, learn about their fears, emotions, patterns of behavior and thinking. All this takes place within an attitude of accommodation and care for oneself. In summary, our task is to accompany the other person from the contemplative perspective as they learn to recognize their own sources of suffering and see how their very neuroses can be the working basis in their journey towards happiness and wisdom.

References

Chödrön, P. (1994). *Start where you are: A guide to compassionate living*. Boston: Shambhala.

Trungpa, C. (1973). *Cutting through spiritual materialism*. Boston: Shambhala.

Trungpa, C. (1976). *The myth of freedom and the way of meditation*. Berkeley, CA: Shambhala.

Trungpa, C. (1988). *Shambhala: The sacred path of the warrior*. Boston: Shambhala.

Trungpa, C. (2004). *Meditation in action*. Boston: Shambhala.

Trunga, C. (2005) *The sanity we are born with: A Buddhist approach to psychology* (C. Gimian, Ed.). Boston: Shambala.

Wegela, K. K. (1988). "Touch and go" in clinical practice: Some implications of the view of intrinsic health for psychotherapy, *Journal of Contemplative Psychotherapy, 5,* 3-23.

Wegela, K. K. (1994). Contemplative psychotherapy: A path to uncovering brilliant sanity. *Journal of Contemplative Psychotherapy, 6,* 27-51.

Wegela, K. K. (1996). *How to be a help instead of a nuisance: Practical approaches to giving support, service and encouragement to others*. Boston: Shambhala.

Zimbardo, P. G. & Gerrig, R. J. (1999). *Psychology and life*. New York: Addison Wesley Longman, Inc.

About the Contributors

Zoë Avstreih, MS, LPC, LP, ADTR, Founder/Director of The Center for the Study of Authentic Movement, is a pioneer in the development of Authentic Movement. She is a Member of the Academy of Dance Therapists Registered, a Licensed Psychoanalyst, and Core Faculty at Naropa University in Boulder, Colorado where she serves as Co-Chair of the Somatic Counseling Psychology Department and Director of the graduate Dance Movement Therapy Program. She lectures and teaches internationally and has published widely in the field.

Lauren Casalino, MA, LPC, is the Chairwoman of the Masters of Arts in Contemplative Psychotherapy Program (MACP) at Naropa University. She co-founded Windhorse Family & Elder Care and has a private psychotherapy practice specializing in couples, infertility, grief, and end of life passage.

Kyle Thomas Darnall, MA. After graduating from the Masters of Arts in Contemplative Psychotherapy Program (MACP) at Naropa University in 1994, Kyle spent ten years working for the Boys & Girls Clubs of Central Minnesota in the area of violence prevention. In 1998 he received the Caritas Award from the College of St. Benedict and St. John's University for his community service. He is currently finishing his doctoral degree in counseling psychology at the University of St. Thomas Graduate School of Professional Psychology. His research activities include the interaction of race, class, culture and gender on diagnostics. His clinical specialties include multicultural counseling and psychological assessment.

Han F. de Wit, PhD, is an Acharya in the Shambhala Buddhist tradition and is an internationally respected Buddhist scholar and teacher. He has taught psychology at numerous academic institutions including the Free University of Amsterdam and Naropa University. He is author of several books including *Contemplative Psychology* and *The Spiritual Path*, and has edited and contributed to numerous other publications.

Michael M. Dow, MA, is a graduate student in clinical psychology at the University of the Rockies in Colorado Springs, CO. After completing the Masters of Arts in Contemplative Psychotherapy Program (MACP) at Naropa University, he has spent the past six years working in community mental health with an emphasis on group and mindfulness-based approaches. He is currently completing his internship at the People's Clinic in Boulder, CO in a program integrating primary care with behavioral health. His dissertation is a qualitative study of different approaches to incorporating mindfulness with psychotherapy.

Mark Epstein, MD, is a psychiatrist in private practice in New York City and clinical assistant professor of psychology at New York University. He is the author of several books including *Thoughts without a Thinker, Going to Pieces without Falling Apart,* and *Psychotherapy without the Self: A Buddhist Perspective.*

James Evans, PhD, has studied, practiced and taught Maitri Space Awareness since 1979. He has taught as adjunct faculty at Naropa University, and taught Maitri and psychology in the United States and abroad. Dr. Evans was one of the early founding members of Maitri Psychological Services in Boulder, Colorado. He is a licensed clinical psychologist and currently supervises clinicians and teams at the Boulder Mental Health Center.

Jeffrey Fortuna, MA, LPC, received his MA degree in Contemplative Psychotherapy at The Naropa University in 1980. He served as a core faculty member in that department until 1989. In 1981, he cofounded and worked with Maitri Psychological Services in Boulder, Colorado. In 1988, he cofounded and directed the Friendship House Project, a residential therapeutic community and a joint project of Maitri Psychological Services, The Naropa University, and the Boulder County Mental Health Center.

Verónica Guzmán, graduated from the Pontificia Universidad Católica de Chile with a degree in Psychology and has been a practicing psychologist and psychotherapist in Santiago, Chile since 1976. She currently teaches at the Psychology School of the Universidad Diego Portales and is the Director of the newly formed Yeshe Institute were she teaches Buddhist Psychology and Contemplative Psychotherapy. Ms. Guzman has been a student of Sakyong Mipham Rinpoche since 1990 and was the Director of the Shambhala Center in Chile from 1996 to 1998 and from 2001 to 2003. Bringing together her practice as a psychotherapist and her Buddhist practice has been a central and essential part of her personal journey.

Silvia Hast, MA, originally from Santiago, Chile, obtained a degree in Business Engineering from the Universidad de Chile in 1973. She became a student of Chogyam Trungpa, Rinpoche in 1978 and graduated from Naropa University with an MA in Contemplative Psychology in 1993. She has been in private practice in Boulder and Longmont, Colorado since then, and is currently owner and director of WEAVE Counseling, LLC. She was also the Meditation Practice Coordinator at Naropa University from 1989 to 1991 and has taught and been a Meditation Instructor there for many years. She believes that her Buddhist training and practice informs her psychotherapy practice.

About the Contributors

Louis Hoffman, PhD, is a core faculty member of the Colorado School of Professional Psychology, a college of the University of the Rockies. Co-author of *Spirituality and Psychological Health* and *The God Image Handbook for Spiritual Counseling and Psychotherapy: Theory, Research, and Practice*, Dr. Hoffman has authored numerous chapters and articles on existential psychotherapy, philosophical issues in psychotherapy, and religious/spiritual issues in psychotherapy. He is also on the editorial board of the *Journal of Humanistic Psychology* and *PsycCRITIQUES: APA Review of Books*. Dr. Hoffman remains active in providing therapy and psychological assessment services at the Center for Growth in Colorado Springs, Colorado in addition to providing training and supervision opportunities through the Depth Psychotherapy Institute, P.C.

MacAndrew S. Jack, PhD, is an Associate Professor at Naropa University in the Masters of Arts in Contemplative Psychotherapy Program (MACP) where he was the director of training. Dr. Jack trained in CBT, behavioral medicine and psychoanalytically oriented psychotherapy at Temple University and Harvard Medical School, and has published and presented nationally on anxiety and the psychophysiology of breathing in panic and wellness. He has worked with students and staff in counseling centers at the University of Tulsa, Temple University, and Swarthmore College. He currently works with individuals and couples in his private practice in Boulder Colorado where he specializes in anxiety, mind/body approaches to health, and depth-oriented psychotherapy.

Francis J. Kaklauskas, MA, graduated from the Naropa University's Masters of Arts in Contemplative Psychotherapy Program (MACP) in 1992 and is a doctoral candidate in clinical psychology at the Colorado School of Professional Psychology, a college of the University of the Rockies. He has presented at numerous professional conferences on topics including group psychotherapy theory and research, comparative psychoanalytic theory, existential psychology, and human sexuality. He recently presented by invitation on Buddhism and Psychotherapy at *The Psychology of International Religion: Western and Chinese Perspective* in Bejing, as well as conducted trainings for psychologists in Hong Kong. He created the *Group Process Inventory*, a psychometric instrument that measures a broad range of group events that link process and outcome. He co-authored the Group Psychotherapy chapter in *The Handbook of Clinical Psychology*. Additionally, he was the primary psychological consultant and on-screen presenter for the United Learning three part video, *Hooked: The Addiction Trap*. He has a private practice in Boulder, Colorado, specializing in group treatment, individual psychotherapy, and clinical supervision and consultation.

Charles Knapp, MA, entered the mental health field in 1982, working with addictions and acute mental illness. He received his Master's degree in Contemplative Psychotherapy at The Naropa University in 1987 and taught at Naropa for several years. He founded Windhorse Community Services with Ed Podvoll in 1990. He has a special interest in exploring the adaptability of the Windhorse model to different diagnostic and recovery needs, and has presented his ideas at numerous professional conferences.

Abigail M. Lindemann, BA, graduated from the University of Pennsylvania with a Bachelors of Arts in Psychology. She is a graduate student in the Masters of Arts in Contemplative Psychotherapy Program (MACP) at Naropa University. In addition to her graduate studies she is involved in a research program looking at the effects of contemplative practice in the training of mental health professionals.

Susan Nimmanheminda, PhD, LCSW, CGP, is an Adjunct Faculty member at Naropa University where she teaches Group Process, and she is the Executive Director of the Colorado Center for Modern Psychoanalytic Studies. She has presented at numerous national conferences on the convergences between Buddhism and psychotherapy. She is in private practice in Boulder, Colorado.

Elizabeth A. Olson, LCSW, received a master of social work degree from the University of Washington at Seattle and completed a Post Master's Internship in Clinical Social Work from the University of California at Berkeley. She is finishing a doctoral degree in clinical psychology at the Colorado School of Professional Psychology, a college of the University of the Rockies. She directs the group training program at the University of Colorado at Boulder's Psychological and Psychiatric Services and serves as an adjunct faculty at the Naropa University's Masters of Arts in Contemplative Psychotherapy Program (MACP). She lectures and presents on issues related to child and adolescent development, parenting, and group treatment. She is working in private practice in Boulder, Colorado specializing in the treatment of women's developmental issues, eating disorders, self harm behaviors, and family and group therapy.

Edward Podvoll, MD, was a graduate and former faculty member of the Washington Psychoanalytic Institute. For nine years, he was a staff psychiatrist at Chestnut Lodge Hospital and the Director of Training and Education at the Austen Riggs Center. He was the Director of the graduate program in Contemplative Psychotherapy at The Naropa University from 1978 to 1990. He was the founding Medical Director of Maitri Psychological Services, the first Windhorse treatment center. Dr. Podvoll presented the Windhorse Project in his groundbreaking book, *Recovering Sanity*. In 1990, Dr. Podvoll entered a long-term meditation retreat in a Buddhist monastery in France. He completed this retreat in

2002 and returned to Boulder to resume his teaching, writing, and consulting activities. He had a special interest in the training of Windhorse team leaders and in meditation experience as the basis for helping others.

Dzogchen Ponlop Rinpoche is acknowledged as one of the foremost scholars in the Nyingma and Kagyu schools of Tibetan Buddhism. Rinpoche is a graduate of Karma Shri Nalanda Institute. He has multiple publications, including the books *Penetrating Wisdon: The Aspiration of Samantabhadra, Wild Awakening,* and *Mind beyond Death.* Rinpoche is president of Nitartha International where he oversees activities in preserving Asian literature and manages Nitartha's educational and preservation programs. He serves as abbot of Dzogchen Monastery, India, and director of Kamalashila Institut, Germany. He has been a visiting professor at Naropa University, as well as lectured at numerous academic intuitions worldwide.

Alexandra Shenpen, PhD, is a mindfulness-based psychotherapist in private practice in Boulder, Colorado. She is a senior adjunct professor at Naropa University and leads Maitri programs in the United States and abroad. Dr. Shenpen mentors and supervises graduate psychology students, and is a certified instructor of the contemplative art of Ikebana/Kado.

Farrell Silverberg, PhD, NCPsyA, is a clinical psychologist, a certified psychoanalyst, and was the first Western student of Taopsychotherapy master Rhee Dong Shik in Seoul, Korea. Silverberg has lectured internationally and has published in journals in the United States and in Asia. He began integrating psychoanalysis and Buddhism thirty years ago, and his 1988 paper on the combined technique is called *Therapeutic Resonance.* Silverberg is currently a Supervising and Training psychoanalyst at the Philadelphia School of Psychoanalysis. His recently published book, *Make the Leap,* distills psychoanalytic concepts into accessible language for the lay public.

Letitia Swann, MA, completed undergraduate work at Barnard College and Middlebury College and completed her Master's degree in counseling psychology from Lesley College. A mother of three children, she has a private practice in Nederland, Colorado, specializing in women's issues and mothering, and is a longtime practitioner of Jin Shin Jyutsu.

Matthew Tomatz, MA, lives and works in Boulder, Colorado as a psychotherapist, addictions counselor, and yoga instructor. Matthew was born in Wyoming; he studied music in Texas and Ohio and holds two degrees in music and music education. Matthew is a graduate of Naropa University, where he is now an adjunct faculty member and continues to cultivate and teach the practice of contemplative psychotherapy. Matthew's life is enriched by his passion for music, nature, yoga, and his wife and son.

Patricia Townsend, MA, is a graduate of Naropa University's Masters of Arts in Contemplative Psychotherapy Program (MACP). She has a private practice in Boulder, Colorado specializing in individual, couple, and group psychotherapy. She is a crisis worker for the Mental Health Center of Boulder County. She also has worked as an editor for Buddhist and psychological texts, including the work of the Dzogchen Ponlop Rinpoche.

Chögyam Trunpga Rinpoche is widely acknowledged as a pivotal figure in introducing Buddhism to the Western world. He was founder and president of Vajradhatu, Naropa University, and Shambhala Training. He has written and published extensively, including the books, *Cutting Through Spiritual Materialism, The Myth of Freedom,* and *Shambhala: The Sacred Path of the Warrior.*

Helena Unger, MA, graduated from Naropa University in 1983 with a Masters in Contemplative Psychotherapy. She has worked for twenty five years with families and children as a custody evaluator, divorce mediator and psychotherapist. Helena works in a contemplative approach with high conflict families to help them better understand the impact on their children. She also teaches at Naropa University.

Robert Unger, LCSW, PhD, has been a practicing psychotherapist and psychoanalyst for 30 years. He is a long-time faculty member in the Masters of Arts in Contemplative Psychotherapy Program (MACP) at the Naropa University and is currently on the leadership team of that program. Pursuant to his special interest in group psychotherapy and group dynamics, he conducts several treatment and supervision groups, consults to organizations on group issues, is a co-founder of the Colorado Center for the Advancement of Group Studies and the Colorado Group Psychotherapy Society, and is a frequent presenter at the national conference of the American Group Psychotherapy Association. He was recently awarded fellowship status in the A.G.P.A., and elected to its national board of directors. His publications include Conflict Management in Group Psychotherapy, and Selection and Composition Criteria for Group Psychotherapy.

Robert Walker, MA, has been a teacher and meditation instructor in the Shambhala Buddhist tradition for over 20 years, working with all levels of students, the majority of whom are health professionals. He developed a complete CRLA approved tutor training curricula, in particular developing original curricula on the psychology of learning and tutoring writing. He currently archives and distributes Pema Chödrön's audio and video teachings, advising groups and individuals about their use.

Karen Kissel Wegela, PhD, has been on the faculty of the Masters of Arts in Contemplative Psychotherapy Program (MACP) since 1981 and served for many years as its director. A psychologist in private practice, she is also the author of numerous chapters and articles and the book, *How to Be a Help Instead of a Nuisance*. She has been a presenter at conferences and programs on the integration of Buddhism and psychology in the USA, Canada, Europe, Australia, Chile, and Mexico.

Name Index

Adler, A., 30, 142, 218,
Agazarian, Y., 142-144, 149
Aronson, H., 171

Bateman, A., 168
Bion, W., 138, 140-141, 143, 145, 162, 169
Billow, R., 141, 146, 148, 162
Bruner, J., 167
Buddha, xiv-xv, 3-7, 9-10, 12, 14, 120, 135-136, 152, 163-165, 224, 197, 309-311, 339, 341-342, 345, 378

Chodron, P., 168, 170, 171, 178, 186, 242, 372

Dalai Lama, 23, 26, 44, 107, 135-136, 152, 239, 362
Davidson, R., 102, 113-115, 118
de Wit, H., 3, 8, 24, 40, 381

Epstein, M., xix, 24, 27, 40, 99, 161, 163, 167-168, 171, 177, 276-277, 322, 337, 340, 342, 382

Fonagy, P., 168-169
Freud, A., 42-43
Freud, S., 4, 8-9, 12, 14-15, 39, 41-42, 100-101, 140-141, 143, 150, 162, 165, 167, 170, 172, 246-247, 250, 266, 338-339, 348, 352
Fromm-Reichmann, F., 43, 92-93, 96

Greene, L., 153
Gunaratana, H., 164-165
Gyatso, T. (see Dalai Lama)

Hanh, T. N., 135, 136, 303
  on interdependence, 226
  on mindfulness, 311-312
Hartmann, H., 43, 318

Hoffman, L., 19, 20, 21, 22, 25, 27, 36, 44, 227, 383
Horney, K., 43, 161

James, W., 42, 102, 122, 161
Jones, M., 136, 140
Jung, C. G., 136, 141, 214

Kabat-Zinn, J., 99, 108, 122-123, 299, 303
Karr, A., 162, 169
Kernberg, O., 143, 147, 343
Kinsley, D. R., 66, 67
Klein, M., 43, 145, 314, 316
Kongtrul, J., 176, 186, 241, 245, 247, 254
Kongtrul, D., 229
Kornfield, J., 340-341
Kohut, H., 43, 215, 318

Langan, R., 172
Luyton, M. F., 175, 189
Le Bon, G., 139-140
Linehan, M., 100, 122, 299, 301, 311, 325

May, R., 24, 26, 30, 72, 37, 80, 230, 236
McWilliams, N., 45, 63
Millon, T., 43, 63
Midal, F., 133, 158, 193, 196, 208, 210
Mipham, S., 108, 119, 123, 127, 162, 174, 177, 178, 180, 193, 277, 297, 382
Mitchell, M., ii, 36, 37
Mitchell, S., 63, 43, 45, 63, 260-264, 268, 272
Murray, H. A., 43, 63.

Ogden, T., 260, 261-264, 272
Ormont, L., xix, 166, 167, 171, 173, 174, 246, 256

Patton, P., 61, 63
Ponlop, D., xiii, 210, 211, 216, 221, 385, 386

Podvoll, E., i, 74, 87, 92, 182, 183, 193, 195-196, 276-278, 281-283, 285, 288, 297, 384

Racker, H., 188, 246, 256, 260-264, 272, 326, 333
Ramachadran, V. S., 112-113, 127, 231
Rahula, W., 20, 37, 135-136, 158, 162, 163, 174, 311, 333
Rubin, J., 165, 167, 174

Safran, J., 45, 63, 161, 164
Segal, H., 162
Segal, Z., 100, 106, 123, 126-128, 164, 174, 299, 302, 303, 307
Schnieder, K. J., 24, 27, 37, 38,
Schneider, S., 143, 147, 151, 155-159
Schore, A., 43, 65, 103, 116, 128, 230, 315-316, 320-321, 327, 328, 332, 333
Siegel, D., 153, 314,
   on successful psychotherapy, 116
Shantideva, 93, 218, 229
Silverberg, F., 175, 185,
   on therapeutic interventions, 187
   on therapeutic resonance, 230, 239-240
Sogyal, R.
   on ignorance, 164
Spotnitz, H., 112, 246, 327-328
Stern, D., 116,
Sullivan, H. S., 43
Suzuki, S.
   on Beginner's Mind, 323
   on Maitri Space Awareness, 196, 227
   on Transformation of Disturbed Emotion, 249
Suzuki, D. T., 338

Trungpa C.
   biographical information, 386
   on Buddha Nature, 268
   on contemplative education, 192
   on ego, 48, 330
   on Five Wisdoms, 210
   on magic, 361
   on maitri, 265
   on meeting of two minds, 233
   on meditation practice, 176-177, 186
   on Western psychology, vi-vii
   on warriorship, 75-76
Valliant, G., 170
Wallace, B. A.
   on compassion, 243
   on mind and brain, 102, 107-108
Walker, R., 176
Watts, A., 161
Wegela, K. K.
   on Exchange, 330
   on getting stuck in the exchange, 242
   on Maitri, 264
   on touch-and-go, 235
Welber, D., 138
Wellwood, J.
   on despair, 70, 71
   on ego, 68
   on the unknown, 77-78, 79, 80
Winnocott, D. W.
   on True Self, 215
   on Mothering Experience, 312
   on the facilitating environment, 316, 317, 318
   on Reparation, 319-320
Yalom, I., 44

Zeisel, E., 147, 326
Zimbardo, P., 43, 149, 367

Subject Index

Abhidhamma/Abhidharma, viii, x
Anicca, 185, 245,
   see also impermanence
Anxiety
   about death, 68-69
   clinical example, 52-54
   cognitive-behavioral therapy, 302
   dreams, 83,
   emptiness in clinical work, 263
   exchange, 248
   groups, 145, 147, 149, 151, 153
   guilt, 319
   letting go, xvi
   meditation, 50, 349-352
   neuroscience, 114-115
   society, 348
   the body, 369
   therapy, 267, 326, 352
   Three Marks of Existence, 6
   warriorship, 75
Anatman, 5
Attachment
   attachment style and groups, 169
   in psychotherapy, 28-29, 47, 327
   mothering, 313, 316, 325-326, 332
   neuroscience, 103, 116-117
   non-attachment to self, 23-26, 50
   suffering, 300-301, 355, 375
   Vajra, 204
Awareness meditation, 176, 182, 186, 209, 226-227, 236, 351
   see also vipassana,

Basic Goodness, also see Brilliant Sanity, Buddha-Nature, x, 226, 313, 330
Bodhichitta, ix, xvii, 51, 123, 229, 234, 267-269, 271
Brilliant Sanity, xix-xx, 47-49, 56, 61, 77, 100, 135, 201-203, 208-210, 226, 228, 232-234, 236, 271, 304
Buddha Families (Five Wisdom Energies), 195-211
Buddha, see Name Index
Buddha-Nature, xiv-xv, xix, 3, 226, 268, 372,
Buddhism, see Preface

Christianity (Judeo-Christian), 22-23, 26, 28, 41
Clarity
   Brilliant Sanity, xx, 47, 77, 88, 135, 265, 372, 379
   emotions, 91
   Islands of clarity, 277, 291, 295,
   meditation, viii, x-xi, 227
   Vajra, 203-204
Cognitive Therapy, 100, 302
   Cognitive Behavioral Therapy, 109, 302
Compassion
   as empathy, 30
   as enlightenment, 61, 218-219
   Brilliant Sanity, xx, 47, 226
   development of, 30, 56, 120, 135-136, 243
   idiot compassion, 316
   in the client, 183
   Maitri Space Awareness, 200
   meditation, 329
   neuroscience, 115
   path, xiii-xvii, 93, 239, 355-357, 362
   psychotherapy, 232, 234, 240, 242, 252-255, 263-264, 267-271, 312-313, 327, 329-330
   Tonglen, 51
   warriorship, 65-66, 68, 70, 73, 76-77, 80, 83-84
   wisdom energies, 197-198, 205, 207, 210
   world religions, 26
Concentration, 168, 312
   Eight-Fold Path, 122, 300
Contemplation, 312, 375
   recovery, 278

Contemplative training, 74, 136, 153, 277
Contract, 165
    groups, 165-168
    resistance, 166
Countertransference, 246, 259-261, 326, 330
    accommodation of, 49
    Maitri, 265

Dalai Lama, see Name Index
Death, 7, 33,
    acknowledgment of, 67-69, 71, 377
Dharma, xvi, 12, 135-136
Dialogue, between
    Psychoanalysis/Western psychology/neuroscience and Buddhism, xix, xxi, 3, 99-100, 119, 161, 191
Diversity, 32-33, 35, 43
Duhkha, 5, 7, 61, 163, 339, 373
    See also suffering

Ego
    antidotes to the problem of, 228, 247
    as true individuation, 352
    Buddhist ego and self vs. Western ego, 170-171
    Buddhist view of, xv-xvi, 8-9, 47-49, 67, 119, 226, 269
    insubstantiability of, as a Mark of Existence, 377
    meditation, 88-90
    the process of, 177, 184,
    reality, 209
    Tonglen, 51
    Western view of, 8, 41, 46, 321
    warriorship, 68-86
Egolessness, x-xi, 4-6, 9, 179, 247, 269, 271, 329-330, 355,
Eightfold Path, 122, 163
Empathy:
    a neural basis for 112-113, 119, 241
    see also mirror neurons
    a technique for development, 268
    as an aspect of the therapist's self-experience, 46, 56;
    developing a capacity for, 30, 208;
    Padma, 206;
    relationship with exchange, 230, 231, 247;
    supervision 242,
Emptiness,
    as a definition of enlightenment, 3,
    as an aspect of brilliant sanity, xx,
    as ultimate truth, 163, 377
    compared with Western usage, 40,
    contemplative group, 171,
    exchange, 234,
    heart sutra, 45, 219 220,
    Jack Kornfeild on, 341
    mind's potential, xiv-xvii,
    recognition of , 268-270,
    suffering, 246,
    warriorship, 70, 72,
Enlightenment, vi, xiii-xvii, 3-4, 6-7, 15, 45, 73, 84, 197, 250, 255, 323, 378
    as defined by Chogyam Trungpa, 61
    as defined by Santideva, 218
    Naropa, xxi
    the age of, 41
    neuroscience, 120
    eros and, 337-345
Eros, 337-345
Existential concerns,
    as a framework, 19-38,
    neurotic suffering, 3-17
    paradox, 78
Existential Psychology,
    see chapter 2
Ethics,
    Buddhist path, xvi, 33,120, 122, 135, 163,
    psychotherapy, 25, 33, 34, 42, 112
Exchange,
    as natural infrastructure of compassion, 93

as obstacle in contemplative
supervision, 188-189,
as web of emotional energy,
260
large group, 142
mirror neurons, 112, 113, 117
therapeutic relationship, 330
touch and go, 48-49, 60
Windhorse therapy, 285
286
See Chapter 12, 225-237
See Chapter 13, 239-257
Experience, direct, 10, 47-50, 61,
74, 176-177, 217, 219, 228,
230, 231, 234, 235, 278, 375

Fear, xvi, 4, 7, 8, 10, 30, 57, 92, 93,
94, 195, 198, 217, 263, 324,
325, 341, 342, 343, 365-366,
376
exchange, 229
fearlessness, 65-86
neuroscience, 113
reality, 144,
resistance, 15,
Folk Psychology, 167
Four foundations of Mindfulness,
164, 312
Four Noble Truths, xiii, 66, 339,
361, 362, 378
Free association, 138, 167
Freedom, 61, 66, 67, 71, 72, 96,
213, 214, 247, 270, 313, 322,
329, 343, 352, 375,
see also liberation, from
attachment, of bare
attention,

Garuda, 71-73, 74, 76, 80, 84
Goals, 144, 145, 148, 305
in group work, 165-168
meditation vs. psychotherapy,
xix, 254
Grief, 11, 253, 270, 355, 360
Group, contemplative,
as a mindfulness practice, 161
174
large group process, 133-160
Guru, 245, 340

Healing, 25, 80, 87, 92, 167, 214,
219, 239, 240, 252, 253, 276
277, 331, 360, 378
authentic movement, 216
community, 227
countertransference, 246
relationship as, 228, 232-233,
357
resonance, 185
Health
as intrinsic nature, 196
Brilliant Sanity, 47, 77,
378, 379
Buddhist psychology view of, ix
xi, 304, 305
development, 317-318,
322
giving and sending, 241-243.
245
myths of self, 25
of ego, 171, 329, 352
social interest, 30
Three Marks of existence, 6,
372
truth, 162
Windhorse therapy, 275
297
Heart sutra, 45, 219
Hindrances, 167
Hindu (ism), 42, 65, 152, 192
Honesty, 162, 178, 264, 265, 293

Impermanence (anicca)-
as a Buddhist viewpoint, xii, 352
as one of the Three Marks of
Existence, 5, 303, 355,
361, 375-377
atmosphere of, annica, 185
being a mother, 310
maitri training, 200-201
meditation and the direct
experience of, 270
suffering of, 8
warriorship, 65-86
William James, 42
Individualism, 21, 192
as a cultural value 25, 142,
149
existential, 27

Interconnectedness, 24, 206, 240, 241, 250, 302, 330
Intersubjectivity, 230-231

Kali, 65-76, 81, 83, 84
Karma, xv, 61, 151-153,
    as a Buddha family, 206-207
Kagu lineage, 347
Knowing, 54. 61, 77, 79, 146, 241, 317
    oneself, viii
    postmodernism, 44
    Vajra, 203-204

Lacanian, 123
Liberation, 4, 90, 342
    acceptance, 61
    impermanence, 72
    mindfulness, 164
    path of or to, xiii, 9, 71, 377, 378

Maitri 123, 195, 197, 209, 233, 234, 264, 277, 292
    cultivating 201, 227-228, 264 265,
    Maitri Project 196-200
    maitri training, 134, 200-201
    space awareness 184-185, 195,
    see also Chapter 10, 227,
Mahayana xvi-xvii, xix, 12, 145, 163, 186, 239-243, 247, 355
Meaning, struggle to create, 49, 70, 170, 310,
Meditation, i-xx, 3, 10, 21, 42, 102 124, 133-138, 146-147, 177 180, 186, 192, 195-198, 200 201, 209, 243-245, 253-255, 260, 264-270, 277, 293, 309 312, 325, 329, 337-340, 347 352, 356, 360-362, 367-380,
    in therapy 28, 3, 31, 34-35, 61, 101,
    psychotherapy 74-76, 79, 87 96, 162-172, 177-180, 185, 214-218, 225-236, 240, 299, 303-305, 343,
    shamatha project, 100
    Shamatha, 49-50

Tonglen 51
Vipashyana, 51, 108, 111, 179, 185,
Mentalization, mentalizing 168-171
Middle Way 46, 247
Milarepa
Mindfulness 22, 30-31, 47-50, 55, 74, 90, 99-101, 106-125,
    see also chapter 8 & 17
Mindfulness Meditation, 100, 107 112, 116-119
Mortality 66
Muslim 32, 34
Mysticism 20, 288

Narcissism 338
Naropa xxi
Naropa University i-ii, vii, xix-xxi, 21, 74-75, 88, 134-136, 144, 148, 150, 153, 161, 166-167, 171 172, 176, 184, 192, 195, 200, 225, 264, 276, 300, 338, 344, 356
Nirvana xiv, 6, 26
Nirvana principle
Nonattachment (non-attachment) 21-29, 50
Non-dual mind xvi, 231, 271, 302
    reality 107
Non-reactive observation. See attentiveness, nonjudgmental
No-self (anatta). 6, 23-28, 45, 220,
    see also emptiness, Impermanence, attentiveness, nonjudgmental

Paradox 24, 45-46, 66-68, 76-80, 84, 95, 119, 145, 149, 153, 214-221
Paramitas 145, 147, 168, 172,
    see also chapter 20

Path vi, xiii-xvii, xxi, 3-10, 15-17, 24, 27, 59, 61, 66-74, 77, 81-84, 89, 120, 136, 138, 145, 148, 162-163, 165, 170-171, 176 177, 183-186, 192, 204, 216, 230, 239, 241, 243-245, 254 255, 263-264, 270-271, 277

278, 286, 292, 295, 323, 342,
347-348, 352, 356-363, 366,
368, 372, 377-379
    Eightfold path 122, 163
Pathology, focus on 43, 57-60, 79,
100, 303, 366,
    psychopathology 68-69, 110,
226, 266,
Peak experiences, personal work
Philosophy –Western v-xii, xix, 3-4,
8, 11-14, 23-27, 39-50, 56, 60
61, 76, 87-88, 99, 108, 115,
122, 133-138, 147-149, 161
165, 170-171, 177, 184, 191,
195-197, 199-200, 207, 216,
225, 264, 300-305, 316-318,
321, 339, 366-367
Pleasure principle 9, 12, 348
Postmodern thought 25-27, 43-46
Prajna v-vi, 50, 122, 146-147, 163
Projection 39, 42, 79, 170, 198,
207, 218, 233, 314, 349, 359
Projective Identification 53, 142
143, 151, 260-263, 314-315,
326, 329-330
Psychology, cross-cultural 43
Psychology, transpersonal 214,
230-231

Realms, Six 8, 10-15
Rebirth (reincarnation) 73, 252
Reductionism vs. non-dualism
Relationships xvii, 29-30, 33, 43,
45, 69, 75, 80, 96, 114, 124,
144, 164, 176, 179-180, 183,
201, 206, 209, 235, 253, 275,
279-284, 289-290, 294-296,
311, 313, 316, 329-332, 357
Renunciation, 80
Resistance,
    compassion, 340
    emotional communication, 327
    328
    Three Marks, 372-373, 378
    to experience of pain, 7-15
    to meditation and Buddhism,
21, 31,
Responsibility/moral accountability,
    case examples, 59, 285,
    diffusion of, 151

discipline, 77
enmeshment, 326

Samadhi, v-vi, 122
Secular,
    Buddhism, 21
    form of meditation, 243
    path, 191
    shila, v
    warriorship, 145
Subjectivity
    ideas of self and, 39-46
    neuroscience, 102
Self, xv, 26-27, 135
    contemplative psychotherapy,
        47-49, 60
    emptiness of, 259
    illusion of, 149, 17
    integrated, 314-315
    interdependence of, 226, 262
    neuroscience, 111
    true self, 214-220
Self and no-self, 6, 23-25
Self psychology, 46, 318
Self-esteem, 11, 25
Self-experience, 39-40
Selflessness, 5, 6, 40,
    realization of, 163, 170
    see also egolessness
Shamata, 311, 49-50, 162-163
    270
Shamata Project, 100
Shila, v
Shunyata. see emptiness
Samsara, xiv, 371
Spaciousness, xx, 72
Spiritual practice.
    psychotherapy, 14-16
    see also meditation, goals of
Suffering
    existential, 7-8
    ignorance, xiiv, xvi, 3-5,
Teachers, spiritual
    psychotherapists, 15-16
Tibetan Buddhism, 107
Therapeutic aggression, 48
Therapeutic community, 136, 196
    197
    meetings, 140
Three Marks of Existence, 4-6, 372

Tilopa, xxi
Tonglen, 51, 241-242, 270-271
Touch-and-Go, 169
Transference, 176, 284, 359
Truth- absolute vs. relative, 40
    first noble, 66
    in therapy, 60
    of impermanence, 67
    of karma, 152
    search for, 162-163

Unbinding and binding, 170
Unconscious,
    collective, 141
    in therapy, 327-328
    social, 142
Upaya, 146-147

Vajrayana, 3, 197, 249
Vipashyana, 51, 164, 179
Visualization, 281
Void, 40, 83

Well-lived life, 253

Yoga, 267-268

Zazen, 323
Zen Buddhism, vi
    authentic movement, 303,
    emphasis on direct experience
        213-214

Printed in the United Kingdom by
Lightning Source UK Ltd., Milton Keynes
137960UK00001B/5/A